Achieving QTS

Primary Computing and ICT

Knowledge, Understanding and Practice

Sixth edition

Primary
Computing
and ICT

Knowledge, Understanding and Practice

Sixth edition

Keith Turvey | John Potter | Jonathan Allen | Jane Sharp

Los Angeles | London | New Delhi
Singapore | Washington DC

Learning Matters
An imprint of SAGE Publications Ltd
1 Oliver's Yard
55 City Road
London EC1Y 1SP

SAGE Publications Inc.
2455 Teller Road
Thousand Oaks, California 91320

SAGE Publications India Pvt Ltd
B 1/I 1 Mohan Cooperative Industrial Area
Mathura Road
New Delhi 110 044

SAGE Publications Asia-Pacific Pte Ltd
3 Church Street
#10–04 Samsung Hub
Singapore 049483

Editor: Amy Thornton
Production controller: Chris Marke
Project management: Deer Park Productions,
Tavistock, Devon
Marketing manager: Catherine Slinn
Cover design: Wendy Scott
Typeset by: C&M Digitals (P) Ltd, Chennai, India
Printed by: Henry Ling Limited at The Dorset
Press, Dorchester, DT1 1HD

First published in 2000 by Learning Matters Ltd.

Reprinted in 2001. Second edition published in
2002. Reprinted in 2002, 2003, 2004 (twice) and
2005. Third edition published in 2007. Reprinted
in 2008 and 2009. Fourth edition published in
2011. Fifth edition published in 2012.
Sixth edition published in 2014.

Library of Congress Control Number: 2014935435

British Library Cataloguing in Publication Data

A catalogue record for this book is available
from the British Library

ISBN 978-1-4462-9586-1 (pbk)
ISBN 978-1-4462-9585-4

Contents

Acknowledgements   vii

Introduction   1

Section A: Primary Computing and ICT: Teaching and Learning   15

1   Organising ICT in your classroom   17

2   Planning for primary computing as a subject   31

3   Planning for primary ICT in other subjects   45

4   Planning ICT in the Early Years Foundation Stage   66

5   Assessment and recording in primary computing and ICT   73

6   Monitoring primary computing and ICT   83

Section B: Using Applications and Technologies   89

7   Word processing and desktop publishing   93

8   Graphics software and digital cameras   111

9   Media production: Video, animation and ICT   127

10   Graphing programs   135

11   Databases and spreadsheets   153

12   Programming and computational thinking   174

13   Mobile technologies   198

14 Interactive whiteboards 205

15 Digital audio and music 214

16 The internet 221

17 Social media: Tools for communicating, collaborating and publishing 235

Section C: ICT and the Professional Teacher 243

18 Professional use of ICT 245

19 E-safety 248

20 Ethical and legal issues 257

Self-assessment questions 262

Answers to self-assessment questions 269

Index 280

Acknowledgements

We would like to thank a number of people for their advice and assistance with this book. Amy Thornton and Helen Fairlie, on behalf of SAGE/Learning Matters, have provided invaluable editorial support throughout the process.

A number of colleagues in Initial Teacher Education have also supported this publication by reading and commenting on drafts of chapters, and also contributing their insights through various vignettes of classroom practice and projects. These include Lis Bundock, Jeremy Burton and Pippa Totraku.

Finally, we owe our gratitude to all of the children, teachers and schools referred to throughout this book, without whose partnerships, the ongoing development of professional practice in computing and ICT would not be possible.

Introduction

About this book

This book has been written to support primary teacher trainees and newly qualified teachers to develop their knowledge and understanding of both computing and the broader pedagogical issues concerning the ways in which Information and Communications Technology (ICT) can support children to develop confidence, capability and competence as lifelong learners in a digital age. The requirements of teachers in England are clearly identified in the National Curriculum and the Teachers' Standards. This book identifies clear links with these requirements, but also addresses the wider context in which ICT has an impact on learning and teaching. For this reason, we use both ICT and computing as terms throughout this book. That is, by ICT we mean the broader context of technology enhanced learning as children learn to use ICT effectively and critically across many domains of learning and curricula. By the term computing we mean the more tightly focused core knowledge and understanding identified in the National Curriculum programme of study (DfE, 2013). As we will explore later, these two are intricately linked, but focusing only on the subject of computing, as now defined in the new National Curriculum (DfE, 2013), does not adequately address the need for 'high-quality training and support that prepares trainees with the skills they need to use a range of approaches to teaching and learning, including information and communication technology (ICT) and educational technology where relevant' (Ofsted, 2012, p.33).

At the time of writing this edition, as at various other times in education, the curriculum has been under review and significant legislation has also been passed that removes the statutory status of the National Curriculum for some schools such as Academies and Free Schools. The government that took office in May 2010 has introduced many reforms to education during its tenure, including reform of Early Years policy that will affect the Early Years Foundation Stage (EYFS) and a review of the primary National Curriculum (DfE, 2013). These significant changes to the National Curriculum or to the EYFS Framework are likely to continue to have a knock-on effect on the assessment of children's attainment in the Early Years and at Key Stages 1 and 2, and there has already been much debate about this. Similarly, despite the introduction of the revised National Curriculum (DfE, 2013), there may well continue to be changes to the curriculum and school curricula in general as well as to the requirements for the subjects within it. This is particularly heightened with regard to ICT and computing as new technologies and practices are continually evolving.

This book includes references to: the statutory programmes of study for computing in the National Curriculum, which should be regarded as a minimum entitlement for children; the areas of learning in the Early Years Foundation Stage; and to the systems of assessment that relate to these. In any period, you will need to understand about what curriculum and assessment requirements were in place before the new arrangements, and teachers you work with may retain in their practice elements of the earlier ways of working. You will certainly hear colleagues discussing the differences between curriculum initiatives and referring to former frameworks, for example the Primary National Strategy for Teaching Literacy and Mathematics, and also to the QCA Scheme of Work for ICT, discussed later in this introduction in the section on curriculum context.

We have focused in this book on giving you insights into the development of the theory behind the core areas of computing and ICT that you will need to inform your practice as you plan to promote the ICT capability of the children you work with and to ensure that they develop effective skills of using and applying ICT as they build on their knowledge and understanding of computing and its broader significance in the digital age.

Features of the main chapters of this book include:

- clear links with the Teachers' Standards;
- references to required knowledge and understanding, both of computing as a subject and of the broader use of ICT to support teaching and learning in other subjects;
- research summaries that give insights into how the theory of ICT and computing has developed, including studies on how children's ICT capability develops and on the development of the use of different applications and technologies;
- examples of practice in the classroom to illustrate important points;
- suggestions for developing the use of ICT in your own practice;
- reminders of how planning for teaching ICT and computing fits in with the bigger picture, across the curriculum and with other aspects of school life;
- reflective tasks and practical activities for you to undertake;
- a summary of key learning points;
- references to key texts and suggestions for further reading.

For those undertaking credits for a Master's Degree, we have included suggestions for further work and extended study at the end of each chapter in a section called 'M-Level Extension'.

This introduction will briefly discuss some of the significant national policies and initiatives regarding the development of ICT and computing in schools in order to set the background. The concept of ICT capability as defined in the 1999 National Curriculum (DfEE, 2000) will be explored, as will the recent shift in emphasis towards computer science in the most recent iteration of the National Curriculum for computing (DfE, 2013). There will then be a discussion of ICT capability and the features of ICT, which make a distinctive contribution to learning and teaching. Consideration will be given to the Professional Standards for QTS, which form part of an ongoing continuum of professional development for pre-service and in-service teachers. The Standards require all teachers in all subjects and phases to use ICT appropriately and effectively in their work. This is a much broader brief than the focus on computing expressed in the National Curriculum. Despite the rebalancing of the programme of study for computing, it remains important to consider the wider application of ICT in some detail in order to develop an understanding of the conceptual framework, which needs to underpin a teacher's professional capability with ICT.

Teachers' Standards

This book has been written with the Teachers' Standards firmly at its core. The *Teachers' Standards in England* (DfE, 2011b) came into force from 1 September 2012, replacing the standards for Qualified Teacher Status (QTS), the Core Professional Standards and the General Teaching Council for England's *Code of Conduct and Practice for Registered Teachers.* These standards define the minimum level of practice expected of all teachers from the point of being awarded QTS.

It is well established that ICT as a tool has the potential to empower children with a wide range of learning needs through its adaptability and interactivity. Indeed, it could be argued that ICT has made most impact in education in the area of special educational needs where software, hardware and peripherals can be designed to bypass a number of physical and cognitive learning difficulties. Thus, technology has a significant role to play with regard to inclusion and facilitating accessibility in education. Consequently, it is the responsibility of thinking teachers to use their professional skills, knowledge, understanding and judgement as to how ICT may or may not be appropriate within these contexts.

Auditing

Your tutor will be able to outline how the audit is carried out in your particular institution. If you feel, in discussion with your mentor, professional tutor or other colleagues, that you have covered aspects of the audit of your development according to the Teachers' Standards, then make a note of it, copy the plan, attach any relevant photographs or printouts as further evidence and cross-reference it with your audit in your portfolio of ICT work. Remember that a good plan, a good lesson activity and detailed evaluation may provide evidence that you are operating at a good level within one or more Standard.

Curriculum context

There has been significant government expenditure on ICT infrastructure, which is indicative of the important role many believe technology can play in education. Now no longer in existence, the National Grid for Learning (NGfL), established in 1998, was managed and funded through the then government's agency for ICT, the British Educational Communications and Technology Agency (Becta). This was essentially an online portal to web-based resources for teachers and children. Similarly, other linked services emerged, such as the Virtual Teacher's Centre (VTC), also no longer in existence. The main thrust of government policy at this time was to connect every primary school to the internet and ensure that all teachers had a basic level of ICT competencies. In-service training was offered to schools by a variety of providers funded through the National Lottery's New Opportunities Fund (NOF). However, the potential of these initiatives was limited by the lack of access to broadband connectivity in schools. This prompted a second wave of national investment that was directed again mainly at infrastructure and hardware, with broadband connectivity and interactive whiteboards introduced into many schools. In the later years of the 1997–2010 Labour government two reviews of the primary curriculum were also undertaken. The Rose Review (Rose, 2009) was commissioned by the 1997–2010 Labour government and suggested among other things, that the status of ICT should be raised to that of core subject in the National Curriculum. The Cambridge Primary Review (Alexander, 2010), an independent review led by the University of Cambridge and funded by the Esmée Fairbairn Foundation, also envisaged an important role of ICT as a tool across eight distinctive domains of learning as well as being located as a subject within the specific domain of 'Language, oracy and literacy'. What these preceding curriculum reviews and national initiatives indicate is the ongoing problematic role of both computing as a subject and the role of ICT more broadly in education.

The contested role of ICT and computing has continued to characterise the most recent curriculum developments and debate under the 2010 coalition government. A report by the expert panel for the National Curriculum Review (DfE, 2011a), recommended that the structure of the Key Stages changed to Key Stage 1 for 5–7 year olds (Years 1 and 2), Lower Key Stage 2 for 7–9 year olds (Years 3 and 4), and Upper Key Stage 2 for 9–11 year olds (Years 5 and 6). The report reaffirmed that the National Curriculum is a minimum entitlement for children and that schools have the flexibility and freedom to design a wider school curriculum to meet the needs of their pupils and decide how to teach it most effectively. In *The Framework for the National Curriculum* (DfE, 2011a), the Expert Panel for the National Curriculum Review recommended that ICT be reclassified from a core subject to part of the Basic Curriculum and that requirements should be established so that ICT permeates all National Curriculum subjects. As a component of the Basic Curriculum, ICT would remain compulsory, but schools themselves would be able to determine the specific nature of the provision.

The establishment of ICT as a component of the Basic Curriculum, underpinning the core and foundation subjects was challenged by two further reports: one by the Royal Society and the Royal Academy of Engineering (2012), and another funded by Nesta (Livingstone and Hope, 2011). These two reports have possibly had the most significant impact on the status and conception of ICT in the most recent iteration of the National Curriculum (DfE, 2013), including its recent renaming as a subject from 'ICT' to 'computing'. Livingstone and Hope (2011), who approached their review from the perspective of the video games industry, made several recommendations regarding ICT in schools, including calls to 'bring computer science into the National Curriculum as an essential discipline' (p.7). This report also recognised the cross-disciplinary and applied nature of ICT and computing, recommending that schools 'encourage art-tech crossover and work-based learning through school clubs' (ibid.). The report from the Royal Society and the Royal Academy of Engineering also suggested a need for greater emphasis on computer science in any new programme of study for ICT. This report also recommended that ICT as a subject in schools be renamed computing to align it more closely with computer science, 'a rigorous academic discipline on an equal footing with other disciplines, such as mathematics, physics, chemistry, geography or history' (p.10). Indeed, the Royal Society and the Royal Academy of Engineering led a group of representatives from organisations such as Naace (ICT Subject Association), ITTE (Association of Information Technology in Teacher Education), BCS (Chartered Institute for IT) and Computing at School (CAS) to produce the initial draft of the new programme of study, which was accepted with some modifications.

The recommendation that ICT as a subject should be renamed computing was accepted by the coalition government and, as we will see next in a closer analysis of the new programme of study for computing, much greater emphasis is placed on computer science both at Key Stage 1 and 2. However, in other ways it can be argued that the focused and specific construction of the new programme of study for computing as a subject (DfE, 2013) now leaves more room for innovation in ICT, which, as mentioned earlier, we define throughout this book as the broader application of digital technologies to enhance learning throughout the curriculum. That is, in freeing the broader application of ICT from specific curricular restraint there can be more scope for the exploration of the ways in which technologies have the potential to enhance learning (Twining, 2013).

A shift in emphasis: computing or ICT?

As suggested earlier in this introduction, this question over whether the subject is best represented by calling it ICT or computing is redundant. In the most recent changes to the National Curriculum (DfE, 2013), ICT as a subject has been renamed computing and, as we will see, it has also been given a tighter focus on a core of knowledge and understanding, with greater emphasis on aspects of computer science. However, ICT as the broad application of technology remains an important concept used widely in the worlds of commerce, business, science, media and the arts, not to mention the many applications within people's leisure and social lives; there are many areas of people's work and leisure lives that require effective and critical engagement with information and communications technologies. There is also a clear indication from the DfE (2013) and Ofsted (2011) that although not detailed in the National Curriculum, teachers are expected to use ICT broadly to enhance their teaching and children's learning where appropriate. So how has the National Curriculum for computing changed other than being renamed?

Table 0.1 sets out the previous programme of study and the new programme of study alongside each other, for comparison. Immediately evident in comparing and contrasting the left and right columns of Table 0.1 is the tighter focus in the scope of knowledge, understanding and skills that is specified. But again it should be emphasised that this is a minimum requirement. Take some time to study Table 0.1.

Table 0.1 Comparison of programmes of study for Key Stages 1 and 2 in 1999 and 2014

Programme of Study (ICT) 1999 – Key Stage 1 *Pupils should be taught:*	Programme of Study (Computing) 2014 – Key Stage 1 *Pupils should be taught to:*
Finding things out ➤ How to gather information from a variety of sources ➤ How to enter and store information in a variety of forms ➤ How to retrieve information that has been stored **Developing ideas and making things happen** ➤ To use text, tables, images and sound to develop their ideas ➤ How to select from and add to information they have retrieved for particular purposes ➤ To try things out and explore what happens in real and imaginary situations **Exchanging and sharing information** ➤ How to share their ideas by presenting information in a variety of forms ➤ To present their completed work effectively	➤ understand what algorithms are; how they are implemented as programs on digital devices; and that programs execute by following precise and unambiguous instructions ➤ create and debug simple programs ➤ use logical reasoning to predict the behaviour of simple programs ➤ use technology purposefully to create, organise, store, manipulate and retrieve digital content ➤ use technology safely and respectfully, keeping personal information private; know where to go for help and support when they have concerns about material on the internet ➤ recognise common uses of information technology beyond school

Reviewing, modifying and evaluating work as it progresses

➢ To review what they have done to help them develop their ideas
➢ To describe the effects of their actions
➢ To talk about what they might change in future work

Breadth of study

➢ Working with a range of information to investigate the different ways it can be presented
➢ Exploring a variety of ICT tools
➢ Talking about the uses of ICT inside and outside school

Key Stage 2	Key Stage 2
Finding things out	➢ design, write and debug programs that accomplish specific goals, including controlling or simulating physical systems; solve problems by decomposing them into smaller parts
➢ To talk about what information they need and how they can find and use it	
➢ How to prepare information for development using ICT, including selecting suitable sources, finding information, classifying it and checking it for accuracy	➢ use sequence, selection, and repetition in programs; work with variables and various forms of input and output
Developing ideas and making things happen	➢ use logical reasoning to explain how some simple algorithms work and to detect and correct errors in algorithms and programs
➢ How to develop and refine ideas by bringing together, organising and reorganising text, tables, images and sound as appropriate	➢ understand computer networks including the internet; how they can provide multiple services, such as the world-wide web; and the opportunities they offer for communication and collaboration
➢ How to create, test, improve and refine sequences of instructions to make things happen and to monitor events and respond to them	➢ use search technologies effectively, appreciate how results are selected and ranked, and be discerning in evaluating digital content
➢ To use simulations and explore models in order to answer 'What would happen if...?' questions, to investigate and evaluate the effect of changing values and to identify patterns and relationships	➢ use technology safely, respectfully and responsibly; know a range of ways to report concerns and inappropriate behaviour
Exchanging and sharing information	➢ select, use and combine a variety of software (including internet services) on a range of digital devices to accomplish given goals, including collecting, analysing, evaluating and presenting data and information
➢ How to share and exchange information in a variety of forms, including e-mail	
➢ To be sensitive to the needs of the audience and think carefully about the content and quality when communicating information	
Reviewing, modifying and evaluating work as it progresses	
➢ To review what they and others have done to help them develop their ideas	
➢ To describe and talk about the effectiveness of their work with ICT, comparing it with other methods and considering the effect it has on others	
➢ To talk about how they could improve further work	

Breadth of study

> ➢ Working with a range of information to consider its characteristics and purposes
> ➢ Working with others to explore a variety of information sources and ICT tools
> ➢ Investigating and comparing the uses of ICT inside and outside school

It is worth considering in more depth how the old and new programmes of study are both similar and different. Both programmes of study avoid a purely skills-based computing curriculum. Such a notion is flawed because the work and leisure spaces that today's children will inhabit throughout their lives will be technologically very different from the present and subject to change; consider how networks have transformed many people's work and leisure practices in the last two decades and, more recently, how mobile technologies such as smartphones and tablets are facilitating new ways of interacting both professionally and socially. Consequently, both programmes of study avoid specific reference to particular hardware, software or skills. This is not to say that teachers do not need to teach or model specific skills to children when operating specific software and applications, but it does indicate that in itself merely teaching a set of skills is not enough to enable children to develop autonomy in their learning with and about ICT and computing. Children need a much deeper knowledge and understanding of the role that technologies might play in their own and others' lives as well as an understanding of how they are designed and created.

This is perhaps where the new and old programmes of study begin to differ in emphasis. The previous programme of study for ICT emphasised the digital literacy elements of ICT. The key strands – finding things out, developing ideas and making things happen, exchanging and sharing information, reviewing, modifying and evaluating work as it progresses (Table 0.1) – place emphasis on the fundamental processes underlying why and how we use technology critically and effectively; that is digital literacy. These four strands within the old programmes of study for ICT encompass a range of skills and higher-order knowledge and understanding. For example, on one level, in order to use ICT to 'find things out' using the internet, children need to know how to use the tools on a navigation bar – whether it be Internet Explorer, Safari, Firefox, Google Chrome, and so on. However, they also need to be able to identify what information they need, search effectively and efficiently for it and interpret that information accurately, taking into account the validity and reliability of the source. This level of higher-order thinking is dependent on a deep understanding of the ways in which information is managed, structured and published online in comparison with other sources of information. Similarly, if children are going to be able to use technology throughout their lives to 'share and exchange information', they will need to develop a deep understanding of the ways in which information can be created and manipulated to communicate effectively with different audiences. In these ways, the old programme of study defined ICT capability broadly in terms of developing children's critical understanding of how they use and apply a range of technologies, placing emphasis on the development of children's digital and media literacy as well as their skills. As Loveless (2003) notes, such a broad ICT capability requires children to develop a deeper understanding of where, when and why to use ICT as well as how.

The new programme of study for computing, in contrast, emphasises some of the fundamental processes of computer science such as programming and using logical reasoning, as illustrated in the first three statements in the new programme of study at both Key Stage 1 and 2 (Table 0.1). There is also a deliberate use of terminology such as 'algorithms' and 'decomposition' in the new programme of study, which are common terms within the specific discipline of computer science and which we explore in more depth in Chapters 2 and 12. However it should be stressed that the new programme of study for computing also recognises the importance of digital literacy which is encapsulated by the aspects of the new programme of study which refer to children being able to use technologies 'purposefully', 'safely', 'effectively', and 'discerningly' across a range of digital devices (Table 0.1). Indeed, e-safety, which is dealt with in detail in Chapter 19, is explicitly mentioned in the new programme of study (DfE, 2013) as this is an extremely important area that schools and teachers need to address with children. Essentially, the new programme of study for computing delineates the computer science and digital literacy elements of computing more precisely than the previous programme of study. As well as developing their knowledge and understanding of digital and media literacy by using technologies effectively and safely with purpose, children are expected to develop a much deeper understanding of how the applications they are using actually work. We often take for granted the technological tools we use in our everyday lives, but the burgeoning array of digital technologies and applications has prompted those designing the new curriculum to question the extent to which we are preparing children to become creators as well as users of new digital technologies. For example, it is argued that learning about computer science has the potential to help children and young people to become the future 'technology designers and creators rather than merely technology users – a philosophy of creativity and expression rather than mere productivity' (The Royal Society and The Royal Academy of Engineering, 2012, p.290).

As suggested in this introduction, this reframing of ICT as computing and the tighter focus on a body of core knowledge surrounding how digital technologies and applications are created as well as their effective use, brings a new opportunity to enrich the teaching of computing as a subject in schools, while also perhaps creating the space for teachers and children to experiment more with new technologies throughout learning and teaching. However, there is also a risk that the good work that many schools have already developed in relation to computing as a subject, and ICT more broadly throughout their practice, are abandoned rather than built upon. Trainees will become aware in schools that there has been much debate around the role and status of ICT/computing in schools and this will no doubt continue to a certain extent as policies develop and change. But it is important also to point out that in relation to the teaching of ICT throughout primary schools in the previous National Curriculum (DfEE, 2000), Ofsted reported that in two-thirds of primary schools inspected from 2008 to 2011 the practice of ICT was 'good' or 'outstanding' (Ofsted, 2011). As with any new policy development in education, it is important to recognise and build on the most successful aspects of what has already been achieved.

From this perspective you may find that some schools and individual teachers you work with are still using whole units, adapted units or elements of schemes of work in their medium-term and long-term planning for computing and ICT. Furthermore, some of these schemes of work may have been adapted from the QCA scheme of work (QCA, 1998, revised 2002, 2003), which was developed to support the 1999 National Curriculum (DfEE, 2000).

The QCA scheme of work for Key Stages 1 and 2

In order to facilitate the implementation of the previous National Curriculum for ICT (DfEE, 2000) and develop children's ICT capability through challenging and relevant experiences, an ICT Scheme of Work was published by the Department for Education and Skills (DfES) and the Qualifications and Curriculum Authority (QCA). However, this was not statutory and many schools developed their own schemes of work as teaching for creativity and creative teaching with ICT requires teachers to think imaginatively about where purposeful links might be made between ICT and other curriculum areas. The QCA scheme of work provided a sequence of units and is still available via the National Archive (Online, see QCA, 1998). While there may be some useful ideas here for trainees to adapt, which could provide opportunities for addressing some elements of the new programme of study, it should be stressed that the QCA scheme of work no longer fulfils the requirements of the new programmes of study for computing (DfE, 2013).

Early Years Foundation Stage

The *Statutory Framework for the Early Years Foundation Stage* (DfE, 2014) identifies features of good practice for the education and care of young children and sets out the early learning goals that most children should achieve by the end of their Reception year. From September 2008, children in the EYFS have been assessed against a comprehensive Early Years Foundation Stage Profile, the main purpose of which is to provide Year 1 teachers with reliable and accurate information about each child's level of development as they enter Key Stage 1. As this edition was written, a number of reforms to the EYFS have been implemented in response to The Tickell Review, *The Early Years: Foundations for Life, Health and Learning* (Tickell, 2011). The six areas of learning in development have now been changed to three prime areas and four specific areas in which the prime areas are applied:

Prime areas:

- personal, social and emotional development;
- communication and language;
- physical development.

Specific areas:

- literacy;
- mathematics;
- expressive arts and design;
- understanding the world.

Developing ICT as a tool for learning

IN THE CLASSROOM

In the corner of a classroom, Albert (a Second World War veteran), is searching the Commonwealth War Graves Commission database (**www.cwgc.org**/) with a group of Year 6 children. They are searching for information about local people from the village who lost their lives in the Second World War; people Albert grew up with and went to school with. The children are fascinated by the information Albert shares with them about these people who until now were merely names engraved on the War Memorial in the centre of the village. However, Albert is equally fascinated as the children demonstrate how they can access information about how, when and where these people fell, and where their graves are. Albert wants to know more and so do the children. These children go on to create a multimedia presentation with images, text and audio from interviews with Albert about the plight of local people during the Second World War.

Encapsulated within this brief extract is the power of technology to act as a catalyst for rich educational experiences for all generations. This snapshot offers a glimpse of the important role technology has to play in lifelong learning; both the children and the 85-year-old were united in their quest for information. Technology can have relevance for all, in different contexts and in whatever phase of life they may be. This raises important and challenging issues for people undertaking primary teacher training and embarking on their careers as newly qualified teachers.

How can ICT enhance teaching and learning?

Such a question prompts us to examine our values and beliefs about the purposes of education, the contexts in which people learn and the roles that teachers might play in facilitating such rich educational opportunities described in this classroom example. Digital literacy will no doubt be a vital factor in enabling both teachers and children to exploit the creative potential of new technologies throughout their learning lives, and this is complicated by the fact that technologies are in a constant state of change and pervade all areas of our lives from work to leisure. Teachers' appropriation of technological tools into their professional practice is a complex process affected by a range of factors (Fisher, Higgins and Loveless, 2006; Somekh, 2007; Turvey, 2013). As Loveless and Williamson state (2013, p.158), 'being *ready, willing and able* to teach, calls for a reading of the world in which content, context and tools can be orchestrated with skill and purpose'. Teachers themselves are linchpins in the turning of technological tools into effective pedagogical tools that support learning.

Although there remains a significant digital divide between those with access to technology in the home and those without, many children in our society enjoy rich digital lives outside school, downloading and sharing music, interacting in online multi-user games environments, and engaging in various forms of communication from e-mail to instant messaging. So, what can we as teachers learn from these informal uses of technology outside school and what effect might the constantly changing technological landscape have on our own uses of technology within school? Teachers need an understanding of the ways in which they can use information and communications technology (ICT) to support and enhance their teaching across the curriculum and in a range of contexts. They also need an understanding of how children develop an ICT capability, which enables them to deal with information critically in a rapidly changing world. These are pedagogical issues, and indeed the development of new technologies often necessitates a shift in pedagogical approach in order to exploit fully the educational potential of the technology. To support your professional judgement about how we integrate ICT into your teaching and children's learning, it is useful to consider the characteristics that any new technology or application bring that can be exploited for pedagogical gain, as we examine now.

Key characteristics of ICT as a learning tool

Many teachers, teacher-educators and policymakers have grappled with the question of what contribution new technologies bring to learning and teaching. The plethora of technological tools now available, from web-based virtual learning environments (VLEs) to mobile hand-held devices such as iPads, smartphones, electronic voting systems and digital video cameras, has led many to look for new ways of describing and classifying the role of information and communications technologies in learning and teaching. The term 'e-learning' is often used in education and encompasses learning and teaching strategies that draw on a range of digital and networked technologies. As teachers, you need to exercise critical judgement, confidence and expertise in applying e-learning strategies throughout your work to improve the quality and standard of children's education. Teachers need to have knowledge, skills and understanding of the ways in which information and communications technologies can support their professional practice. That is, teachers should be able to make informed decisions about when, when not and how to use e-learning strategies effectively in their teaching and children's learning. In order to unpick this issue, it is useful to begin to consider the features of ICT that can make a distinctive contribution to practice or a specific subject; that is, the characteristics that can be exploited in order to make a contribution as a resource, as a tool and as a catalyst for new ways of working in the curriculum.

Interactivity can engage users at a number of levels, from the playing of a computer game in a child's bedroom to investigating the geographical features of the Himalayas via Google Earth. Both of these activities have in common the ways in which ICT can give immediate and dynamic feedback to decisions and actions made by the user. Whether undertaking a search of the internet, investigating a graph of the changes detected by a temperature sensor over a period of time or editing a multimedia presentation, these activities enable children to make decisions, see the consequences and act on feedback accordingly. However, the degree to which children engage and interact will very much depend on the way in which the teacher has framed these activities. Furthermore, the role of the teacher in encouraging the children to explore, to learn from dead ends and frustrations and to develop perseverance in trying out ideas and learning from feedback is vital in maximising the educational value of the experience for the children.

The **provisionality** of ICT enables users to make changes, try out alternatives and keep a track of their developmental ideas. The advantages of this can be recognised immediately in the writing of text with a word processor, which can facilitate continual editing and development of ideas. Advances in the speed and storage capacity of computers have extended this feature to the digital manipulation of still images, moving images and sound or the designing and programming of a computer game. Such advances put within children's and teachers' grasp a range of new modes of expression and enable them to become creators of rich multimedia. However, as with interactivity, teachers have a vital role to play in promoting positive attitudes to working with and exploiting the provisionality of ICT. They can model, discuss and make explicit the processes of evaluation, changing ideas and reviewing work, whether this is with text, still images, moving images, sound or adapting debugging an algorithm that is not providing the expected outcome in a game they have created.

Another key characteristic of ICT is the **capacity and range** of ways in which children and teachers can access vast amounts of digital information in the form of text, visual images and sound. The modes by which information is communicated with technology continue to diversify as file capacity and processor speed increase across the range of technologies from mobile phones to desktop computers. However, with this increasing multi-modality comes the need for children to be able to make sense of this information and critically evaluate its authority and authenticity. While teachers continue to play a vital role in enabling children to make sense of text from an early age, reading images (still, moving and animated) and considering the impact of sound in a multi-modal text will also be key to children's capacity to make sense of an increasingly rich multi-modal world.

The **speed and automatic function** of ICT allow tasks of storing, changing and displaying information to be carried out by technology, enabling users to read, observe, interrogate, interpret, analyse and synthesise information at higher levels. Many routine activities, such as capturing and organising data, monitoring change, carrying out calculations, drawing graphs and presenting findings, can be done using ICT, leaving the children time to ask questions and think about the meaning of the information with which they are presented.

These distinctive characteristics of ICT offer a useful framework for teachers in thinking about the broader contribution of ICT to learning and teaching throughout the curriculum as well as their wider professional role. However, it is important to understand that these features do not lie solely within the technology. It takes a thinking teacher to realise and exploit the full potential for interactivity, provisionality, capacity and range or speed and automatic function offered by an interactive whiteboard or any piece of hardware or software.

Outcomes

As you read this book it will become clear that it is grounded in a view of computing and ICT as both a subject and a powerful teaching and learning tool throughout the school curriculum and beyond, into many areas of children's learning lives. The emphasis is placed on children becoming discerning and creative users of technology as opposed to passive consumers. In order for children to develop such critical, confident and expansive dispositions towards technology they need opportunities to develop their capabilities over time, through using and applying their skills, knowledge and understanding across a range of purposeful and meaningful contexts. The new National Curriculum for computing (DfE, 2013) has introduced the need for children to develop a knowledge and understanding of how technology works through aspects of computer science as well as how it is used effectively and critically (digital literacy). However, it is also clear that there is an expectation that schools will continue to create opportunities for children to develop a broad ICT capability through the integration of a range of digital technologies into their learning, which reflect the 'increasingly digital and connected world' in which they live (DfE, 2013, no page). The challenge for teachers is to develop children's knowledge and understanding through planning and providing meaningful opportunities for sustained engagement with technology, opportunities in which children themselves are required to explore, create, reflect, review, ask questions and share ideas openly. Trainees and new teachers also need to take responsibility for the development of their own capability, through personal study, working with others, planning classroom experiences and developing networks of professional support, providing strong role models for the children as they themselves become confident, informed and critical users of technology.

By using this book to support your own subject knowledge development, you will be able to learn the knowledge and develop the understanding that you require to teach primary computing, develop your professional use of ICT and consider the appropriate elements of the EYFS areas of learning.

So that you can check on how well you have assimilated the subject knowledge and test your understanding, you may wish to try the self-assessment questions related to the different aspects of computing and ICT application that we address. You will find these in a section at the end of the book. The answers follow.

For those undertaking credits for a Master's Degree, we have included suggestions for further work and extended study at the end of each chapter in a section called 'M-Level Extension'.

To support you in understanding the curriculum context, you may find it helpful to refer to some of the documentation that we have mentioned in this introduction (see References).

REFERENCES REFERENCES **REFERENCES** REFERENCES REFERENCES REFERENCES

Alexander, R. (2010) *Cambridge Primary Review Final Report: Children, Their World, Their Education.* Available online at **www.primaryreview.org.uk/**

DfE (2011a) *The Framework for the National Curriculum. A Report by the Expert Panel for the National Curriculum Review*. London: DfE.

DfE (2011b) *Teachers' Standards.* Available at **www.education.gov.uk/publications**

DfE (2013) *Digital Technology in Schools.* Available at **www.education.gov.uk/a00201823/digital-technology-in-schools**

DfE (2014) *Statutory Framework for the Early Years Foundation Stage.* London: DfE. Available at: **www.education.gov.uk/publications**

DfEE (2000) *National Curriculum Handbook for Key Stages 1 and 2*. London: HMSO.

Fisher, T., Higgins, C. and Loveless, A. (2006) *Teachers Learning with Digital Technologies: A Review of Research and Projects*. Bristol: Futurelab.

Livingstone, I. and Hope, A. (2011) *Next Gen: Transforming the UK into the World's Leading Talent Hub for the Video Games and Visual Effects Industries*. London: NESTA. Available online at **www.nesta.org.uk/publications/assets/features/next_gen**

Loveless, A. (2003) *The Role of ICT*. London/New York: Continuum.

Loveless, A. and Williamson, B. (2013) *Learning Identities in a Digital Age: Rethinking Creativity, Education and Technology*. London/New York: Routledge.

Ofsted (2011) *ICT in Schools 2008–11*. Available at **www.ofsted.gov.uk/resources/ict-schools-2008–11**

Ofsted (2012) *Initial Teacher Education Inspection Handbook*. London: Ofsted.

QCA (1998, revised 2002, 2003) *Scheme of Work for ICT*. London: QCA. Available online at **webarchive.nationalarchives.gov.uk/20090608182316/http://standards.dfes.gov.uk/schemes2/it/?view=get**

Rose, J. (2009) *Independent Review of the Primary Curriculum Final Report.* Available online at **www.educationengland.org.uk/documents/pdfs/2009-IRPC-final-report.pdf**

The Royal Society and The Royal Academy of Engineering (2012) *Computing in Schools: Shut Down or Restart? The Way Forward for Computing in UK Schools*. Available online at **http://royalsociety.org/education/policy/computing-in-schools/report/**

Somekh, B. (2007) *Pedagogy and Learning with ICT: Researching the Art of Innovation*. London: Routledge.

Tickell, C. (2011) *The Early Years: Foundations for Life, Health and Learning. An Independent Report on the Early Years Foundation Stage to Her Majesty's Government.* London: DfE.

Turvey, K. (2013) *Narrative Ecologies: Teachers as Pedagogical Toolmakers*. London/New York: Routledge.

Twining, P. (2013) *ICT is Dead – Long Live ICT*. Available online at **http://edfutures.net/ICT_is_dead_-_long_live_ICT**

FURTHER READING FURTHER READING FURTHER READING FURTHER READING

Duffty, J. (2006) *Primary ICT: Extending Knowledge in Practice*. Exeter: Learning Matters.

Selwyn, N. (2011) *Schools and Schooling in the Digital Age: A Critical Analysis*. London/New York: Routledge.

Section A
Primary Computing and ICT: Teaching and Learning

This section is concerned with issues related to planning, organising, assessing and recording ICT and computing throughout the whole of the primary age phase. The curriculum for the Early Years will also be addressed in a separate chapter on ICT in the Early Years Foundation Stage. As good planning depends on a thorough analysis of the situation before you even start working, the opening chapters provide a consideration of the background knowledge you need to acquire in order to deliver appropriate learning opportunities for the children you teach.

In 'Organising ICT in your classroom' we will consider the physical management of a range of technologies in learning areas. The different levels of resourcing will be characterised so that you can begin to assess the situation in your placement school more quickly. We will consider what the various strategies are for dealing with high-, medium – and low-resource situations. For example, we will consider the very different management strategies to be employed when working with children in a primary school with a network room full of computers or when working with one stand-alone machine in the classroom. We will also look at the implications of recent initiatives in primary schools and see how some of these have taken ICT in UK schools forward at a very rapid rate.

As far as possible throughout the parts of chapters which are concerned with resources, we have attempted to be completely generic; that is to say, we have not specified a particular platform (PC, Mac, etc.). Some example titles of software or other specific resources may be given, but only where absolutely necessary to explain a concept further. There is so much software available for schools at all levels for all of the computer platforms that it would be impossible to create a list that would be applicable or viable in all settings. Local authorities (LAs) and schools themselves will have such lists and justifications for the choices they have made in terms of ease of use, applicability to the age phases they are being used with, and so on. They may use their own sites to explain connections between specific titles and curriculum content, thereby aiding in the planning process.

In the chapters 'Planning for primary computing as a subject' and 'Planning for primary ICT in other subjects', we will consider the curriculum context and its impact on the teaching and learning of the subject. We will also address the ways in which some LAs and schools have planned for ICT to suit local needs and priorities. There is the potential to integrate ICT in all subjects of the National Curriculum, so this section will also look at how to plan within the core curriculum (English, maths and science) and within the foundation subjects in order to maximise the potential of ICT for all learners.

'Planning ICT in the Early Years Foundation Stage' will look specifically at ICT in the context of the Early Learning Goals (DfE, 2014).

'Assessment and recording in primary computing and ICT' will look at how to go about evaluating children's development in ICT and computing in order to inform planning. It will consider a range of strategies designed to provide a quick overview of a class as well as a more detailed and individually targeted assessment of the needs of a given learner.

'Monitoring primary computing and ICT' will be of particular interest to those training in the primary phase as ICT specialists or who are undertaking an assignment during their training, perhaps as part of M-level work or as a research project validated within their degree or PGCE. It includes an activity looking at classroom-based case studies.

REFERENCE REFERENCE **REFERENCE** REFERENCE **REFERENCE** REFERENCE

DfE (2014) *Statutory Framework for the Early Years Foundation Stage*. London: DfE.

1
Organising ICT in your classroom

Chapter objectives

When you have completed work on this chapter, you will have:

- thought about the organisational issues around teaching ICT and computing in your primary classroom;
- considered the practical aspects of locating equipment and how this impacts on planning;
- looked at organising the different levels of resources present in schools/settings;
- examined how best to meet children's needs and to enable them to benefit from and enjoy using ICT in their learning.

TEACHERS' STANDARDS

A teacher must:

1. **Set high expectations which inspire, motivate and challenge pupils**

- establish a safe and stimulating environment for pupils, rooted in mutual respect
- set goals that stretch and challenge pupils of all backgrounds, abilities and dispositions
- demonstrate consistently the positive attitudes, values and behaviour which are expected of pupils.

5. **Adapt teaching to respond to the strengths and needs of all pupils**

- have a secure understanding of how a range of factors can inhibit pupils' ability to learn, and how best to overcome these
- demonstrate an awareness of the physical, social and intellectual development of children, and know how to adapt teaching to support pupils' education at different stages of development
- have a clear understanding of the needs of all pupils, including those with special educational needs; those of high ability; those with English as an additional language; those with disabilities; and be able to use and evaluate distinctive teaching approaches to engage and support them.

7. **Manage behaviour effectively to ensure a good and safe learning environment**

- manage classes effectively, using approaches which are appropriate to pupils' needs in order to involve and motivate them.

Introduction

First, to look back at the recent past, new entrants to the teaching profession are fortunate to be joining it at a time following continuing, well-funded change in ICT in schools. Since the late 1990s in England, there has been significant spending on ICT infrastructure, hardware and software in schools. However, change on such a large scale is not without its logistical difficulties and much still depends on how the additional spending on ICT in schools has been managed at school level and at local authority (LA) level.

The national background

The evidence, from inspections by Ofsted and others, has suggested year on year that the use of computers and other ICT resources in schools, such as interactive whiteboards, is, in some cases, becoming more prevalent and better integrated into subject teaching. However, there is concern at the widening gap between schools that are at the cutting edge and using ICT widely and pervasively and those that have not yet fully integrated it into their teaching and learning. Even in areas where there is rich provision of resources, it is possible to find evidence that ICT is not always fully or usefully integrated into the curriculum. For a fuller discussion of these reports and the relevant research into ICT in education, please see Chapter 6.

Part of the issue lies with the variation in the quality of the development plans at local and at school level as well as with the wide variation in advisory support to schools. In turn, some of the variation can be put down to the 'bid culture' in which the innovation has taken place. In some initiatives, LAs made bids for funding to central government on the basis of a costed development plan. Schools sometimes had to bid to LAs for a share, and so on. No two neighbouring LAs managed this in exactly the same way, so you will notice variations when you move between your placement schools.

Allied to the expansion in hardware provision was the connection of every school to the internet and to subsequent opportunities for collaboration communication, as well as home–school links. This used to be referred to as connecting schools to the National Grid for Learning (NGfL) and you may still see references to this now-defunct initiative in school documentation. To this end, LAs in many parts of the country aligned themselves with the emergent 'Regional Broadband Consortia' (RBCs), which were public–private partnerships providing fast, relatively low-tariff internet access for schools and, in many cases, a virtual learning environment (VLE) of one kind or another through which the learning community interacts. Most LAs also assisted schools in protecting children from unsuitable content through the deployment of firewalls and servers which screen sites and searches.

A further major element of spending early on was an acknowledgement of the need to train teachers in schools. The New Opportunities Fund (NOF) was set up with Heritage (Lottery) money. Again, although NOF funding and training have now ceased, you may well encounter references to it in staffroom documentation or in conversation.

A further intention of government policy has been to provide subsidised laptops for teachers. Significant pilot projects, such as the Becta multimedia Portables for Teachers pilots had found that giving teachers laptops greatly increased their use of ICT in the curriculum for teaching and administration. In order to benefit from the scheme teachers had to be part of a school which was registered with the above-mentioned NOF training scheme. Some of the teachers with whom you will be working may well have benefited from this scheme.

Other major initiatives have had differing levels of emphasis in different local authorities. In some LAs, personal ownership of computers was pursued in the form of projects which focus on the use of hand-held equipment such as PDAs (personal digital assistants). In other LAs, the use of laptops was seen as something to be encouraged through bulk purchase schemes alongside trolleys for storage and charging of the equipment. The aim here was to diversify

ICT provision away from the static fixed computer lab and put the technology in the hands of the learners. More recently, some schools have moved towards exploring the use of tablet devices such as iPads and other such devices, in order to exploit the mobility and flexibility offered by such devices. Similarly, trainees might come across schools that operate what is called a 'bring your own device' strategy (BYOD), in which children may be encouraged to bring their own devices to school (e.g. smartphones, iPod Touch) so that they can be linked to the school network and used for researching on the internet. This is more common in secondary schools and does of course bring with it issues of equal opportunity for learners.

You may well also encounter local projects and initiatives based in the realm of digital media, recording and presenting video and audio resources, digital movie-making, podcasting, and so on. There is a fuller discussion of this in future sections. Finally, interactive whiteboards are having an influence on pedagogy in schools.

The local background

There has been a perceived lack of confidence with ICT and computing on the part of some teachers. Occasionally, this is characterised as 'reluctance'. It is certainly true that some teachers find it enormously threatening to be delivering a subject or using technological tools that employ skills which they do not feel they themselves have, but which the children may possess.

There may also be no support structure for teachers in their school situation. At school level, there may be no ICT co-ordinator. Good ICT and computing subject leaders who attend training and pass it on to colleagues, and give generously of their time and knowledge are not always readily available. At LA level, it may be that there is no active advisory team encouraging good practice and recommending hardware and software. In both these cases, there has been a failure of management to see the necessity of putting money into human resources. Too much time and money can sometimes be spent on hardware and software and not enough on the human resources needed to develop and promote excellence in ICT and computing in the classroom. You may well see evidence of this in your placement school. The recent emphasis on computer science and programming in the National Curriculum has also exacerbated this issue.

One other issue to note is the perceived 'skills gap' between teachers and children at home. Year on year, home ownership of computers is increasing. It would be wrong to assume that it was all going into the study bedrooms of middle-class students. It is possible to find levels of computer ownership in deprived areas of Inner London, for example, where 6-year-old children are experienced users of the latest software. As alluded to above, it would be wrong for teachers to allow the feeling to grow that children know more than they do. What children do not know, and the reason why they need the teacher to be using ICT with them, is how to apply it in their developing subject knowledge. They require the teacher to be a guide or facilitator.

Resource levels in schools: a rough guide

This section attempts to categorise schools according to the resource settings at different levels. Three types of resource setting are described on a continuum from high resource to medium resource to low resource. It is useful to characterise resource settings in this way because you will be able to make a judgement about particular organisational strategies if you can learn to observe and sum up the situation in a placement school quickly.

The school in which you are placed will be somewhere along the line of development and will not necessarily have all elements of the different resource settings represented. Furthermore, schools develop and change year on year.

A further issue – which is partly included below – is the human resource levels in the school. A school with very low levels of ICT equipment may still be doing well in ICT and computing due to excellence in organisation and involvement of all staff. Similarly, a school which looks good with a network room full of computers may in fact be keeping the door locked and doing nothing with them. The situation is complex.

Table 1.1 Resource level definitions

High-resource setting

Portable computers such as laptops or tablet and handheld devices are used to distribute ICT around the school. There is a network room used by groups and the wider community (sometimes) as a hub for ICT development activities.
Printing – in colour when necessary – is available at every station.
There is a fast broadband connection and wireless connectivity throughout the school.
There is a technician who regularly attends to maintain equipment in good working order.
Digital cameras and digital video cameras are available for use by teachers and children. There are interactive whiteboards or visualisers in most teaching spaces and their use is informed by good pedagogical decisions, not always teacher-led; children often have control of the resource.
A range of appropriate software is available for every age phase.
There are also stations connected to the network available in the classroom to carry on with work begun in the network room. These may be in the form of rechargeable laptops or tablet devices such as iPads.
Programmable toys and other robotics or electronics equipment are available for exploring programming and aspects of computer science.
The school is implementing a cohesive strategy for the use of ICT and the teaching of computing, including an ongoing development plan.
There is a policy for acceptable internet use and comprehensive safeguarding procedures.
There is a fully implemented scheme of work that is regularly reviewed and updated.
Teachers, children and the wider community make use of the VLE where the school has a vibrant and well-used web presence.

Suitability for placement as a trainee:

This is an excellent setting for learning how to integrate ICT fully into the curriculum and develop your ICT capability at the same time.

Medium-resource setting

There is a working computer and printer in every classroom.
There is a network room with computers connected to the internet that is partially timetabled for each year group.
Some programmable toys are available.
A digital camera is available to borrow and some short video clips are sometimes used.
Repairs to equipment are dealt with fairly promptly.
Interactive whiteboards are present in some classrooms and are sometimes used by children, often in a didactic and limited way to reinforce teacher-directed pedagogy.
A scheme of work for computing is being implemented.

The school has a development plan in operation and is considering how to integrate ICT more fully through the use of flexible and mobile technologies such as laptop trolleys or class sets of tablet devices.

ICT and computing are valued and within the next two or three years the school will move forward and become a high resource setting.

A policy on safe and acceptable internet use is being developed and there are plans to upgrade the school website soon.

Suitability for placement as a trainee:

Although not at the very cutting edge, this is a good situation in which to develop skills of organising for ICT and a trainee may still learn and even contribute something to the placement school.

Low-resource setting

There is an older, frequently broken computer in the classroom or one between two. There are a few interactive whiteboards that are used infrequently or ineffectively.

Overhead projectors are used on the whiteboard surface.

There may be low staff morale, low spending on ICT, no ICT co-ordinator, no technician. There is no scheme of work in place.

Printers are shared and are not always properly serviced.

Poor software results in children from Year 1 to Year 6 doing the same thing on the computer (copy typing, doodling in a Paint package, playing a number or spelling game, possibly the same one each time).

The school website is rarely updated.

In Ofsted terms, the school is not providing the full entitlement to computing and ICT for its children and staff are not receiving their entitlement to professional development.

Suitability for placement as a trainee:

Hopefully, there are very few settings like this left as this is a very difficult placement in which to gain the required standard in ICT in subject teaching and you would be heavily dependent on your institution for support.

PRACTICAL TASK   PRACTICAL TASK   PRACTICAL TASK   PRACTICAL TASK

Observing the ICT setting 1: The computers and other hardware

Schools have a degree of choice over how they organise their resources for computing and ICT and this early observation task is designed to raise awareness about the organisation and use of ICT in teaching and learning. The sections which follow will take up issues around school organisation and discuss how they may have come to certain pedagogical decisions.

Although in itself computing is a foundation subject, ICT can be integrated into every subject area across the curriculum and you will see it being used in a range of settings, including in areas of learning in the Early Years Foundation Stage. Make notes on what is being used and on where it is being used. Use these questions as prompts for your note-taking. Have a look at all of the places in the school where ICT may be in operation.

- **What do you see?**
- **Is there a computer in the classroom?**
- **Or are all the computers grouped in an ICT suite?**
- **Is there a mixed provision of some in the classroom and some in an ICT suite?**

- Are there any portable computers available, either laptops or tablets?
- Is there an interactive whiteboard in the classroom or the EYFS setting?
- How is it being used?
- Who is using it?
- Are there scanners or digital cameras or digital video cameras?
- Can children and teachers access the internet easily?
- Is the internet available in the classroom or ICT suite or both?
- Does this appear to be a quick connection?
- Is there wireless connectivity throughout the school?
- Is the internet filtered in any way to protect the children?
- Does it go straight onto the internet or special local authority network?
- Does the school use a virtual learning environment (VLE)?
- Does there appear to be interesting primary school software around in the school?
- How does it appear to be organised?
- Has the school subscribed to appropriate web-based software for learning?

Find out what is available and, if you can, list six to eight titles with their subject area and age range.

The notes which you make should be brief and comprise up to two sides of A4. They should be written with enough detail to give you a snapshot of ICT in use across the curriculum in your school. Read them again in the context of the opening sections of this chapter. What do your observations and reflections tell you about the kind of ICT setting in which you will be operating?

Observing the ICT setting 2: Human resources for ICT
Observe how the class teachers organise the ICT for their children.

Observe the children themselves as they work with ICT in the school. They are the best source of information about what is going on with ICT in the classroom. They know about the equipment. If it is old, they know which keys stick. They tend to know how to get round the deficiencies of the equipment, such as the printer which jams regularly. The games-playing children, those who have computer games consoles at home of one kind or another, often have a robust attitude towards computers of all sorts. They are aware of 'cheating' to get to different levels. Sometimes they will indulge in various key presses which may cause havoc with onscreen displays; sometimes they may discover for the class, newer, more efficient ways of doing things. Whatever the situation, it is always worth listening to what children say about computers and considering and valuing their contributions to the whole class body of knowledge about computing and ICT.

Observe the classroom and learning support assistants wherever possible. Where available, they are a valuable source of knowledge and support about ICT in the classroom. Listen to what they say and involve them in your planning. Mutual respect and good communication are the keys to working well with teaching assistants in all areas of the curriculum.

How do the children and adults use the interactive whiteboard? Is the teacher always in control? Which curriculum areas predominate? Do they use the software that comes with the board or do they sometimes show web pages, images and DVDs through the projector?

Find out about the parents and governors and ICT. Parents, like children, have a wide range of ability and experience and an even wider range of concerns with computing and ICT. Some parental concerns will be around the use of the internet in your school, how it is organised, and so on. They may ask whether or not the school has an acceptable use policy and adequate protection for their children from unsuitable material. Governors may raise many of the same issues with you as the school will be held responsible for the materials that the children may, in all innocence, be accessing if the school is not providing access through an education provider or through a filter which it is maintaining itself.

Make notes about your findings, including who the computing and ICT subject leader is, how to report faults/maintenance issues, for example to a technician or via the school office, and who you can talk to if you have queries on ICT policies.

RESEARCH SUMMARY   RESEARCH SUMMARY   **RESEARCH SUMMARY**   RESEARCH SUMMARY

Bridget Somekh (Somekh and Davis, 2007) characterises three ways in which teachers approach the use of ICT. In the first two of these, teachers either use ICT as a tutorial tool, delivering content to pupils or as a tool for carrying out tasks in 'content-free' software that does not necessarily depend on fully exploiting the features of ICT (she calls the computer a neutral tool in this mode). Finally, the third way of using the computer is as a cognitive tool to support active learning on the part of the children concerned (see Somekh and Davis, 2007). These provide a useful framework for examining practice, either your own or practice observed in school.

Organisational strategies for different resource settings

Computing as a subject and the appropriate use of ICT in teaching and learning is an entitlement no matter which situation you are working in. In all settings there are organisational issues which need to be addressed. This section looks at organising ICT in low resource and high resource settings.

Organising ICT in high resource settings

In a high resource setting, it is quite likely that you will be able to share the experience of the lesson with the children by means of a large display. This will be in the form of a large monitor, projector and screen or an interactive whiteboard (IWB). It could be by being able to take control of the screens at the individual stations and replacing them with the teaching screen via the network software. In any school where there is no such display facility, you will have to gather the children together in a space in front of one of the monitors. Teaching in network rooms without a large display is very difficult and you will need to learn strategies for overcoming this from observing the other teachers and/or teaching assistants.

Remind the children that they do not have to sit at the same machine each week and about the importance of their password. Here are some different models of practice.

- Whole-class logon with the same username and password into a general area on the network for that class.
- Children with a unique username and password.
- Children with group logon names and passwords.

Before teaching the children on a network, make sure that you understand the process of logging on yourself. Ask the computing and ICT subject leader or technician before starting (remember to ask for your own username and password as a guest on placement at the school). Children are often given their own area on the network in which to save their work. It is important that you follow the same protocols that they are used to. Every school network is organised slightly differently and you will need to take time to learn this for yourself so as not to make potentially serious mistakes, such as losing work. Also, when working as a whole class in a computer suite, children should be encouraged to develop independent problem-solving skills. Strategies such as 'ask three and then me' are useful in managing the learning environment so that the teacher is not seen as the only source for support and learning. For example, a child who is stuck with a task or technical issue considers first if they can solve the problem themselves, secondly if another child can help them and thirdly perhaps another child or teaching assistant can help, before asking the teacher.

As a rule, unless the children are very young, they should be taught how to log on and log off by themselves. This is part of learning about network literacy. One strategy is to have all the passwords and usernames on index cards, used at the beginning of the session and collected at the end.

Whole-class demonstrations can, and should, still take place, but they need to be a sensible length, enabling the children to make the best use of the time available.

In a school where there is access to distributed technology, such as laptops or tablet devices, many of these issues do not arise at all. In their place, other factors need to be taken into account, such as battery life, ownership, sharing, storing, and so on. At any rate, it is important that you follow the protocols of the school in this area as in others. Many teachers remark on how much simpler it is to integrate the use of technology when mass access to portable or hand-held computers is available, rather than having to take everyone down to a computer suite. It becomes as much a part of the provision as the use of traditional items in the classroom.

Later chapters will look in detail at how to manage ICT resources to approach knowledge and skills across the curriculum as well as when teaching computing as a subject. It is important to remember that children can contribute to the whole-class understanding and skills development in ICT and that there should be an opportunity for them to do so at times during, or at the close of, the session. The plenary, for example, can really come alive in a networked environment if the children are encouraged to use software for presentation of their projects for all to see. Schools in high resource settings which are capable of publishing on the internet or their own intranet will be able to further enrich the motivational opportunities for children writing or creating multimedia presentations for a wider audience.

Organising ICT in low resource settings

Lower resource settings are far less common. However, they still exist and can also pertain in a school when a network room or set of laptops is out of use or block-booked by another teacher. In a setting in which a single computer is shared by a class of 30 children, first bring the computer to the carpet area where it can be seen by everybody.

There may, of course, be physical reasons why you cannot do this. If there are, do what you can to overcome them or borrow areas big enough to do it somewhere else in the school. Just getting started with a piece of software should involve the whole class. When beginning with software that children have not encountered before, and screens look very unfamiliar to the class, it would be worth spending time on them.

The aim is still to allow the computer to be a part of the general resource provision of the classroom more fully. A question-and-answer style lends itself to this situation. Allow the children to contribute, even to provide tips for other users. Discuss with them the difficulties that they have overcome in familiarising themselves with the onscreen layout of the particular piece of software. Whole-class sessions can be enhanced by the following examples and principles.

- Ask the children to discover during the session, and then report back on, different ways of doing the same thing. In a writing program, for example, how can they make text appear in a different font size or colour?
- Stress regular, practical instructions. One such regularly repeated instruction should be 'Save before you print', in order to avoid the inevitable heartache which arises when a document gets lost.
- As is the case with all good primary practice, question children who don't always jump up and down with the answer (don't favour the loud over the quiet).
- Do not allow one gender or group of children to dominate.
- Stress the team-building aspects of sharing strategies so that they/we can all use the computer efficiently and safely.
- Involve children in a discussion about safety – monitor position, length of time, seating, and so on.
- Value what children contribute even when it is patently wrong. Help them to discover a better way constructively (e.g. 'That's a good suggestion but. . .').
- Draw on children's experience of ICT at home or in other community settings.

The suggestions in the list above are part of good practice for any teaching situation. There is no reason why the use of technology should result in adopting different values around communication and sharing. Technology sometimes challenges assumptions that we have of teaching and learning; indeed it often stimulates debate about the first principles of education, but it should never be an end in itself. There has to be a sound pedagogical reason for using ICT in a given situation.

Regular whole-class input increases the shared level of knowledge in the classroom about the use of ICT and will reduce the number of times that you have to say the same thing over and over again to groups of two to three children.

Becoming independent and increasingly competent in basic ICT skills will engender in the children a sense of responsibility for their work. It may be something that many of the children know from home, but there will be others for whom you are providing the only access to newer technology. From an early age, as children progress through the school, they are expected to take on more responsibility for knowing where their equipment is, where their possessions are, where they're going next, and so on. It should be the same for ICT. Children can be shown the importance of looking after electronic forms of their work, just as they learn the importance of looking after their books. They will often need to be shown how to save and retrieve their work and the importance of backing up work.

An alternative model of instruction, a version of the cascade model, whereby one or two children learn it and teach others, allows the more negative messages about ICT to be disseminated and should therefore be avoided. Among these more negative messages are:

1. There are ICT experts who know everything and must always be consulted before you do anything.
2. ICT is something that happens in a corner of the room away from the mainstream and is never discussed and nothing to do with the rest of the school day.

Show children that you are also a learner. ICT will be less threatening to you as a teacher if you enter into the situation as a learner alongside them. It is wrong to give children the impression that you or anyone else know all they need to know about computers. Frustrating as it may be, the truth of the matter is that we are all always learning about ICT. Once one thing is learned you can be sure another parameter will enter the equation. It is OK to make mistakes. If the basic care of the equipment is known and respected, there is not much harm that can be done by trying different solutions to problems.

At the same time it is important in the low resource setting to establish and maintain a rota. Rotas ensure that there is equality of access and of opportunity in the classroom. However, they should not be set in stone. The acquisition of ICT skills is a dynamic process, always changing. After whole-class input, in the beginning of working with a new piece of software or hardware, children need time to practise. Longer rota periods can be gradually shortened as children gain more skills and independence.

Organising ICT for children with special educational needs

Children who have special educational needs have the right of access to the whole curriculum, including computing and ICT. Often, the use of ICT as a tool has been identified as being of particular benefit to a given learner in a given situation. Sometimes, if the child is on the SEN register, they will have ICT hardware and software use identified as part of their Individual Education Plan (IEP) and you will need to incorporate this in your planning and organisation. Some examples might include:

- software which addresses the needs of a dyslexic child;
- hardware which allows access to the computer for a child with motor impairment;
- browser windows which open up in larger fonts for visually impaired children;
- portables or laptops with specialist software loaded for very particular needs (this might include one specialist device or laptop assigned to one child in particular);
- specialist hardware for those who are wheelchair users, e.g. specialist keyboard mounts or switching devices.

THE BIGGER PICTURE   THE BIGGER PICTURE   THE BIGGER PICTURE   THE BIGGER PICTURE

Some companies are dedicated to finding solutions for access for children with SEN and they will welcome enquires about their software and suggestions for future development. They are usually smaller companies who depend on a close relationship with the schools and children with whom they work. The annual British Educational Technology and Training exhibition (known as the BETT show and held in January in London each year) includes a Special Needs Village for you to examine at first hand such solutions.

For children with SEN in your class, it is important to discover if they require any additional access to the computer in the form of hardware that makes it easier to point and click at menu items or enter text. Some examples include:

- A Concept Keyboard – a device which allows touch-sensitive areas to be created on a flat A4 or A3 board which can be set up to input particular items of text or commands. Teachers can tailor the Concept Keyboard to the particular needs of an individual child using the authoring software provided. The software also includes printing facilities.
- A Touch Window – a device which attaches to the front of a monitor allowing the user to touch areas of the screen as a replacement mouse click to gain access to the menus in given software.
- Big Keys – a larger-format keyboard for children with fine motor control difficulties.
- Switches – on/off rack-mounted switches for wheelchair users and others which equate to left and right mouse clicks.
- Trackballs – large inverted mouse systems where the user is able to move a larger ball over a bigger area to point and click.
- Small mice – smaller point-and-click devices for those children with motor control difficulties, for example children with muscular dystrophy.

In terms of software for special educational needs, there is a very wide range available. There is also a case for appropriate tutorial software for some children with dyslexia or language delay because it will address very specifically the multi-sensory approach needed to allow such children to acquire strategies to catch up with language development.

REFLECTIVE TASK

When organising ICT for children who have special educational needs:

- **Find out about children in your class with SEN.**
- **Does their IEP require that they use ICT?**
- **Is there dedicated equipment for use by one child?**
- **Would this be hardware, software or both?**
- **Does the child have a special needs assistant who will work with them on their ICT?**
- **How does their need for specialist ICT input impact on your organisation of the class?**
- **Is there a programme of review for determining success levels of the ICT equipment with their special educational need?**
- **Is there someone you can discuss the situation with, for example the ICT subject leader or the special needs co-ordinator (SENCO)?**
- **What are the feelings of the parent on the use of ICT by their child during the week? Do they have materials or equipment at home which they are using to support their child? Does it complement what you are doing or do you need to make adjustments?**

RESEARCH SUMMARY

Research by Lie, O'Hare and Denwood (2000) in Scottish schools showed that, although word processing is believed to have a positive effect on the compositional process for children with specific writing difficulties, there are further significant background factors around motivation, cognition, medical factors and the whole learning environment.

The argument throughout this book and this chapter in particular is about seeing the possibilities for ICT use within the context of the whole class, or, in this case, the individual learner with special educational needs. ICT is a tool for the enhancement of the learner's education within the context of the whole child and not simply an intrinsically 'good thing'.

Organising ICT for children with English as an additional language

ICT offers many benefits to young learners in the primary classroom who are learning and using English as an additional language (EAL). The internet brings many audio and video resources across the curriculum within reach. Children who are learning English at the earliest stages can access parts of the curriculum by means of such media.

As a child begins to acquire more English, the computer, if properly managed, allows them to experiment with forms of written and spoken English in an unthreatening and motivating environment. Some additional tutorial software may be appropriate but talking word processors can be just as effective, with immediate feedback provided on composition. The biggest benefit is in areas where the child can experiment with open-ended software alongside peers.

Community languages with their own alphabets and letter systems are available through font add-ons in Office software. Among other uses, these can be employed to produce signs and instructions in the appropriate language. In turn, this goes some way to demonstrating that the language of that child is valued in the context of the school.

For younger children in this context, sensitive adult intervention and peer support are crucial. There should be plenty of opportunity to try to move conceptual development along by talk in the home language alongside support for learning English.

The choice of software or web-based resource should include elements which allow for the child to choose menu items by pointing and clicking, to have sections of text spoken, to allow access to pictures, music and video. Multimedia authoring packages, including some digital video activities, can be useful in this context. There is enormous potential for producing home-grown resources in dual language format. This would be an exciting project for a Year 6 class undertaking a unit on multimedia authoring. Resources could be created for any age in the school by the older children asking parents, siblings, and other adults to help to record in the home language.

Organising ICT for children with English as an additional language carries the same responsibilities and requirements as for organising any area of the curriculum for them, namely:

- Never assume the level of language-learning – find out.
- Differentiate for levels of English appropriately; do not assume that all EAL learners are the same.
- Make sure that children with EAL understand all of the processes involved in switching on and off, logging on and off and saving work.
- Check and recheck understanding with sensitive questioning.

THE BIGGER PICTURE   THE BIGGER PICTURE   THE BIGGER PICTURE   THE BIGGER PICTURE

Lani Florian writes 'It has been suggested that technology is a great equalizer, that for many people with disabilities technology can serve as a kind cognitive prosthesis to overcome or compensate for differences among learners' (Florian and Hegarty, 2004, p.10). While she advises caution over fixed and finite approaches to SEN and ICT, she also identifies several useful ways in which ICT may be exploited for meeting the different needs of children with SEN. She describes these as:

- **Used to tutor**
- **Used to explore**
- **Applied as tools**
- **Used to communicate**
- **Used for assessment**
- **Used as a management tool**

While these should not be seen as mutually exclusive or exhaustive, think about the ways in which ICT can be used to support children with a range of SEN and explore this within your school-based context.

A SUMMARY OF **KEY POINTS**

➢ **There has been significant investment in ICT initiatives nationally.**

➢ **Progress in these varied from local authority to local authority and school to school.**

➢ **Teachers differ in their levels of ICT capability and their confidence in using ICT to support children's learning and their own teaching.**

➢ **Schools vary in their levels of resourcing, both in terms of equipment and human resources, and this will impact on your planning.**

➢ **When organising ICT for children with SEN, there are ranges of hardware, software and peripherals available to support their access to the curriculum and to enhance their learning.**

➢ **When organising ICT for children with EAL, there are many resources available that will support their language development and allow them to participate in lessons alongside their peers.**

M-LEVEL EXTENSION > > M-LEVEL EXTENSION > > M-LEVEL EXTENSION

Research further the range of ways in which ICT can be used to support various special educational needs. Read the introductory chapter of *ICT and Special Educational Needs* by Lani Florian and John Hegarty (2004), which is available as a sample chapter at the following link **www.mcgraw-hill.co.uk/html/033521195X.html**.

REFERENCES REFERENCES **REFERENCES** REFERENCES REFERENCES REFERENCES

DfE (2011) *Teachers' Standards.* Available at **www.education.gov.uk/publications**

Florian, L. and Hegarty, J. (2004) *ICT and Special Educational Needs: A Tool for Inclusion*. Buckingham: Open University Press.

Lie, K., O'Hare, A. and Denwood, S. (2000) Multidisciplinary support and the management of children with specific writing difficulties. *British Journal of Special Education*, 27 (2) June.

Somekh, B. and Davis, N. (eds) (2007, Kindle edition) *Using IT Effectively in Teaching and Learning: Studies in Pre-service and In-service Teacher Education*. London: Routledge.

FURTHER READING   FURTHER READING   **FURTHER READING**   FURTHER READING

Ager, R. (2003) *ICT in Primary Schools.* London: Routledge.

Duffty, J. (2006) *Primary ICT: Extending Knowledge in Practice.* Exeter: Learning Matters.

Florian, L. and Hegarty, J. (2004) *ICT and Special Educational Needs: A Tool for Inclusion*. Buckingham: Open University Press.

Freedman, T. (1999) *Managing ICT*. London: Hodder & Stoughton.

Lie, K., O'Hare, A. and Denwood, S. (2000) Multidisciplinary support and the management of children with specific writing difficulties. *British Journal of Special Education*, 27 (2) June.

Somekh, B. and Davis, N. (eds) (1997) *Using IT Effectively in Teaching and Learning: Studies in Pre-service and In-service Teacher Education*. London: Routledge.

2
Planning for primary computing as a subject

Chapter objectives

When you have completed work on this chapter, you will have:

- examined some of the key principles to focus on when planning for the use of new technologies;
- considered the elements of effective planning;
- looked at a possible lesson-planning pro forma;
- thought about how to plan for computing as a National Curriculum subject.

TEACHERS' STANDARDS

A teacher must:

1. Set high expectations which inspire, motivate and challenge pupils

- establish a safe and stimulating environment for pupils, rooted in mutual respect
- set goals that stretch and challenge pupils of all backgrounds, abilities and dispositions
- demonstrate consistently the positive attitudes, values and behaviour which are expected of pupils

2. Promote good progress and outcomes by pupils

- plan teaching to build on pupils' capabilities and prior knowledge
- guide pupils to reflect on the progress they have made and their emerging needs

3. Demonstrate good subject and curriculum knowledge

- have a secure knowledge of the relevant subject(s) and curriculum areas, foster and maintain pupils' interest in the subject, and address misunderstandings
- demonstrate a critical understanding of developments in the subject and curriculum areas, and promote the value of scholarship

4. Plan and teach well structured lessons

- impart knowledge and develop understanding through effective use of lesson time
- promote a love of learning and children's intellectual curiosity
- set homework and plan other out-of-class activities to consolidate and extend the knowledge and understanding pupils have acquired
- reflect systematically on the effectiveness of lessons and approaches to teaching
- contribute to the design and provision of an engaging curriculum within the relevant subject area(s).

Introduction

There are some key principles on which to focus when thinking about planning in the light of new technology.

High expectations must extend to the use of technology in schools in an era of continual change and adaptation and in which young learners may have access to all sorts of ICT at home and elsewhere away from the classroom. Having high expectations means knowing where the children are up to in the first place. It presupposes that some kind of conversation has taken place which locates the children's knowledge and experience of computing. In this way, computing is no different from any other area of learning. It needs to be mapped accurately by reference to the learners and what they bring to the setting. It will not do, for example, to teach how to underline fonts to someone who is designing and creating their own website at home. There will have to be a different set of expectations for these learners.

You need to have a **secure knowledge and understanding of your subject** and related pedagogy. This means being aware of where to go for support in knowledge and understanding and not simply in the way of finding appropriate 'content' for subject teaching, but when and how to use that content, and with what sort of pedagogy in mind. There are very many resources produced by LAs, software publishers and the government (as well as informally through the networks which teachers establish for themselves) which lend themselves to particular visions of pedagogy.

You need to design **opportunities for learners to develop their computing skills**. This means being able to see opportunities in whatever sessions you are designing for the convergence of skills and purposeful learning with the technology in a given subject. As a concrete example, publishing small books in the classroom will give a sense of writing for a purpose, for a target audience and perhaps focusing on particular aspects of literacy teaching. At the same time, the mix of text and graphics, the negotiation with scanners, printers, cameras and other peripherals helps to develop children's computing capabilities within a real context.

You need to **use a range of teaching strategies and resources,** including e-learning. E-learning is defined here in its broadest sense for the use of both online and offline resources and as both a resource and a subset of skills in its own right. It means seeing opportunities for using web-based learning platforms, online software, and resources in the classroom (including IWBs).

You need to plan for **a purposeful and safe working environment**. The word 'safe' means being physically well organised in the space, whether you are in a network room or bringing a portable resource to the classroom. It is about being aware of everything that can contribute to a safe working environment around technology. A fuller discussion appears in Chapter 19 but, at this juncture, it's worth demarcating the range of thinking in health and safety as starting from who plugs and unplugs the equipment to dealing with trailing cables, to safe, possibly height-adjustable seating, and monitoring levels of screen-time.

The word 'purposeful' relates to having some clear idea of what is happening and where it is taking the learners in terms of their knowledge and experience. More than that, as in other subjects, it means being able to communicate this. In planning terms, this means being very clear about the learning objectives. We will see in Chapter 3 how we might identify these learning objectives and opportunities in subject teaching in all subjects.

You need to ensure that **other adults in the classroom are fully briefed** as to your planning and their role within it. There are many occasions in classrooms where you will be responsible for the work of other adults in the setting. With ICT and computing, this means being sensitive to the needs of those teachers and helpers and being fully apprised of the situation regarding skill levels and expectations of everyone in the setting.

Effective planning – analysing the situation

Effective teaching depends heavily on effective planning. ICT in subject teaching and computing as a subject in its own right are no exception to this rule. In turn, effective planning depends on a thorough analysis of the situation at the outset. Many writers have identified this link and some have produced books for teachers in training which summarise and synthesise the best of the available research.

RESEARCH SUMMARY RESEARCH SUMMARY **RESEARCH SUMMARY** RESEARCH SUMMARY

Chris Kyriacou (2009) provides an overview of studies which have looked at lesson effectiveness. One of the studies reported, that of Cooper and McIntyre (1996), looked at the teaching and learning in a series of lessons in terms of what both the teachers and the pupils felt. Analysis produced the following list of key items which contributed to lesson effectiveness.

- **Clear learning goals for pupil learning.**
- **Helping pupils to contextualise the content in terms of their own experience and knowledge.**
- **Providing a supportive social context for learning.**
- **Enabling pupils to engage in the learning process in a number of different ways.**
- **Willingness of the teacher to modify learning tasks in the light of pupil circumstances.**

All of these factors are of immediate direct relevance to teachers planning for any subject in the curriculum. When it comes to the use of ICT in subject teaching or computing in its own right, there is an added layer of complexity because of the impact of the resource setting of the school (see Chapter 1). Some questions need to be raised to take account of this and added to the generic areas above. At the outset, as a minimum, trainees preparing to teach computing or use ICT in their teaching need to be asking these questions.

- What do we know about the children's existing knowledge, skills and understanding in the subject?
- What has been their previous experience with ICT or computing?
- What does the computing curriculum set out for the children in this year group?
- What does the school's scheme of work require?
- What am I therefore expecting the children to achieve?
- How will I differentiate the activity to reflect the different needs and abilities in the class?
- What relevant pieces of theoretical writing and/or case studies are there to support my planning?

- What will be the demands on me in terms of my own knowledge, skills and understanding of computing?
- What is the resource setting for the school and how does this impact on what I can plan for the class?
- What are the additional time costs and constraints on me when planning to use ICT or teach computing?
- What kind of grouping or organisation am I planning to use?
- How do I go about the physical management of the activity?
- Are there any further cross-curricular links?
- How will I go about including the whole class in the activity?
- What are the assessment and record-keeping opportunities in the activity?

Planning is, of course, cyclical in nature. No sooner have you reached the last question than you realise it must be used to answer the first question in the next batch of planning. Good planning should create assessment opportunities because good assessment informs good planning.

THE BIGGER PICTURE THE BIGGER PICTURE THE BIGGER PICTURE THE BIGGER PICTURE

When you are planning differentiation as part of your duty to ensure the inclusion of all children, remember that there are sources of advice within your school (class teachers and teaching or learning support assistants who work with the children, and the inclusion leader or special educational needs co-ordinator) and from local authority services (such as those for children with additional and special educational needs, for those with English as an additional language and for traveller and minority ethnic children, and a 'virtual headteacher' with responsibility for looked-after children).

It makes sense to try to collect these questions into headings which you can use to ensure that you cover all of the necessary elements each time you plan. As part of your training year, you will develop, or be given assistance in developing, lesson-planning pro formas of various kinds. Some will provide very detailed outlines of what is going on in a session, whereas others will be shorter. As you gain experience through the year, what seems like a very detailed and time-consuming activity initially will become part of your professional life and second nature to you as a practising and reflective teacher.

Without attempting to prescribe a model which works in all settings, on all courses and in all classrooms, we set out later in this chapter an example plan for a computing lesson in Key Stage 1. Most of the headings are in common use for curriculum planning in all subjects and are relatively easily adapted to ICT in subject teaching and computing as a subject in its own right. However, before examining more closely what a computing lesson in Key Stage 1 might look like in practice, we want to take a more detailed look at computing as expressed in the National Curriculum programme of study.

Computing as a National Curriculum subject

This chapter is concerned principally with the computing curriculum as it is outlined for children entering Year 1 of primary school up to Year 6. The curriculum for the Early Years Foundation Stage is covered in Chapter 4. We give an overview here of the computing programme of study, but more detailed information on specific activities can be found throughout the chapters in Section B of the book.

The most recent version of the National Curriculum for schools in England was published in 2013 for implementation from September 2014. As discussed in the Introduction to this book, compared to the previous Programme of Study, the latest iteration of the computing National Curriculum places more emphasis on children learning to program computers and developing computational thinking. The revised National Curriculum (DfE, 2013) sets out the purpose for computing as a subject stating that:

> *A high-quality computing education equips pupils to use computational thinking and creativity to understand and change the world. Computing has deep links with mathematics, science, and design and technology, and provides insights into both natural and artificial systems. The core of computing is computer science, in which pupils are taught the principles of information and computation, how digital systems work, and how to put this knowledge to use through programming. Building on this knowledge and understanding, pupils are equipped to use information technology to create programs, systems and a range of content. Computing also ensures that pupils become digitally literate – able to use, and express themselves and develop their ideas through, information and communication technology – at a level suitable for the future workplace and as active participants in a digital world.*

(DfE, 2013, no page)

It is clear that the purpose of this Programme of Study is to give children a greater understanding of the ways in which computers actually work by addressing some of the fundamental concepts of computer science. However, there also remains a clear expectation that the curriculum will enable children to become creative and discerning users of technology, that is digitally literate.

Looking briefly at resource provision for planning with the National Curriculum, as a minimum, the table below indicates the kind of indicative resources (hardware and software) and activities you would expect to see provided in order for children to have their entitlement to computing met. Important terms from the Programme of Study are also defined. Subsequent chapters in Section B of this book explore these aspects of the programme of study in more depth.

Key Stage 1

Area of knowledge, skills and understanding. Children should be taught to:	Resource entitlement, indicative activities and definitions	Sections B & C – Chapter cross-reference
Understand what algorithms are; how they are implemented as programs on digital devices; and that programs execute by following precise and unambiguous instructions. Create and debug simple programs.	***Resources and indicative activities:*** Children should use programmable toys such as Bee-Bots, Roamers, giving them instructions to navigate a floor map or maze. On the computer they could use programs that allow them to give instructions to control an onscreen turtle or other controllable object. For example, programs such as 2Simple's 2Go or Logo could be used. Or they could create a game using software such as Kodu or Scratch.	Chapters 10, 11, 12

Use logical reasoning to predict the behaviour of simple programs.	**Definitions:** Algorithm – a sequential set of instructions to achieve a specific goal Debug – to identify and remove errors, e.g. in an algorithm Logical reasoning – being systematic when writing algorithms or debugging programs	
Use technology purposefully to create, organise, store, manipulate and retrieve digital content.	**Resources and indicative activities:** Children should use a range of hardware and software, such as word processors, desktop publishing, multimedia software, digital cameras (still and video), music/audio editing software, scanners, monitoring and data-logging equipment. **Definitions:** Digital content – this could be any kind of digital content, e.g. data collected as part of a survey on how children travel to school; photographs and text for a presentation about a recent school trip to a local museum; and digital audio that the children have recorded and edited	Chapters 7, 8, 9, 10, 11, 13, 15
Use technology safely and respectfully, keeping personal information private; know where to go for help and support when they have concerns about material on the internet. Recognise common uses of information technology beyond school.	**Resources and indicative activities:** Children should use the internet for finding and critically evaluating information. Opportunities can also be available for children to discuss safety issues by engaging in communication through a range of communication tools, such as e-mail or online forums, in the relative safety of the school's virtual learning environment. Teachers should discuss with the children what is meant by personal information (i.e. passwords, usernames, home town and address details) and when this should not be shared. There should be opportunities to discuss children's use of technologies beyond school. For example, safety issues surrounding the use of online games or technologies in the home, such as mobile phones and tablet devices, can be addressed positively through the discussion and modelling of appropriate use of such devices.	Chapters 16, 17, 19, 20

Planning for computing as a subject

Schools must have a scheme of work in place as a fundamental aid to planning, a map of the learning outcomes for computing in their school and as a statement of intent and entitlement. In the past, many schools used a QCA Scheme of Work for ICT (QCA, 1998). Some have schemes which are based on the QCA model or are based on a similar, local authority one. Try to obtain early on in your placement a copy of your school's scheme of work and use it in your planning. However, please note that if based on the QCA model (QCA, 2000), this no longer meets key aspects of the new programme of study.

Key Stage 2

Area of knowledge, skills and understanding. Children should be taught to:	Resource entitlement, indicative activities and definitions	Sections B & C – Chapter cross-reference
Design, write and debug programs that accomplish specific goals, including controlling or simulating physical systems; solve problems by decomposing them into smaller parts. Use sequence, selection, and repetition in programs; work with variables and various forms of input and output. Use logical reasoning to explain how some simple algorithms work and to detect and correct errors in algorithms and programs.	*Resources and indicative activities:* Children should have the opportunity to work with a range of programming environments/languages. For example, they could work with block-based visual programming tools (e.g. Scratch, App Inventor, Kodu, Lego WeDo) to design, create and control simulations, apps, games and physical models or systems including robots (e.g. Pro-Bot). Similarly, they could work with flow-chart programming tools (e.g. Flowol) to control simulations such as automated lighthouses, pedestrian crossing and traffic light scenarios, which illustrate how computers can be used to automate aspects of the physical environment. Logo could also be used to create onscreen graphical objects which can be controlled and animated using a text-based programming language (e.g. MSW Logo, Testease Turtle CT). *Definitions:* Program – a collection of related algorithms/instructions with specific outcomes Control/Simulate physical systems – this refers to any simulated or physical system or model that can be linked to a computer or has a computer embedded within it, e.g. traffic light system Decomposition – the process of isolating or breaking down the various constituent parts of a computer program or algorithm to solve problems and debug any errors in it Sequence – the order of events in a program or algorithm Selection – the point within a computer program or algorithm where there is more than one possible output (e.g. conditional IF, THEN, logic) Repetition – loops in programs are often exploited by programmers. Repeat commands can also be used to make programming more efficient Input – a signal or data entered into a computer (e.g. via the keys on a keyboard; buttons on a mouse; button on a pedestrian crossing; or a hotspot on a touchscreen device) Output – what results when data or signals are processed and sent from a computer or program (e.g. a letter on a screen when a key on a keyboard is pressed; the wait light, amber, red and green lights on a pedestrian crossing)	Chapters 10, 11, 12

	Variable – a place in a computer program where data is stored and remembered (e.g. a score in a computer game uses variables; a sold out sign in a drinks vending machine would also depend on variables that monitor how many of each drink has been sold)	
Understand computer networks, including the internet; how they can provide multiple services, such as the world wide web; and the opportunities they offer for communication and collaboration. Use search technologies effectively, appreciate how results are selected and ranked, and be discerning in evaluating digital content. Use technology safely, respectfully and responsibly; know a range of ways to report concerns and inappropriate behaviour.	*Resources and indicative activities:* Children can learn about and discuss how information is sent and received via the internet. Processes such as packet switching could be explained and explored with children through role-play activities. They should also explore the difference between the internet and the world wide web. There are a number of online videos that explain this (e.g. **www.youtube.com/ watch?v=VXg_HGgo7Qs** and **www.youtube. com/watch?v=C3sr7_0FyPA**) Children should use a range of web browsers (e.g. Google Chrome, Firefox, Safari, Internet Explorer) and search engines to support their research. They could explore Boolean search strategies to narrow their searches. They could also explore how different search engines (Google, Bing, Yahoo, Ask, Duck Duck Go) deliver different results and consider the reasons for this. They could also compare and check information from a range of different sources, e.g. books, people, information leaflets and the world wide web. Children should have hands-on experience of strategies for keeping themselves safe online as well as opportunities to discuss issues of e-safety. They could take part in an online simulation game where they have to make decisions about how to respond to a range of scenarios (e.g. from how to deal with spam e-mail to what to do if they receive threatening or abusive text messages). *Definitions:* Packet switching – this is the process by which data is transferred so speedily on the internet by being broken down into millions of smaller pieces of data by the sender's device and then reassembled by the receiving device. For a more detailed explanation, see **www.explainthatstuff. com/internet.html** World wide web – the content or the billions of digital pages on the internet Internet – the infrastructure of the network, e.g. the interconnected cables, computers, servers, routers and connected networks Search engine – a web-based program that acts like an index in a library, returning a list of web-based documents or resources according to a keyword used to search	Chapters 12, 13, 16, 17, 19, 20

	Web browser – a program that enables users to locate, access and present information on the internet	
	Boolean search strategies – these are specific strategies that enable users to perform more specific or targeted searches	
Select, use and combine a variety of software (including internet services) on a range of digital devices to accomplish given goals, including collecting, analysing, evaluating and presenting data and information.	*Resources and indicative activities:* Under the supervision of the teacher, children could create and maintain a class blog (e.g. WordPress, Edublogs, Tumblr) to keep the wider school community (other classes, parents and family, partner school in another location or country) up to date with news of trips and what they have been learning about. This could include presenting relevant photographs provided appropriate safety procedures have been followed. Children could use moving or still images combined with digital audio to create a short e-safety video or presentation for other children (e.g. presentation software, video/audio editing software). Children could investigate how the school could become a more environmentally friendly community by carrying out a survey of how children travel to school. They could design a survey and make it available to the wider school community via an online form (e.g. Survey Monkey). They could evaluate and analyse the data using a database and then present their findings about the school's impact on the environment. *Definitions:* Blog – the word is a contraction of 'web log'. A blog is an online chronological journal/diary of individual or group reflections and observations. The most recent blog post or entry is at the top of the home page	Chapters 7, 8, 9, 10, 11, 13, 15, 16, 17

Planning example for Key Stage 1

An example follows of a suggested longer-format lesson plan. It assumes a high resource setting; a school with a networked suite of computers and multiple programmable toys/robots. The specific lesson is adapted from an idea by Kristine Kopelke (see **http://elresources.skola.edu.mt/wp-content/uploads/2010/06/doc_669_2468_beebotguideA4v2.pdf**). The context is a unit for Year 1: Journeys – Robot Routes. This lesson could also be adapted for different contexts or smaller groups. For an example of the kind of outcomes from the lesson, watch this video (Kopelke, 2012).

LONGER LESSON PLAN FOR COMPUTING AT YEAR 1

UNIT: Journeys – Robot Routes

CROSS-CURRICULAR LINK: Mathematics

OVERVIEW: In this unit of work the children have been finding out about journeys in a range of contexts (e.g. in stories, their own lives, historical journeys). In computing they have been working with programmable toys (Bee-Bots), exploring how they can be controlled using the input keys (e.g. forward, backward, right, left). To support this work they have also been exploring non-standard units of measure in mathematics. For example, Bee-Bot moves 15cm so this unit of measure has been used to estimate the distance Bee-Bot travels. The children have also begun to explore routes on maps, using maps/plans of familiar places (e.g. plan of the school layout and simple map of the local area). In this lesson the children will design and create their own route for Bee-Bot. They will also be challenged to predict and program multi-step instructions (algorithms) for Bee-Bot to carry out as it navigates the routes they have designed. The lesson will be in two parts. In the first part, the children will work in groups to design and create a simple but multi-step route or maze for the Bee-Bot to follow. In the second half of the lesson they will devise algorithms using adapted playing cards to program the Bee-Bots to navigate the mazes/routes they have created.

SCHOOL/CLASS CONTEXT

The school is a large, inner-city primary school with a wide range of ability. Some 20 different languages are spoken, of which the majority speak Sylheti-Bengali. There are 29 children in the class, an average size for the school. The children are all in Year 1.

LEARNING NEEDS OF THE CHILDREN

FOR COMPUTING: Most children are confident at logging on and using the computers in the network suite. They have also explored programming Bee-Bots both onscreen and through programmable toys, giving single-step instructions (algorithms) to navigate a short route or floor map. The aim of the lesson is to develop the children's ability to give precise multi-step instructions, which show their understanding of the importance of sequence.

FOR MATHEMATICS: The aim of the lesson is also to develop the children's ability to estimate distances using non-standard units, as well as to understand quarter, half and full turns.

GROUPING/TIMING

The lesson will last one hour, not including a 10-minute outline to recap on what they know about giving instructions to Bee-Bot. We will go into the hall at about 1.30 and leave at about 2.45 in time for the afternoon break. The class will be split into groups of 3–4. Groupings should be based on the teacher's knowledge of the children and the children should be reminded about how to work well together. There will also be a Teaching Assistant to support the task who has been briefed on the aims of the lesson.

RESOURCES

The hall will be used for this activity as it allows the children to work with the Bee-Bots on the floor. However, the activity could also be done outside using chalk to create different routes on the playground surface or in small groups using an area of the classroom. Each group will need an A1 sheet of paper and large pencils (chalk if outside), erasers and a non-standard Bee-Bot measure. Each group will need a Bee-Bot. Also each group will need a set of algorithm playing cards with the various Bee-Bot instructions on them (Forward, Backward, Right Turn, Left Turn or arrows). As an alternative, Bee-Bot routes could be created from 3-dimensional objects such as building blocks or found objects.

THEORETICAL CONTEXT

From Avril Loveless' *The Role of ICT* (Chapter 2 in Loveless, 2003, p.45): 'Control technology offers the opportunity for an investigative approach to problem solving and a development in the complexity of giving and modifying instructions. …. They can learn the importance of testing systems to make them foolproof in all circumstances – procedures essential to designers and engineers.'

NC/EYFS CONTEXT

Understand what algorithms are; how they are implemented as programs on digital devices; and that programs execute by following precise and unambiguous instructions.

Create and debug simple programs.

Use logical reasoning to predict the behaviour of simple programs.

SCHEME OF WORK CONTEXT

Lesson ideas Year 1 unit: Journeys – Robot Routes

YOUR OWN LEARNING NEEDS

Make sure I am confident programming multi-step instructions into Bee-Bot.
Make sure that I know how to model using the Bee-Bot non-standard unit measure, to model the design and creation of a Bee-Bot route.

ORGANISATIONAL MEMORY JOGGERS

Make sure all of the Bee-Bots are working properly and have enough battery life for the activity. Remember to collect enough paper, large pencils and erasers. Make sure I have briefed the Teaching Assistant and that they are familiar with how to program Bee-Bot. Make sure the children know their groups for the activity.

OTHER ADULTS

Remember to copy the lesson plan and talk to the Teaching Assistant before the lesson takes place if at all possible. Give them access to a Bee-Bot before the lesson if necessary.

LEARNING OBJECTIVES/INTENTIONS

FOR COMPUTING: The key idea is that children understand that robots/computers can be controlled using instructions (algorithms) and that they can receive and respond to multiple instructions (algorithms). Children will also develop their understanding of the need for precision and correct sequencing when working with algorithms to program Bee-Bot to complete a given route.

FOR MATHEMATICS: Children develop their estimations skills using non-standard measures and use the vocabulary of quarter, half and whole turns.

DIFFERENTIATION

Children will be organised in mixed-ability groupings based on their previous work with Bee-Bots. Lower attainers may need to break the Bee-Bot route into two-step algorithms but challenge them to combine or extend this to a multi-step algorithm to complete the whole route. Higher attainers can be challenged earlier in the process to predict and develop multi-step algorithms to navigate through the route. Lower attainers can also record their algorithms using the adapted playing cards whereas higher attainers will be encouraged to record their algorithms by writing them down fully or in pseudo code.

LEARNING NEEDS – SEN

For the child with difficulties with motor control, remember to ensure that they are given more time to physically program the Bee-Bot.

LEARNING NEEDS – EAL

Children who have English as an additional language are all at different stages of acquiring English. Partner the children appropriately according to language needed to access the activity. Remember to check and re-check understanding of the task.

ASSESSMENT OPPORTUNITIES

Complete observation pro formas on targeted children or on the whole class profile as appropriate (see Chapter 5).

KEY QUESTIONS

Remember to focus on the language being developed for computing, i.e. can they predict and make a recording of their algorithms or say their algorithms before testing them with Bee-Bot? With higher attainers, can they write or record multi-step algorithms to predict the Bee-Bot's route? Can they identify and debug errors in their predictions and algorithms? Can they estimate distance accurately using the non-standard unit (Bee-Bot unit)? Can they use the appropriate language for turns (e.g. quarter, half, full turn, left, right)?

LESSON FORMAT

10 minutes: Opening with demonstration on IWB/visualiser/flip chart, use Bee-Bot unit to draw a simple route for Bee-Bot. Invite some participation from the children. Ask questions. Explain that they are going to create their own routes. Model the use of language (e.g. right quarter turn, left quarter turn) while drawing a route. Check and re-check understanding of the task. Share the learning objectives with the children.

15–20 minutes: In groups, children devise and draw their routes for Bee-Bot on large sheets of paper.

10 minutes: Re-group and use one of the groups' Bee-Bot routes. Remind the children how to program Bee-Bot using the input direction keys. Explain to the children that you want to challenge them to program the Bee-Bot in as few attempts as possible, e.g. try to predict the algorithm to get Bee-Bot to the end of the route in one go.

20 minutes: Using the routes they have created, children collect a Bee-Bot and predict the algorithm they think they need to help Bee-Bot complete the route. Encourage them to offer different solutions before trying it, listening to everyone's suggestions in the group. If there is time, groups could swap Bee-Bot routes.

10 minutes: Plenary with contributions/questions from children. Allow the children themselves to demonstrate and talk through their work. Remember to allow for questions from across the ability range. Possibly also use photographs of the children working and their algorithms to highlight their achievements.

EVALUATING THE LESSON (1) – OPERATIONAL ISSUES

Note here any changes during the lesson which might affect the way you work on this unit in the future. Issues which might have arisen include any of the following.

- **All children needed more time to share the equipment.**
- **The two 20 minute activities were fine as it occurred, but some children needed more support within the groups to make it work.**
- **The plenary was too rushed and there was insufficient time to draw the understanding together and revisit the learning objectives with the children.**

EVALUATING THE LESSON (2) – LEARNING OUTCOMES

Note in this section any particular achievements which children demonstrated. Were you able to carry out the assessments planned for during the session?

EVALUATING THE LESSON (3) – NEXT TIME

What aspects of this work (if any) need to be repeated? How could you deepen understanding of the computing concepts behind the work? What will you do next time in the light of the organisational changes you had to make?

PRACTICAL TASK   PRACTICAL TASK   PRACTICAL TASK   PRACTICAL TASK

Identify a unit in the school's scheme of work for computing for the age group you are teaching. Find an activity which fits in with the current units of work being undertaken in either computing or any of the other subject areas. Follow the pro forma for the example lesson plan from above, identifying the cross-curricular links if relevant, and plan a lesson for your class.

A SUMMARY OF **KEY POINTS**

- ➤ There are some key principles to focus on when planning to teach computing, including maintaining high expectations, having secure knowledge and understanding of the subject and designing opportunities for learners to develop their skills.
- ➤ You need to use a range of teaching strategies and resources, including e-learning (e.g. IWB, visualiser, digital camera to capture any assessment opportunities), planning for a purposeful and safe working environment and ensuring that other adults in the classroom are fully briefed.
- ➤ Effective planning is underpinned by some key questions, including asking what is known about children's current knowledge, skills and understanding, what is required by the curriculum, what are the objectives for children's learning and how any activity will be assessed.
- ➤ A comprehensive lesson-planning format is recommended that draws on these key questions and is closely related to the school's scheme of work for computing.
- ➤ Computing must be taught as a National Curriculum subject in its own right but meaningful links can be made to other subjects, as in the example Year 1 lesson plan.

> ➤ When planning for computing as a subject, it is important to set out the context of the lesson, and to set clear learning objectives/intentions against which you can assess children's progress.
>
> ➤ Links to other subjects should be noted if relevant.
>
> ➤ Differentiation for children of all ability levels, for those with additional and special educational needs and children with English as an additional language promotes the inclusion of all children.
>
> ➤ The lesson should be evaluated to complete the planning cycle.

M-LEVEL EXTENSION > > M-LEVEL EXTENSION > > M-LEVEL EXTENSION

When you have the opportunity to observe your class teacher or other colleagues, ask to look at their planning and discuss how they set about planning the lesson you saw and the series of lessons that it was a part of. Ask how they planned the differentiation that you observed. After reflecting on your discussion, decide how you would differentiate this activity for children of differing levels of ability. What about those children with specific learning difficulties or particular needs, for example children with English as an additional language? Would they require any particular support or additional resources? Remember that you may also have in the same group or class children who are able, gifted and talented. When you have made your decisions, discuss your notes with your mentor/class teacher and ask for feedback specifically on planning when a colleague observes you teaching.

REFERENCES REFERENCES **REFERENCES** REFERENCES REFERENCES REFERENCES

Cooper, P. and McIntyre, D. (1996) Effective teaching and learning. *British Educational Research Journal*, 22 (5) December.

DfE (2011) *Teachers' Standards.* Available at **www.education.gov.uk/publications**

DfE (2013) *National Curriculum in England: Primary Curriculum.* London: DfE. Available at **www. gov.uk/government/publications/national-curriculum-in-england-primary-curriculum**

Kopelke, K. (2012) *Making Your Classroom Buzz with Bee-Bots*. Available at **http://elresources. skola.edu.mt/wp-content/uploads/2010/06/doc_669_2468_beebotguideA4v2.pdf**

Kyriacou, C. (2009) *Effective Teaching in Schools.* London: Nelson Thornes.

Loveless, A. (2003) *The Role of ICT*. London: Continuum.

QCA (1998, revised 2002, 2003) *Scheme of Work for ICT.* London: QCA. Available at **http:// webarchive.nationalarchives.gov.uk/20090608182316/http://standards.dfes.gov.uk/schemes2/ it/?view=get.**

FURTHER READING FURTHER READING **FURTHER READING** FURTHER READING

Department for Education website, **www.education.gov.uk**

Duffty, J. (2006) *Primary ICT: Extending Knowledge in Practice.* Exeter: Learning Matters.

McFarlane, A. (2007, Kindle e-book version) *Information Technology and Authentic Learning: Realising the Potential of Computers in the Classroom.* London: Taylor and Francis.

3
Planning for primary ICT in other subjects

Chapter objectives

When you have completed work on this chapter, you will have:

- considered planning for the use of ICT in subject teaching, beginning with the subjects themselves rather than the programmes of study for ICT;
- looked at opportunities for the use of ICT in the core subjects;
- examined opportunities for cross-curricular use of ICT to support the foundation subjects;
- noted the differences in school settings with different levels of resourcing.

TEACHERS' STANDARDS

A teacher must:

2. **Promote good progress and outcomes by pupils**

- demonstrate knowledge and understanding of how pupils learn and how this impacts on teaching
- encourage pupils to take a responsible and conscientious attitude to their own work and study

3. **Demonstrate good subject and curriculum knowledge**

- have a secure knowledge of the relevant subject(s) and curriculum areas, foster and maintain pupils' interest in the subject, and address misunderstandings
- demonstrate a critical understanding of developments in the subject and curriculum areas, and promote the value of scholarship

4. **Plan and teach well structured lessons**

- impart knowledge and develop understanding through effective use of lesson time
- promote a love of learning and children's intellectual curiosity
- contribute to the design and provision of an engaging curriculum within the relevant subject area(s).

Introduction

While learning how to plan for ICT in subject teaching, you will be cognisant of the need to know about the children's ICT capability in order to pursue opportunities to exploit and extend it. It will be part of a set of factors that make up good lesson planning, in the same way that planning a useful mathematics lesson in shape and space, for example, takes into account the children's wider experiences, mathematical capabilities and opportunities to enhance and develop them. They do not exist in a separate world; they are inextricably linked. You must look at the context of the features of ICT which make it a learning tool – one among many – and decide on whether it is appropriate to the learning outcome for which you are currently planning. At the same time, unless other factors are taken into account (and, as previously stated, this means, as a minimum, knowing about the children's existing ICT capability and the resources available in the school), planning will be, at best, ineffective and, at worst, potentially counterproductive.

This chapter addresses the context of ICT in subject teaching, beginning with the core curriculum and moving through to the foundation subjects. Throughout, while the emphasis is on how the ICT supports the learning in each of these subjects, there is clearly a parallel development going on of your own skills.

Planning ICT in English and literacy

In support of the requirements for National Curriculum English, lessons in literacy were introduced as part of the National Literacy Strategy, and continued under the Primary National Strategies (DfES/QCA, 2006). Although the requirement to have regard for the Primary National Strategies has been discontinued and a new National Curriculum has placed a greater emphasis on systematic synthetic phonics in decoding language, you may find that schools and individual teachers you work with are still using elements of the national strategies. For example, it is likely that the three-part literacy lesson will still be used to some extent, which included a whole-class starter session on text-level, sentence-level or word-level work, main follow-up activities often with group or individual work, and a plenary review. The National Curriculum for English (DfE, 2013) breaks the subject into:

Spoken Language

Reading

1. word (decoding)
2. comprehension (reading for meaning)

Writing

1. transcription (spelling, handwriting)
2. composition
3. vocabulary, grammar and punctuation

The main differences between the recent National Curriculum for English and the Primary National Strategy (DfES/QCA, 2006) is a greater emphasis on systematic synthetic phonics but many of the previous requirements can still be traced if you compare the new structure with the previous requirements. For example:

Speaking and listening for a wide range of purposes in different contexts

- *Speaking*
- *Listening and responding*
- *Group discussion and interaction*
- *Drama*

Reading and writing for a range of purposes on paper and on screen

- *Word recognition: decoding (reading) and encoding (spelling)*
- *Word structure and spelling*
- *Understanding and interpreting texts*
- *Engaging and responding to texts*
- *Creating and shaping texts*
- *Text structure and organisation*
- *Sentence structure and punctuation*
- *Presentation*

(DfES/QCA, 2006)

The issue for those planning to work with ICT in literacy sessions is how to integrate it effectively. The solution to this issue, will, as usual, be different in almost every setting and contingent on the resources available in all the categories: human resources, hardware resources and software resources.

Here, we look at how you might approach the use of ICT in support of literacy sessions in low- and high-resource settings.

Group activities – low-resource setting

To take an aspect of a literacy session – the group activity – we can see that this lends itself to the use of the computer. In a low-resource setting, with one computer in the corner of the classroom, there will need to be some creativity with the planning. Depending on the nature of the task and of the software being used, it could be possible to split a group of six into two lots of three with 10 minutes each. This group would then become part of the working week in the normal way and the whole class rotated through in a week.

In some ways, this is an example of the atomised curriculum at its worst, with children not being able to develop any real ICT skills in such short bursts. It also has high planning 'overheads' because of the need to plan something for the children to do while they are waiting for their turn. On the other hand, there are activities which lend themselves to shorter amounts of time at the computer. With tutorial software there might be short activities and investigations around a particular learning objective, such as learning the sounds of English. The most recent debates in teaching literacy in primary schools has brought to prominence the teaching of synthetic phonics in a systematic way. Software publishers have not been slow to exploit this and a whole range of titles and online areas is emerging which aim to provide multimedia reinforcement for learning sounds. An onscreen exercise, for example, to identify parts of words and break them down into constituent sounds would be one. Clearly, pointing and clicking on items in a menu or a game in such software is not doing a great deal to advance the knowledge and understanding of ICT. However, literacy provision itself might be enhanced by the regular presence of reinforcement of learning objectives which rely on heard sounds and take children away from the daily provision of photocopied worksheets.

Another idea is to use open-ended software in this situation to create your own short activities. For example, using a word processor, a document template could be created which allowed children to search and replace nouns with pronouns, or the thesaurus facility might be used to develop a wider vocabulary. Another could allow children to highlight all the verbs in sentence-level work and change the font in some way. At this level of resourcing, activities are going to be low level with some element of repetition and reinforcement. However, in the example with open-ended software, the ICT is being used to provide stimulus and variety and one more planning option for the hard-pressed class teacher. It can also legitimately be said to be providing variety for the children and giving them different ways to access the curriculum.

THE BIGGER PICTURE   THE BIGGER PICTURE   **THE BIGGER PICTURE**   THE BIGGER PICTURE

When you are planning to use ICT to support cross-curricular literacy work, consider how writing frames developed for literacy sessions could help to support less able or less confident writers in your class, including those children with additional and special educational needs. For example, a frame to structure and record research could be useful when undertaking a project on healthy lifestyles that includes work in science (healthy eating – food as fuel), personal, social and health education (good mental health, the dangers of alcohol, drug and substance abuse) and PE (the benefits of health-related exercise). If considering such a project, you may find it helpful to visit the MEND programme website (see www.mendprogramme. org). MEND (Mind, Exercise, Nutrition ... Do it!) is a joint initiative between local authorities, NHS primary care trusts and other partners to work together to combat the causes of child obesity, and successful elements include the healthy schools programme, extended schools activities and school sport partnerships.

The plenary in a low-resource setting

If you have access to presentation software and the computer is accessible to the carpet area, then in a given week children could be preparing small presentations on the learning objective for the plenary each day. This is potentially the highest-order development of ICT skills, and perhaps also of the literacy focus. As the class teacher familiar with the children concerned, you would be in a position to determine which of the children would benefit from this. It need not always be the most able. In this situation, having an adult helper who is also familiar with the software would allow the children who are struggling with a given concept to reinforce their learning by having to construct a presentation for others.

The situation in this resource setting could be described in the following table:

Activity	Software	Literacy/ICT potential
Ten-minute onscreen reinforcement of learning objective	Tutorial program, focused aims, revision in a game-style environment	High literacy Low level ICT skills
Ten-minute onscreen search and replace, reinforcement of learning objective	Word processing	High literacy Higher level ICT skills
Collaborative work on presentation for the plenary about a particular learning objective	Presentation Word processing	High literacy High level ICT skills

A literacy lesson in a high-resource setting

Looking at the other extreme, where a school has very rich provision for ICT, there is inevitably more room for using ICT in a literacy lesson.

In the simplest example, if there are more computers in the classroom (perhaps three), then a group can work in pairs for the whole of the 20 minutes of group activity, undertaking any of the examples illustrated above at a higher level due to the extended time available.

If the high-resource setting manifests itself in the form of a collection of hand-held devices, laptops or tablets (Apple or Android), there is very great potential. If working with tablet devices, children might work with mind-mapping tools to plan a piece of writing. There are various apps to support literacy work, including tools for story-boarding. Apps such as Puppet Pals HD allow the children to create and record an animated puppet show, creating their own characters and backgrounds, and recording their own narrative. Such tools can be extremely motivating for children. A collection of wirelessly connected laptops or tablet devices allows much more flexibility for integrating ICT in English or literacy.

In a network room, it could be possible to run an entire literacy hour there at regular intervals. Each child would have access to the computers, and plenaries could be held using the large monitors, interactive whiteboards, visualisers or screen control software. The opening sections of the literacy hour could be presented to the children using hyper-media resources, perhaps containing scanned parts of books. These activities have a high overhead in terms of staff training and confidence. In a high-resource setting which fully integrates ICT into the good practice of the school and where the children are using the network room confidently, ICT has much to offer literacy, specifically:

- it provides a different resource base for the literacy session, a break from the classroom;
- it allows children to develop ICT skills alongside literacy skills (except in the case of tutorial software);
- it reinforces the message that ICT is a medium in which to carry out work of different kinds;
- it provides the opportunity for children to combine text, graphics, sound and video in different software packages.

The following table summarises literacy teaching in the high-resource setting:

Activity	Software and hardware	Literacy v. ICT potential
Group activity reinforcing learning objective for 20 minutes	Three computers, tutorial program or word processing	High literacy Low level ICT skills (tutorial) Higher level ICT skills (word processing)
Group activities on search and replace, guided writing, story-boarding/mind mapping	Tablet devices (Android/IOSApple) or laptops available for groups	High literacy Higher level ICT skills
Collaborative work throughout literacy session on learning objective, used on the interactive whiteboard and perhaps published online on the school website	Network room Presentation software, html editors, etc. Word processing software Authoring templates provided by the online supplier (local grid for learning or regional broadband consortia)	High literacy High level ICT skills

The internet and literacy – publication and exhibition issues

In a reliable high-resource setting, the internet is an area of significant potential. Very large numbers of teachers and children are already sharing ideas online. Many of these are downloadable without charge and provide a basis for planning, though some require subscription. Other sites provide onscreen activities with immediate feedback. School web pages or local authority intranets can provide rich sources of material and opportunities for publication, including many examples of good practice in literacy teaching and learning. In many schools, teachers are using blogging tools such as WordPress, Edublogs and Tumblr to create school or class blogs. These can offer incentives and an authentic context for writing, especially if used in collaboration with a partner school in another location or country. Similarly, there are new opportunities for collaborative writing through facilities such as Googledocs, which allows multiple users to edit the same document at the same time, or various wikis, which also allow multiple editors albeit at different times. Such tools can be particularly useful for collaborative homework tasks, allowing small groups of children to share and work on a document beyond the normal school times and at a distance. Of course, as with any online tools, these need to be monitored carefully by teachers and an appropriate code of conduct set up with the children.

Finally, as noted above, the idea that children can now publish their own work within secure online environments means that the distance between objective, idea and final publication is shortened. There is a real meaning in which this publication and the commentaries provided on it allow for a sense of audience and purpose to be built up, which motivates and increases children's concept of personal authorship (see Chapters 16 and 17 for more on this).

Planning to use ICT to support literacy teaching

PRACTICAL TASK PRACTICAL TASK **PRACTICAL TASK** PRACTICAL TASK

Look at your school's scheme of work for literacy and choose a particular year group. Consider the learning objectives in relation to the children you are working with.

- **Decide on what level of activity you could aim at, according to whether you are in a high-resource setting or a low-resource setting.**
- **Design an activity for five or six children for the 20 minutes of group activity.**
- **Remember to discuss the levels of ability of the group with the class teacher and to target the actual content appropriately.**

Here is an example of a Year 3 activity for sentence-level work on verbs, which is planned to support the following learning objective:

children should learn to use verb tenses with increasing accuracy in speaking and writing, e.g. catch/caught, see/saw, go/went, etc., using past tense consistently for narration...

For the ICT element in a low-resource setting, where there is one computer to the 30 children in the class, consider getting the children to work on a pre-prepared Word template file which contains, say, 10 sentences with verbs in the present tense. Have a series of regular and irregular examples differentiated for ability groups through the week. Ask the children to identify the verbs in the text and change them into the past tense using the features of the word processor.

In a high-resource setting, in a network room, prepare templates for the whole class, differentiated according to ability, and ask them to search and replace. Alternatively, ask children to investigate the patterns in pre-prepared onscreen texts and prepare a presentation about it.

Some questions to ask yourself after the activity, some of which form the usual pattern for the use of ICT, and some adapted for the purpose of this activity, could be as follows:

- How was the activity integrated into the normal running of the classroom?
- What skills did I need in order for the activity to succeed?
- What skills did the children need?
- How did I ensure that all children had access to the activity?
- What were the learning outcomes for the children in literacy?
- What were the learning outcomes for the children in ICT?
- What assessment opportunities were there?
- How does this experience add to my understanding of ICT in subject teaching?
- What will I do next time?

Planning ICT in English and literacy across the curriculum

It is worth spending some time considering briefly how to use ICT in the teaching of English in a wider sense. Beyond the structure of their literacy lessons, children are using English in a cross-curricular way, for example:

- publishing a science report;
- creating a local area guide book in geography;
- writing school web pages;
- writing a class news blog;
- generating a historical account;
- writing about their beliefs in RE;
- creating rules for classroom and playground behaviour in PSHE;
- generating captions to explain findings in maths data handling;
- reading for information in any of the foundation subjects, science and maths.

The issue for planning for ICT to support these wider uses of English is, as usual, how to operate in the differing resource settings. Higher-resource settings are going to allow for much greater exploration of the provisional nature of information, simply because faster, more distributed internet access through a school means that greater numbers of teachers and children can become involved. In lower-resource settings, where one computer is shared between the class, there are still opportunities for engagement with the wider English curriculum; for example, in speaking and listening (encouraging children to defend choices made in simulations and adventure games), reading (whole-class reading sessions from the screen) and writing (using the word processor as an aid to drafting materials and understanding the writing process better).

The cross-curricular opportunities for developing English teaching which uses ICT are many and varied and the limit to what is feasible will be determined largely by the access to the software, hardware and the internet which the children have.

REFLECTIVE TASK

Consider a curriculum area in which you are expecting the children to write at the computer. It could be taken from the list already suggested:

- **publishing a science report;**
- **creating a local area guide book in geography;**
- **writing school web pages;**
- **generating a historical account;**
- **writing about their beliefs in RE;**
- **creating rules for classroom and playground behaviour in PSHE;**
- **generating captions to explain findings in maths data handling;**
- **reading for information in any of the foundation subjects, science and maths.**

Create a lesson plan which focuses on the specific areas of development of the writing itself which you are developing using the ICT. You may wish to use the pro forma for a lesson plan that was suggested in Chapter 2, an example of which, for a Year 4 geography lesson, is provided below.

LESSON OVERVIEW

Include here the English element, the ICT element and the element from the other subject. For example, a lesson overview for 'Creating a local area guide book in geography' for Year 4 might describe the ICT element as using desktop publishing software and digital images. The geographical element could be from the work on localities described in the National Curriculum (see below). The English element is the developing sense of audience and of how to present information in a clear and accessible manner as well as assessing and evaluating their writing.

SCHOOL/CLASS CONTEXT As described previously.

LEARNING NEEDS OF THE CHILDREN

Note these in the cross-curricular contexts.

GROUPING/TIMING

Think about different groupings from literacy lessons if your class employs ability groups. Children should experience a range of working partnerships and not always be grouped with the same children. We know from our understanding of the ways in which children learn that they need to interact with one another and learn in the context of talk with a whole range of peers of different abilities.

RESOURCES

Make the most of information collected on local area trips, in particular, digital images, video clips and sound recordings, which could be incorporated into the work on the computer. Consider working with a multimedia-authoring package to produce a multimedia version of the guidebook if you are fortunate enough to be in a highly resourced setting.

THEORETICAL CONTEXT As described previously.

NC/EYFS CONTEXT

One example for ICT could be from the computing programme of study Key Stage 2 'select, use and combine a variety of software (including internet services) on a range of digital devices to accomplish given goals, including collecting, analysing, evaluating and presenting data and information'.

For Geography: from the programmes of study for Key Stage 2, in their study of localities and themes pupils should: 'understand geographical similarities and differences…'. For English: from the programmes of study for Key Stage 2, children should 'assess the effectiveness of their own and others' writing, suggesting improvements…'.

SCHEME OF WORK CONTEXT

Make reference here to the school's schemes of work for ICT, English and geography.

Make notes under the following headings as described previously:

- **YOUR OWN LEARNING NEEDS**
- **ORGANISATIONAL MEMORY JOGGERS**
- **OTHER ADULTS**
- **LEARNING OBJECTIVES/INTENTIONS**
- **DIFFERENTIATION**
- **LEARNING NEEDS – SEN**
- **LEARNING NEEDS – EAL**
- **ASSESSMENT OPPORTUNITIES**
- **KEY QUESTIONS**
- **LESSON FORMAT**
- **EVALUATING THE LESSON (1) – OPERATIONAL ISSUES**
- **EVALUATING THE LESSON (2) – LEARNING OUTCOMES**
- **EVALUATING THE LESSON (3) – NEXT TIME**

Planning ICT in mathematics

In support of the requirements for National Curriculum mathematics, lessons in numeracy were introduced as part of the National Numeracy Strategy, and continued under the primary national strategies (DfES/QCA, 2006). Although the requirement to have regard for the primary national strategies has been discontinued, you may find that schools and individual teachers you work with are still using elements of them, including the three-part mathematics lesson, which included a whole-class starter session on mental mathematics, main follow-up activities often with group or individual work, and a plenary review. The new programme of study for mathematics (DfE, 2013) differs mainly in the way it breaks down the various thematic topics and nomenclature, and sets out the programme of study on a year-by-year basis. For example, at Key Stage 1, the topic of number is broken down into place value, addition and subtraction, multiplication and division, and fractions. Also, there is a renewed emphasis on children developing fluency in mental arithmetic. The new National Curriculum for mathematics also advises against using calculators until the end of Key Stage 2 where they are recommended for developing 'pupils' conceptual understanding and exploration of more complex number problems, if written and mental arithmetic are secure' (DfE, 2013 no page). Consequently it is anticipated that many teachers will continue to draw on previous materials using whole or adapted units in their planning for:

- *Using and applying mathematics*
- *Counting and understanding number*
- *Knowing and using number facts*
- *Calculating*
- *Understanding shape*
- *Measuring*
- *Handling data*

(DfES/QCA, 2006)

Technology can be incorporated into most parts of the mathematics lesson. An opening section on mental maths can be varied in its use of resources by the inclusion of an interactive whiteboard (see also Chapter 14 on using the IWB). The same applies to the plenary, where the strands of the lesson can be drawn together by the use of electronic media, either by the teacher or by groups of children presenting their work to the rest of the class. Tablet devices with screen capture apps such as Explain Everything (see **www.explaineverything.com**/) could be utilised by children or the teacher to reinforce and model understanding of mathematical processes.

However, it is the central part of the lesson which lends itself most readily to the integration of appropriate ICT, including all of the available audio-visual aids and, of course, calculators should the teacher judge that such devices can add to or develop children's understanding. For the computer, several different types of program are suitable for this section of the lesson, including:

- software to explore number patterns, including the use of spreadsheets;
- tutorial software for practising a particular skill, with rapid assessment;
- data-handling software;
- software for giving instructions of movement and turn in order to develop subject knowledge in, for example, measurement of distance and angle;
- software for transforming shapes;
- software for branching and sorting in order to develop logical thinking and problem-solving;
- screen capture software to model processes.

Some of these possible uses have the potential to develop high-order ICT skills. However, it is worth remembering that the focus of the lesson has to be mathematics specifically and the lesson succeeds or fails partly by the way in which the teacher can draw the class together in a plenary at the end of the session. If the activity has moved out of the realm of the initial focus and is meeting some other planning requirement, the quality of the mathematical experience may decline.

The potential for ICT skill development and maths together is summarised in the following table, where, as for literacy, it is possible to see little in the way of such skill development in the use of tutorial software.

Software type in mathematics	ICT skills, knowledge and understanding
Software to explore number patterns (tutorial)	Low-level ICT skills
Tutorial software for practising a particular skill, with rapid assessment	Very low-level ICT skills
Software for transforming shapes	Middle-range ICT skills (depending on the package being used – some are much more complex than others)
Data-handling software	High-level ICT skills
Using spreadsheets to explore number patterns	High-level ICT skills
Software for giving instructions of movement and turn in order to develop subject knowledge in, for example, measurement of distance and angle	High-level ICT skills (link with programming)
Software for branching and sorting in order to develop logical thinking and problem-solving	High-level ICT skills

THE BIGGER PICTURE   THE BIGGER PICTURE   THE BIGGER PICTURE   THE BIGGER PICTURE

When you are planning for mathematics, you need to plan suitable activities that will include all children and ensure that every child makes progress. You are likely to have children in your class or group who have additional and special educational needs. You may also have in the same group or class children who are mathematically able, gifted and talented. Talk to class teacher colleagues, take advice from the inclusion leader or teacher responsible for children with special needs and discuss the children with any teaching or learning support assistants who know them well to see what they suggest will help. See also *Teaching Primary Special Educational Needs* (Glazzard et al., 2010). When you have identified links from your mathematics topics to other areas of the curriculum, don't forget to look out for opportunities to develop mathematical learning when planning other subjects. It is important to include mathematics in other subjects to improve all children's transference skills and allow them to rehearse, reinforce, consolidate and extend what they have learned in mathematics lessons. Seeing the uses and applications of mathematics in other areas of the curriculum makes it more 'real' and often more enjoyable, and demonstrates the need for functional numeracy. Examples could include opportunities to apply number work and calculation in science, use concepts of shape, space and measures in design technology, identifying patterns and sequences in music and art, and handling data in geography and history.

In a low-resource setting it is possible to become dependent on poorer-quality tutorial software of a very basic drill-and-practice type. Where this is focused (on reinforcing a topic which is under development) and targeted (at children who need it), such software can be useful. As we have seen in earlier chapters, where this software is used to keep certain children busy or as a reward or sanction, there is little justification for using it in pursuit of real learning objectives.

In a high-resource setting, in a network room or similar, all children could experience some mathematics lessons with access to the relevant software and hardware. The whole lesson could be run in the computer suite from time to time (timetabling allowing).

In a low-resource setting, or one where the children's experience of using ICT is limited, collect simple data about the packed lunches brought to school across a given week. Ask children to enter the information and display it in data-handling software. This could be done using a simple graphing tool or using a more complex data-handling package.

For a medium-resource setting, where there is regular access to the computer and the children have already gained experiences of simple graphing, extend their knowledge by building a more complicated database based on the different methods which children use to come to school each day.

In either case, in your planning, develop questions which exploit the ICT learning opportunities alongside the mathematical learning opportunities. The following table characterises some of these sorts of questions:

Example ICT knowledge questioning	Example mathematics knowledge questioning
Which graph shows the information best?	Do most children walk to school? How do we know?
What did we have to do after entering each piece of information?	How many more children walk to school than come by car?
How did we add to the file the next day?	What would happen if it were a wet day?

In this way, the ICT supports the subject and the subject supports very important conceptual developments in ICT.

Questions worth asking as a result of the activity include the following:

* How was the activity integrated into the normal running of the classroom?
* What skills did I need in order for the activity to succeed?
* What skills did the children need?
* How did I ensure that all children had access to the activity?
* What were the learning outcomes for the children in mathematics?
* What were the learning outcomes for the children in ICT?
* What assessment opportunities were there?
* How does this experience add to my understanding of ICT in subject teaching?
* Did the ends justify the means in terms of time costs?
* What will I do next time?

Planning ICT in science

There is the opportunity to make good use of the very wide potential of ICT to support the teaching of science. There is ample opportunity for both subjects to support each other. Planning for science with ICT means identifying the sorts of activities where ICT can support and enhance the learning of science. As with the rest of the core subject provision discussed above, some activities develop the scientific knowledge, skills and understanding of children but do not necessarily generate further ICT skill development. There are other activities which develop much higher-level ICT skills alongside scientific skills of enquiry and hypothesis. To take a simple example, programs which are tutorial in nature and which describe and then question the user about certain concepts do not necessarily advance the ICT skills of the user who is, as in all tutorial software, rehearsing skills of navigation over and over again. On the other hand, an activity which requires that the user set up and maintain a monitoring situation with data-logging equipment and software is clearly requiring a higher level of skills in both subjects.

Whether low-level ICT skills or much higher-level ICT skills are being employed, the decision to make in terms of lesson planning is to focus on the appropriate activities in the whole scheme of work for the children. Is it the case that you need a context for developing their awareness of databases? Have they browsed websites at length? Do you now need, in terms of the science, to deepen their awareness of subject knowledge in classification by asking them to work with the data they are collecting? Scientific enquiry and the application and development of ICT skills and understanding can usefully go hand in hand within many particular science units of work, as can be seen by the following table, which breaks down some of the various units of work for science in the new National Curriculum (DfE, 2013) and highlights some indicative activities for integrating ICT.

There are many ways in which ICT can support science in a more general way, with the use of templates, for example, scaffolding as a form of writing so as to further structure scientific thought and develop skills of planning and enquiry.

Above all, the use of ICT in science should be seen as something in which the scientific learning is the focus; it should be a key to opening up the world of scientific development and not an end in itself. There are benefits for both subjects in close integration.

Key Stage	Science unit of work	Indicative links and activities integrating ICT
1	Plants	Use digital microscopes to look closely at the different parts of plants found in their locality.
		Use digital cameras to take photographs and compare different plants.
		Label pictures using publishing software.
		Explore examples of time-lapse photography illustrating how things grow, e.g. seed germination.
	Animals, including humans	Use various 3D apps on a tablet device to explore and compare the different parts of the body of various animals.
		Use story-boarding software on a desktop computer or a tablet to represent various life-cycles.
		Create a poster with a graphics package to illustrate life-cycles.
	Everyday materials	Use a branching database to classify different materials and their properties.
	Seasonal changes	Use a simple database to keep a record of the weather throughout the year.
	Living things and their habitat	Use the internet and video to explore local and non-local habitats to identify how living things are adapted to their environments.

2	Plants	Use a digital microscope to observe the different parts of flowering plants.
	Animals, including humans	Capture or use existing digital film footage of animals on the move, e.g. film some of the pupils running and use editing software to slow the footage down to compare and analyse movement in different animals.
	Rocks	Examine different rocks and soils under a digital microscope. Use publishing software to label and explain the physical properties of different rocks and soils.
	Light	Test the reflective properties of different materials by setting up a fair test and using a data-logger to measure and record light levels. Use graphing software to analyse the results.
	Forces and magnets	Capture the effects of different forces, including magnetism on different objects, using a video camera. Playback and analyse the results.
	Living things and their habitat	Use a database and digital camera to capture and classify a wide selection of living things and their habitats. Keep a diary to monitor changes to the environment over time.
	States of matter	Use a temperature probe and data-logger to record, capture and observe the melting of ice in a cool environment (e.g. outdoors). Repeat the experiment but in a warmer environment (e.g. indoors). Compare and analyse the results.
	Sound	Use a digital audio recorder that captures sounds waves and represents them graphically. Analyse and compare the relationship between the graphical representation and the features of the sounds created, e.g. volume, pitch.
	Electricity	Use a simulation package to explore and construct different types of circuit. Record these circuits using conventional symbols for components. This should not replace the actual constructing of physical circuits using batteries, bulbs, wires and switches.
	Earth and space	A simulation package or app could be used to explore and model phenomena such as night and day, changes of seasons, phases of the moon.
	Evolution and inheritance	Children could use the internet and other sources to research evolution and the work of key scientists such as Mary Anning, Charles Darwin and Alfred Wallace.

PRACTICAL TASK   PRACTICAL TASK   PRACTICAL TASK   PRACTICAL TASK

Choose a unit of work from your school's science scheme of work for which you have access to the appropriate software and hardware. Plan for one session within the unit to have a major input from ICT. Use the links suggested in this section to help you. When you evaluate the session, consider the following aspects.

- Make a judgement, in conversation with your mentor and/or tutor, about the contribution of the ICT to the subject knowledge in the sessions.
- Did the ends justify the means?
- Would you use ICT to work with this particular concept or unit again?
- If yes, would you do anything differently?
- If no, why would you prefer not to use ICT in this way again?

Planning ICT in the foundation subjects

Planning for ICT in the foundation subjects, as for the core curriculum, means identifying those activities where ICT provides an essential part of the learning experience. In other words, it means identifying the lessons in the foundation subjects where, with ICT, the learning opportunities are enhanced in depth, range and quality. The following examples, given under the relevant subject headings, are by no means an exhaustive list. They are intended to be starting points for planning for ICT in the foundation subjects.

Art and design

Some of the foundation subjects depend on a sophisticated understanding of how the ICT works and of how it uniquely contributes to the learning in that subject area. One example would be art, where the understanding of what is happening in a graphics package is crucial to understanding the contribution which it makes to the subject.

Image-editing packages, in spite of their onscreen appearance with virtual canvases and paint pots and virtual pencils, represent a different medium for artists. They may look as though they are replacing the physical world of brushstrokes and charcoal marks. The fact is that they are not. The way that they work is by arranging digital information on screen.

RESEARCH SUMMARY   RESEARCH SUMMARY   **RESEARCH SUMMARY**   RESEARCH SUMMARY

Avril Loveless in 'Working with images, developing ideas' (in McFarlane, 2007) builds an argument about helping children and teachers to understand that they are interacting with a new medium, rich with different possibilities. She writes that 'IT has the potential to be a catalyst in the development of new ways of expressing a visual language' and goes on to define the central role that the teacher has in the process:

It is the interaction of the facilities of IT, the children's ability to explore and extend their visual ideas and the teacher's pedagogy that can improve the quality of teaching and learning.

(Loveless, 2007)

The use of digital and video cameras to record observations and keep a diary of the creative process and ideas can go hand-in-hand with more traditional forms of working, such as developing a sketchbook for experimenting with different media and processes. Similarly, the internet can be used as a medium for children to explore the work and styles of many different genres across the world. With bandwidth and distribution of the internet around schools improving all the time, virtual art galleries represent a significant contribution to the art and design curriculum. The faster transfer of much bigger files is of particular benefit in this area because the files are so much larger than with other uses of ICT, for example, word processing.

In terms of planning appropriately, the usual judgements apply about how the subject is enhanced and which ICT skills are being utilised and developed. Purposeful exploration of painting packages, image-recording devices and websites which bring art into the classroom in ways which were not possible before are all unique to ICT and can enrich children's learning in art and design. The important thing to remember for your planning is the word 'purposeful' and all that implies. Of particular importance is the notion that the ICT is adding to the potential achievement and learning by the children in the given subject.

Geography

History and geography are two subjects in which ICT can make a contribution to the enhancement of the learning process. We have seen, in the section on English and literacy across the curriculum earlier in this chapter, an example of a connection between a geographical activity and a unit of work integrating ICT.

The internet brings much potential to the teaching of geography. The subject itself offers a context for developing skills of searching, e-mailing and publishing. Similarly, early understanding of mapping and routes can be enhanced by the use of a programmable toy. The National Curriculum for geography (DfE, 2013) organises the curriculum into the specific area of:

- Locational knowledge
- Place knowledge
- Human and physical geography
- Geographical skills and fieldwork

Clearly, as a tool, ICT has much to contribute to the enrichment of these areas. From the local to the global, digital cameras could be used to record events outside the classroom, while the internet could be used to obtain comparative weather information from around the world.

THE BIGGER PICTURE   THE BIGGER PICTURE   THE BIGGER PICTURE   THE BIGGER PICTURE

When you are planning to use ICT in support of geography, the internet has a wide range of sources that you will find useful (see also Chapter 16). Try some of the following:

Blogs on geography http://primarygeogblog.blogspot.com

Google Earth www.google.com/earth/index.html

Google Street View http://maps.google.co.uk/

Worldmapper www.worldmapper.org/index.html

Beyond comparative weather data come the whole series of possibilities raised by e-mail or video conference contact with children and teachers in other localities. E-mailed questions about what you can see from your window on a given day generate vast amounts of interesting information between children of the same age, across the world, very quickly. Similarly, a class blog could be used to facilitate links with other schools and children from other locations and countries.

Geographical resources which were not available before – detailed maps and aerial photographs of most of the world – are now accessible online and offline. The skill in terms of the teaching will be to integrate these resources usefully into planning. You will need to identify opportunities for learning which are uniquely offered by the technology. As for all areas, if you are in a high-resource setting with large numbers of computers and good internet access, your problems are significantly reduced. In some cases the availability of tablet or hand-held devices with mapping software connected to global positioning satellites (GPS) can also enhance the experience of geography.

History

History can be brought to life by the carefully planned use of ICT. The internet brings not only art galleries into the school, but also museums and archival resources of all kinds, many of which are free to use in educational settings. Incorporating ICT into history lessons, as with all subject areas, becomes an issue depending on the resource setting in which trainees, teachers and children are working.

Some of the links between history and ICT are simply related to the resource capabilities of ICT, as in finding out about significant people in the past, for example. Another example of quite low-level ICT use would be in using digitised maps in local enquiry.

Higher-level ICT skills are demanded by the sophisticated use of databases which could be exploited at Key Stage 2 to study patterns of change over time. History provides us with an example of the need to be very clear about the sort of order of skills in both the curriculum subject and ICT which are to be developed in a given lesson. This area was explored previously in the section on planning for mathematics, where we saw a trade-off between higher-level ICT skills and content browsing.

Design and technology

ICT, and specifically computing, offers much to teachers of design and technology in the primary school. The area of most potential is probably that of computing and control technology, where children learn that they can control devices and models which will respond to external instruction and inputs. Children already know that such devices exist. A quick concept map at the start of work on this subject will bring to mind TV remote controls, washing machine programmes, central heating timers, burglar alarms and a whole host of other devices.

Additionally, when creating or developing ideas for themselves, children could be encouraged to make use of ICT in the design process as well as think about how they can incorporate computing into their creations. The programmes of study for Key Stage 2 (DfE, 2013, no page) make explicit reference to this idea, pointing out the link back to ICT and computing in the following statements:

Pupils should be taught to:

- *generate, develop, model and communicate their ideas through discussion, annotated sketches, cross-sectional and exploded diagrams, prototypes, pattern pieces and computer-aided design*

- *apply their understanding of computing to program, monitor and control their products*

It is difficult to imagine being able to meet the needs of young learners in design and technology and their curriculum entitlements without significant levels of ICT use. It is important to find out what is available to resource control technology in your placement school.

A further issue is the availability of support in terms of expertise. Although relatively simple-to-use software is involved, many teachers are deterred from including this area in their planning. Most teachers who do take it on find that the equipment and software working together are highly motivating for children and stimulate a great deal of interest and creative learning potential. Further support for this area can be found in Chapter 12, *Programming and Computational Thinking.*

Music

ICT has for a long time enjoyed a close relationship with music in primary schools. Tape recorders and CD players have been used in schools for many years to:

- bring children into contact with music from different times and different cultures;
- record children's own compositions;
- provide resources for learning songs;
- provide a resource for budding instrumentalists to record and assess their work;
- provide accompaniment to dance (link to PE);
- provide a source of music for assemblies and performances.

Additionally, schools with electronic keyboards have been able to extend the performance aspects of music. Keyboards with sound modules in which real instrument voices have been stored allow children to explore the different timbres and possibilities of different instruments.

In terms of computer use, there are software packages available which allow children to explore composing. The feedback which they gain from such software is immediate and the performing and appraising aspects of the curriculum are therefore made similarly immediate. As was the case for art and design, there is no suggestion of the computer-based musical tools replacing hands-on experience with the whole range of instruments found in primary schools. Instead, the suggestion is that ICT be used to enhance the learning process.

Children learn that computers are capable of storing more than just text and images and that they can be used to record and manipulate sound. They learn that sound can be represented and stored digitally, in which form it can be transformed in many different ways.

Computers are now the medium of choice in professional and home recording studios for composing and arranging music. Children will be aware of the possibilities of mixing and remixing songs as they hear different versions of their favourite songs produced. Some children may have access to simple tools on mobile phones or tablet devices for music editing or at least know of them. The learning curve for non-specialist teachers who are seeking to use music composition software and keyboards at this higher level is sometimes perceived to be quite steep and requiring specialist INSET. However, once the basic concepts are mastered, such devices open up a whole range of possibilities for young composers in both key stages, but particularly upper Key Stage 2 and there are increasingly simplified yet powerful tools to use for this (see Chapter 15 for more on this).

The links between ICT and the programmes of study for music are numerous. For example, at Key Stage 1 (DfE, 2013) children should be taught to:

- *listen with concentration and understanding to a range of high-quality live and recorded music*

- *experiment with, create, select and combine sounds using the interrelated dimensions of music*

ICT can enrich both of these areas of activity and understanding. Similarly, at Key Stage 2 children should be taught to develop their level of performance, as expressed in the statement that they should be taught to:

> *play and perform in solo and ensemble contexts, using their voices and playing musical instruments with increasing accuracy, fluency, control and expression*

The link here is the use of recording equipment for analysing and reviewing work so that they can further develop their level of performance.

The resource setting is one potential obstacle to fully exploiting these links between music and ICT. Another is teacher confidence and appropriate training, as well as access to hardware and software. However, at even the most basic level of using recording equipment, ICT enhances subject teaching in music in powerful ways.

RE, PSHE and citizenship

In terms of its access to resources on the internet, ICT is a major contributing factor to growing subject knowledge and understanding in the interlinked areas of RE, personal, social and health education (PSHE) and citizenship. The diversity of world religions can be explored and children can have a context for their writing which extends their sphere of personal expression into that of personal belief.

The potential of the internet to link to other cultures and belief systems can engender respect. ICT brings these worlds within reach in a unique way.

For the non-statutory areas of PSHE and citizenship, ICT remains an important tool. One example is that of developing relationships through work and play, for example communicating with children in other countries through video calls, online discussion or e-mails.

Children are aware that the school holds information about them from the earliest years. They can be explicitly made aware of the uses of ICT in gathering and processing this information. Later, they could discuss the confidentiality issues raised by large databases being held by companies and government agencies full of personal information.

PE

There is a place on the PE curriculum for ICT, certainly in terms of devices which can help to record movement for children to analyse later. For example, in dance and gymnastics children could use videos of movements and actions to develop their ideas and improve their performance.

Further cross-curricular opportunities exist in the analysis of the effects of exercise which can be carried out using sensors. The potential link to science has already been outlined above. The potential to link with maths in the exploration of data in spreadsheets is also there.

Clearly, it would be unwise to make strong claims for all-day, everyday pervasive links in planning between ICT and PE. However, there will be times, particularly when tackling the issue of assessment in PE, when ICT can make a vital contribution. The contribution of digital video in particular is noted in Chapter 9.

Languages and primary ICT

ICT has great potential to support the teaching of languages in primary schools. The National Curriculum (DfE, 2013) introduces the teaching of a foreign language at Key Stage 2. It should be noted that some schools introduce a foreign language in Key Stage 1. The teaching of European and other languages can be supported and enhanced by the use of high-quality CD and DVD-based resources, which, alongside websites, can be incorporated into lessons.

Some learners will benefit from simpler drill-and-practice vocabulary reinforcement and extension. For others, the opportunity to explore scenarios and solve problems in other languages online and in collaboration with other learners will be highly significant and a genuinely useful context for technology, such as video-conferencing.

Increasingly, the sophisticated operating systems of both Windows and Mac computers have simplified the use of a variety of language fonts both European and worldwide, making multilingual publishing in the classroom a real possibility. Similarly, tools such as Google Translate have emerged but these should be used with caution due to issues of accuracy. Such tools may have their place from time-to-time but should not replace the practice of learning to speak and listen to a foreign language. Where ICT has the most potential is perhaps in putting children in direct contact with native foreign language speakers through, for example, a school-to-school video conference link.

REFLECTIVE TASK

If you are in a course which requires you to develop a specialism, use your specialist subject as the basis for the following activity. Use the school scheme of work for the subject to complete it.

Identify a unit of work. Cross-reference it to an ICT unit. Decide on the balance between the two and plan a series of four to six lessons or activities which develop the subject knowledge of the children alongside an identified aspect of ICT capability.

At the end of the sequence, address the following issues as an overview of all the sessions:

- Were the learning objectives achieved? How?
- Which aspects of ICT capability did the children develop, rather than just reinforcing?
- What operational difficulties were encountered (if any) during the activity?
- Make a judgement, in conversation with your mentor and/or tutor, about the contribution of the ICT to the subject knowledge in the sessions.
- Was this an effective use of time for both subjects?
- Would you use ICT to work with this particular concept or unit again?
- If yes, would you do anything differently?
- If no, why would you prefer not to use ICT in this way again?

A SUMMARY OF **KEY POINTS**

➢ As well as planning for computing as a subject in its own right, it is important to plan for ICT within other subjects to support children's learning.

➢ The use of ICT can promote knowledge, skills and understanding in both core and foundation subjects.

➢ The levels of resourcing available in the school setting can affect how ICT can be used within other subjects and this must be taken into account in your planning.

➢ Planning should ensure that ICT capability is enhanced as well as learning in the other subjects, even where there is only the potential for lower levels of ICT skills.

M-LEVEL EXTENSION > > M-LEVEL EXTENSION > > M-LEVEL EXTENSION

Look back over the sections on the use of ICT to support the core subjects. Is it possible to devise schemes of work that develop higher-order skills in both the subject and ICT? Would this be viable for all groups of children? Would there be any drawbacks in such schemes of work?

REFERENCES REFERENCES **REFERENCES** REFERENCES REFERENCES REFERENCES

DfE (2011) *Teachers' Standards.* Available at **www.education.gov.uk/publications**

DfE (2013) *National Curriculum in England: Primary Curriculum.* London: DfES. Available at **www. gov.uk/government/collections/national-curriculum#programmes-of-study-by-subject**

DfES/QCA (2006) *Primary Framework for Literacy and Mathematics.* London: DfES.

Glazzard, J. et al. (2010) *Teaching Primary Special Educational Needs.* Exeter: Learning Matters.

Loveless, A. (2007, Kindle edition) Working with images, developing ideas, in A. McFarlane (ed.), *Information Technology and Authentic Learning: Realising the Potential of Computers in the Classroom*. London: Taylor and Francis.

FURTHER READING FURTHER READING **FURTHER READING** FURTHER READING

DfE (2011) *Religious Education in English Schools: Non-statutory Guidance.* London: DfE.

4
Planning ICT in the Early Years Foundation Stage

Chapter objectives

When you have completed work on this chapter, you will have:

- considered the differences between the Early Years Foundation Stage and the National Curriculum;
- thought about the theories of child development that underpin the organisation of the Early Years environment;
- noted the importance of talk in relation to the use of ICT in the Early Years Foundation Stage;
- examined the opportunities for using ICT to support young children's learning in the Prime and Specific areas of learning set out in the EYFS curriculum (DfE, 2014).

TEACHERS' STANDARDS

A teacher must:

1. Set high expectations which inspire, motivate and challenge pupils

- establish a safe and stimulating environment for pupils, rooted in mutual respect

2. Promote good progress and outcomes by pupils

- be accountable for pupils' attainment, progress and outcomes
- demonstrate knowledge and understanding of how pupils learn and how this impacts on teaching

3. Demonstrate good subject and curriculum knowledge

- have a secure knowledge of the relevant subject(s) and curriculum areas, foster and maintain pupils' interest in the subject, and address misunderstandings
- demonstrate a critical understanding of developments in the subject and curriculum areas, and promote the value of scholarship

4. Plan and teach well structured lessons

- contribute to the design and provision of an engaging curriculum within the relevant subject area(s).

Introduction

Under the Labour government (1997–2010), the *Statutory Framework for the Early Years Foundation Stage* (DCSF, 2008) identified features of good practice for the education and care of young children and set out the early learning goals that most children should achieve by the end of their Reception year in the context of six areas of learning. From

September 2008, children in the EYFS were assessed against a comprehensive Early Years Foundation Stage Profile, the main purpose of which is to provide Year 1 teachers with reliable and accurate information about each child's level of development as they enter Key Stage 1. The current coalition government has brought in some changes to the EYFS curriculum (DfE, 2014) but, in terms of the EYFS curriculum, the reforms do not mark a significant change of direction, as we will see.

The Early Years Foundation Stage (EYFS) continues to be based on an entirely different structure from the National Curriculum. If you are not an Early Years specialist but you find yourself in a placement in an Early Years setting, you need to familiarise yourself with the guidance provided. In particular, you need to become attuned to a setting which looks at key early learning goals for young children, rather than at explicit programmes of study and schemes of work.

The definition of the early learning goals is informed by Early Years specialists' under-standing of the ways in which young children think and learn. They are also intended as laying the foundation for the child's future engagement with the curriculum in the mainstream primary setting. The table below shows the early learning goals as they were mapped out for the EYFS in six developmental areas in 2008 and as they are now defined (DfE, 2014).

EYFS (DCSF, 2008)	EYFS (DfE, 2014)
• personal, social and emotional development; • communication, language and literacy; • problem solving, reasoning and numeracy (PSRN); • knowledge and understanding of the world; • physical development; • creative development.	Prime areas: • communication and language; • physical development; and • personal, social and emotional development. Specific areas: • literacy; • mathematics; • understanding the world; and • expressive arts and design.

The changes highlighted above were triggered by The Tickell Review, *The Early Years: Foundations for Life, Health and Learning* (Tickell, 2011), which recommended a number of changes for EYFS reforms. The Tickell Review prompted the change of the six areas of learning in development into three prime areas and four specific areas in which the prime areas are applied (DfE, 2014).

Key issues

The key issue for practitioners who are seeking to use ICT to support young children's development in these areas of learning is how to merge its use with the philosophy and methodology of planning for young learners.

Adults who work in EYFS settings, planning for and interacting with young children, set out their environment to maximise the opportunities for learning to take place. This is not a simple template for daily use of a space with young learners; it is an environment under-pinned by knowledge of how children develop skills, explore and grow in understanding of key concepts. Learning happens both in the opportunity for play and in the interaction between people – all people – in learning spaces.

The theories of Vygotsky are important here as a major component of the theory underpinning the mapping out of Early Years settings. He believed that children are continually refining their growing understanding through a sort of innate, inner speech or dialogue. Learning potential is enhanced in settings where children verbalise their inner speech and test and retest it in their interaction with others. This happens in what Vygotsky characterised as the 'zone of proximal development'. Many texts are available which explore these concepts in some depth. One example would be the book by David Wood, *How Children Think and Learn* (Wood, 1997). Early Years specialists will also be familiar with the work of Sandra Smidt in *A Guide to Early Years Practice* (Smidt, 2007), which looks at the theories of how very young children learn.

Vygotsky's theories underpin the Early Years setting. As a result, such environments are rich in opportunities for play (the context for the inner speech of children) and in opportunities for interaction (in the zone of proximal development).

Where does ICT fit into this environment? With its associated certainties and appearance of rigidity and non-fluid thinking, the computer appears to contradict this widely held view of the way in which children learn in the zone of proximal development. Some writers (Crook, 1996; Mercer and Fisher, 1997) have, however, attempted to analyse the working of the computer in the zone of proximal development and to look at the key features of talk around children working with computers. Their work suggests that computers are particularly rich in their possibilities for collaborative learning in the zone of proximal development.

The above research suggests that the best organisational strategies for the Early Years are the same, in many respects, as for the classroom. At the most basic level, this means making the computer more a part of the general experience of play and dialogue alongside the writing area, the modelling, the books and the play equipment. It means making the computer accessible for use in a range of contexts, both collaboratively and singly, with an adult and without an adult, in the same way as any Early Years activity might be designed to maximise learning opportunities.

When teaching children in the Early Years Foundation Stage, remember to build on their high levels of engagement by giving them opportunities to interact with a wide range of media and technologies. When you are developing a dramatic play area, remember to make this as realistic and up to date as possible by including a range of information and communication technologies. In the hairdressing salon or boarding kennel, include a laptop so that the children can take bookings and make appointments. In a coffee shop or restaurant, include an electronic till, a basic calculator to add up the bills and an up-to-date looking telephone or mobile. In a hotel reception area, include a computer so that the children can print customers' accounts. Photocopy or scan and print the children's work to include in a class book or to be sent home to share with parents.

Clearly, giving children and the adults around the computer the space to talk and to play is crucial. Placing the computer in, for example, a role-play situation, building a small office play environment around it and running open-ended software on it could be a starting point for stimulating much of the inner dialogue and talk in the zone of proximal development.

From the planning point of view, it is important to be clear about how each of the defined areas of learning can be enriched and enhanced. It means thinking about ICT through-out the areas of learning and development (DfE, 2014). With regard to the prime areas of learning and development, the following activities are indicative of the kinds of experiences that practitioners could facilitate.

Encouraging children's development of 'Communication and language' in the Early Years means planning opportunities for children to participate in the following activities.

- Write messages, label pictures with their name and otherwise engage with the communicative aspects of ICT. They do not have to get it right in the same way as a writing area doesn't exclude children who can't yet form letters. The uncritical nature of the ICT can prove extremely motivating (particularly when the computer is in a role-play area and the child is experiencing an impetus to try from the imaginative play).
- Experience the notion that computers (including any device, e.g. IWB, smartphone, tablet) can communicate words and pictures from books. If an adult helper, parent or older child is present, much useful talk and discussion about books and print, words and sounds, computers and communication can occur.
- Communicate with friends, relatives and peers in other settings nearby and very far away if possible. Children know that the computer is one among many tools for communication over distance and time. If the computer cannot deliver the necessary experiences, then other ICT equipment, such as a digital camera, video camera or tape recorder, may be able to.

For children's 'physical development' it can be useful to consider some of the following.

- Encourage children to monitor and regulate the amount of time they might spend using and exploring ICT.
- Use technologies such as digital cameras to capture and celebrate the physical outdoor activities the children engage with.
- Digital cameras could also be used to capture and celebrate the healthy choices children make in relation to food.
- The use of ICT equipment can promote and develop fine motor skills for all children, in particular, the use of the mouse.
- For children who are experiencing difficulties in fine motor skills across the whole range of severity, access devices such as brightly coloured, larger keyboards, touch windows and trackballs can all be used. Concept Keyboards which contain teacher-defined touch areas, touch screens and big switches which can be wheelchair-mounted and others all allow for inclusion and development within the Early Years setting.

For 'Personal, social and emotional development' this could mean planning opportunities for any of the following to occur.

- Learning how to share the ICT equipment and take turns to allow children to establish constructive relationships with each other and with other adults.
- Using the computer to encourage collaboration between children, and between adults and children in problem-solving (even at the basic level of switching on, selecting an item from a menu, clicking on a name).
- Using ICT to explore worlds beyond the Early Years.
- Using the computer as a tool to encourage collaboration between children who are experiencing difficulties and others in the Early Years setting (using alternative access devices alongside mice and keyboards).

In terms of the specific areas of learning and development there may well be cross-over with the activities and ideas suggested above. For example, in terms of 'literacy', the strategies discussed above for 'communication and language' may be relevant.

For children's 'mathematics', the following strategies might be useful.

- Plan to use software which allows children to experience situations of counting and sharing and identifying numbers, e.g. in counting items for a picnic.
- Use software which relates a counting song or nursery rhyme known to the children to reinforce early counting concepts and which allows the children to have some free play. If children are working with parent helpers or other adults and making conscious what they understand, much constructive dialogue can take place, which takes the child forward.

ICT can develop children's 'understanding of the world', including their skills of enquiry in many ways. Some of the following might be used to plan to address this key learning area.

- As mentioned above, include ICT within a role-play area. Consider settings with which the children are familiar, such as libraries, doctors' surgeries, and any kind of office. This creates a powerful context for imaginative play because the computer reinforces the 'reality' of the situation for the child. It is a powerful stimulus for the inner speech and the outer dialogue in the zone of proximal development.
- The computer provides everyone in the Early Years setting with a means of recording in writing, orally and visually (still and full motion), the children's experiences as learners. Digital cameras are highly significant tools in this context, with their capacity for immediate feedback.
- The capacity for ICT to provide access to activities for many children with special educational needs (including sensory impairment, physical and behavioural problems) allows for activities which promote knowledge and understanding of the world to be planned for all.
- There is plenty of scope for the internet to bring experiences of other cultures and other worlds into the Early Years setting.

For children's 'expressive arts and design', ICT brings into the world of the Early Years setting, experiences with new media which can be used alongside the range of traditional, hands-on experiences. For example:

- The use of graphics software is an area of great potential in the Early Years setting. The medium in which the learner operates is infinitely editable and scalable. Colours in areas of the onscreen canvas can be varied at the click of a mouse. Shapes can be created with and without filled areas. With support from an adult or working with a friend, the child can be encouraged to verbalise their thoughts on the image they are making. Digital cameras allow images of the child themselves and other people and objects from the environment to become part of the onscreen canvas.
- ICT also offers the Early Years setting the potential to be creative with sound and with video. Simple musical composition software allows young learners to see that you can do more than just paint and write at a computer. A recording studio is another imaginary scenario in which to explore and develop.

REFLECTIVE TASK

Choose one of the EYFS areas of learning and development. Identify, with the help of the Early Years team at the school, an appropriate piece of software with which the children are already familiar.

Set up the computer within some kind of role-play context if possible (if space allows and if it fits with the current planning in the setting). Observe the children working with the software over a period of a few days for a few minutes each day. Ask for one or other of the co-workers in the setting to do the same. Collate your observations.

How has the presence of the computer assisted in generating talk around the area of learning? Have you been able to observe any interactions in which peer learning was evident? Did the children work in the ways in which you expected? Were there any surprising outcomes?

Were there any overlapping areas of development from the other areas of learning and development?

THE BIGGER PICTURE   THE BIGGER PICTURE   THE BIGGER PICTURE   THE BIGGER PICTURE

When you are planning in the Early Years, think about planning across all of the areas of learning rather than just one. For example, when planning for mathematics, think about how mathematical concepts might fit into a wider topic or unit of work. Comparing eye and hair colour and measuring heights and using a basic graphing program (see Chapter 10) to display results might fit in with the theme of 'Ourselves' that also includes creative development work on drawing self and others and communication, language and literacy work on children's families. Investigating patterns and tessellations might form part of a half-term's focus on 'Buildings' that includes finding out about homes in different parts of the world or at different times in history. Collecting data on favourite foods or numbers of different types of animal might both be included in a cross-area plan based on 'Food and farming' that includes research on farming in different parts of the world.

RESEARCH SUMMARY   RESEARCH SUMMARY   RESEARCH SUMMARY   RESEARCH SUMMARY

Research has been carried out on the importance of talk around the computer which is of particular interest to Early Years practitioners as they plan for contexts in which young learners express their 'inner speech' (Smidt, 2007). In Wegerif and Scrimshaw's *Computers and Talk in the Primary Classroom* (1997), a number of projects are outlined which analyse talk in and around computers according to a variety of frameworks. In one example, Eunice Fisher reports on the influence of software type on the kinds of talk generated (Mercer and Fisher, 1997). A pattern of talk emerges in the use of less open-ended software which is quite different from the wide-ranging exploratory talk in evidence when open-ended software is being used by children. Wegerif responds in the chapter which follows, making a case for exploratory talk which is generated around closed software and which actually extends children and 'leads to the educationally valuable combination of directive teaching software with children's active peer learning' (Wegerif, 1997, p.99).

A SUMMARY OF **KEY POINTS**

➢ **Planning for ICT should be based on an understanding of the ways in which young children think and learn.**

➢ **The talk and play around ICT is an important element in the planned outcomes.**

➢ **Each of the areas of learning and development can be supported with planned use of ICT.**

M-LEVEL EXTENSION > > M-LEVEL EXTENSION > > M-LEVEL EXTENSION

Look back at the Research Summary near the start of this chapter. Find out more about the seminal work of Vygotsky and how this influences the organisation of the Early Years Foundation Stage. What impact does the Vygotskian approach have on your planning for the use of ICT in the EYFS?

REFERENCES REFERENCES **REFERENCES** REFERENCES REFERENCES REFERENCES

Crook, C. (1996) *Computers and the Collaborative Experience of Learning.* London: Routledge.

DCSF (2008) *Statutory Framework for the Early Years Foundation Stage.* London: DCSF.

DfE (2011) *Teachers' Standards.* Available at **www.education.gov.uk/publications**

DfE (2014) *Statutory Framework for the Early Years Foundation Stage*. London: DfE. Available at **www.education.gov.uk/publications**

Mercer, N. and Fisher, E. (1997) The importance of talk, in R. Wegerif and P. Scrimshaw (eds), *Computers and Talk in the Primary Classroom.* London: Multilingual Matters.

Smidt, S. (2007) *A Guide to Early Years Practice.* London: Routledge.

Tickell, C. (2011) *The Early Years: Foundations for Life, Health and Learning. An Independent Report on the Early Years Foundation Stage to Her Majesty's Government.* London: DfE.

Wegerif, R. (1997) Children's talk and computer software: a response to Fisher, in R. Wegerif and P. Scrimshaw (eds), *Computers and Talk in the Primary Classroom.* London: Multilingual Matters.

Wegerif, R. and Scrimshaw, P. (eds) (1997) *Computers and Talk in the Primary Classroom.* London: Multilingual Matters.

Wood, D. (1997) *How Children Think and Learn.* London: Wiley Blackwell.

FURTHER READING FURTHER READING **FURTHER READING** FURTHER READING

Basford, J. and Hodson, E. (2008) *Teaching Early Years Foundation Stage.* Exeter: Learning Matters.

5
Assessment and recording in primary computing and ICT

Chapter objectives

When you have completed work on this chapter, you will have:

- understood the place of assessment in the planning cycle;
- considered the main principles of assessment and how it is used in practice in computing as a subject and when ICT is used to support the teaching and learning of other subjects;
- thought about the main tools used to assess computing and ICT;
- looked at observing and profiling individual children, including considering a detailed pro forma for this purpose;
- examined how whole-class snapshots can help you to gauge quickly the range of ICT capability of the group you are working with;
- thought about assessment in the EYFS.

TEACHERS' STANDARDS

A teacher must:

2. **Promote good progress and outcomes by pupils**

- be accountable for pupils' attainment, progress and outcomes
- plan teaching to build on pupils' capabilities and prior knowledge

6. **Make accurate and productive use of assessment**

- know and understand how to assess the relevant subject and curriculum areas, including statutory assessment requirements
- make use of formative and summative assessment to secure pupils' progress
- use relevant data to monitor progress, set targets, and plan subsequent lessons.

Introduction

Assessment is vital because it allows teachers to track progress and plan appropriately for children to achieve. Without proper assessment and recording in a given subject, there is no real evidence or knowledge of where the children are up to, and planning becomes empty and meaningless. In the worst cases, it leads to the same activities being undertaken year on year by children who will underachieve because of it. In computing, this means seeing the same basic word-processing activities going on at Year 6 as happened at Year 2 or perhaps a superficial understanding of the principles of programming.

The planning and assessment cycle is incomplete in a school where this occurs and the children make no real progress in the subject or in its use in other subjects.

It may be that the school in which you are placed is still working with paper-based assessments of children's work and progress. The suggestions for pro formas in this chapter make this assumption. However, it may also be that you are working in a school that stores examples of work electronically, possibly with the involvement of the children. It could be that the school keeps an electronic portfolio for each child or for a group of children. Either way, the online examples of children's work can be used to help you to make judgements about children's work.

Principles of assessment

The principles which underpin good practice in assessment apply equally to computing as a subject in its own right and to ICT in other subject teaching. As teachers, we are looking for ways to make judgements about achievement which, at the same time, allow us to identify a child's future learning needs. These methods of assessment, in turn, will allow us to plan efficiently and appropriately in order to create opportunities for pupils to consolidate their understanding, undertake further practice or take on new challenges. Ways of assessing children in computing, as in other subjects, include some or all of the following:

- observing how the child goes about tackling a piece of work;
- diagnosing difficulties which become apparent over a series of lessons;
- observing which planning strategies appear to work and allow the child to succeed in a given area;
- collecting significant pieces of work in a portfolio of development;
- noting the context of the work and any factors which were significant: the grouping, the time taken, the level of concentration, their understanding of the concepts involved;
- noting the views of the child about the piece of work and asking them what made the activity so successful/ significant/challenging;
- feeding the information back into the planning process;
- when appropriate, making a judgement about the child's progress in terms of the key knowledge and understanding identified in the National Curriculum programme of study for computing;
- at all times keeping a clear focus on key learning objectives; this is very important as well as having a general awareness of other learning taking place.

Nevertheless, assessment and record keeping in computing and ICT are complicated by the fact that meaningful work samples are harder to come by than in most other subjects, with the possible exceptions of PE and RE. Printouts of work by themselves are not useful. Similarly, a final product, such as a game that has been designed and programmed by the child, may not in itself offer much evidence of the process with which the child has engaged. ICT is often used as a tool to present work in its best possible light. Any revealing errors and misconceptions are often lost along the way. The finished product is only the final element of a much longer, more complex process. The process itself is what provides the real assessment opportunities. To borrow an example from another subject, English, a writing sample which contains only the finished ('best') copy is similarly without any real use. Teachers need to go back through the draft book to understand the process the child went through. The child also needs to see and understand this in order to move forward.

How computing and ICT can be assessed effectively

Some ICT tools do allow for processes to be explored. Word processors, for example, allow changes to be tracked and printed. Some record how many times the child accessed the online help in a particular software package. Browser software tracks the user through the various sites and links they follow. This might provide useful assessment information. In some local authorities and schools, there are systems which allow children to select pieces of work and store them in an electronic portfolio. Taken together, in context, these are useful tools for the teacher assessing a child's achievement and identifying their learning needs. If we add connectivity to the home computer into the equation we have a powerful, fluid record of achievement which is also accessible to parents and to children out of school hours.

Tutorial software, including software produced as part of an integrated learning system (ILS), can record the units of work which the child has covered and can produce tables, graphs and collections of statistics. These relate to the software itself and closely to the subject being taught. They are of very limited use in assessing the child's ICT capability, however, and should not usually be presented as evidence of attainment in ICT. They record particular progress through an onscreen worksheet or tutorial. As we have seen in the planning chapters, the ability to use tutorial software only demonstrates the ability to use tutorial software. True ICT capability or knowledge and understanding in any subject are much more than the ability to follow onscreen instructions and click on the button which says 'Next' or 'Continue'.

The most useful tool in assessment in computing and ICT is the teacher's own observation of the child in all contexts and interaction with them about their work. In all of the resource settings we have discussed, this presents real logistical difficulties and requires systematic planning and the use of other adults in order that it is carried out effectively. Many schools, for example, operate an assessment week with samples being collected across the curriculum at the same time, in each class, in each half term. Extra adults are sometimes drafted in to support the class teacher in this work. Collection of ICT evidence and observation could also be planned for in this way.

However, on teaching placement with all of the course demands being placed on trainee teachers and their mentors and tutors, any assessment activity has to be focused and manageable. The course requirements which follow the prescribed curriculum for initial teacher training will spell out the number of assessments to be made of children and at what particular level in each curriculum area.

It is important to bear in mind that a further difficulty is the collaborative nature of work in computing and ICT. It is sometimes hard to separate out the individual contributions to a joint project. There will be times when this is irrelevant and unnecessary. However, while collaboration itself is usually to be encouraged, there comes a time, at the end of a unit of work or at other key times, such as the end of the year and, more formally, at the end of the relevant key stages, when a teacher will need to make a judgement about the extent to which children have grasped and understood important areas of knowledge and understanding outlined in the programme of study for computing. As Berry (2013, p.22) points out, 'national curriculum assessment has undergone considerable change for the new framework'. The National Curriculum review by the expert panel (DfE, 2011b, p.9) recommended that descriptive levels of attainment should be disregarded as they can often 'inhibit overall performance' and even 'undermine learning' if applied to pupils too rigidly as labels. Despite this, Berry (2013, p.23) also notes that level descriptors have become 'ingrained in many teachers' professional practice, as well as in the systems schools have in place to monitor pupils' progress'. Berry goes on to point out (ibid.) that 'nothing in the DfE's guidance prevents schools from continuing to use levels to monitor progress'. This may well be the case in the short term, but trainees should also recognise that the new programme of study for computing identifies new areas of knowledge and understanding, as discussed hitherto, and these aspects of the programme of study are not adequately captured by the disapplied level descriptors.

It becomes important, therefore, to develop skilled observations of individual contributions to partner work in computing and ICT in order to determine what children know and understand about computing and the extent to which they are able to apply this knowledge and understanding as they develop their skills with a range of ICT tools. Developing skills in monitoring children's progress in this way also protects quieter, less dominant children from being overlooked. However, it is also important to approach any assessment of children's learning, knowing what it is we are actually assessing. While this may seem an obvious statement, it is complicated by the fact that computing has several different facets of knowledge, understanding and skills, notwithstanding the different contexts within which these different facets may be applied.

What is being assessed?

For the purposes of assessing children's progress in computing against the programme of study it is useful to look in more detail at the way the knowledge, understanding and skills can be categorised in the National Curriculum programme of study for computing. Three key areas underpin the programme of study for computing. These are: Computer Science (CS), Information Technology (IT) and Digital Literacy (DL). Twining (2013) offers a clear definition and discussion of these at the following link: **http://edfutures.net/ICT_is_dead_-_long_live_ICT**. Also, Berry (2013, p.6) breaks the programme of study down, as represented in the table below.

	Key Stage 1	Key Stage 2
CS	Understand what algorithms are; how they are implemented as programs on digital devices; and that programs execute by following precise and unambiguous instructions. Create and debug simple programs. Use logical reasoning to predict the behaviour of simple programs.	Design, write and debug programs that accomplish specific goals, including controlling or simulating physical systems; solve problems by decomposing them into smaller parts. Use sequence, selection, and repetition in programs; work with variables and various forms of input and output. Use logical reasoning to explain how some simple algorithms work and to detect and correct errors in algorithms and programs. Understand computer networks including the internet; how they can provide multiple services, such as the World Wide Web. Appreciate how [search] results are selected and ranked.

IT	Use technology purposefully to create, organise, store, manipulate and retrieve digital content.	Use search technologies effectively. Select, use and combine a variety of software (including internet services) on a range of digital devices to design and create a range of programs, systems and content that accomplish given goals, including collecting, analysing, evaluating and presenting data and information.
DL	Recognise common uses of information technology beyond school. Use technology safely and respectfully, keeping personal information private; identify where to go for help and support when they have concerns about content or contact on the internet or other online technologies.	Understand the opportunities [networks] offer for communication and collaboration. Be discerning in evaluating digital content. Use technology safely, respectfully and responsibly; recognise acceptable/ unacceptable behaviour; identify a range of ways to report concerns about content and contact.

Breaking down the programme of study in this way (Berry, 2013, p.6) is useful when assessing computing because it can help us to develop a clearer focus for what is being assessed. Thus, it is possible to get a clearer idea of what to look out for and listen for in children's responses to tasks. For example, if we think back to the example lesson given in Chapter 2 (Robot Routes), it is clear that the main focus in this lesson was Computer Science. For example, the lesson was designed to develop pupils' understanding of what algorithms are and how they are implemented in programs. So in this lesson we were looking for how confidently the children could work with single and multi-step algorithms as well as how effectively they were able to identify any errors in the algorithms they devised to get the Bee-Bot through the route they had designed. While the main focus of this lesson concentrated on working with algorithms and one element of the programme of study, other lessons and tasks we plan for pupils may well incorporate several aspects of the programme of study. Furthermore, even in a lesson that is tightly focused on developing children's capabilities when working with algorithms, links can be made to digital literacy by asking children to think about other important applications of algorithms in computing, for example the inconspicuous use of searching algorithms to harvest data as people use social networks.

In Section B of this book, you will find many other ideas for lessons and different approaches to the teaching of computing. Other examples require assessment of different areas of the programme of study for computing. For example, in Chapter 12, *Programming and Computational Thinking*, we look at how various programs, such as Scratch, could be used to teach programming and computational thinking. One example involves children in Key Stage 2 designing and programming their own game. Such activities offer the opportunity to assess children in multiple areas of the programme of study. With regard to the Computer Science element, we would be assessing how effectively children were able to use computational thinking to 'design, write and debug programs that accomplish specific goals' in the game they are creating. However, there would also be an opportunity to assess elements of Information Technology, because in designing and building a game the pupils would need to make effective use of various graphics software to create the graphical objects and backgrounds for their game. Similarly, in terms of Digital Literacy, there would be the opportunity to teach pupils about the importance of respecting others' intellectual property when sourcing any graphics or images they used in their game. So when assessing the pupils' final products or games, the opportunity arises to assess numerous aspects of the programme of study and not just their programming skills in Scratch.

The examples which follow detail two very different forms of assessment. The first, individual profiling, provides a means of systematically tracking an individual child in some detail. The second, taking a whole-class snapshot, provides a means of assessing ICT capability at a very basic level in order to gain a picture of where each child in the class is at a given moment in time. These need to be employed together in order to gain the maximum benefit in terms of the assessment and planning cycle. Also, these examples should not be seen as a blueprint. It may be necessary to adapt them according to the specific context or unit of work being assessed.

Individual profiling

Individual profiling of children in curriculum subjects provides a means of mapping their progress through the various work samples collected and observations made. It makes a link to the child's own view of their developing capabilities and a link back to planning, thus completing the planning and assessment cycle.

The following pro forma is intended to be completed two or three times in a term and should take no longer than five or ten minutes, once it becomes familiar. Ideally, it should be completed with the child in discussion about a particular work sample. The number of these completed in a teaching practice would need to be negotiated in terms of the overall course requirements for assessment. The questions next to each of the cells provide an *aide-memoire* of how to complete the form. As you can see, the areas covered include the child's individual progress alongside notes about the school context and an opportunity to record the child's own response to the piece of work. It is intended that the same sheet is used for each child and that the columns are completed for each observation so that it is possible to check progress across the two or three observations made.

THE BIGGER PICTURE   THE BIGGER PICTURE   THE BIGGER PICTURE   THE BIGGER PICTURE

When you are planning opportunities to assess computing or ICT, remember that peer- and self-assessment strategies that are useful in other areas of the curriculum, such as maths and English, can also be helpful here. You may use talk partners in literacy and other subjects, and many teachers build on these relationships to extend them to peer assessment. However, it is important that any feedback shared between children is constructive and you will need to have agreed guidelines for the children to work to.

RESEARCH SUMMARY   RESEARCH SUMMARY   RESEARCH SUMMARY   RESEARCH SUMMARY

Cook and Finlayson (1999) argue for the involvement of the child in recording progress in ICT. Tunstall and Gipps (1996) place great importance on the need to feed back to young children, identifying it as a 'prime requirement for progress in learning'. Both of these statements imply interaction and active involvement in the assessment process on the part of the child.

Date	
Name of child	
Computing/ICT context (computer in class/ network room, tablet/handheld device)	Was the child working in the network room or on one machine? What was it?
How the software program was used	Using software stand alone or on the internet? Was a range of software used?
Type (tutorial, office tool, etc.)	If the child was using software, write the type here
Unit of work	Which unit was the child studying?
Working with partner? Who?	Was the child working alone, with a peer, with the teacher, teaching assistant, parent helper or other adult?
Length of time	For how long?
Confidence with hardware, mouse, keyboard, etc.	Rate the child's confidence with the hardware listed and/or with printers or other devices if relevant. Very, fairly, not very, needing support, etc.
Software navigation (use of menus)	As above but for navigation within the particular piece of software
File management: saving, opening, renaming work, etc.	As above but for working with files, reopening them, knowing where to find work, etc.
Computing programme of study	What knowledge, understanding and skills have been developed in relation to the different elements of the programme of study for computing, e.g. CS, IT, DL?
Cross-curricular context: using ICT to support work in English, science, maths or a foundation subject	How was the child operating within the curriculum context? Did the computer support the subject? Were there particular difficulties? Did the use of ICT help to improve the outcome?
Child's view of their ICT work	Ask the child about their view of themselves as a user of ICT. Were there significant things about this piece of work that pleased them?
Where next?	What activities with ICT would move the child forward?

Taking whole-class snapshots

To gain a picture of the whole class over a shorter period of time, in order to map out their skills, knowledge and understanding of computing and ICT, it would be useful to complete a very basic skills matrix. This is in no way suggested as a substitute for the detailed profiling and sampling suggested in the previous section. This gives you a quick overview on which you can build some basic planning. The more detailed observations of individual children will be needed to gauge more accurately the effectiveness of the planning in raising the achievement of the class. Also, whole-class skills matrixes like the one detailed below should be adapted to suit the unit being studied. The example below is a general skills matrix which can be adapted accordingly to suit different ages and different units of work.

Make best-guess judgements on a consistent value scale in order to provide a snapshot of the children in the class. Remember that this is merely an *aide-memoire* to help you write a short comment on the form for the rest of the class. The best practice in assessment is the longer form where curriculum contexts are taken into account alongside technical skill development. Use the longer format for the identified children.

Name	Date	Mouse	Keyboard skills	Switch on or logon	Switch off or logoff	Open	Save	Cut/ paste	Graphics	Independence	General comment

For the snapshot, use a 1–4 scale for, for example, mouse skills and keyboard skills, switching on/off, opening and saving, cutting/pasting, inserting graphics, etc., as follows: 1 (not at all confident), 2 (developing confidence and accuracy), 3 (accurate and confident), 4 (very accurate and confident).

Assessing Early Years ICT

We saw in Chapter 4 that very young children are working in a different context, that of the Early Years Foundation Stage. The different areas of learning for planned activities were mapped out.

In the EYFS, the criteria will be the Early Learning Goals and the observations you make will be referenced to the 'prime' and 'specific' areas of learning:

Prime areas:

- communication and language;
- physical development; and
- personal, social and emotional development.

Specific areas:

- literacy;
- mathematics;
- understanding the world; and
- expressive arts and design.

From September 2008, children in the EYFS have been assessed against a comprehensive Early Years Foundation Stage Profile (QCA, 2008), the main purpose of which is to provide Year 1 teachers with reliable and accurate information about each child's level of development as they enter Key Stage 1.

The individual profiling sheet described above is of potentially greater use in the Early Years setting than the 'whole-class snapshot'. With the more detailed observation sheet, the background to the activity and the grouping become the more significant fields in which to enter any observations. If you are working in this context, you may even find it easier than in the mainstream school since so much assessment and recording in Early Years settings depends on collating team observations of children across a period of time in different situations.

The Tickell Review, *The Early Years: Foundations for Life, Health and Learning* (Tickell, 2011), recommended a number of changes for EYFS reforms. One of these is a reduction of the number of Early Learning Goals (ELG), from 69 to 17. Furthermore, in order to make the profiling system described above less burdensome, Tickell recommended that there are three definitions for each ELG to explain 'emerging', 'expected', and 'exceeding' the ELGs. These reforms have been implemented in the updated handbook for the EYFS profile (DfE/Standards and Testing Agency, 2013).

REFLECTIVE TASK

At Key Stages 1 and 2 or in the EYFS, use the pro forma for individual observations to look in detail at the work of three children of varying levels of ability. Complete the pro forma during a unit of work from the school's ICT scheme or from a subject scheme with heavy ICT content. Carry out three observations on each child. Collect work samples and cross-reference your observations with them. Did the assessment reveal any strengths and/or areas for development? How helpful was the assessment?

Were there questions which you wished to see answered which were not on the form? If yes, what were they?

Were you able to track development through the lessons?

How did you differentiate your questioning for the focus children?

THE BIGGER PICTURE

ICT can be used not only as a direct support to the assessment of children's learning during planned activities, but it can also help teachers with their ongoing assessment for learning, their regular record keeping and in reporting on children's progress to their parents. There are commercially available programs to support all of these applications, but many local authority administration systems now have data-handling functions to track individual pupils' progress, their attainment as measured through summative assessments, and other important data, such as attendance records. You may find that your school has pro formas that it uses as part of its assessment procedures and these may be available on the school's intranet or virtual learning environment (VLE). Ensure that you are familiar with the assessment policy and any forms used, and that you understand how they are used. Before using any of them, discuss them with your mentor/class teacher or the assessment co-ordinator.

A SUMMARY OF KEY POINTS

➢ Assessment is a vital part of the planning cycle.

➢ The principles and processes of good assessment apply equally to computing as a subject in its own right and to the use of ICT to support children's learning in other subjects.

➢ Computing can be assessed using ICT tools in software packages and by collecting examples of children's work, but the best way of assessing computing and ICT capability is via the teacher's own observation.

➢ By discussing their work with them, children can be involved in their own assessment.

> ➤ In profiling individual children's progress, it is important to record information on the context of the observations, including whether the child was working alone or with a partner or small group.

> ➤ Taking a whole-class snapshot can be a quick way of identifying the range of levels of ICT capability present in your group/class.

> ➤ Individual observations can also be useful in assessment in the EYFS to assess/record progress towards the Early Learning Goals and in the planning cycle for the 'prime' and 'specific' areas of learning.

M-LEVEL EXTENSION > > M-LEVEL EXTENSION > > M-LEVEL EXTENSION

Choose a sample of your children and ask if you can have permission to look at the assessment records kept for each child over time, which may include seeking parental permission in some cases. Note the types of assessment that have been undertaken on each child and whether there are any differences between the range of assessments carried out on children of different abilities, or on particular groups, such as able, gifted and talented children, those with additional and special educational needs, children learning English as an additional language or looked-after children. Reflect on the different ways in which assessment is being used to monitor and promote children's learning. What assessments use ICT as a tool? What assessments are there of computing or children's ICT capability? Find out about Assessing Pupils' Progress (APP) (The National Strategies, 2010). Reflect on how APP could influence your assessment for learning (AfL). Will there be a knock-on effect on how you plan for computing or cross-curricular activities with ICT. Should there be?

REFERENCES REFERENCES **REFERENCES** REFERENCES REFERENCES REFERENCES

Berry, M. (2013) *Computing in the National Curriculum: A Guide for Primary Teachers.* Available at **www.computingatschool.org.uk/data/uploads/CASPrimaryComputing.pdf**

Cook, D. and Finlayson, H. (1999) *Interactive Children, Communicative Teaching: ICT and Classroom Teaching.* Buckingham: Open University Press.

DfE (2011a) *Teachers' Standards.* Available at **www.education.gov.uk/publications**

DfE (2011b) *The Framework for the National Curriculum. A Report by the Expert Panel for the National Curriculum Review.* London: DfE.

DfE/Standards and Testing Agency (2013) *Early Years Foundation Stage Profile: Handbook 2014.* London: DfE/Standards and Testing Agency.

The National Strategies (2010) *Assessing Pupils' Progress: A Teacher's Handbook.* London: DCSF.

QCA (2008) *Early Years Foundation Stage Profile Handbook.* London: QCA.

Tickell, C. (2011) *The Early Years: Foundations for Life, Health and Learning, An Independent Report on the Early Years Foundation Stage to Her Majesty's Government.* London: DfE.

Tunstall, P. and Gipps, C. (1996) Teacher feedback to young children in formative assessment: a typology. *British Educational Research Journal*, 22 (4), 389–404.

Twining, P. (2013) *ICT is Dead – Long Live ICT.* Available online at **http://edfutures.net/ICT_is_dead_-_long_live_ICT**

FURTHER READING FURTHER READING **FURTHER READING** FURTHER READING

Briggs, M., Woodfield, A., Martin, C. and Swatton, P. (2008) *Assessment for Learning and Teaching in Primary Schools.* Exeter: Learning Matters.

Perrotta, C. and Wright, M. (2010) *New Assessment Scenarios.* Available from www.futurelab.org.uk/resources (accessed 12 May 2011).

6
Monitoring primary computing and ICT

Chapter objectives

When you have completed work on this chapter, you will have:

- considered the role of Ofsted in the national monitoring of primary computing and ICT;
- learned about the role of local authorities in the local monitoring of computing and ICT;
- examined how primary computing and ICT is monitored in schools and by whom.

TEACHERS' STANDARDS

A teacher must:

2. **Promote good progress and outcomes by pupils**

- demonstrate knowledge and understanding of how pupils learn and how this impacts on teaching

3. **Demonstrate good subject and curriculum knowledge**

- have a secure knowledge of the relevant subject(s) and curriculum areas, foster and maintain pupils' interest in the subject, and address misunderstandings
- demonstrate a critical understanding of developments in the subject and curriculum areas, and promote the value of scholarship

4. **Fulfil wider professional responsibilities**

- develop effective professional relationships with colleagues, knowing how and when to draw on advice and specialist support
- take responsibility for improving teaching through appropriate professional development, responding to advice and feedback from colleagues and communicate effectively with parents with regard to pupils' achievements and well-being.

Introduction

If you are training as a computing or ICT specialist and one day hoping to lead this subject in a primary school, it is worth knowing about the various ways in which computing and ICT are monitored. This is done at various levels, from the Department for Education nationally to the local level and the school level. It is useful to know how computing and ICT are measured and why and with what results.

The government used to publish an annual survey which tracked the trends of ICT use and hardware-buying in schools. You can find examples of this up to 2004 online, after which point the reports were superseded and subsumed into Becta annual reviews (see Condie and Munro, 2006).

Becta closed on 31 March 2011 and its website and some of its work has been archived (see **www.nationalarchives.gov.uk**). Becta has not been replaced but there are a number of computing and ICT subject associations that advise the government from time to time and monitor the development of the subject as well as the broader use of ICT in education. For example, some of the related subject associations that include links to their websites are:

- Naace, which explains that it is 'the National Association for all of us who wish to advance education through the use of technology' (see **www.naace.co.uk/**);
- ITTE, which is the association for Information Technology in Teacher Education (see **www.itte.org.uk/**);
- CAS, or Computing At School (see **www.computingatschool.org.uk/**), which is an organisation whose aim is 'to promote the teaching of computer science at school'.

The role of Ofsted in the national monitoring of computing and ICT

The Office for Standards in Education (Ofsted) has a statutory duty to report on standards in education and teacher education across phases and across the curriculum. Every year, Her Majesty's Chief Inspector of Schools produces a summary report and commentary on inspection findings in the previous year, which attempts to draw together trends and developments into a picture of education in England.

Each year in the Annual Report, the Chief Inspector reports on different areas of the curriculum. The early reports from 1996 and 1997 were critical of the implementation of teaching and learning with ICT in primary schools. There have been changes year on year, but there continued to be evidence that the use of ICT in schools was highly variable and inconsistent. The report on inspections in 2005–06, for example, noted that:

> *Ofsted found that most schools in the survey made at least satisfactory curricular provision for ICT, including some balance between teaching ICT capability and its application across subjects. However, none of the schools surveyed embedded ICT to the extent that it was an everyday aspect of pupils' learning. Typically, pupils' use of ICT varied from subject to subject or from year to year.*

(Ofsted, 2006)

We have seen the importance of a school's scheme of work as a map of the teaching and learning. Where schools do not have such a scheme in place, the same low-level activities and skills are being rehearsed year on year and Ofsted is reporting that fact. You can find comments on these issues in the Annual Report for most years in some form. Similar comments arose in the 2005 special report by Ofsted, *Embedding ICT in Schools*, which looked at the situation in more depth than the Annual Report and included in its summary the following comment:

> *The project highlighted continuing inconsistencies within and between schools. In particular, there was wide variation in the extent to which ICT was embedded in the work of schools, although ICT as a tool for learning was expanding in all.*

(Ofsted, 2005)

The situation has improved in primary schools, although there is evidently more work to be done in terms of addressing key areas of the new programme of study, namely those relating to computational thinking and programming. For example, in the most recent report (Ofsted, 2011) it was noted that:

> The teaching of ICT was good or outstanding in nearly two thirds of the primary schools visited, with many teachers and teaching assistants increasingly confident and able to support pupils effectively. There were weaknesses in the teaching of more demanding topics such as data handling or control, but in many of the schools this gap had been identified and was being addressed.

The role of local authorities in the monitoring of ICT

As we saw in Chapter 1, local authorities took a role in the development of ICT resourcing in their schools and in providing some of the training for teachers. Local authority advisers have also been involved in the supporting of schools as they develop and improve ICT provision and until recently in collecting and collating schools' targets for ICT at the end of Key Stage 2.

REFLECTIVE TASK

Find out about the latest Ofsted inspection evidence on schools' ICT. Visit your LA inspection report and discover what information there is about ICT support in the area. Then visit your placement school's Ofsted report and see how the school fits into the pattern of inspection evidence. Answer the following questions:

What is the trend in English schools' ICT inspection reports by Ofsted? Towards higher or lower standards?

How does your placement school perform in its most recent Ofsted report?

Does the report match up with the current state of provision?

Find out about your specialist subject in relation to the ICT (if ICT is not your specialist subject). What does the national and local picture appear to be on the teaching of your subject with ICT?

School-level monitoring by senior managers and ICT subject leaders

Senior managers have a role in leading and monitoring the curriculum. In many schools this is delegated to the subject leaders. Computing and ICT subject leaders may be given additional time during the week to monitor the curriculum. We have seen, however, in earlier chapters that there are as many different kinds of computing and ICT leader as there are kinds of school organisation for the subject itself. It may be useful to carry out the following practical activity.

This activity focuses on the people who impact on the organisation and use of ICT in the school. Find out who they are in your particular school situation. Interview them and discover more about their influence on the whole-school development of computing as a subject in its own right and ICT as a tool to enhance learning.

You could ask them, sensitively, if they are considered to be members of the core or extended senior leadership team of the school.

Find out whether they are working solely on developing computing as a subject or combining it with one or more of science, maths, technology or, less usually, English or a creative arts subject. It may even be part of a deputy or assistant head's role or assessment co-ordinator's remit.

For the computing subject leader or senior managers in charge of ICT, try to discover the following information about them.

- **Their training.**
- **How they got the job.**
- **What contact they have with their LA advisory team (if indeed there is an advisory team).**
- **Their role in the management structure of the school.**
- **Their budget.**
- **How they pass on their expertise.**
- **Do they report faults or have a system for doing so?**
- **Is there a service contract?**
- **Crucially, is there a development plan for computing and ICT and how was it constructed?**
- **How do they involve parents and carers, teaching assistants, governors and others in ICT in the school?**
- **What was the outcome of the most recent inspection in terms of computing/ICT and how is the school addressing the issues?**

Relate your findings to the development of computing/ICT in your specialist subject (if it is not ICT). Are there policy statements or schemes of work which outline how ICT can be developed in the subject? Is there evidence to suggest that it is happening in the school?

THE BIGGER PICTURE THE BIGGER PICTURE THE BIGGER PICTURE THE BIGGER PICTURE

When you are undertaking the practical task above, ask if it is possible to talk to one of the school governors who has responsibility for computing or ICT (perhaps a member of the Governing Body's Curriculum Committee or someone with a similar role). Talk to them about how it is funded, how they plan to move the subject forward and how they monitor provision in the school to ensure that it is providing good value for money.

RESEARCH SUMMARY RESEARCH SUMMARY RESEARCH SUMMARY RESEARCH SUMMARY

In the literature researching computing and ICT in education, you will find useful discussions of a range of different aspects of social and cultural factors in the use of technology. Areas of research activity include some of the following:

- Technology and innovative pedagogy.
- The use by teachers and learners of online environments.
- Creativity, technology and education.
- Politics and technology – the selling of new technology in education.
- The use of computer games in educational settings, formal and informal.
- Digital video in education.
- The uses of social networking in education.
- Mobile learning.
- Interactive whiteboards and display technologies in education.
- Various emergent forms of literacy, such as media literacy, visual literacy and information literacy.

There is an introduction to research and debates in technology and education in another Learning Matters publication, *Education Studies: An Issues-based Approach* (see Potter, in Sharp, Hankin and Ward, 2009). In addition to these kinds of summaries, there have been reports which have attempted to prove a direct causal link between networked technologies in schools and rising standards (Becta, 2002).

The Futurelab site (**www.futurelab.org.uk**) promotes the innovative use of technology in education and includes a number of interesting and useful reports. For research purposes, there are many literature reviews commissioned by Futurelab, most of which are freely downloadable about areas such as thinking skills, games, e-assessment and mobile technologies (Futurelab, 2011). A number of leading figures in research into ICT in education have put together sources which they regard as key to ways of thinking about technology and education and you can use the reviews as starting points for your own enquiry.

A SUMMARY OF **KEY POINTS**

> Primary computing and ICT is monitored at a range of levels.

> Nationally, Ofsted monitors and reports on trends in computing and ICT provision and the quality of teaching and learning in the subject.

> At the local level, LAs have played a role in monitoring the upgrading of ICT provision and in supporting schools to raise children's attainment in computing and ICT.

> In schools, senior managers and subject leaders monitor the quality of computing and ICT.

> Arrangements vary from school to school.

M-LEVEL EXTENSION > > M-LEVEL EXTENSION > > M-LEVEL EXTENSION

Look again at the section on Ofsted's role in monitoring computing and ICT and reflect on the Research Summary in this chapter. Then go to Ofsted's website (see www.ofsted.gov.uk) and download a copy of *ICT in Schools 2008–11* (Ofsted, 2011). Consider the discussion of the particular demands of ICT and compare the findings described with practice that you have observed in schools. What implications are there for your own knowledge and understanding, and for your teaching strategies to develop children's ICT capability? What are the implications of the changes from ICT to the subject of computing with a new emphasis on programming and computational thinking?

REFERENCES REFERENCES **REFERENCES** REFERENCES **REFERENCES** REFERENCES

Becta (2002) *ImpaCT2 – The Impact of Information and Communication Technologies on Pupil Learning and Attainment*. Coventry: BECTA.

Condie, R. and Munro, B. (2006) *The Impact of ICT in Schools: A Landscape Review*. Coventry: Becta.

DfE (2011) *Teachers' Standards.* Available at **www.education.gov.uk/publications**

Futurelab publications available at **www.futurelab.org.uk** (accessed 12 May 2011).

Ofsted (2005) *Embedding ICT in Schools: A Dual Evaluation Exercise*. London: Ofsted. Available at www.ofsted.gov.uk/resources/embedding-ict-schools-dual-evaluation-exercise (accessed 11 March 2014).

Ofsted (2006) *Annual Report 2005/06: Ofsted Subject Reports – Primary and Secondary.* London: Ofsted. Available at **www.ofsted.gov.uk** (accessed 12 May 2011).

Ofsted (2011) *ICT in Schools 2008–11.* Available at **www.ofsted.gov.uk/resources/ict-schools-2008–11**

Sharp, J., Hankin, L. and Ward, S. (2009) *Education Studies: An Issues-based Approach.* Exeter: Learning Matters.

FURTHER READING FURTHER READING **FURTHER READING** FURTHER READING

Cuthell, J. (2002) *Virtual Learning: The Impact of ICT on the Way Young People Work and Learn.* London: Ashgate.

Gamble, N. and Easingwood, N. (eds) (2000) *ICT and Literacy: Information and Communications Technology, Media, Reading and Writing.* London: Continuum.

Heppell, S. (2001) Preface, in A. Loveless and V. Ellis (eds), *ICT, Pedagogy and the Curriculum: Subject to Change*. London: Routledge Falmer.

Kempster, G. (2000) Skills for life: new meanings and values for literacies, in N. Gamble and N. Easingwood (eds), *ICT and Literacy: Information and Communications Technology, Media, Reading and Writing*. London: Continuum.

Selwyn, N. (2002) *Telling Tales on Technology: Qualitative Studies of Technology and Education.* London: Ashgate.

Twining, P. (2002) Conceptualising computer use in education: introducing the computer practice framework (CPF). *British Educational Research Journal*, 28 (1), 95–110.

Section B
Using Applications and Technologies

Generic software is software that is considered to be content-free and consequently has a wide range of applications across the primary curriculum. In the same way, a lot of ICT equipment beyond the standard desktop computer is now available at a cost which schools can afford to enrich the children's work in all subject areas. This section explores some key categories of software and hardware that now should be part of every child's experience at primary school.

The chapters in this section of the book will inform your development towards meeting ICT aspects of the professional standards as well as the computing-specific subject knowledge. However, because of the great diversity available, subject-related educational software cannot be treated comprehensively here. Nevertheless, it is helpful to recognise how it differs in nature from generic software. Content is obviously a major element of such packages, presented in a variety of imaginative ways: adventure games and other modelling investigations, multimedia encyclopaedias and other reference works all ultimately intended to convey knowledge and understanding of their themes.

Each chapter in this section includes:

- a brief introduction and definition;
- reference to relevant sections of the National Curriculum for computing;
- background information as appropriate;
- examples of the ways in which teachers may work with the software or hardware;
- details of the specific functions of the software or hardware with which teachers should be familiar;
- examination of the contribution the software or hardware can make to teaching and learning;
- exploration of any limitations of the software or hardware;
- examples of ways in which the software or hardware can be utilised in the teaching and learning of the core subjects and any relevant foundation subjects;
- references and further reading.

It is envisaged that you will dip into the various chapters in this section based upon your own needs and also the requirements of your course. There is no implied hierarchy in the order with which the various topics are introduced. Topics covered in Section B are:

- word processing and desktop publishing;
- graphics software and digital cameras;
- media production: video animation and ICT;
- graphing programs;
- databases and spreadsheets;
- programming and computational thinking;
- mobile technologies;
- interactive whiteboards;
- digital audio and music;

- the internet;
- social media: tools for communicating, collaborating and publishing.

Much software covered in this section takes on a certain character. Its freedom from a particular context means that the child may well start working with a clean slate on which they must fashion a finished product. The blank page of a word processor or art program epitomises this situation. The child may then go through a creative journey which culminates in an outcome that represents the harnessing of the software's capability to the child's purpose. However, just as with a blank paper page, the child needs support from the teacher. This is necessary not just to set the objective and guide the process, but perhaps also by providing the scaffolding, such as a writing frame, that enables the child to start in the first place.

The hardware that features in this section is similarly broad in its scope, and gives rise to all sorts of creative opportunities, some of which are described in the chapters and some of which you will think of yourself.

You can find the relevant references in *Teachers' Standards* (DfE, 2011) applying to all of the chapters in this section as follows:

TEACHERS' STANDARDS

A teacher must:

2. **Promote good progress and outcomes by pupils**

- **plan teaching to build on pupils' capabilities and prior knowledge**
- **demonstrate knowledge and understanding of how pupils learn and how this impacts on teaching**

3. **Demonstrate good subject and curriculum knowledge**

- **have a secure knowledge of the relevant subject(s) and curriculum areas, foster and maintain pupils' interest in the subject, and address misunderstandings**
- **demonstrate a critical understanding of developments in the subject and curriculum areas, and promote the value of scholarship**

4. **Plan and teach well structured lessons**

- **impart knowledge and develop understanding through effective use of lesson time**
- **contribute to the design and provision of an engaging curriculum within the relevant subject area(s)**

5. **Adapt teaching to respond to the strengths and needs of all pupils**

- **know when and how to differentiate appropriately, using approaches which enable pupils to be taught effectively**
- **have a secure understanding of how a range of factors can inhibit pupils' ability to learn, and how best to overcome these**
- **demonstrate an awareness of the physical, social and intellectual development of children, and know how to adapt teaching to support pupils' education at different stages of development**

- have a clear understanding of the needs of all pupils, including those with special educational needs; those of high ability; those with English as an additional language; those with disabilities; and be able to use and evaluate distinctive teaching approaches to engage and support them.

8. Fulfil wider professional responsibilities

- take responsibility for improving teaching through appropriate professional development

REFERENCES REFERENCES **REFERENCES** REFERENCES REFERENCES REFERENCES

DfE (2011) *Teachers' Standards.* Available at **www.education.gov.uk/publications**

7
Word processing and desktop publishing

Introduction

Word processing is a key medium through which we communicate information using ICT. It is also one of ...
foremost implement... ...
ways in which we co... ...
and desktop publishi... ...
lap in functionality be... ...
sors and desktop pub... ...
course, but also sour... ...
can be used for pres... ...
recent developments ...
wikis, and synchrono... ...
ple users to edit a do... ...
media: Tools for com...

This chapter explore... ...
teaching and learning ...
current word process... ...
included in most wor... ...
word processing is re... ...
teaching and learning.

Handwritten note:
→ mainly used for communication
→ most common uses of ICT globally
→ two types of software which are often overlapped:
  • word processing
  • desktop publishing
→ most word processors have included the use of multimedia elements, images, videoes etc.
→ word processing can be used as an electronic presentation or paper based
→ collaboration tools- wikis
→ synchronous w/p tools - googledocs
neu.org.uk

What is word processing?

Word process... ...of text,
and increasin... ...of processes which ...

What is ...

Desktop publi... ...ing text
and graphics, ...rtant, to
a greater exte... ...ind the
overall 'look' ... ...nce, initially, desktop ... ...design-
ers in the pres... ...ns both
of cost and us... ...each of
any computer ...

Handwritten note:
WORD PROCESSING
→ entry, storage, retrieval & manipulation of text, graphics & sound
→ electronic format
→ "facilitates a variety of processes which can SUPPORT & ENHANCE COMMUNICATION

DESKTOP PUBLISHING
→ design of documents containing text & graphics
→ often used for publications
→ more accessible now
neu.org.uk

93

What do the programmes of study for Key Stages 1 and 2 include?

In the aims of the National Curriculum for computing, it is emphasised that the teaching of computing 'ensures that pupils become digitally literate – able to use, and express themselves and develop their ideas through, information and communication technology – at a level suitable for the future workplace and as active participants in a digital world' (DfE, 2013, no page). A key aspect of digital literacy is the responsible and safe use of technologies and, with the ease with which it is possible to publish online, it is also important to consider these ethical dimensions when creating and publishing text. The specific aspects of the programme of study which relate to this are highlighted as follows.

At Key Stage 1, the new programme of study for computing (DfE, 2013) states that, children should be taught to:

- Use technology purposefully to create, organise, store, manipulate and retrieve digital content;
- Use technology safely and respectfully, keeping personal information private; know where to go for help and support when they have concerns about material on the internet;
- Recognise common uses of information technology beyond school.

The old programme of study broke this down in more detail and is worth considering. For example, it stated that children should be taught: to use text, tables, images and sounds to develop their ideas; to select from and add to existing information; to share their ideas by presenting information in a variety of forms; and to present their work effectively (DfEE, 2000).

At Key Stage 2 (DfE, 2013), children should be taught how to:

- Use technology safely, respectfully and responsibly; know a range of ways to report concerns and inappropriate behaviour;
- Select, use and combine a variety of software (including internet services) on a range of digital devices to accomplish given goals, including collecting, analysing, evaluating and presenting data and information.

What do teachers need to know about word processing?

Teachers apply their knowledge, skills and understanding of word processing in two distinct ways. One is concerned with teaching and learning with and about word processing, and the other relates to the use of word processing to support more general aspects of their professional role.

It could happen that teachers use different word processors for these different purposes. Several word processors have been marketed specifically for primary age children, and feature facilities such as simple, easily modified interfaces, speech facilities and word banks. Alternatively, many schools have adopted Microsoft Word, possibly in its adapted form, RM Talking First Word, which enables the teacher (or child) to set levels of complexity for the interface along the same lines as the word processors designed for children. There are arguments in favour of both approaches. Some educators would prefer software designed for children, while others would argue that drawing children into the use of adults' 'industry standard' software has benefits. Another word processing and desktop publishing package designed specifically for primary age children can be found in the Textease Studio CT suite of software.

Whichever word processing package is used in the classroom, teachers need to be competent and confident users. This does not mean that they need to know the answer to every question. Rather, they should have a working knowledge of the software so that they are able to plan, support and assess appropriate activities as well as predict likely difficulties and assist with problem solving.

Word processing will impact in several different ways in the classroom.

- Selecting appropriate opportunities – in which word processing software can facilitate, enhance or extend children's learning, such as the importance of presentation in communication. In some instances, the focus will be on teaching and learning in computing (how to enlarge text, make newspaper-type columns or add a border to a poster); in others, ICT will be used as a resource in the teaching and learning of another curriculum area (writing for a specific audience).
- Making explicit links between related knowledge, skills and understanding – word processing is closely associated with literacy and language work at all levels, and as a consequence has a contribution to make across the primary curriculum.
- Modelling appropriate use of ICT – for instance, scribing and amending shared writing with the whole class or a group using the interactive whiteboard.
- Demonstrating or intervening – for example, inserting an image into a word processing document, cutting and pasting, or deciding how and when to use the spell-checker. Explicit teaching of word processing knowledge, skills and understanding requires demonstration and intervention as with any other curriculum topic. Children may gain word processing skills by themselves, but without the guidance and direction of their teacher the acquisition of such capability will be haphazard.

To support their wider professional duties, teachers use word processing in a number of contexts.

- Preparing resources – such as an electronic writing frame to support writing in history, a word bank to support an individual child or a troubleshooting help-sheet or interactive display to improve children's independence when using the spell-checker. Alternatively, teachers may use ICT to prepare resources for activities which do not involve children utilising ICT, such as a shared text, a range of three differentiated worksheets or number lotto cards to support a group mathematics activity. Some of these examples focus on using ICT as a tool for teaching and learning (in another curriculum area); others focus on the teaching and learning of computing.
- Administering and managing – for example, correspondence with parents, creating and amending schemes of work or school policies, using templates to prepare weekly planning, recording children's progress and producing banners for display boards.

The list below attempts to identify the knowledge, skills and understanding of primary word processing software teachers need in order to teach effectively with and about word processing:

- creating, opening, saving, closing, deleting and printing documents;
- selecting font, font size, colour, style (italic, bold), line spacing and justification;
- inserting, deleting, selecting, cutting, copying, pasting and undoing;
- utilising help;
- inserting bullet points, tables, clip art, borders, shading and columns;
- altering page orientation (landscape, portrait), background colour, page size and margins;
- altering defaults;

- forcing page breaks;
- utilising tabs and indents;
- utilising spelling- and grammar-checkers (including how to switch on and off), thesaurus, print preview, highlighter and talking facilities (including how to switch on and off) and find and replace;
- connecting alternative input devices (overlay keyboards, touch screens);
- constructing and utilising on-screen word banks;
- inserting page numbers;
- inserting text, graphics, tables and documents from other applications;
- inserting symbols, headers and footers;
- creating macros and templates;
- utilising dynamic links between documents;
- customising the word processor;
- merging documents;
- formatting graphics;
- protecting documents.

What are the key features of a word processor?

Word processing software has become increasingly sophisticated in the range of features offered. In contrast, the interface has become progressively more user-friendly and accessible. As with any application, it is important to have an understanding of the capabilities and limitations of the software in order to use it effectively. This is not to say that it is essential or even preferable to be familiar with all the possible functions of the software. If you consider your personal use of a word processor such as Microsoft Word, it is likely that on a regular basis you use only a small proportion of its functionality, while nevertheless using it as an effective and efficient aid to communication.

Word processors, like any category of software, are defined by their common features. These features could be listed, but it is important to understand that there may be good reasons to restrict the number of functions available. For example, if the software is to be used by young children who are not likely to wish to insert footnotes or track the modification of a document over time, then these facilities may not be included, so reducing the complexity of the interface. In different circumstances, in a hand-held portable computer (tablet), functionality may have to be balanced by available memory.

In general terms, the key features of word processing software can be categorised as follows:

Editing: *Editing features allow the entry and manipulation of text or images, such as insertion and deletion at any point in the document, and cutting, copying and pasting to reorder and reorganise. It is important in the context of word processing for children to grasp the concept of provisionality: that anything created is easily modified or changed.*

Formatting: *Formatting features allow the utilisation of a range of fonts, text sizes, text styles (such as italicising and emboldening), page size, page orientation (landscape and portrait), tables, boxes and other graphics options.*

Tools: *There is a range of tools which complement and enhance the editing and formatting features of word processors. These include spelling and grammar checkers, speech capability, templates and word counting.*

As indicated earlier, many word processors now incorporate desktop publishing and even multimedia and web-authoring tools; Textease Studio CT and Microsoft Word are examples. The advantage of such packages is that children (and teachers) are able to extend their ICT capabilities without the need to learn new software for specific tasks. Instead, they can build on their existing knowledge, skills and understanding.

Word processing's contribution to the writing process

The obvious context through which to explore the contribution word processing can make to teaching and learning is writing. If the writing process is broken down into its elements, then we can see what word processors offer at each stage.

The writing process can be considered to comprise:

- planning and drafting: the initial composition of the ideas, the facts, the emotions being communicated through the writing;
- editing: attention will be given to:

  - the structural aspects of writing, such as sequencing and style (text level work);
  - the technical aspects of writing, such as sentence construction, punctuation, grammar and spelling (word and sentence level work);

- proofreading: the final revision to check for errors in spelling, punctuation and grammar, and for any omissions and repetitions;
- presentation: formatting the material to offer a neat, clear final copy. At this point – and probably not before – the focus will be on the layout and look of the writing.

When children write by hand, they must be resigned to a number of complete reworkings of their texts, or must address each element of the writing process simultaneously. While this latter is a valuable life skill in certain situations, it can also be a considerable challenge. For example, attention to presentation may detract from attention to the content. The fact that editing on the computer is provisional and facilitates presentation to such an extent can be key motivations for the use of a word processor in the classroom and beyond. We will now look at word processing's contribution in more detail.

Planning and drafting

Unless carefully guided, children tend to write sentence by sentence with little overview of the text as a whole, rarely rereading previous sentences to check the progress of the narrative. Indeed, many children find difficulty in retaining the thread of their thoughts while they also grapple with the physical aspects of writing, be they handwriting or keyboard entry. For some, the challenge of rereading their writing may prove a further distraction. The speech facility in some word processing packages can help some children to focus on the progress of their writing as a continuous whole, rather than as a series of disjointed statements. However, such facilities should not be relied upon and will not be appropriate for all children.

A range of text input strategies may be utilised in association with word processing software to enable children's speed of writing to match better their thought processes. These include overlay keyboards, word banks, and even voice recognition, and are discussed in greater depth below.

Clearly, keyboard skills, particularly speed relative to handwriting, are also relevant. It is suggested that children engage in the writing process for longer when ICT is involved, thus producing extended and perhaps more sophisticated narratives.

The use of writing templates (electronic writing frames), an extension of the widely used non-fiction writing strategy, may assist children to produce writing, providing the support which they need in order to embark on the project.

Editing: structural aspects

Once text has been entered into a word processor, there is clearly much scope for revision and development to enhance the quality of the writing. Since making alterations will require thought and some manipulative skill, but not a lengthy rewrite by hand, children can experiment with a view to improvement. Text can be re-sequenced, rephrased, extended and enriched. Meaning can be clarified. Attention can be paid to style, structure, genre, audience and purpose. Alternatives can be explored and compared, and changes can be reversed. The act of writing becomes a process rather than an end point; a temporal dimension is introduced, with the opportunity for reflection, even research to influence subsequent amendments. Printouts can be a useful record of the stages of the process and can provide a teaching and learning opportunity in themselves. A text thus revised should far better reflect the writer's intentions than a first draft that has not undergone revision. Children will be encouraged to write more when the prospect of subsequent redrafting is not associated with the physical effort of copying out by hand.

However, children may not automatically use the editing possibilities afforded by word processors to improve the quality of their writing in this way. In practice, they are easily distracted by the technical editing opportunities associated with presentation rather than content. Refined outcomes depend on focused and explicit teaching and task-setting.

Editing: technical aspects

Perhaps the most obvious contribution that word processing can make to the writing process is the opportunity for children to focus in the initial stages of a writing activity (composing) on communicating ideas, safe in the knowledge that attention can be paid to grammar, spelling and punctuation (as well as structure and style) at a later stage. Word processors now incorporate functions to address each of these phases, but the built-in tools do not even have to be utilised for children to review and amend these aspects of their word-processed work. Frequently, a range of such secretarial adjustments can result merely from rereading the text, again safe in the knowledge that changes will not result in lengthy rewriting or untidy work. Often, this rereading and the selection of items for amendment can be done away from the computer on printouts. This arrangement serves to maximise effective use of computer resources, but equally importantly, it may be easier to see typographical errors on paper than on screen, especially when **proofreading** the final draft. If word processors are to provide the opportunity for children to write in a sustained and purposeful way, drafting and redrafting work, then children need access to the range of facilities word processing has to offer. This includes printing out and using drafts of writing in progress, rather than printing only when writing is judged to be finished. Pedagogic considerations should not be sacrificed to financial constraints.

Presenting

The options for presentation through word processing are practically endless, and nowadays it is in this area that the overlap with what was formerly the province of DTP software is most pronounced. Children can adjust the font and size of their text to be accommodated in the space available, in keeping with the genre of the work, the intended method of presentation (display on the wall, or on a class blog, for instance) and the audience. Colour can be added, as can borders, backgrounds and bullet points.

Text can be arranged in columns to replicate newspaper or magazine layout. One of the most significant developments in word processing software is the facility to incorporate images, be they clip art, children's compositions in drawing and painting software, digital photographs or images scanned or copied and pasted from other locations such as the internet (subject to copyright). We live in an age of changing and evolving literacies, in which children are surrounded by presentations of high quality, so it is important that they too have access to the means through which to communicate their ideas. Teachers similarly need to take advantage of presentation features to provide good models as well as visually engaging resources. However, care must be taken to ensure that children realise the value that teachers place on the content of writing relative to its presentation. While good presentation can significantly enhance communication, it is usually not the primary learning outcome of a writing activity.

There is evidence that for some children being able to word process their writing, at least some of the time, makes a substantial contribution to the development of self-esteem and confidence in their own abilities, a key determinant in children's progress. As previously indicated, the physical effort involved in handwriting at times may be an active deterrent to the creative process. For some children the struggle to provide tidy or even legible work may seem insurmountable. Access to a word processor may allow such children to produce writing which they feel can stand alongside that of their peers. They may also be enabled to communicate what they really want to say, but may not be able to commit effectively to paper by hand.

THE BIGGER PICTURE THE BIGGER PICTURE THE BIGGER PICTURE THE BIGGER PICTURE

When you are planning guided writing activities as part of the process of developing children's independent writing, these need not always be traditional 'literacy' texts. Guided writing techniques can be part of many other areas of the children's learning. For example, you may want to introduce children to the correct way to write up a science experiment or present the findings of a maths investigation or technology project. The move from short pieces of writing to extended writing does not have to take place solely in English sessions, but can be developed in history, geography or RE. Similarly, electronic writing frames, research-recording grids and other scaffolding methods can be useful in all subject areas, including when undertaking cross-curricular topic or theme work. Using guided writing in other parts of the curriculum reinforces the expectation that literacy skills are not just for use in English sessions, but are for all written work.

Progression of knowledge, skills and understanding

We have already alluded to the range of word processing software available, with the most significant contrast being in packages designed for children compared with those intended for adults working in business environments. This diversity in turn leads to there being variety in functionality among different word processors, and so differences in the ease with which particular outcomes are achieved. For example, Microsoft Word has a button to create bullet points which is situated clearly and conveniently, while finding a command for a bullet point in some children's word processors may be difficult. It is consequently problematic to attempt to identify skills development, and in particular to link skills development with levels of attainment or year groups. With this proviso in mind, however, it is possible to identify progression as children progressively use a wider range of tools to improve both the quality of the content and presentation of their writing.

RESEARCH SUMMARY RESEARCH SUMMARY **RESEARCH SUMMARY** RESEARCH SUMMARY

Helen Smith (1998) identified some specific and particular knowledge young children need in order to use word processors. Some of this knowledge is quite different from that needed to write by hand, for instance:

- **that the space bar must be pressed after each word, but not before punctuation marks such as full stops and commas;**
- **that the shift key provides access to capital letters and some punctuation;**
- **that the backspace can be used to correct errors;**
- **that text wraps around automatically onto the next line and that line breaks can be forced using the Enter/Return key.**

She also details knowledge necessary for the basic editing of word-processed work:

- **that the mouse is used to position the cursor (caret) and the importance of this;**
- **that arrow keys, page up, home, etc. can be used to move around the text;**
- **the use of strip highlighting for copying and pasting, cutting, etc.**

To this should perhaps be added:

- **the value of the undo function;**
- **any variations to the above when editing text on tablet devices, which can differ significantly compared to using a fixed PC.**

What are the capabilities and limitations of word processing?

Document sizes and their implications

Text documents do not, on the whole, take large amounts of memory for storage. However, the inclusion of formatting features such as page borders, tables and images may considerably increase the size of a word-processed document. This will result in longer saving and retrieval times.

Text entry

Most text entry into word processing (and other) software is effected by use of the standard QWERTY keyboard. Supplementary technology, such as overlay keyboards, touch screens and word banks, can be deployed to support children entering text. In some circumstances, it is appropriate to use adult scribes (amanuenses). Voice input is available, too, and its accuracy has improved greatly of late. These alternatives to the keyboard often have an important role to play, particularly in special educational needs or disabilities (SEND) contexts. However, it remains that the keyboard itself is the predominant input mechanism for text.

Developing keyboard skills which facilitate text entry and other aspects of ICT use would seem to be a worthwhile investment for the future. Yet, despite the self-evident importance of text entry, there is little consensus about how keyboard skills should best be developed. Teachers have expressed concern over the inefficiency of 'hunt and peck' typing and, particularly in the early stages of keyboard use, the relative time required to enter text. It can be argued that children need to learn keyboard familiarity early on in their computer use, otherwise typing will take more time and concentration than handwriting the equivalent text. Timing is crucial because once habits are learned it is very hard to change them. If children do not develop skills which make word processing accessible as an activity, they will not be able to take advantage of the opportunities word processing provides to enhance communication. Keyboard skills do feature increasingly in Individual Education Plans (IEPs) of children with statements of special educational needs, particularly where the IEP also provides for the regular personal use of a portable word processor or computer.

Some knowledge, skills and understanding relating to text entry have already been discussed. There is a wide range of software available dedicated to the development of children's keyboard skills. In addition there are paper-based materials which provide keyboard familiarisation exercises. These can be used with word processing software or even paper keyboards for children to practise either in the classroom or at home.

Most of these strategies focus on **touch-typing** – learning to use the full range of fingers to access the standard keyboard, with the aim of being able to use the keyboard without looking first to locate letters. When compared with the commitment required to gain some mastery of a musical instrument, for instance, touch-typing may not appear as such an unattainable goal, and some children will particularly benefit from practice in hand-eye co-ordination. However, touch-typing, as taught to secretaries and other adults, is based on the span and stretch of a full-size adult hand, and for younger children modified strategies will be more appropriate. These include:

- knowledge and use of the 'home' keys (*asdf* for the left hand and *jkl* for the right; *f* and *j* often have a raised dot or line on the keyboard to help the fingers in locating them);
- encouraging the use of the first fingers of both hands, and then of at least two fingers on each hand, the thumb for the space bar and the little fingers for the Shift key;
- the use of the number pad, usually located to the right of the keyboard, for the entry of numbers.

For younger children, stickers to replace the standard capital letters of the keyboard with their lower case equivalents are available, and may simplify early familiarisation.

When schools are devising their schemes of work for computing and ICT, consideration should be given to the enhancement of children's keyboard skills and the identification of progression. Clearly there is an important role for teachers in the diagnosis and remedy of inefficient or ineffective keyboard techniques.

The physical demands that handwriting places on children and the consequent contribution word processors can make to writing when some of these are removed has already been discussed. However, it is worth remembering that some children (and adults) may prefer to write by hand or may prefer to do certain, perhaps more personal, types of writing by hand.

REFLECTIVE TASK

REFLECTIVE TASK

Think about your own use of word processing. Do you edit directly onscreen, or are there circumstances in which you prefer to prepare a handwritten draft initially? Talk with other adults about their choice of approach. What implications do the differences you identify have for teaching children?

Overlay keyboards have been available in schools for many years. Using a serial link, the overlay keyboard is an external input device that can be used as an alternative to, or in conjunction with, a standard keyboard. It is programmed such that, when a particular area is touched, a letter, image, word, sentence or paragraph is entered (the same principle is used at some retail tills, for example in fast-food outlets). In the classroom, different overlays can be constructed for different purposes, typically designed on paper or thin card. The overlay is designed and organised into areas representing the effect intended by touching them, and then the keyboard itself is programmed to correspond. For instance, a picture of a horse on the overlay could result in the input of the word 'horse' into a word processor when the area is pressed. Some software comes with pre-programmed keyboard overlays, for example to support writing activities related to talking books. Teachers may also make their own overlays using the editing software that is usually provided with the overlay keyboard itself. This process does take time, though soon it becomes quicker. Designing and making overlays locally allows them to be customised to the requirements of particular activities or individuals. Overlay keyboards are particularly well suited to Key Stage 1 to support writing activities and at all stages for children with certain special educational needs or disabilities (SEND).

Word banks provide some of the functionality of overlay keyboards. These are typically integrated within a children's word processor, and, quite simply, facilitate the choice of appropriate vocabulary (and, by association, spelling). Word banks can be quickly prepared by the teacher to support specific activities; equally, a graduated range can provide differentiated support. For instance, a word bank of specific vocabulary could be used in the recording and reporting of a geographical or historical enquiry, enabling children to concentrate on articulating their understanding rather than being diverted by the spelling of new words. Equally, children may access personalised word banks.

Clicker (Crick) is an interesting and valuable onscreen alternative to the overlay keyboard, with at the same time greater versatility than a conventional word bank. Unlike a word bank, Clicker is separate software that can be used in conjunction with a word processor (and some other applications). Grids can be prepared by the teacher (or children) to the same effect as overlays, dividing the workspace into text, images, sound and even video and animations. Crick have also developed a wide range of ready-made grids to support established curriculum activities such as the Oxford Reading Tree materials. The grid occupies part of the computer screen space, appearing as a separate window, and the children make selections, usually with the mouse.

PRACTICAL TASK PRACTICAL TASK PRACTICAL TASK PRACTICAL TASK

Find out how to prepare and use a word bank or Clicker to support a science activity. Identify teaching and learning objectives with regard to both science and ICT. Note how you would organise and manage this activity:

- in a computer suite;
- in a classroom with two computers.

Touch screens can be used in conjunction with word banks or Clicker to assist text or graphic entry. In these contexts, they may be crucial in overcoming physical obstacles posed to some children by the standard keyboard and mouse. Indeed, software such as Clicker is now available in tablet format (Apple iPad).

Adult scribes are used to assist children with emergent writing and there is no reason why this practice cannot be extended to word processing. This arrangement can provide another strategy to assist children during the composing phase of the writing, allowing them to concentrate on the communication of ideas. Equally, an adult scribe (or the teacher) could record contributions from a whole-class discussion, quickly printing and distributing them to groups to facilitate a follow-up activity.

Voice recognition software has been available for some time but has proved difficult to implement in practice, partly because of the necessity for the software to recognise the particular inflexions of individual users. This involves training the software by reading prepared texts and lists of words and phrases. The software builds up a profile of how words and sounds are pronounced by the user. Although invaluable in some special needs contexts, voice recognition software has yet to arrive in primary schools as a mainstream technology. The need to spend time training the software is one obstacle, but there is also the more mundane concern of background noise, which will interfere with the process.

Speaking word processors

Most word processors designed for the primary school now incorporate a speech facility. They are usually referred to as 'talking' word processors. Since talk carries connotations of a dialogue or discussion, 'speaking' may be a more accurate description, but the increased interaction between a child and a word processor which has a speech facility does indeed carry some of the characteristics of conversation, in which the child responds to what is being said.

Speaking word processors can be used to assist children's writing by reading back each sentence as it is completed, or the entire narrative so far, reminding children of what they have written and prompting them to take the writing forward. It is suggested that the writing of children who are still emerging as readers may as a result be more coherent. Similarly, the computer will read back what the children have actually written, as opposed to what they thought or wanted to write, alerting them to opportunities for revision. This support clearly works to provide word level feedback, too.

If used indiscriminately, speaking word processors can be a distraction both for children writing electronically and for those working close by. Children need to be clear how the speech can assist them to develop their writing and when and where not to use it. Choosing the appropriate settings (whole words or sentences, or individual letters and sounds) is also important. Explicit communication of learning outcomes and classroom protocols is essential for such tools to be used effectively – for instance, completing a first draft and then listening to the computer read the text to assist with the identification of errors and opportunities for improvement. Headphones may also be useful for individual work.

Teachers need to understand and make explicit to children the limitations of the speech facility. Words are uttered through the word processor by concatenating small chunks of recorded sound that correspond to the phonemes represented by letters or short combinations of letters. This can lead to the speech facility occasionally failing to pronounce properly words that are correctly spelled.

Spell-checkers and thesauruses

Spell-checkers can be useful to draw attention to possible errors, though they are far from infallible. Concern has been expressed about over-reliance on such tools, which can act as a disincentive to children to improve spelling. Additionally, used indiscriminately, spell-checkers may not only want to correct spellings which do not require correction (are merely not within the spell-checker's memory) but, more importantly, provide a distraction to writers in the early stages of the writing process. Much time can be wasted adjusting and readjusting spellings, diverting children's attention from the ideas they are seeking to convey. Most spell-checkers allow for new words to be added and teachers should make use of this facility to ensure that the vocabulary associated with current curriculum work is recognised by the word processor. Some watchfulness should be used in encouraging children to add new words – perhaps these should first be checked by the teacher or teaching assistant, to avoid the obvious difficulties associated with inaccurate suggestions being offered by the spell-checker.

Spell-checkers, like speech facilities, may be easily turned off. It may be appropriate for children to complete their initial writing and only then use the spell-checker. Teachers must employ discretion about when and to what extent these facilities should be used.

A spell-checker may provide for a valuable learning experience in itself where unfamiliar words are suggested, particularly if used in association with a dictionary or thesaurus, enriching vocabulary. Likewise, **thesauruses** can be used as part of a structured learning activity to promote independence.

Grammar- and style-checkers

For similar reasons to those discussed in relation to spell-checkers, grammar- or style-checkers, though generally helpful, need to be treated with some caution, especially in software which originated outside the UK, where syntactic conventions may be different. The grammar-checkers in many adult word processors were originally designed for the business market, and the suggestions made reflect this. Additionally, they are unable to evaluate usage in context. Some grammar-checkers can be customised so that they will pick up particular errors and overlook others, and can be very useful for identifying over-long sentences or inappropriate use of apostrophes.

Portable computers

Word processing software is frequently used in conjunction with portable computers. However, it is important to consider health and safety issues and ergonomics when using small devices for carrying out such tasks with mobile technologies. There is a range of portable devices available, including the following.

Notebooks/laptops: These are portable versions of desktop machines, running from the mains or rechargeable batteries. They run standard software and usually have multimedia capability. However, users working at speed often find the laptop keyboard less ergonomically convenient as it is not raked. A mouse and standard keyboard can be attached if preferred.

Dedicated word processors: There are a number of machines available that function only as word processors, such as AlphaSmart and DreamWriter. They allow the entry, storage, downloading and usually direct printing of documents. They do not facilitate much in the way of text formatting, though they do incorporate a small screen which will allow rereading and elementary editing. Text can be downloaded into a word processing program on a desktop computer to provide greater options for revisions and printing. Because of the limited functionality, dedicated word processors formerly had a price advantage by comparison with desktop computers, but the fall in computing costs over recent years has eroded that advantage.

Word processing using portable computers can have a range of benefits for schools. Portable equipment, by its very nature, enables trips outside, to the hall or music room, and even home to be supported. In cramped classrooms, the possibility of using computer equipment on standard tables, rather than specially adapted and located furniture, can be attractive.

Portable word processors have proved effective tools for the support of struggling writers, often bringing associated gains in terms of improved behaviour and social confidence, particularly when used to provide differentiated support for children with SEND. Children gain confidence from the privacy and support provided by the technology. Portable machines have also been useful tools in encouraging parental involvement in children's writing, with children taking the equipment home to continue their writing.

Of course, word processing is also undertaken on various smaller devices such as smartphones and tablets, which is discussed in more depth in Chapter 13.

Explicit skills teaching

One key area for children (and teachers) is their developing understanding of the scope and range of word processing software – what is possible and what isn't. The swiftly evolving nature of the software and hardware means there is no lasting answer, but a developing appreciation of the possibilities goes hand-in-hand with a developing sophistication of use.

The nature of the ways in which we learn about the various functions of word processing (and other) software can lead to inefficient and ineffective practices. Much of the time we learn new skills by experimentation ourselves, by asking our peers or our teachers, by using built-in help, by observing others and by accident when we are trying to achieve something quite different. Some software also allows the same effect to be generated by a range of different strategies; for instance, in Microsoft Word, highlighted text can be copied by accessing the copy command from the edit menu, by using the copy icon on the standard tool bar, by using the keyboard shortcut Ctrl-C and by using the right mouse button to access a mini-menu of options, again including copy. Some of these may work in some other word processing packages and some may not. All are effective. Some are more efficient in terms of time and number of mouse clicks than others. Some suit some individuals and the ways in which they work better than others.

It is important sometimes to watch children working with word processing software and to note and confront inefficient and ineffective practices. For instance, many children access capital letters via the Caps Lock. This requires them to put on the Caps Lock, type the letter and take off the Caps Lock, a three-stage process. Very often children forget the final stage and may have typed several more words before they notice. Changing capitals to lower case letters once typed requires a quite detailed knowledge of some word processing software; it is just not feasible in others. In practice, children tend to delete the offending words and retype them. Time and continuity are lost. Use of the Shift key can be taught explicitly, either informally on a one-to-one basis or demonstrated to a whole class. This alternative makes the capitalisation of letters a two-stage process (Shift and the letter) and avoids unwanted capitals. Similarly, if children are typing in a number of figures, they may find the number keypad at the right-hand side of the keyboard easier than the numbers at the top of the keyboard. Many young children get into the habit of forcing their own line breaks via the Enter key or a mouse click when they notice they are getting towards the right-hand side of the typing area and do not realise that the text will wrap around automatically. This becomes a problem when children subsequently edit their text and the line breaks are not then in the best positions.

A regular 'tips' slot where children demonstrate useful strategies to their peers, or the teacher models a new idea, can easily and fruitfully be incorporated into classroom practice. It should not be assumed that children will learn word processing unaided. As in any subject, they will benefit from explicit teaching and guidance.

Children need to be aware of the limitations of software tools: that the spell-checker is not always right (likewise the grammar- or style-checker); that some words may not be in its dictionary; and that some of its suggestions may not be appropriate. Some understanding of the clues that spell-checkers use to offer alternatives may be useful to enable children to make best use of such facilities. Similarly, the talking function may mispronounce words not in its memory, potentially giving children the false impression that something is incorrect.

Word processing and the core subjects

The ideas and activities introduced below are intended to give a feel for the range of ways in which word processing can be utilised to support and enhance teaching and learning in mathematics, science and English. They are not intended to be comprehensive; they merely to go some way towards illustrating the breadth of possibilities and to provide starting points for the customisation of ideas and the generation of others. Examples introduced under mathematics, for instance, may be just as applicable to one or more of the other areas and vice versa.

Word processing and mathematics

Children can use word processing software to present the results of mathematical investigations. Writing can make a valuable contribution to the development, and particularly the articulation, of meaning and ideas, which is no less important in mathematics and science than in English-language development work. The word processor allows children to import graphs from graphing or database programs and images from painting and drawing packages or a digital camera. They can add commentary, perhaps to pose questions for their peers or to produce fact sheets to contribute to a whole-class reference document.

Of course, many graphing and database packages allow text to be added and amended for the recording and presentation of results. Children need to know that they can transfer their skills from one to the other, but also to recognise the potential limitations of such software; for instance, word banks or bullet points may not be available. Accordingly, children, and their teachers, need to make an informed choice.

Word processing and science

The strategies discussed for mathematics can similarly be applied to the teaching and learning of science. Children at all stages can use word processing software to assist with sequencing and sorting information. The degree of preparation and structuring required may vary with the development of the children. Young children may begin by using an onscreen word bank featuring images with text labels, to sort materials into hard and soft, for instance. An obvious extension for such an activity may be the writing of a sentence of explanation, with adult assistance as necessary.

Sequencing the stages of an investigation can be supported at a range of levels. Children can use cut and paste to sequence and re-sequence the elements of a prepared text. Children may enter their own text and use the facilities of the word processor to revise and reorder their work until they are satisfied. Activities such as these are appropriate for pairs or small groups, since the associated discussion and decision-making should be a fertile ground for rehearsing explanations, justifying opinions and articulating ideas.

One of the principal conventions of science is the systematic recording of investigations. Children begin early in their school careers to develop this skill and word processing can be used to support this writing in various ways. A word bank can be used to access new or difficult vocabulary, allowing children to concentrate on articulating their developing understanding. Electronic writing frames or templates, prepared files with headings and sometimes questions of a general nature which can be used in a variety of contexts or customised for particular activities, can be useful.

Word processors can be useful tools when children are seeking information from databases. Children can make their own notes about what they have found, supplementing these as appropriate with images or text copied and pasted from electronic sources. Children may then use their notes in either an electronic or paper-based format to develop their work further.

The examples given above focus predominantly on using the features of word processors to assist in the development of writing associated with science. Each of these can be taken a stage further by using the tools and facilities to improve the technical and presentational aspects of children's writing in science. The word processing and desktop publishing facilities of the software can be used to good advantage when children produce posters to communicate important facts, such as why we should clean our teeth or which foods we need for a healthy diet. Equally, information can be prepared in a word processing document with a view to linking it with the work of others to form a multimedia document, for the school's VLE or to make a non-fiction talking book or reference guide for younger children. At this point it is particularly important that teachers are clear about their primary learning objectives, which might reside in any combination of English, science and computing.

Word processing and English

Word processing has a range of features which support writing activities, some of which have already been discussed. Editing offers powerful possibilities, and may be structured in ways that develop both English and ICT capability. For example, under a heading such as *All about me*, young children could select and enter words, sentences and images from Clicker or an onscreen bank. Alternatively, or as an extension, children could delete descriptions from a prepared text which do not apply to them. Such an activity promotes skills in working with text on the screen.

A wide range of sentence-level literacy activities can be facilitated – for instance, highlighting direct speech from a prepared text. Some children might use the word processor to complete this activity, while others could use a highlighter and a printout, thus making practical and effective use of classroom resources. Likewise, a prepared text could be changed from reported to direct speech. Word-level work could involve inserting punctuation into a continuous narrative to produce sentences or using search and replace to substitute alternatives for *said*.

Shared text-level work on instructions may focus on *How we clean our teeth*, with the teacher fielding suggestions and acting as scribe as the class or group look on. The interactive whiteboard provides an ideal medium for modelling the writing and editing process. A more complex instructional text, such as a recipe for shortbread biscuits, can be supported at different levels according to need – a prepared list requiring reordering for some, a partial list or a blank sheet for others. Word processing allows children to insert, delete, reorder and present their work.

Prepared texts can be turned from prose into note form, or notes turned into prose. Interesting comparisons can result if one group of children perform the inverse task on the work of others (once it has been saved or printed). A competitive element can be introduced as children seek to use the fewest number of words while still conveying meaning. Debate on what is and is not considered to be important may ensue.

There are opportunities for work focusing on the importance of layout, for instance in the writing and presentation of poetry. The effects of inserting line breaks and capital letters, centring, illustrating or font selection and size can be examined. Cartoons and newspaper layouts can be supported at various stages. Teachers can prepare paper versions for planning and electronic templates to support some children with the layout of their work. Designing front and back covers and title pages for books can provide an alternative to the book review, although children can make use of a prepared electronic writing frame to support such writing.

Children of all ages can work with tables, to compile ongoing lists of synonyms for common adjectives.

Many of the activities suggested above make use of prepared word-processed documents. Teachers should ensure that they manage the use of these carefully. Always have a backup copy and agree with the children how the prepared document will be used. Clearly, having the first pair of children making adjustments and then saving their work over the original is to be avoided. Protect the master document so that changes cannot be saved and encourage children to save the document with a new name before they do anything else or to print out their work and then close the document without saving.

PRACTICAL TASK   PRACTICAL TASK   **PRACTICAL TASK**   PRACTICAL TASK

Use the template facility of a word processing package to design:

- **headed notepaper for your home or school address;**
- **a lesson-planning pro forma;**
- **a writing frame to scaffold work in one of the core subjects.**

Consider whether and how each of these could be utilised electronically or as printouts.

Desktop publishing

Software is now available which enables the non-expert to produce high-quality desktop-published documents. Through the use of wizards, birthday cards, invitations, calendars and newsletters can be generated by following the onscreen instructions, inserting the required text or graphics as directed. Publisher, from Microsoft, is one example. Textease Studio CT, widely adopted in some local authorities, is another.

THE BIGGER PICTURE   THE BIGGER PICTURE   THE BIGGER PICTURE   THE BIGGER PICTURE

When you are planning to use desktop publishing, remember that it is not just useful for literacy texts but also to publish children's work in other subjects, for example the results of investigations in maths, science and PE, and research projects in geography, history, RE and PSHE.

Many schools are now using such applications for half-termly newsletters, prospectuses, fliers, display banners and other publicity and display materials. They can also be usefully deployed in the classroom, for instance in newspaper activities. DTP software does not always allow for changes to be made easily, particularly in text. This mirrors the professional DTP process, where graphics and text are comprehensively edited and considered to be finished before being incorporated in the layout.

A SUMMARY OF **KEY POINTS**

➢ **Word processing and DTP can be used both in children's learning and to support aspects of the professional teaching role.**

➢ **Teachers need to be confident users themselves in order to use word processing and DTP to create a range of learning resources.**

➢ **They also need to be conversant with the features of word processing programs designed for use by primary children, and to be aware of the capabilities and limitations of word processing.**

➢ **Word processing can support every stage of the writing process, but effective use depends on the explicit teaching of skills.**

> ➤ Word processing can support learning in all areas of the curriculum, especially the core subjects.

> ➤ Although many word processing programs now incorporate DTP features, there are separate DTP programs for more advanced presentation needs.

M-LEVEL EXTENSION > > M-LEVEL EXTENSION > > M-LEVEL EXTENSION

Word processing is such a fundamental aspect of ICT that we tend to accept it somewhat unreflectively as a given way in which we work with computers. However, as a primary teacher, it is important to consider that the word processing software that you use on a daily basis does not represent the only approach to what we have seen is a complex and involved creative process. Try to test out other word processing software, particularly packages designed for children, and make comparisons with the application that you use regularly. Using the suggestions for Further Reading and your own research, start an evaluation of how word-processing skills can be properly developed as part of a scheme of work showing progression from the EYFS through Key Stages 1 and 2 to Year 6 and beyond.

REFERENCES REFERENCES **REFERENCES** REFERENCES **REFERENCES** REFERENCES

DfE (2011) *Teachers' Standards.* Available at **www.education.gov.uk/publications**

DfE (2013) *Digital Technology in Schools.* Available at **www.education.gov.uk/a00201823/digital-technology-in-schools**

DfEE (2000) *National Curriculum Handbook for Key Stages 1 and 2.* London: HMSO.

Smith, H. (1998) *Opportunities for ICT in the Primary School.* Stoke-on-Trent: Trentham Books.

FURTHER READING FURTHER READING **FURTHER READING** FURTHER READING

Abbott, C. (2002) *ICT and Literacy Teaching.* Reading: National Centre for Language and Literacy.

Andrews, R. (ed.) (2004) *The Impact of ICT on Literacy Education.* London: RoutledgeFalmer.

Archdeacon, T. (2005) *Exciting ICT in English.* Stafford: Network Educational.

Leask, M. and Meadows, J. (2000) *Teaching and Learning with ICT in the Primary School.* London: Routledge.

Loveless, A. and Dore, B. (2002) *ICT in the Primary School.* Buckingham: Open University Press.

Martin, F. and Asprey, E. (2001) *Double Click on Word Processing.* Oxford: Heinemann Educational.

Monteith, M. (ed.) (2002) *Teaching Primary Literacy with ICT.* Buckingham: Open University Press.

8
Graphics software and digital cameras

Introduction

Images, patterns, shapes and colours are key features of children's early learning. Logos and icons are increasingly important in making sense of the world, from choosing breakfast cereal to operating computer software. Children learn to communicate and interpret visual imagery and ICT has a significant contribution to make to the development of visual literacy.

Recent advances (and cost reductions) in hardware have readily made accessible computers with sufficiently large memories for the storage and manipulation of complex graphics. At the same time, graphics software has become more sophisticated in the range of features and functions supported. The continued move towards icons and toolbars for controlling these functions has improved accessibility for children and their teachers. Most generic software applications, such as word processors and databases, now support graphics. Associated peripherals, particularly scanners and digital cameras, are also increasingly available in primary schools. There has been considerable convergence of software and hardware in the last five years to such an extent that moving and still images can be edited and manipulated using smartphones and tablet devices as well as laptops and PCs.

In this chapter we shall introduce some basic technical considerations that are important for the successful use of graphics software and digital cameras in the classroom, and then identify some straightforward applications, both in activities designed for children and to meet teachers' own professional needs and demands.

What are graphics software and digital cameras?

Graphics software allows the entry, storage, retrieval and manipulation of images and their constituent elements – line, colour and texture – in an electronic format. Generic graphics software is considered to encompass painting and drawing software, although a range of other related software, such as clip art and digitising software for scanners and digital cameras, is becoming increasingly important. Many of the tools for the manipulation of images are also becoming available for tablet devices such as iPads (Apple) and other Android tablet devices.

Digital cameras share a common purpose with film-based cameras: they both record images. However, the technical means by which this end is achieved differs. The traditional camera uses film. The film is sensitive to light, and changes on exposure. The film is then processed, outside the camera, resulting in paper- or transparency-based pictures. In a digital camera the image is taken, or 'captured', but then it is also processed and stored as a file within the camera itself (Ang, 2008). In a digital camera, processed images are held on a memory card. From this medium the images may be transferred to a computer, usually by a USB cable or, on recent computers, by inserting the memory card into a drive on the computer, for further manipulation or incorporation in other files. Alternatively, many recent printers can accept the memory card directly and print from it, so bypassing the computer altogether. Furthermore, more recent devices bypass the need for storing images on a memory as the images are automatically uploaded to a cloud-based storage facility.

What do the programmes of study for Key Stages 1 and 2 include?

In the aims of the National Curriculum for computing it is emphasised that the teaching of computing 'ensures that pupils become digitally literate – able to use, and express themselves and develop their ideas through information and communication technology – at a level suitable for the future workplace and as active participants in a digital world' (DfE, 2013, no page). A key aspect of digital literacy is the responsible and safe use of technologies, which has particular resonance in relation to the use of digital images. The specific aspects of the programme of study which relate to this are highlighted as follows.

At Key Stage 1, the new programme of study for computing (DfE, 2013) states that, children should be taught to:

- Use technology purposefully to create, organise, store, manipulate and retrieve digital content;
- Use technology safely and respectfully, keeping personal information private; know where to go for help and support when they have concerns about material on the internet;
- Recognise common uses of information technology beyond school.

The old programme of study broke this down in more detail and is worth considering. For example, it stated that children should be taught: to use text, tables, images and sounds to develop their ideas; to select from and add to existing information; to share their ideas by presenting information in a variety of forms; and to present their work effectively (DfEE, 2000).

At Key Stage 2 (DfE, 2013) children should be taught how to:

- Use technology safely, respectfully and responsibly; know a range of ways to report concerns and inappropriate behaviour;
- Select, use and combine a variety of software (including internet services) on a range of digital devices to accomplish given goals, including collecting, analysing, evaluating and presenting data and information.

What do teachers need to know about using digital cameras in the classroom?

Unfortunately, the ease with which images can be recorded, transferred and stored by digital cameras has led to their misuse by unscrupulous individuals. Both trainees and serving teachers need to be aware and respectful of parental concerns about images of their children being taken. Schools will have their own policies in respect of photography, frequently guided by their local authority. A regular strategy is for the school to obtain written parental permission for their child to be involved in photography at the beginning of each school year, or when the child enters the school. The understanding will be that the images are used only in the course of educational activity. Before using a digital camera in school, it is vital to ensure that you will be complying with your school's policy on photography (see also Chapter 9 on digital video).

From the perspective of the teacher's own professional needs, a digital camera can be a helpful ally. For example, a picture of the outcome of a design technology project, or a photograph of PE or a dance or drama production will serve as a helpful record for assessment purposes. It is certainly quicker to create than a written account, and is likely to convey what was happening much more clearly.

For a teacher's own continuing professional development, photographic documentation can bring to life their work in the classroom and their contribution to the wider life of the school. It is also first-hand testimony; evidence in a form that is much more convincing than a written claim can be.

There are two significant technical parameters that are typically used by manufacturers to describe digital cameras: resolution and zoom. The resolution of which the camera is capable is measured in pixels – or more usually megapixels (one million pixels). A pixel is a rectangular dot in a single colour. Putting lots of pixels together in an image provides the illusion of continuous gradations of colour. The smaller the pixel, the better defined the image will appear. If the same size of picture is rendered in 1024×768 pixels it will look better, and, dependent in its size, is less likely to appear 'blocky' than if it is shown in 640×480 pixels. However, in this example the image file at higher resolution will be two and a half times larger than the same image at lower resolution, so taking up proportionately more space on the memory card. If the children are using the images they create for desktop publishing, incorporation into web pages or to send by e-mail, then small images at relatively low resolutions will be sufficient and more economical in every respect, not least ink.

It is worth noting that, conventionally, images are recorded with dimensions in a ratio of 4:3, consistent with the usual proportions for computer monitors. Some cameras have the capability for other settings, such as 3:2.

A digital camera usually incorporates a **zoom lens**, typically allowing the image to be enlarged up to three times, and so enabling the user to change the field of view between wide angle and telephoto. The camera may also offer a digital zoom function, which takes over when the limit of the optical zoom is reached. However, because of the way it functions, the digital zoom tends to deteriorate the picture quality.

Most digital cameras are provided with an **LCD screen**. This is helpful in enabling the user to review immediately the images that have been taken, providing the opportunity to ensure that appropriate images are captured before returning to the classroom and to delete those that are not needed, so freeing up space on the memory card. This facility enables the adoption of a totally different approach to photography in contrast to film technology, where mistakes are costly in terms of developing unwanted pictures. Digital photography allows a much more spontaneous experimental attitude to be embraced.

Other important features that are usually found on a digital camera include a **flash**, which can be utilised to assist recording images in poor light or at night. As with a conventional film camera, there are limits to the capability of the flash in an open space, but the technology now enables good-quality close-up shots to be achieved in the dark. The camera is also likely to have various **controls**, such as a timer, options for close-up and distance work, and adjustment of the white balance.

Graphics software

Graphics software can be characterised under two main headings: drawing and painting packages. Each has different strengths and limitations. One of the key differences is in the storage mechanism for the images created and manipulated within them.

Painting programs produce bitmap images. Bitmap images are minutely detailed, essentially recording separately every pixel (tiny dot) displayed on the screen, including blank areas. This results potentially in very large documents.

Drawing programs, sometimes called vector graphics programs, operate a completely different method of storing information. Drawings are stored as a series of vectors. These are mathematical descriptions of lines determining their magnitude and direction from the points at which they originate to their ends – and including all the curves and changes of direction in between. This is a more economical way of describing a simple image, and it results in smaller file sizes.

There has, however, been considerable convergence in graphics software. Most graphics programs are now painting programs which also support drawing features, such as lines, arrows and shapes. Drawing features have also been included in other software applications. For example, most word processing software supports a range of drawing functions which enable the user to incorporate diagrams and other line art into their documents.

PRACTICAL TASK   PRACTICAL TASK   PRACTICAL TASK   PRACTICAL TASK

It is worth exploring the characteristics of different image file types using an adult's image manipulation software such as Paint Shop Pro, Photoshop or Fireworks. Alternatively, the free utility PixResizer (http:// bluefive.pair.com/pixresizer.htm) is specifically designed to support the resizing of images and their subsequent saving in alternative file formats. Compare the differences in file size. Paste an image into a graphics or word processing program and enlarge it significantly. What do you notice? Could you explain what is happening, and why, to children?

Teachers need to be competent and confident users of primary graphics software in order to facilitate children's learning. This does not mean that they need to know the answer to every technical question, but they do need a working knowledge of the software so as to be able to plan, support and assess appropriate activities. They also need to have strategies to support the children in their discovery of how the software works, as well as to assist with problem solving.

Teaching with and about graphics software involves teachers:

- **Preparing resources** – such as a worksheet to support early mathematics work, a prepared graphics document in which children may explore and reinforce early symmetry work, or illustrations to accompany a wall display. Some of these examples focus on using ICT as a tool for teaching and learning in another curriculum area, while others focus on the teaching and learning of computing.
- **Selecting appropriate opportunities** – in which graphics software can facilitate, enhance or extend children's learning, such as the importance of presentation in communication. In some instances, the focus will be on teaching and learning in computing (e.g. aspects of digital literacy such as optimising images

for different publication formats: web, print poster), while in others, ICT will be used as a resource in the teaching and learning of another curriculum area (e.g. creating a presentation on a history trip for a whole-school assembly).

- **Making explicit links between related knowledge, skills and understanding** – graphics software has applications across the range of the primary curriculum and as a consequence may provide opportunities to make explicit links in knowledge, skills and understanding in mathematics and art, for instance.
- **Modelling appropriate use of ICT** – cropping an image from a digital camera and transferring the result into a word processor to illustrate an activity sheet is an example where modelling is appropriate.
- **Demonstrating or intervening** – for example, demonstrating a new skill, such as altering the size of painting tools or intervening to assist a child to delete multiple copies of a saved image to save memory space.

The list below attempts to identify the knowledge, skills and understanding that teachers need in order to teach effectively with and about graphics software. Many graphics programs support only a subset of these functions. This is no reflection on their usefulness – in most instances, simplicity is a strength. However, it does signal that teachers must be aware of the capabilities and limitations of any program as these will be significant in the choice of software for any teaching and learning activity.

Painting and drawing programs:

- creating, opening, closing, deleting and printing documents;
- selecting file type and saving documents;
- selecting page size, margins and page orientation;
- inserting, modifying and deleting background colours and textures;
- selecting, modifying and utilising tools from the tool bar (spray, round brush, shapes, line);
- utilising fill;
- utilising the pipette/choose a colour tool;
- utilising undo/redo;
- selecting, modifying and utilising the text tool (font, font size, colour);
- selecting areas (for cropping, scaling, reshaping, deletion);
- selecting, modifying, utilising and saving repeated images (stamps);
- selecting and utilising more advanced features such as tiling, flipping and rotation;
- switching grid on and off;
- utilising zoom/magnifier and understanding how it differs from image resizing;
- inserting, deleting, manipulating and saving imported images;
- exporting images/drawings to other applications;
- clearing the screen;
- utilising help;
- altering defaults;
- customising set up;
- connecting alternative input devices (overlay keyboards, touch screens, graphics tablets);
- protecting documents.

What are the key features of graphics software?

Graphics software makes use of a variety of tools, editing functions and effects for the creation and manipulation of electronic images.

Tools include brushes, lines, shapes and colour filling among many others. The variety of tools supported varies between software. Much painting software includes a selection of drawing features, although these cannot be manipulated in the same way as is possible in drawing programs because once laid down they are converted into pixels in the same way as the rest of the image.

The distinguishing feature of drawing software is that drawings are composed of a series of layered elements (shapes, for instance) and these may be reordered as required. Similarly, the elements may be grouped together to be edited. In painting software, **editing functions** and effects can be applied to a selected area of an image, but it is not possible to isolate the elements of the image in the same way. This is because each pixel is treated essentially independently of its neighbours.

Figure 8.1 was created with the drawing tools available in Word. Objects were reordered to create the desired overlapping circle effect. Elements were grouped so that the image could be copied, the copies then being resized and rotated. Many drawing and painting packages support a range of common editing functions, including, for example, scaling, reflecting, rotating, cropping and editing. Figure 8.2 demonstrates the effect of each of these on a simple image.

Painting software provides a range of artistic **effects**, the variety and sophistication of these varying between packages. Common effects include a spray can, watercolour, colour blending, stamping (multiple copying), tinting and diffusing.

PRACTICAL TASK   PRACTICAL TASK   PRACTICAL TASK   PRACTICAL TASK

Explore the tools, editing functions and effects of two common painting packages for children. Decide the most appropriate age range for each. If your school were purchasing a paint package, which would you recommend and why? Produce an A4 help sheet to assist children in the use of a few key effects.

Figure 8.1 Shape-based worksheet designed using the drawing features (Microsoft Word)

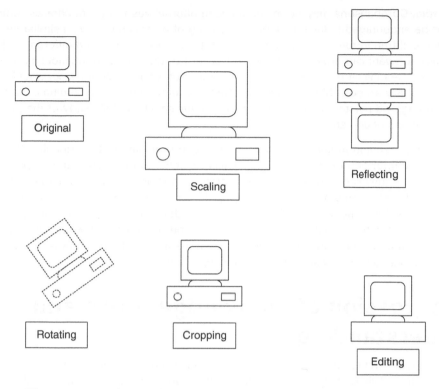

Figure 8.2 The effects of common editing functions (Microsoft Word)

What does graphics software contribute to teaching and learning?

Use of graphics software provides a quite different aesthetic and kinaesthetic experience compared with traditional art media. The outcomes produced are also different and there is a completely distinct physical experience associated with creating outcomes. Some children may be frustrated at the difficulties associated with using the mouse as a drawing tool; others may delight in the potential to create difficult shapes, such as curves, exactly as they wish them to look. In order to develop understanding and inform choices, children need a range of experiences on which to base their decisions.

Drawing and painting software facilitates a range of starting points for graphic activities, from a blank screen to a photographic image to be manipulated and developed. Similarly, the sheer variety of tools, editing functions and effects available provide challenges in themselves. The range of tools, editing functions and effects can, however, be limited in order to promote specific learning outcomes. Use of graphics software provides an opportunity to introduce and develop children's understanding of related technical issues, such as file size and file extensions, in a relevant and meaningful context.

Most graphics software allows users to undo the previous action. Many primary packages, though not all, support repeated undoing. This feature allows children to use the software to explore and experiment with effects in ways which are not possible with traditional art media. Comparisons may be made between alternatives to inform choices. Children should be encouraged to take risks. Regular saving of work can provide a similar security, allowing children to return to an earlier stage in their work and follow a different pathway. Graphics software can provide children with access to tools, editing functions and effects which may be difficult or impossible to achieve with other arts resources commonly available in primary schools. Children may be able to develop their understanding of watercolour painting and painters by simulating watercolour effects and similarly of the potential and limitations of pop art.

Graphic representation is an important area of communication. Experiencing the creation and manipulation of electronic images assists children to interpret the graphics they encounter, be they sporting goods manufacturers' logos or sophisticated film animations. Similarly, the electronic nature of some graphics enables global sharing and exchange through e-mail and the internet. Graphics software does not in any way replace children working with the traditional range of art media; rather it increases the choices available. In certain situations the software features or even the nature of the outcome, in electronic format for instance, may make it the appropriate selection.

Progression of knowledge, skills and understanding

Graphics work will focus on the development of children's graphical communication and interpretation skills as well as software skills. Very young children may use touch screens and concept keyboards to control the software, developing their understanding of the relationship between their actions and the effects on the screen. A range of early language, number and science activities can be supported; for instance, using fill tools to colour in prepared drawings; the boat red, the fish orange and the seaweed green. With adult help, children might draw party hats on digital photographs of themselves. With increasing independence, children will be able to engage in a range of painting and drawing activities, such as producing a new label for their tray or coat hook.

Children will be increasingly able to make their own choices about the creation, manipulation and presentation of images, extending their repertoire of knowledge, skills and understanding through structured activities and interventions. Older children will be able to make appropriate choices related to the task and its audience. The variations in both software and the intended outcomes make ordering and ascribing particular skills and techniques difficult. Consideration is more appropriately focused on the development of knowledge and understanding which underpins the use of skills. In addition to directly teaching a limited range of skills, it is important for the teacher to encourage children to explore the software purposefully for themselves, to think of an effect that they want to create and then discover how to achieve it.

THE BIGGER PICTURE   THE BIGGER PICTURE   THE BIGGER PICTURE   THE BIGGER PICTURE

When you are planning graphics work, it is helpful to incorporate practical activities into real-life situations around school and in the community. For example, many schools take part in charity and fundraising events, such as sponsored walks or silences, and end-of-term or summer fairs that are open to parents, friends and other members of the community. There are lots of opportunities for older Key Stage 2 children to get involved in organising these. Think of the possibilities in drawing a plan to show where the stalls will go, designing signage and instructions for each stall, price lists and menus for customers requiring refreshments, and posters and fliers advertising the event.

What are the capabilities and limitations of graphics software?

Drawing with graphics software

The features of drawing software enable children to produce shapes and arrows, for instance, rapidly and accurately. An oval can be drawn by selecting the appropriate tool and clicking to locate the centre of the shape or edge of the shape (depending on the program), holding the mouse button down until the desired size and shape are shown. A perfect circle can be achieved by holding down Ctrl or Shift (depending on the program) while moving the mouse. Drawing software also allows objects to be deleted, redrawn and resized. The process is ideal for the creation of diagrams in science, for example, or for simple maps. However, the scope is limited; subtleties of colour and realistic, rather than abstract, representations are difficult to achieve.

Freehand drawing is tricky, requiring a high degree of hand-eye co-ordination. The computer mouse is not a sensitive drawing tool and freehand drawing can be very difficult. There are a number of strategies teachers can use to mediate this problem. Using the zoom or magnifying tool to enlarge the drawing area, drawing the required image, and then reducing the zoom may have the effect of disguising hand-wobble. Some graphics software includes smoothing utilities that provide curves of best fit.

It is possible to adjust the sensitivity of the mouse, but a more effective alternative is to use a simple graphics tablet. A graphics tablet is made up of a small plastic board and a light pen. The light pen allows the user greater manipulative control than is possible with a mouse. Inexpensive graphics tablets are available, such as those from Wacom. Tablet devices, with which it is possible to use a stylus pen, have the significant advantage of direct contact between pen and screen, which makes hand-eye co-ordination much easier, although the sensitivity can vary between different devices and types of stylus.

Colour handling

Painting software is based on a combination of pixels (derived from 'picture elements'), the 'dots' of an image, which are arranged on a rectangular grid (raster). Each pixel shows a colour, the information about which is stored in the image file. Viewed together, the pixels create the illusion of a picture but in reality they are distinct one from another.

Computers work with colour by mixing different proportions of red, green and blue light – the 'RGB' that gives its name to the cable linking the computer to the monitor. The mix is determined by a scale running from 0 to 255 for each of these primary colours. White, then, is 255, 255, 255, while black – the absence of colour – is defined as 0, 0, 0. All other colours are represented by varying combinations of red, green and blue falling between these values. For example, Red 80, Green 105 and Blue 50 together make a shade of olive. In total 16,777,216 different shades, calculated as 256 × 256 × 256, or 2^{24} (2 to the power of 24) can be defined in this way – more than are discernible by the human eye. It is from this calculation that the term '24-bit image' derives. A bit (binary digit) is either 1 or 0, with current in the computer switched on or off accordingly. Each pixel on which the computer needs to hold information is allocated 24 bits, eight bits (2^8, or 256) for each of the red, green and blue components. In the example given above, the amount of Red (80) is understood by the computer in binary as 01010000, the amount of Green (105) as 01101001 and the amount of Blue (50) as 00001110, together making up twenty-four pieces of information that together generate the olive colour.

Compression and resolution

Graphics software, particularly packages designed for image manipulation, should enable the user to make choices about the resolution at which an image is saved, and the amount of compression that is applied.

It is usually helpful to identify the width and height of an image. Accordingly, an image that is 2048 pixels wide and 1536 pixels high holds altogether 3,145,728 pixels, which can be expressed alternatively as 3.1 Megapixels – the unit by which digital cameras are often described.

An image of this size is very big. Let's consider why. Our computer screens are also set at a particular resolution. This might range from an older 17" monitor set at 800 × 600 pixels to a larger (19" or more) high-quality screen set at 1280 × 1024 pixels. However, our 2048 × 1536 image will not come close to being viewable in its totality on even this more highly specified equipment. A scroll bar or the software's zoom-out facility will have to be utilised. Similarly, if an image is to be incorporated into a PowerPoint slide it will only take up a relatively small proportion of the displayed area. It is sensible to import the image at that optimum size, by using image manipulation software to reduce the size. Given that the monitor has a limit to the number of pixels per inch (PPI) of display (sometimes known as the pixel density) that it offers, if the images that are created are essentially for use onscreen, then there is no need for them to be larger than the pixel dimensions that they occupy. Larger files occupy more storage and memory space, which may be a significant factor on school computers if they are not built to a high specification. Similarly, large image files are slower to transfer on the internet or by e-mail.

Resolution takes on a different shade of meaning when printing is involved. The instruction to the printer is given to render a specified number of dots per inch (dpi). Accordingly, an image that is 800 × 600 pixels printed at 200 dpi will result in a printed picture measuring 4 inches × 3 inches. In this way, the same file could be used to create different-sized pictures. Printing the same file at 96 dpi will produce a larger picture than if it is printed at 200 dpi, but the latter will probably appear to be better quality. 200 dpi is considered a minimum for prints of reasonable quality.

The basic file used by painting programs is the bitmap (file extension: .bmp). The term derives from the organisation, or mapping, of the pixels (composed of bits), which we examined earlier. However, another format, jpeg, which is pronounced 'jay-peg', and has the file extension usually .jpg, sometimes .jpeg, is now a popular alternative option. This is because jpeg files can be compressed, so reducing their size. Painting or image manipulation software usually effects the compression through a slider tool at the point of saving the file. There is a trade-off between quality and file size, though, as the compression technique necessitates some loss of graphical information. However, judicious use of jpeg compression can substantially reduce file size without compromising quality unduly.

The .jpg format follows standards set by the Joint Photographic Experts Group, and is particularly useful when dealing with photo-realistic images. The file type is not so well suited to images containing large areas of flat colour such as cartoons and maps. Here the preference will probably be for GIFs (file extension: .gif), which are economical files in terms of size, because they use a maximum of only 256 colours. In consequence, they take up much less storage and memory space. The appropriate limited range of colours is identified as a palette and attached to the file. GIFs also support transparency, allowing one of the palette's colours to be defined so that the background appears through wherever that part of the GIF appears on a page.

In summary, determining the variables of resolution and compression will depend on the way in which the image is to be used. The size of files is not as critical as it used to be, given the increased storage and memory capacity of the computers sold today. Nevertheless, it is good practice to be aware of the implications. Generally, images to be displayed on screen, in PowerPoint or other presentations, or in web pages, can be saved in lower resolution or compressed format. Graphics which are to be enlarged or which require high-quality printouts, such as photographs, should be high resolution or uncompressed – or both. Low-resolution images which are subsequently enlarged often become 'blocky' or pixelated.

By contrast, despite occupying less memory, drawing images do not suffer quality reductions when they are enlarged. The vectors which describe the drawing images can be scaled to any size.

Settings without access to a network server, or with older computers, may have difficulty in saving and storing quantities of large graphics file. Teachers should ensure that children avoid saving multiple copies of large documents and that documents which are no longer needed are either deleted or saved in a way which will not occupy large amounts of memory. CD writers have become commonplace and these allow documents to be quickly and permanently stored on CD-ROMs.

Sourcing images and ethical use

In addition to drawing and painting their own graphics images, children can source prepared images or photographs from a variety of locations. Websites, CD-ROMs and scanning are common sources of images produced by others. Similarly, pictures can be downloaded from digital cameras. Children often find it daunting to begin with a blank screen and the manipulation of an existing image can be a useful starting point, or a teaching and learning activity in itself where the emphasis is on exploring the features of the software. It is important to remember that any image other than clip art is likely to be subject to copyright. Children should also be taught about Creative Commons and how to source such images through image libraries such as Flickr (see **www.flickr.com**), carrying out an advanced search for images that are available under Creative Commons. Essentially, these are images whose creators give consent for others to use their work as long as there is no commercial or financial gain involved, and that the original creator is acknowledged. There are different kinds of Creative Commons licences which can be explored with children (see also **http://creativecommons.org/**). In addition to this, children should be taught that they have a responsibility to use images ethically. For example, while a classroom visitor may be content to have their photograph displayed on the wall of the classroom, they may not want it to be published on the school website or class blog. Consequently, children should consider how the images they are sourcing will be used and published in order to ensure ethical and responsible use and that they have the appropriate permissions for how they intend to use the images.

Clip art

Clip art, which is widely used in primary schools, is usually copyright-free artwork, although it may come as exemplar material as part of a program and so be licensed within that. Clip art is typically simple in execution and offered as GIFs or Windows Metafiles (.wmf) in order to minimise file size. Most word processing software now comes with a range of clip art. There are also websites from which free clip art can be downloaded, though these should be mediated by an adult as they frequently need some negotiation of pop-up advertising. Publishers of educational software also produce CD-ROMs of associated clip art images, e.g. Oxford Reading Tree Clip Art.

Clip art may be used for a range of purposes, such as illustrating notices around the school, computer room and wet play area. Clip art images may also be a useful starting point for children to practise image-manipulation techniques in painting packages. However, clip art is to a certain extent a short cut to create visual impact; its originality lies with the artist who created it rather than with the child who imports it into their work.

Scanners

Scanners allow digital images to be made of hand-drawn diagrams, existing photographs, autumn leaves and everyday (flattish) objects such as scissors. Scanners also come with software which enables images to be captured and saved in a range of file formats. The software will conduct a preliminary scan of the original and allow the user to select and save just the parts of the image that are required. Scanners all accommodate images, and are

Figure 8.3 Image created with a scanned leaf and painting software effects (Dazzle 03, Indigo Learning)

usually provided with optical character recognition (OCR) software, which enables printed pages of text to be converted into a digital format that can be fed into word processing or text-editing applications. This technology has become very accurate, but it is not infallible, so documents must be carefully checked.

Scanners are useful for translating children's artwork, for instance, into an electronic format to allow it to be displayed on the school VLE. Similarly, scanned images can be the starting point for a range of activities. Children may scan leaves (see Figure 8.3), import them into a graphics package and manipulate them to produce a border for a poem. Alternatively, they could attempt to replicate a leaf using the drawing and painting tools in an activity designed to increase facility with these, displaying the scanned and the drawn images side by side. Due caution must be exercised to ensure that scanning does not breach copyright.

PRACTICAL TASK PRACTICAL TASK **PRACTICAL TASK** PRACTICAL TASK

Use a scanner or a digital camera to produce a resource to support a science activity. How will you use the resource? How will you differentiate? How will you assess the resource's effectiveness?

Printing

The large size of many graphics documents has implications for printing. Printers have memories into which documents are sent from the computer. Documents which are too large for the printer's memory will not print out. They will also prevent the printing of other documents sent subsequently to the printer until the problem document has been cleared from the print queue. Children may be disappointed to find that importing a number of graphic images into a word processing document, for instance, renders the file size too large to print. Problems with memory are usually associated with older printers.

PRACTICAL TASK PRACTICAL TASK **PRACTICAL TASK** PRACTICAL TASK

Find out how to delete jobs from the print queue. NB Sometimes switching the printer off and on again will not be effective.

Images, particularly those which are uncompressed or high resolution and therefore contain the most detail, take a long time to print out on conventional inkjet printers. Waiting for printing can be frustrating and time-consuming if such eventualities are not anticipated. Further, if a backlog of print jobs accumulates in the print queue because documents are taking time to print, the printer's memory may become overloaded, causing it to crash.

Although the price of printers has fallen in recent years, colour printing is still expensive. Inkjet cartridges have only a small ink capacity and cost a lot. Colour lasers have become more affordable but again their maintenance is not cheap. If very high-quality images are required, photographic-quality paper is available, but this too is expensive for regular use in schools. Nevertheless, if children are to work with images, then the likelihood is that at least some of their work should be printed, and schools need to take the consumables involved into account with their budgeting.

Digital images and the core subjects

The ideas and activities introduced below are intended to give a feel for the range of ways in which graphics software and digital cameras can be utilised to support and enhance teaching and learning in mathematics, science and English. They are not intended to be comprehensive, merely to go some way towards illustrating the breadth of possibilities and to provide starting points for the customisation of ideas and the generation of others.

Examples introduced under mathematics, for instance, may be just as applicable to one or more of the other areas.

Science

Children may use painting software to produce images which illustrate the effects of light sources, such as street lights at night, fireworks in the sky or sunlight reflected in water. The particular qualities of graphics software, which enable light colours to be easily imposed on top of dark ones, make ICT a suitable medium for such representations, allowing children to create an artistic effect otherwise only accessible to very practised artists.

Very often, science work at all levels requires illustration to aid communication. Graphics software enables images to be created, imported and modified as required. It also supports the addition of labels to aid identification and explanation. Posters may be designed to illustrate scientific understanding – the importance of a healthy breakfast or regular cleaning of teeth, for instance. Such posters can be created using traditional media, although graphics software allows revision and reorganisation to maximise presentational impact. It also enables children to incorporate images from a range of electronic sources, including digital cameras. Digital cameras can also be used to record key findings or observations from experiments.

Experience with graphics software in the manipulation of images – resizing or cropping, for instance – is an important skill which can be applied to the incorporation of graphics across the range of generic applications, most notably word processing and desktop publishing.

Mathematics

Drawing programs may be used to support mathematical modelling activities. A teacher may prepare an electronic file containing a plan view of the classroom and the outlines of a range of furniture to be included. Children could explore possible arrangements. Extension activities might include conditions (the computer cannot be located by a south-facing window) or additions (two new children are starting on Monday; where should the extra table and chairs be located?).

Graphics software sometimes includes a grid which can be switched on and off. Grids may help children use graphics software to develop their mathematical understanding of shape. A teacher may prepare graphics files incorporating a grid, lines of symmetry and shapes in one quadrant. Children can make use of the grid to help them draw the shape reflected or rotated (see Figure 8.2). Similarly, a teacher may use a regular shape on a grid to demonstrate rapidly and effectively the effect of increasing perimeter on area. The incorporation of images into mathematics work mediated through the interactive whiteboard presents particularly rich opportunities, simply because of the greater visual impact that an image commands by comparison with text.

Graphics programs can be used to produce repeating patterns for wallpaper or wrapping paper. The stamping facility in many paint packages enables a design to be rapidly duplicated and arranged. The suitability of various shapes for geometric sequences can be explored – an investigation that can be extended into consideration of Islamic art, offering valuable opportunities for cross-curricular work.

English

Children's books are usually enhanced by their illustrations and, logically, their own writing will be made more attractive and perhaps clearer through the incorporation of digital images that they have composed. It is important that the pictures the children use do genuinely complement and enrich the text, and are not just a technological version of the borders with which teachers encouraged children to decorate their work if they finished their writing quicker than anticipated. Talk to the children about how the words and pictures interplay to give meaning. Images can be imported into painting software – children may paint themselves into a Viking village scene, with appropriate clothing and props, for instance, and from there create a story of their life as a Viking.

PRACTICAL TASK PRACTICAL TASK **PRACTICAL TASK** PRACTICAL TASK

Create a resource bank of photographic images that might be used in the classroom, but which it may be impractical for the children to take themselves. For example, photographs of your town – the station, the market place, the park, key buildings such as the fire station and hospital – will be invaluable for a local study in geography. You will be able to use the photographs for whole-class work, perhaps on an interactive whiteboard, while the children will be able to include them in their reports or presentations.

Images are frequently used to communicate information in newspapers and magazines. Children can select and manipulate images from a wide range of sources, including digital cameras, scanners and websites, to illustrate news stories. Possible challenges include manipulating a photographic image, or creating a photo montage, to give a misleading or contrary impression.

The communication of information in cartoon-type format can be particularly enhanced using graphics software. A common background may be prepared and used as the basis for six or eight images telling the story of the child's journey to school or the adventures of a cat. A series of digital images may be sequenced and captioned to provide an account of the class's visit to the fire station or a record of a drama production.

A SUMMARY OF **KEY POINTS**

➤ Graphics can be incorporated in a wide variety of electronic documents.

➤ Sources of graphics include images composed in painting and drawing software, as well as scanned images, digital camera pictures, clip art and (copyright permitting) CD-ROMs and the internet.

➤ Graphics occupy large amounts of computer memory space relative to text documents, which can cause difficulties in file management and printing.

➤ Graphics software complements more traditional art media; it does not replace them.

➤ The functions, effects and tools incorporated in graphics software provide exciting opportunities for image creation and manipulation.

➤ There are safeguarding issues regarding using the images of children without parental permission and relevant policies and protocols should be followed on the dissemination of these.

➤ There are ethical issues to consider when capturing and manipulating images. Children should be made aware of the ethical responsibilities they assume when working with digital images.

M-LEVEL EXTENSION > > M-LEVEL EXTENSION > > M-LEVEL EXTENSION

Go to the Futurelab website at **www.futurelab.org.uk** and download a copy of the report *'It's Not Chalk and Talk Anymore'* (Hague, 2010). This is a comprehensive review of a project that looked at school approaches to developing children's digital literacy. Look at the sections on digital literacy and the curriculum, pedagogy and school-based interventions and the impact of these. Study the examples of digital literacy interventions in different schools. How does the use of digital cameras, digital video and other technologies and applications contribute to the development of children's digital literacy? The term itself has caused some controversy – what is digital literacy? Is it a valid focus in an already crowded curriculum? How will you build in your findings to your own ICT practice?

REFERENCES REFERENCES **REFERENCES** REFERENCES REFERENCES REFERENCES

Ang, T. (2002) *Digital Photographer's Handbook.* London: Dorling Kindersley.

DfE (2011) *Teachers' Standards.* Available at **www.education.gov.uk/publications**

DfE (2013) *Digital Technology in Schools.* Available at **www.education.gov.uk/a00201823/digital-technology-in-schools**

DfEE (2000) *National Curriculum Handbook for Key Stages 1 and 2.* London: HMSO.

Hague, C. (2010) *'It's Not Chalk and Talk Anymore': School Approaches to Developing Students' Digital Literacy.* Available at **www.futurelab.org.uk** (accessed 5 January 2014).

FURTHER READING FURTHER READING **FURTHER READING** FURTHER READING

Ang, T. (2008) *Digital Photographer's Handbook.* 4th Edition. London: Dorling Kindersley.

DfE (2011) *Teachers' Standards.* Available at **www.education.gov.uk/publications**

Hague, C. (2010) *'It's Not Chalk and Talk Anymore': School Approaches to Developing Students' Digital Literacy.* Available at **www.futurelab.org.uk** (accessed 5 January 2014).

Hague, C. and Williamson, B. (2009) *Digital Participation, Digital Literacy and School Subjects: A Review of the Policies, Literature and Evidence.* Available at **www.futurelab.org.uk** (accessed 5 January 2014).

Key, P. and Stillman, J. (2009) *Teaching Primary Art and Design.* Exeter: Learning Matters.

9
Media production: Video, animation and ICT

Introduction

The aim of this chapter is to introduce the reader to the various productive uses of digital media in educational settings. It discusses some of the key concepts, the theoretical perspectives and some of the relevant tools. The place of media in the orders for the primary curriculum in England has never been as central as in other countries which recognise the primacy of the main communicative mode of the twenty-first century. In any case, whether or not it is present in the formal school curriculum, it is present everywhere else in the lives of learners, parents, carers and teachers. It can also be found in a diffuse form in the curriculum in the use of media clips as audio visual aids for accessing forms of curriculum content. There is recognition in this that teachers and children can access knowledge in school contexts which is presented in familiar forms with high modality, such as they see every day in their use of the internet, television and sound. Used in this way, and only in this way, this has the effect of closing the door on understanding the ways in which such media are constructed and used to convey meaning. Arguing against this nonsensical position to take in the twenty-first century, many commentators point out that this is similar to restricting literacy teaching to reading and never learning to write (for a more sophisticated and elaborated take on this, see David Buckingham's book, *Media Education* (Buckingham, 2003), in which he discusses the notion of learners as producers, not simply consumers).

Further arguments for making media in various forms as opposed to simply viewing them, are made in research which shows that working creatively with film and media, like all arts subjects, enhances learning in a range of other curriculum areas (Burn and Durran, 2007; Parry, 2013; Potter, 2012). It gives children access to higher order thinking about the decisions they make, promotes clear written and verbal communication, encourages teamwork and allows them to experience something of the field to which the UK is a major contributor: film-making and its associated industries. These arguments, or similar, were made by lobbyists subsequent to the welcome addition of computing to the curriculum and there are a number of UK organisations that promote the use of film and media in educational settings which have advocated media production in education (The British Film Institute, Film Nation UK, The Film Space, The Media Education Association, Learn About Film and more; it is certainly worth searching online for the homepages of these organisations). So, whether you are simply viewing clips in the classroom, or critiquing them and learning about how they are made, and/or making media with children, it is useful to know something of the ICT resources which are out there to support that work, and where you can go for help in learning more about how moving images work to support teaching and learning.

What do the programmes of study for Key Stages 1 and 2 include?

While the word 'media' in the programmes of study for 2014 is missing, there are several instances in the orders where Animation and Digital Video, particularly in the productive sense, can find a location in the prescriptions of the National Curriculum. Aside from the general requirement that schools meet the aim to ensure pupils 'are responsible, competent, confident and creative users of information and communication technology', there is ample opportunity in media production to meet the following aims from the programmes of study:

Key Stage 1

- Use technology purposefully to create, organise, store, manipulate and retrieve digital content;
- Recognise common uses of information technology beyond school.

Key Stage 2

- Select, use and combine a variety of software (including internet services) on a range of digital devices to accomplish given goals...

Media production in schools has been made possible and accessible in recent years thanks to the proliferation of affordable equipment and software. Simple editing software and the ease of sharing short film creations have given non-specialists access to areas which were previously in the domain of media professionals. As seen in the chapters on social media and on digital audio and music, a further set of possibilities has been opened up by the ease with which productions can be shared and exchanged through the medium of the internet or by swapping commonly formatted media files. It is also more than likely that some children in schools in which you work have begun to experiment with making both video and animation with cameras and/or on smartphones or tablets. They may never have considered editing these and perfecting them as short films but will undoubtedly have drawn on the wider culture of the moving image in designing them and making them.

For formal educational settings, the production of digital video images of children and their work raises ethical considerations and internet safety issues. Sensible discussion of these safeguarding issues with school governors, parents, children, teachers and all stakeholders, together with an agreed protocol for making and distributing these productions, can result in children being given access to the very powerful medium of digital video within a school context. There are schools that regularly publish their children's work within password-protected areas in their local authority online learning environment. Others distribute material to parents on DVD. Some make sure that children can safely use the medium without being identifiable but that they can still engage with work such as animation or simple video production. In any case, simply closing the door, as noted above, denies children and young people access to a productive engagement with contemporary culture and further widens the gap between educational spaces and home.

RESEARCH SUMMARY RESEARCH SUMMARY **RESEARCH SUMMARY** RESEARCH SUMMARY

Whatever the means by which the concerns raised above can be addressed, there is little doubt that working with moving images in the classroom brings huge benefits in a number of areas of the curriculum and broadens our understanding of children's experience of literacy and the role of media in shaping learner identity. There are a growing number of studies and texts which explore this in more depth, including Becky Parry's *Children, Film and Literacy* (Parry, 2013), with a foreword by Jackie Marsh, and John Potter's *Digital Media and Learner Identity* (Potter, 2012), which reports on a digital video production project by children in Year 6 which was autobiographical in nature. Burn and Durran's *Media Literacy in Schools* (Burn and Durran, 2007) is an invaluable source of advice in the field for both live action and animation production.

Some curriculum uses of digital video

Some of the potential sites of this work in school settings include the following.

- Curriculum-based projects which allow children to make media productions of project work, either for assessment purposes (e.g. their portfolios) or for use within the school setting with other age groups ('Make a movie which tries to explain gravity to a younger class').
- Autobiographical and/or creative productions which allow exploration of the medium in a more creative context, including the use of sound assembled for the project (see also Chapter 15).
- Shorter clips produced with assessment in mind, including peer- and self-assessment (e.g. for movement within a PE lesson).
- Shorter unedited pieces used to review movement on a shared space in the classroom (using the interactive whiteboard).
- Self-produced clips used to explore popular culture and emergent media literacy concepts, through parodies or references to popular programming on TV or online (in areas such as YouTube). Also used to reinforce ICT concepts around media filetypes and simpler skills applicable across all digital media (cutting and pasting, etc.).
- Comparison of different tools of production from digital video cameras through to solid-state recorders (discussed later in this chapter), mobile phones and PDAs.

Whatever the location in the curriculum, there are teaching points to be made throughout about how moving images work together to make meaning. The pedagogical discussion which you have with children should be as much concerned with simple rules of moving image grammar and editing for clarity as it is with the curriculum content of the activity. If you are not confident in teaching some of these aspects of production, there is likely to be increased support for this in the years to come through the Film Nation UK initiative and other organisations listed in the first section. For example, a search for 'making movies make sense' should take you to the latest version of the excellent resource originally created by Tom Barrance for Media Education Wales.

THE BIGGER PICTURE   THE BIGGER PICTURE   THE BIGGER PICTURE   THE BIGGER PICTURE

When you are planning opportunities for peer- and self-assessment, remember that some subjects lend themselves to the use of digital video to support this. For example, in drama you could record improvisational exercises for children to discuss and make suggestions for improvement, and in PE you could film clips of movement sequences to review. Longer portions of team games could be filmed so that attacking shots, passes or defensive moves can be analysed. In English, debates can be filmed so that speaking and listening skills can be assessed, and in geography role-play activities about ethical issues can be recorded to review the quality of the arguments put forward by the characters.

Animation production in education

It should be apparent by now that the applications of digital video to the curriculum are potentially wide and varied and offer something to all subjects of the curriculum. Animation in particular has a place in schools that is potentially highly significant. It is a form of cultural production with which children and young people are highly familiar and which is ubiquitous in their daily life. Two main kinds of experience are usually available: working with stop-frame animation in which objects are moved steadily through frames in front of a camera, recording their changing position over time to create the illusion of movement, or the use of software to create and shoot the animation inside the computer itself, with no movement of objects in real space. This kind of production is enabled by software which borders on programming, using, for example, Flash or HTML 5 or by user-friendly mock-ups of film and animation stages such as Moviestorm, the machinima software for schools.

For stop motion animation, the more widespread availability of simple equipment to shoot animation productions (still digital video cameras, tablet computers, smartphones) and the presence in schools of many things to animate with (toys, LEGO, classroom objects and more) combined with the availability of low heat steady light sources (cheap LED lights) make this, for some, an even more viable option than film-making with live action. Indeed, for schools with deep anxieties about children featuring in video made at school or without a safety policy on such images, animation can circumvent the issue by having only objects visible in the frame.

Animation itself can be used to teach concepts of framing more widely, along with camera angle and so on. In addition to the organisations already listed above, advice and support can be found from others specific to the form, such as **www.animationforeducation.co.uk**.

RESEARCH SUMMARY RESEARCH SUMMARY **RESEARCH SUMMARY** RESEARCH SUMMARY

From Australia comes evidence that the use of animation production in learning concepts of science and other curriculum areas is particularly successful (see the website and associated papers from **www. slowmation.com**).

In England there have been a number of projects which refer directly to children's experience of animation and machinima, some of which are reported on the website of the DARE collaborative (**www.darecollaborative. net**) and the Media Education Association (**www.themea.org.uk**). These include a year-long study into the pedagogical benefits of children engaging with animation production to learn about the teaching of poetry (and vice versa) at Key Stage 1; this was called 'Persistence of Vision' and was carried out by Cary Bazalgette, Becky Parry and John Potter (see the MEA website above).

Starting points for working with digital video production or animation

In order to undertake video production in the classroom, there are a number of starting points. Digital still cameras often include the facility to make short movies which can be quickly reviewed and used in a spontaneous way in an unedited form. This could be useful in lessons which require the facility to go back and review live action to make a learning concept explicit (a science experiment, a piece of classroom drama or performance – see the classroom example below – or a PE lesson on making shapes). For animation, the same kinds of cameras or tablets could be used (especially with appropriate grips) or webcams, which can be attached by USB cable (such as the HUE webcam). Indeed, whereas there was previously difficulty at the uploading stage, smaller solid-state digital video cameras are available which shoot a small amount of material for downloading directly to the computer via a USB connection for editing or via a small memory storage card. Simple editing interfaces allow children to add effects and to export a finished version.

The widespread and growing availability of tablet computers is a further source of useful equipment. They are capable of producing high-quality results in good definition and require that children are holding them steady. In this regard they are perhaps more useful than smartphone or small handheld cameras for younger children. They also have the possibility to enable children to frame action better than looking through a small eyepiece. Both Apple and Android products have a substantial array of editing software apps available, meaning that the whole production can be enabled with one device for shooting, editing and exporting. The further reading list contains a list of possible suppliers and sources of further advice for both live action and animation use in the classroom.

IN THE CLASSROOM – A VIGNETTE

A teacher has distributed lines from a poem to a Year 4 class, two to each of five tables in the classroom. The task is interpreting the lines in a rhythmic way, to perform them to the rest of the class. The teacher reminds them to think about each word and how it contributes to the whole, and to think about how the overall pattern of the piece reflects a particular form (in this case, Calypso). The class comes out table by table, after a short time rehearsing, and the children record each table's two-line performance in turn. The whole thing is played back on the interactive whiteboard in sequence and the children appraise the overall class performance in terms of its communicative and dramatic aspects. This has been a literacy lesson which has featured a huge amount of excitement, and allowed for speaking and listening activities exploring aspects of poetry and performance. Motivation has been high. There have been no worksheets. Nothing has been recorded in a written form, but the movies can be saved as part of the class portfolio on the school's VLE and the teacher has had time to review contributions for her own record keeping.

Developing digital video work further

The next, and slightly more complex, stage of video production involves some editing and post-production. Once inside the computer, via USB cable or a memory card, software allows for the scenes to be trimmed to appropriate lengths and joined using a variety of transitions simply by dragging them and dropping them onto a timeline or working with them as whole clips. You may already be familiar with this from your own use of free software to edit clips and images on a smartphone or tablet. In any case, if you have used the free audio editing software Audacity, recommended in Chapter 15, you will be familiar with the timeline concept and also the idea that because, like sound, video is stored digitally, it can be manipulated, cut and pasted in the same way. Effects such as titles can then be added and the whole production can be exported as a finished file for exhibition on the internet, the LA or school VLE, or for distribution home on disk.

It is worth mentioning at the outset that sound is a big problem in all kinds of animation and video production by learners. An audience will put up with poor camerawork (to an extent) over poor sound. Sound quality, whether in the form of a soundtrack or speech to camera, is closely bound to an audience's ability to construct meaning from a video production. You should draw attention to this and investigate the possibility of using microphones in noisier settings to record crucial speech or dialogue. Using Audacity, it might be possible to clean up poorer audio after shooting. However, in the interests of keeping the process simpler, it should be a consideration at the beginning of any project.

There is free software available to edit on a PC (Windows Moviemaker Live). On a Mac, as part of the same suite of software which provides Garageband for music production (see Chapter 15), there is also free and powerful videoediting software called iMovie. There are some difficulties with certain filetypes due to the ways in which these have been compressed. The key to working successfully with these and overcoming difficulties is, obviously, to practise their use in advance of working with a class of children.

Teachers must always have a view of the pedagogy and a reason for using any resource, and software is no different. There are possible mappings onto all curriculum areas for digital video production and animation, which make it ideal for cross-curricular work in school. At the same time, there are powerful reasons for using it as a way to extend learner knowledge in an exciting and motivating context and in a form which is culturally significant and authentic for them.

As stated above, a key factor that you must consider is the extent to which you will enable improvements in the quality of children's work by engagement with the language and techniques of film-making.

REFLECTIVE TASK

Using Google (UK) search online for Dingwall Primary School's weblog. Here you will find videos made by children at Dingwall School in Scotland. If you cannot locate this resource, search on BAFTA – BE Very Afraid. Here you will be able to view work produced by students and exhibited on the web – with permission – by Stephen Heppell, who has been actively involved in championing children's creative use of technology, including digital video production, for a number of years (see also **Heppell.net**). Once you have some examples of children's video, try to respond to the following questions:

- Which curriculum area (or areas) is represented?
- What genre is the film operating in?
- Has the teacher given the children input into film-making?
- What do you think the plan for this activity looks like?
- What skills would you personally require to carry out work like this with children?

THE BIGGER PICTURE THE BIGGER PICTURE THE BIGGER PICTURE THE BIGGER PICTURE

When planning the use of digital video, a useful resource can be found at **www.filmstreet.co.uk**. Film Street is an organisation aimed at getting children involved in film-making, and the site includes video-based workshops, stop-frame animation and information about different animators and film-makers.

A SUMMARY OF **KEY POINTS**

➤ More affordable equipment and software has made video production in schools possible and accessible.

➤ The production of digital video images of children and their work raises ethical considerations and internet safety issues under the safeguarding of children agenda.

➤ You need to adhere to agreed school/LA protocols.

➤ Digital video production can support many subject areas and cross-curricular work and can also develop children's ICT capability.

➤ As a starting point, the short movie facility of digital still cameras may prove a useful introduction.

➤ You could then move on to using smaller solid state digital video cameras.

➤ There are editing programs available that allow children to include titles, sound effects and music on the finished film.

➤ The internet is a useful source of video examples from other schools.

M-LEVEL EXTENSION > > M-LEVEL EXTENSION > > M-LEVEL EXTENSION

Choose a year group or Key Stage and look at the school's schemes of work for the age group in all subjects. Make a note of all activities that could benefit from the use of digital video to enhance the teaching and learning, including for assessment of these opportunities. Is it possible to develop these into a cohesive scheme of work that develops children's capability with digital media production progressively? Are there connections you can make between Digital making and working with coding and programming?

REFERENCES REFERENCES **REFERENCES** REFERENCES REFERENCES REFERENCES

Buckingham, D. (2003) *Media Education: Literacy, Learning and Contemporary Culture*. Oxford: Polity Press.

Burn, A. and Durran, J. (2007) *Media Literacy in Schools*. London: Paul Chapman.

DfE (2011) *Teachers' Standards.* Available at **www.education.gov.uk/publications**

Parry, Becky (2013) *Children, Film and Literacy*. London: Palgrave.

Potter, John (2012) *Digital Media and Learner Identity*. New York: Palgrave.

Reid, M., Burn, A. and Parker, D. (2002) *Evaluation Report of the Becta Digital Video Pilot Project*. London: Becta/BFI.

FURTHER READING FURTHER READING **FURTHER READING** FURTHER READING

Ang, T. (2008) *Digital Photographer's Handbook*. 4th Edition. London: Dorling Kindersley.

Duffty, J. (2006) *Primary ICT: Extending Knowledge in Practice*. Exeter: Learning Matters.

Futurelab Create-A-Scape – Creating and Using Mediascapes. Available at **www.createascape.org.uk** (accessed 10 May 2011).

Hague, C. (2010) *'It's Not Chalk and Talk Anymore': School Approaches to Developing Students' Digital Literacy.* Available at **www.futurelab.org.uk** (accessed 12 May 2011).

Hague, C. and Williamson, B. (2009) *Digital Participation, Digital Literacy and School Subjects: A Review of the Policies, Literature and Evidence.* Available at **www.futurelab.org.uk** (accessed 12 May 2011).

OFCOM (2004) *Ofcom's Strategy and Priorities for the Promotion of Media Literacy – A Statement.* Available at **www.ofcom.org.uk/consult**/ (accessed 10 May 2011).

Pearson, M. (2005) Splitting clips and telling tales. *Education and Information Technologies*, 10 (3), 189–205.

Schuck, S. and Kearney, M. (2004) *Students in the Director's Seat: Teaching and Learning across the School Curriculum with Student-generated Video.* Sydney: Faculty of Education, University of Technology, Sydney.

10
Graphing programs

Introduction

Graphical representations of data are everywhere: in newspapers, magazines, books, on television programmes and on websites. Children are constantly exposed to information communicated in this manner. If they are to interpret this in any meaningful way, they need to develop appropriate knowledge, skills and understanding.

Graphing programs have been available in primary schools for many years. Recent developments, particularly the move towards the use of icons rather than keyboard commands to access common functions, have improved the accessibility of such software for children and teachers. The range of features and functions supported by many graphing programs has also been significantly enhanced.

This chapter explores graphing programs and their potential for the enhancement and extension of teaching and learning in the primary classroom. Cross-curricular applications are explored and links made to other generic data-handling software.

What are graphing programs?

Graphing programs facilitate the communication of information through graphical representation. They enable data to be entered, stored, presented and interpreted graphically in an electronic format. Some allow the rudimentary sorting of data, into ascending or descending order of frequency, for instance. Graphing programs do not, however, support sophisticated sorting, searching or modelling. Such data-handling activity requires database software.

What do the programmes of study for Key Stages 1 and 2 include?

In the aims of the National Curriculum for computing, it is emphasised that the teaching of computing 'ensures that pupils become digitally literate – able to use, and express themselves and develop their ideas through, information and communication technology – at a level suitable for the future workplace and as active participants in a digital world' (DfE, 2013, no page). A key aspect of digital literacy is the responsible and safe use of technologies, which also applies when children are collecting data for representation in graphing programs. The specific aspects of the programme of study which relate to this are highlighted as follows.

At Key Stage 1, the new programme of study for computing (DfE, 2013) states that, children should be taught to:

- Use technology purposefully to create, organise, store, manipulate and retrieve digital content;
- Use technology safely and respectfully, keeping personal information private; know where to go for help and support when they have concerns about material on the internet;
- Recognise common uses of information technology beyond school.

The old programme of study broke this down in more detail and is worth considering. For example, it stated that children should be taught: to use text, tables, images and sounds to develop their ideas; to select from and add to existing information; to share their ideas by presenting information in a variety of forms; and to present their work effectively (DfEE, 2000).

At Key Stage 2 (DfE, 2013), children should be taught how to:

* Use technology safely, respectfully and responsibly; know a range of ways to report concerns and inappropriate behaviour;
* Select, use and combine a variety of software (including internet services) on a range of digital devices to accomplish given goals, including collecting, analysing, evaluating and presenting data and information.

What do teachers need to know about using graphing programs?

In order to teach with and about graphing programs teachers need to be confident about their subject knowledge related to the handling of data. In this area, there is a substantial and obvious overlap in terms of subject knowledge between science, mathematics and computing. Relevant issues include:

* choice of variables;
* types of data;
* grouping data;
* collecting and recording data;
* presenting data.

Many data-handling activities begin with consideration of what data to collect. In science, the choice of variables is often a key teaching and learning objective. For instance, the growth pattern of a seedling may be explored by comparing its height at 9:00am each day over a three-week period. Two variables are involved here: seedling height and time. Alternatively, the investigation could be limited to one variable by measuring the height of a number of seedlings once only three weeks after sowing. The exploration would, in this instance, focus on the distribution of heights achieved. It should also be noted that there is potential for children to confuse the meaning of the word 'variable' as it is used in the process of scientific investigation compared to its usage in computing and programming (see Chapter 12).

There are three types of data: categorical, discrete and continuous. **Categorical data** fall into distinct named categories which do not overlap and cannot be ordered. For example, children's eyes may be blue, brown, hazel, green or grey. Where **discrete data** are concerned, the classes are defined by discrete whole numbers. An example might be the number of siblings class members have. **Continuous data** cannot be so easily segregated. The height of seedlings is measured on a continuous scale and each seedling's height is, potentially at least, slightly different from that of the others. The type of data collected influences how it is collected, recorded and presented in graphing software.

Before data are collected and recorded, decisions should be made about grouping. In the case of categorical and discrete data, the categories or classes will usually be quite obvious. Where continuous data are involved, there is a choice: either to record and then plot each individual item (each seedling's exact height) or to attempt to group the data into classes, effectively translating continuous data into discrete data. For instance, rather than recording a seedling's height as 8cm, another as 8.5cm, another as 6cm, each of these three seedlings could be entered into the category 5.0–9.9cm, with other categories for 10.0–14.9cm, etc.

Decisions about the grouping of data will affect recording and presentation. To continue the example above, further decisions about accuracy, number of decimal places and use of rounding will be required, and a suitable recording format must be chosen. Data may be collected and recorded in a number of ways, counting and tally charts being the most common for categorical, discrete or grouped data.

Once data have been collected and recorded, consideration can be given to presenting them graphically. It is important that the choice of graph is consistent with the data type. Categorical and discrete data are conventionally represented by bar charts, with each bar representing one discrete category or number. Bar charts can be arranged horizontally or vertically or as bar line graphs. Pie charts are also suitable for the presentation of categorical or discrete data, particularly where consideration of relative proportions is important – for example, in comparing the ways in which members of a class travel to school. However, caution should be exercised in the use of pie charts, especially where there are two or more categories containing similar or equal amounts of data, since it may be difficult to distinguish their relative size by eye. The representation of datasets where one or more category has a value of zero is also problematic, since these will not be represented on the pie chart.

Line graphs and scatter graphs are suitable for the presentation of continuous data. Continuous data may include two variables. For example, the growth of a plant may be measured over time, with its height plotted against the day on which each reading is taken. Such graphs are sometimes called xy graphs. A scatter graph represents the actual data in this instance, whereas a line graph may be used to join the individual points to give some indication of rate of growth over time. However, children need to understand

How we travel to school

Figure 10.1 Pie chart with one category (Train) having a zero value

that joining such plots by a line represents an approximation. If data had been collected at intermediate points they would not necessarily fall directly on the line. Further, if some data-collection opportunities are missed, for instance over the weekend or half-term, the graphing program may interpret no data as having a value of zero. In this case, the line graph will return to the *x*-axis. Spreadsheets, which also enable graphs to be plotted from such data, may cope better with this situation.

Teaching with and about graphing programs involves teachers:

- **selecting appropriate opportunities** – in which graphing programs can facilitate, enhance or extend children's learning, such as exploring the impact of graphically representing one set of data using a range of scales. In some instances the focus will be on teaching and learning in computing and ICT (how a graphing program can facilitate such an investigation), while in others ICT will be used as a resource in the teaching and learning of another curriculum area (the effect of choice of scale);
- **exploring the full range of data-handling activities** – it is important that data-handling work does not always end with the production of a graph. In many instances data-handling work will begin with a graphical representation and learning will be focused on interpretation and analysis;

Figure 10.2 Line graph showing the effect of a break in data collection

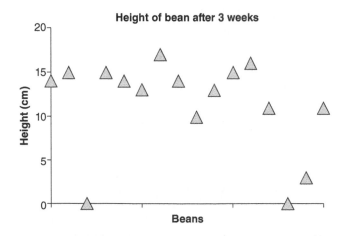

Figure 10.3   Scatter plot showing distribution of seedling heights

- **making explicit links between related knowledge, skills and understanding** – data-handling has applications in many areas of the primary curriculum; teachers thus have opportunities to make explicit and reinforce the links between children's previous experiences and new learning across the range of contexts;
- **modelling appropriate use of ICT** – for instance, the joining of individual plots of data by a line graph to assist in the analysis of the pattern or trend the data represent;
- **demonstrating and intervening** – for instance, intervening to assist a child to export a graph to the appropriate place in a word-processed record of a science experiment; similarly, demonstrating and discussing the potential difficulties of interpreting data represented in a pie chart.

The list below attempts to identify the knowledge, skills and understanding of graphing software teachers need in order to teach effectively with and about graphing programs.

Many graphing programs support only a subset of these functions. This is no reflection on their usefulness – in most instances it may be a strength. However, it does signal that teachers must be aware of the capabilities and limitations of any program as these will be significant in the choice of software for any teaching and learning activity.

- Graphing program knowledge, skills and understanding;
- creating, opening, saving, closing, deleting and printing documents;
- adding, modifying and deleting data;
- plotting and replotting graphs;
- selecting and displaying graph types, including more than one graphical representation of the same data;
- selecting and modifying constituent elements of graphs, such as changing the colours of bars in a bar chart to correspond with the data represented;
- selecting, resizing, cutting, copying and pasting graphs;
- selecting and modifying graph scales and autoscaling;
- selecting two-dimensional or three-dimensional representations;
- inserting graph titles, axes labels, key and text;
- selecting font and font size for graph and axes headings;
- exporting graphs into other applications;
- importing information from other applications, such as clip art;
- utilising help;
- altering defaults;
- customising the graphing program, switching off functions not needed;
- utilising alternative input devices (particularly data-loggers);
- selecting appropriate colours or patterns depending on printer availability (black and white or colour);
- protecting documents.

There will be occasions on which other data-handling software, such as databases or spreadsheets, will be more suitable. Teachers need to be confident in making decisions about the most appropriate application for a particular situation.

What are the key features of a graphing program?

Graphing programs:

- produce graphs directly from data entered;
- offer a range of graph types;

- usually automatically select the scale;
- provide opportunities to reinforce the relationship between numerical and graphical representation of the same data;
- allow children to focus on using the information contained in a graph rather than the process of construction;
- do not replace children constructing graphs manually – this is an important developmental stage in the process of understanding;
- facilitate a range of learning outcomes – for instance, emphasis may be on data collection (planning, organising, recording, entering), interpretation, or on the effect of scale;
- facilitate work on equivalence and differences between graph types, such as bar charts, pie charts, bar line charts, line graphs, scatter graphs;
- facilitate work on progression in graphical representation.

Graphing programs can be divided into two categories:

- pictogram programs, which support early graphing activities and usually allow for the representation of data only as pictograms or block graphs;
- more sophisticated graphing programs, which support a range of graph types and functions.

In order to facilitate the exploration of the features and contribution of each of these, they will be referred to as pictogram programs and graphing programs respectively.

What do graphing programs contribute to teaching and learning?

One of the key advantages of working with graphing programs to handle data is that much of the time-consuming work of planning and plotting graphs is automated, allowing the user to focus on the information contained in the graph. Which is the most frequently owned pet in Year 3, and how does this compare with pet ownership of children in Year 6? Other questions may then be raised, such as what might be the influences on choice of pet? What constitutes pet ownership where there is more than one child in a family? How is double-counting avoided? The emphasis should be on investigation and analysis as much as on representation.

An important aspect of work in handling data surrounds choosing the most appropriate graphical representation. Graphing programs facilitate immediate comparisons between the different graph types. Would pie charts be the most suitable method of representing the pet ownership information? What if some animals are owned by children in Year 3, but not by children in Year 6? Using graphing programs enables children to make independent choices of graph types, safe in the knowledge that the graph can be redrawn speedily if necessary. When hand-drawing is involved, there may be a tendency for the teacher to direct children towards a shared class decision in order to avoid wasting time.

Most pictogram and graphing programs also enable data to be sorted at a simple level, for example, into ascending or descending order of frequency. This can be a very useful facility, especially if there is a wide range of categories, or the scale is marked in intervals of two, or five or ten. Using a sorting function does not obviate the need for children to be able to read information accurately from graphs; it can provide another opportunity for teaching or reinforcing that skill.

Graphing programs can be used to demonstrate the relationship between data, their recording in a frequency table and their representation or as a graph. Most programs allow the frequency table to be shown alongside a graph. Making these connections is vital if children are to handle data in a meaningful way.

Developing children's understanding of the equivalence of information represented in different graphs can be facilitated by showing, for instance, a horizontal bar chart, a vertical bar chart and a bar line graph side by side.

Graphing programs have autoscaling features which choose the scale of the graph, usually depending on the highest value or frequency. Most programs replot graphs each time new data are entered. In this way the development of a graph and the effect of each new piece of data can be powerfully demonstrated. Autoscaling often results in graphs where scales are marked in intervals of 2, 5 or more. The construction and interpretation of such graphs are important stages in the progression of children's understanding of data handling. Sometimes the autoscaling feature can be disabled to enable children to make their own selections as appropriate.

Similarly, the connection between choice of scale and the effectiveness or impact of a graph can be explored. There can be valuable learning associated with attempting to 'misrepresent' information, choosing a scale that will make a small variation look large or a large variation look insignificant. This also brings in the ethical dimensions surrounding the ways in which such data is used. For example, when collecting data about other people, children should be taught about their responsibilities in using and storing the data appropriately and responsibly. Almost any newspaper, magazine, website or TV news programme will contain some graphical representation of information. Making links with real-life applications of knowledge and understanding which children could otherwise view as quite abstract in nature can be a powerful learning tool.

Many of the issues discussed above, such as choice of graph type, equivalence, comparison and scale, also have relevance for the exchange and sharing of information. Additionally, if a group of children presents the results of a science investigation for display on the classroom wall, decisions need to be taken not only about the most suitable type of graph for the data, but also about its readability at a distance. The advantages of a horizontal bar chart over the more common vertical, where the labels might more obviously correspond with the data, might also be explored. There are instances where two or more graph types may be equally appropriate and children can justify their personal selections and discuss the merits of each (see Figure 10.4).

Copying and pasting a graph into a report or other document is a useful function and many pictogram and graphing programs support this. Graphs can usually then be moved and resized as any other image. It is important that children know that they can transfer their skills in this way within and between applications.

Progression of knowledge, skills and understanding

Early data-handling activities will relate closely to children themselves and their own experiences. 'Ourselves' is a common theme and many pictogram programs, such as

Counting Pictures 3 (BlackCat) and Pictogram 3 (Kudlian Soft), have a predetermined range of relevant topics to select from, for example pets, favourite foods and hair colour. Having chosen a suitable focus, such as children's eye colour, and discussed the likely alternatives, the teacher can call up a blank pictogram on screen and ask each child in turn their eye colour. The children may need to consult with a friend and the teacher (or a child) can click or drag the appropriate icon to include the information in the graph. The pictogram will be built in front of the children and the connection between each child's answer and the appearance of an icon in the relevant column made explicit. This method of data collection is appropriate for young children and the immediate building of the graph reinforces the connection between the data (the answers the children give) and the graphical representation of the data (see Figure 10.5).

At its simplest, a pictogram drawn with a graphing program will consist of columns of icons indicating a one-to-one representation. The teacher can lead the children in counting to establish how many children in the class have blue eyes. There is no need for text labelling as each category is identified by an icon, although the software usually allocates a title based on the subject selected.

Pictogram programs have a variety of features which facilitate their use at various stages in supporting children's knowledge and understanding of data-handling. These might include:

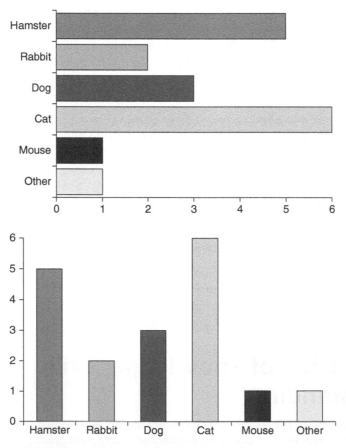

Figure 10.4 Horizontal and vertical bar charts showing the same data

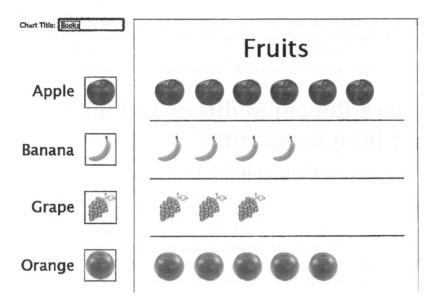

Figure 10.5 Building a pictogram (Pictogram 3 courtesy of Kudlian Software)

- **adding a scale** – reading from a scale requires a more sophisticated understanding of number than does counting icons;
- **adding axes** – the addition of $\times$ and y axes represents a stage in the development from a straightforward pictorial representation of data towards the more abstract model generally recognised as a graph;
- **transforming the pictogram into a block graph** – again, this is a development from the straightforward pictorial representation of data towards something more abstract in nature. Each block in a block graph clearly represents an individual piece of data, which distinguishes it from a bar chart in which the divisions between the data are not distinct. Pictogram 3 (Kudlian Soft) also supports bar charts, representing a further progression.

REFLECTIVE TASK

Following the compilation of a Year 1 class pictogram of favourite foods, what questions would you ask to probe and develop the children's understanding? How would you follow up the activity?

Programs such as DataPlot (Kudlian Soft) and Counter (BlackCat) facilitate more sophisticated data-handling activities. Data are entered through a frequency table and a graph is drawn and redrawn as new data are added. Text labels are transferred from the frequency table to the graph and these are necessary to identify and interpret the graph. There is a range of graph types to choose from, allowing children to experiment and select the most suitable. Scales marked at intervals greater than one can result, although such graphs can also be drawn in some pictogram packages. Options for saving, adding text and exporting to other applications are easily accessible. A further level of sophistication (DataPlot and CounterPlus) enables each axis to be separately titled and choices to be made about colours and/or patterns. Two- and three-dimensional representations are often possible and selection can be made from a wider range of graph types. Negative and decimal numbers are usually supported. Effective utilisation of graphing programs may facilitate the development of children's knowledge, skills and understanding of handling data independently of the motor skills required for the hand-drawing of graphs.

What are the capabilities and limitations of graphing programs?

Selecting appropriate graph types

Graphing programs do not automatically select the most suitable graph type to represent data. The choice remains with the user. Nor will the software warn against unsuitable selections. Teachers will need to ensure that children make appropriate choices based on the data. Many graphing programs automatically represent data as vertical bar charts unless another graph type is specifically selected. This default risks reinforcing the use of this most common graph type at the expense of consideration of alternatives.

IN THE CLASSROOM

A trainee teacher had carefully prepared a lesson on graphing programs. His teaching objectives were appropriately described in terms of computing. He was familiar with the software and had selected data related to current geography work. He took the class to the ICT suite and proceeded to introduce the activity, describing the process. The children were required to access a graphing program, enter into it data relating to average temperatures across a year in a distant place and the UK, and produce pie charts for comparison.

The trainee teacher provided pairs of children with a help sheet he had prepared and the lesson proceeded. After 35 minutes, each pair had produced two pie charts. These were printed out and the class returned to the classroom. Questioning the children, however, suggested that they had little understanding of the information the graphs represented. Although the data had been chosen to relate to a current geography study, the links between that and the computing session had not been made explicit to the children. Further, there was little examination of the finished pie charts in order to interpret the data. This would in any event have been difficult using the graph type selected.

PRACTICAL TASK   PRACTICAL TASK   PRACTICAL TASK   PRACTICAL TASK

Prepare a display to demonstrate:

- **an appropriate use of each of the graph types supported by a particular graphing program;**

or

- **how to print a completed graph, including making appropriate selections to cater for the available printer;**

or

- **children's top tips for using the particular graphing program you are focusing on.**

Frequency tables and tally charts

Most graphing programs allow data to be viewed through a frequency table as well as a graph. In many, the data are entered through the frequency table. This feature provides an opportunity for teachers to reinforce the correspondence of the information represented in these different ways. Many programs also have a tally chart function which can be used to facilitate the progression from simultaneous data collection and entry, as in the eye-colour example described previously, to recording and subsequent entry, for which the tally chart is the most frequently used mechanism.

PRACTICAL TASK PRACTICAL TASK **PRACTICAL TASK** PRACTICAL TASK

Plan a sequence of lessons to introduce the concept of tally charts for the recording of data. Choose a suitable subject context. Note how and why ICT can be used, making reference to assumptions about the availability and location of resources. Note prerequisite knowledge, skills and understanding with respect to mathematics and ICT.

3-D graphs

Most graphing programs have the facility to display graphs in three dimensions as well as two. The third dimension allows children to produce sophisticated-looking representations which compare with those they see on television or in the press.

However, the 3-D effect can be problematic for children when reading information from scales. This concern is particularly apparent in respect of bar charts. Children may experience confusion in deciding which lines to follow to read off information. Similarly, a bar with a zero value will still contain a block of colour. The interpretation of 3-D graphs

Figure 10.6 3-D bar chart showing category with zero value (CounterPlus, BlackCat)

may thus require explicit teaching. There is an argument for avoiding them altogether as strictly speaking the 3-D perspective distorts the areas that should represent the individual fields, so that they no longer comprise an accurate proportion of the whole. This problem is most clearly evidenced by 3-D pie charts.

Pictogram programs

Pictogram programs tend to have a limited range of possible graph subjects, such as pets, journeys to school or favourite colour, determined by the icons available. It is entirely appropriate that young children's data-handling experiences involve data which have some relevance to them, rather than the rainfall patterns in a distant location, for instance, and most of these are catered for. Some packages provide the opportunity for the range to be extended, although this involves drawing appropriate pictures using the tools provided. Within each graph subject there is also a limited range of categories; 'hamster', for instance, may not always appear as a pet choice, although 'horse' often does. Again, these can be customised and software houses enhance their products over time, most welcoming feedback on such issues. Similarly, there may be restrictions on the amount of data that can be entered. With class sizes even in Key Stage 1 of around 30, such a limitation on numbers can be important as the result might be that it is impossible for a record to be entered for each child.

Selecting colours

Graphing programs often allocate predetermined colours to bars in bar charts; thus the first bar may be blue, the second green, and so on. Clearly this may be problematic if the data have some link to colour – for instance, children's favourite colours, hair colour or eye colour – and there is a mismatch. A graphing program will not be helpful if it represents the number of people with blue eyes with a red bar. Better software will allow colours to be changed once the initial graph has been drawn up, but there is some software in which this option is not available.

Teachers need to ensure that they explore such issues when selecting software for particular tasks. The writers of the DataPlot (Kudlian Soft) software saw this as a potential difficulty and incorporated some programming that ensures that if data are identified by colour (e.g. eye colours, blue 6, green 3, brown 7), it is represented by those colours. The software also identifies hair colours such as ginger, fair and blonde and makes appropriate choices (assuming the colours have been spelt correctly).

Printing considerations

Most graphing programs make extensive use of colour. This helps children differentiate between different groups of data and aids the visual engagement with the graphic representation. However, when graphs are to be printed out this may become an issue. Colour printing is expensive. Printing a coloured graph in black and white usually results in various shades of grey. These may be difficult to distinguish. There are two potential solutions available to teachers and most graphing programs will support at least one of these. Sometimes it is possible to choose to print out a graph without any colour, enabling the children to colour in by hand. DataPlot (Kudlian Soft) provides an option to switch off the colour function. Alternatively, it may be possible to change the various colours to white, producing the same effect when printed out. Secondly, some programs provide a range of pattern options which can be selected instead of colours.

Links to other generic data-handling software

Some software allows multiple columns of numeric information to be incorporated and thus represented on the same graph, enabling comparisons to be made. This type of function is usually only possible using a spreadsheet.

Many software houses have linked ranges of data-handling programs, so that the transfer of children's skills from one to another is facilitated by familiar icons and functions. Kudlian Soft produce Pictogram 3 and DataPlot, facilitating progression from one to the other. Additionally, DataPlot is a constituent of DataSweet, which also includes the spreadsheet DataCalc as well as database software. Similarly, Counting Pictures uses the same icons as Pick a Picture, BlackCat's early database program.

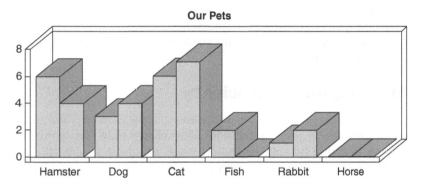

Figure 10.7 Block graph and frequency table demonstrating comparison between two sets of data (BlackCat Numbers, Words and Pictures)

Common errors and misconceptions

Although using graphing programs reduces some of the demands on children relating to graphical representation of data, it is important to ensure that emphasis is placed on interpretation as well as presentation. The graph is not the end product. Children need to be able to analyse, discuss and summarise what the graph means. A display of the children's graphs alone indicates that this process may not have happened. The display will be far more convincing if it includes a record of the children's commentaries.

The scale of data-handling activities deserves consideration. The availability of ICT might prompt the collection of far more data than would otherwise be contemplated. This might be its advantage, for instance in the monitoring of environmental conditions. However, caution should be exercised to ensure that the time taken to collect data does not distract from the teaching focus. On the other hand, especially for older children familiar with the basic principles of data handling, it is important for the challenge to be authentic. Entering the colours of cars from the staff car park into graphing software to establish which shade is the most popular is poor use of the power of ICT to handle data.

Autoscaling can often be disabled to allow children to select their own scale and consider the implications of differing intervals.

Graphing programs and the core subjects

The ideas and activities introduced below are intended to give a feel for the range of ways in which graphing programs can be utilised to support and enhance teaching and learning in mathematics, science and English. They are not intended to be comprehensive, merely to go some way towards illustrating the breadth of possibilities and to provide starting points for the customisation of ideas and the generation of others. Examples introduced under mathematics, for instance, may be just as applicable to one or more of the other areas and vice versa.

There is extensive overlap between science, mathematics, English, computing and other subject knowledge, skills and understanding in this area of data handling. Teachers need to be clear about their primary teaching objective for any particular task or sequence of activities and maximise the opportunities for making explicit links between learning in the various curriculum contexts.

Graphing programs and science

Graphing programs have many possibilities in science for the recording and representation of experimental data. A number of possibilities have already been discussed. Most graphing programs allow text to be entered and displayed alongside graphs, and graphs can usually be copied and pasted into other applications, such as word processing software.

Some activities will involve the collection, entry and representation of data, while others may start with prepared data looking for patterns, causal links and evidence to test hypotheses.

Environmental monitoring and sensing

Data-logging is the process of monitoring and recording environmental data such as temperature, light, movement and sound using sensors. The data are displayed through software which can be considered to be a special application of a graphing program, having many common features and functions, such as choice of graph types and scale.

Sensors are linked to the computer through a buffer box interface (for example from Deltronics) or through more portable equipment, such as the LogIT Explorer, which provides an integrated interface between the sensors and the computer. The software, which is often supplied with the hardware, or may be purchased separately (such as Junior Datalogging Insight from Longman Logotron), is used to set the timescale for the logging of the data, which can be very short or very long, and the intervals at which data are collected are automatically adjusted. Data-logging can take place with the interface connected to the computer, enabling the results to be simultaneously displayed on screen, or, with LogIT, remotely (even outside) and subsequently downloaded.

Data-logging offers a variety of possibilities both inside the classroom and beyond. Key Stage 1 children can hold temperature sensors in their hands and watch the screen as the sensor warms up. Similarly, they can observe the instant and dramatic effects of clapping, singing or being very quiet near a sound sensor. Recording the sound levels in a classroom over the school day can provide interesting discussion as the teacher and children attempt to identify peaks and troughs and relate these to particular activities or incidents.

Older children may insert a temperature sensor into a defrosting bread roll and record data over a 24-hour period. (Temperature sensors fall into two broad technical categories and not all are appropriate for contact with damp conditions.) Two temperature sensors connected to the buffer box can record the temperature inside and outside a window overnight. Similarly, away from the classroom the temperature in the school pond may be monitored night and day over a week or even longer. Another long-term project might involve placing a movement sensor in a pot with a bulb while it sprouts, flowers and dies.

Data-logging can make a valuable contribution to children's data-handling experiences. Its principal advantages are:

- speed – data can be recorded more quickly than by hand;
- electronic data entry – the data recorded are automatically entered into the software, removing the time-consuming manual entry of data;
- memory – large amounts of data can be stored;
- persistence – data can be logged over extended periods.

Data-logging can be used to facilitate children becoming more scientific in their experimental technique:

- enabling the realistic repetition of experiments to achieve consistency in results and appreciate the concept of experimental error;
- enabling the testing of variables over greater ranges of values and similarly wider ranges of variables to be tested.

PRACTICAL TASK PRACTICAL TASK PRACTICAL TASK PRACTICAL TASK

Find out how to:

- **connect the sensors to the data-logging interface and the interface to the computer; select the duration and/or intervals of data collection;**
- **collect data remotely and download to the computer;**
- **save and retrieve collected data.**

Briefly outline activities involving the logging of environmental data suitable for Year 1, Year 3 and Year 5 children. Relate these to your school's scheme of work for science.

Graphing programs and mathematics

Graphing programs should contribute to the development of children's understanding of the graphical representation of data. Almost any activity involving graphs draws on children's existing mathematical knowledge and provides opportunities for reinforcement and extension work. As already indicated, graphing programs can make a substantial contribution where the speed and automatic function of the software enable teachers and learners to focus more specifically on a particular mathematical objective, be it choice of appropriate graph type or scale, the grouping of data or recording technique.

When you are planning to teach children about data handling using graphing programs, make sure that you are confident with this area yourself so that you are able to deal with any misconceptions that children may have. Check out some of the useful revision sites, such as BBC Bitesize, to practise your own skills in this area. See Chapters 3 and 6 of *Primary Mathematics Knowledge and Understanding* (Mooney et al., 2014) for more on this.

Teachers can also make use of graphing programs to provide prepared documents as starting points. Children might use printouts for work away from the computer or complete activities involving data that has been pre-prepared. Such strategies maximise the contribution of limited ICT resources.

Some really useful interactive programs (ITPs) were developed to support the Primary National Strategy for Mathematics and, although the requirement to have regard for the strategies has been removed, these materials are still available. The ITPs were designed to support the modelling of various aspects of mathematics:

Data handling (www.taw.org.uk/lic/itp/itps/datahandling_2_9.swf) enables you to enter data into a table and then create a vertical or horizontal bar chart or a pie chart. Existing datasets can be amended to show the impact on the charts.

Line graph (www.taw.org.uk/lic/itp/itps/line_graph_1_1.swf) enables you to enter data into a table or select from existing datasets and then create a line graph to represent the data. Data and values on axes can be changed to explore the impact on the graph.

Graphing programs and English

Most media make extensive use of the graphical representation of data to communicate information. On at least some occasions there is an element of selection, either of the data themselves or of the means by which they are presented, in order to persuade the audience to reach a particular conclusion. If children are to engage with information critically, they need a range of opportunities through which to explore the issues of selection and presentation of data – taking information presented in a local news story and reinterpreting it to support an alternative slant, for instance. This might involve the selective omission of data, choice of scale, or even choice of graph type to accentuate or mask certain aspects.

Find out how to switch the autoscaling facility on and off. Represent one set of data using a range of scales and comment on the selection of the most appropriate. Collect a range of graphical representations of data from the media. Plan a speaking and listening activity to explore the issues associated with the impressions conveyed.

Children can develop and apply their knowledge of genre and the classification of literature by analysing the books in the class library. A range of data-handling questions arises relating to the selection, grouping and presentation of data. Similarly, children will be involved in prediction, articulating their ideas, supporting their views and decision making. The results can be considered in the light of children's preferences. Further exploration might focus on the similarities or differences in girls' and boys' tastes.

RESEARCH SUMMARY RESEARCH SUMMARY RESEARCH SUMMARY RESEARCH SUMMARY

Phillips (1997) reviewed three experiments conducted by others into Key Stage 2 children's abilities to interpret graphical representations of information where ICT is involved.

In the first, children were asked to interpret a car's journey on a distance/time graph. They were able to identify when the car was travelling rapidly forwards, when stationary and when going slowly backwards, although very much more difficulty was experienced with associating these movements to time. In the second study, children were readily able to distinguish and interpret data-logging sensor readings for light, sound, movements and temperature on a time graph, telling the story of the various features of the data. The last involved children investigating paper spinners to determine the optimum length of wings to maximise distance travelled. Scatter graph plots were discussed and a line of best fit used to identify the v pattern in the data and consequently the optimum wing length.

Phillips contrasts these results with data which show poorly-developed graphical interpretation skills among secondary children. He concludes that it takes time for children to develop graphical interpretation skills and that the increasing use of ICT for data-handling in primary schools is likely to increase the children's exposure to graphic representations with consequent positive effects. He cautions against well-presented but meaningless graphs which are all too easy to produce with ICT, highlighting informed decision making in this respect as a key issue for intending teachers.

PRACTICAL TASK PRACTICAL TASK PRACTICAL TASK PRACTICAL TASK

Work that children undertake with graphing programs in the classroom will become more meaningful if it can be related to examples of the use of graphs in the world around them. Try to collect instances that the children may have encountered, for example voting on a TV game show or graphs in a newspaper. Discuss these with the children. Why are graphs used rather than text? Talk about how graphs can be manipulated; an example of breaks in a bar chart which result in differences in the bars being exaggerated is a good starting point.

A SUMMARY OF **KEY POINTS**

➤ **Effective teaching with graphing programs requires careful consideration of the selection, collection and recording of data.**

➤ **Graphing programs enable learners to focus on the interpretation of graphical representations of data.**

➤ **Graphing programs facilitate work on the equivalence and differences between graph types.**

> ➤ Data-logging software can be considered to be a special application of graphing.

> ➤ Graphing programs have very specific features. For some data-handling activities, spreadsheets or other types of database will be more suitable.

M-LEVEL EXTENSION > > M-LEVEL EXTENSION > > M-LEVEL EXTENSION

Download a copy of *Mathematics: Understanding the Score – Improving Practice in Mathematics Teaching at Primary Level* (Ofsted, 2009) from **www.ofsted.gov.uk**. As you read it, think about teachers' use of questioning in areas of the mathematics curriculum, including handling data, and the need for regular 'real-life' problems to develop children's skills in interpreting data. Start to devise a series of real-life problems for each year group from the EYFS to Year 6 that can be used to develop children's knowledge, understanding and skills in the area of handling data and that will generate datasets that can be used with graphing programs. For each investigation, write a list of relevant questions that will probe children's understanding and challenge them to use appropriate vocabulary in their responses. Can the same questions be used as part of your assessment of this aspect?

REFERENCES REFERENCES **REFERENCES** REFERENCES REFERENCES REFERENCES

DfE (2011) *Teachers' Standards.* Available at **www.education.gov.uk/publications**

DfE (2013) *Digital Technology in Schools.* Available at **www.education.gov.uk/a00201823/digital-technology-in-schools**

DfEE (2000) *National Curriculum Handbook for Key Stages 1 and 2.* London: HMSO.

Mooney, C. et al. (2012) *Primary Mathematics Knowledge and Understanding.* Exeter: Learning Matters.

Ofsted (2009) *Mathematics: Understanding the Score – Improving Practice in Mathematics Teaching at Primary Level.* Available at **www.ofsted.gov.uk**

Phillips, R. (1997) Can juniors read graphs? A review and analysis of some computer-based activities. *Journal of Information Technology for Teacher Education*, 6(1), 49–58.

FURTHER READING FURTHER READING **FURTHER READING** FURTHER READING

Bennett, R. (2006) *Learning ICT with Maths.* London: David Fulton.

Clark-Jeavons, A. (2005) *Exciting ICT in Maths.* Stafford: Network Educational.

Frost, R. (2006) *Dataloggerama: Ways with ICT in Science Education.* Available at **www.rogerfrost.com/** (accessed 10 May 2011).

Higgins, C. et al. (2002, 2003) *ICT Connect* (Years 1–6). Oxford: Harcourt Education Limited.

Loveless, A. and Dore, B. (2002) *ICT in the Primary School.* Buckingham: Open University Press.

Meadows, J. (2004) *Science and ICT in Primary Education: A Creative Approach to Big Ideas.* London: David Fulton.

Mooney, C. et al. (2014) *Primary Mathematics Knowledge and Understanding.* Exeter: Learning Matters.

Way, J. and Beardon, T. (2002) *ICT and Primary Mathematics.* Buckingham: Open University Press.

Williams, J. and Easingwood, N. (2003) *ICT and Primary Science.* London: RoutledgeFalmer.

Williams, J. and Easingwood, N. (2004) *ICT and Primary Mathematics.* London: RoutledgeFalmer.

11
Databases and spreadsheets

Introduction

Among the first purposes to which computers were widely applied was the systematic handling of data. That the modern world is so information-rich in so many ways is largely due to the facility with which computers can store and process large amounts of data. Through understanding the concepts underlying data handling, children will not only develop computing and ICT skills, but also will become familiar with key principles through which knowledge and information are now managed. Working with data-handling programs can provide insights into how computers use different types of searching algorithms to sort and find information efficiently.

What are databases and spreadsheets?

Databases are structured stores of information. They allow large amounts of data to be stored, organised, sorted, searched and retrieved quickly and easily. They provide for more sophisticated interrogation than the graphing programs that we explored in Chapter 10. Databases as repositories of information abound, from the school library catalogue to television listings to government records, and almost all are now in digital format. In order to access, analyse, synthesise and interpret information, children need to develop appropriate knowledge, skills and understanding, including a basic understanding of how computers utilise search algorithms to retrieve information efficiently. The electronic databases used in school take a variety of forms, from branching tree identification keys to multimedia CD-ROMs and various web-based databases.

Spreadsheets are another kind of data-handling software that is widely used by adults. While they may share some features with databases, spreadsheets are usually not as adept for sorting and searching data, nor are they as effective for storing long text strings. However, where they come into their own is in the manipulation of numerical data, which makes them well suited to mathematical calculations and modelling.

As software development continues, the distinctions between many generic categories blur and fade. Spreadsheets may share many of the features and functions of databases. Similarly, many databases also incorporate spreadsheet functions. This chapter explores the variety, features and functions of databases and spreadsheets and their potential contribution to teaching and learning in the primary school. Clear links are made to other generic aspects of data handling.

What do the programmes of study for Key Stages 1 and 2 include?

Key Stage 1

- Use technology purposefully to create, organise, store, manipulate and retrieve digital content.
- Recognise common uses of information technology beyond school.

Key Stage 2

- Use search technologies effectively, appreciate how results are selected and ranked, and be discerning in evaluating digital content.
- Select, use and combine a variety of software (including internet services) on a range of digital devices to accomplish given goals, including collecting, analysing, evaluating and presenting data and information.

What do teachers need to know about using databases and spreadsheets?

Vast amounts of data are collected, from the various meanings of words, to the amount of rain that falls in a particular location, the daytime telephone numbers of families with children at a particular school and the school's annual repair budget. In order for these data to be of any use, they must be organised and stored in some way, usually as an electronic database. The choice of a database is important to ensure that information can be accessed and manipulated as required.

The types of data-handling software utilised in some primary schools can appear quite distinct from those employed in the world at large. However, there has also been a contrasting tendency for educational ICT to move towards 'industry standards'. The argument, used particularly in secondary schools, is that children should be encouraged to learn the software that they will encounter in the world of work. As an example, the RM spreadsheet Number Magic has many features which will be familiar to users of Excel. It is important to remember, though, that data-handling software used in schools is designed to facilitate learning about the processes and possibilities of data handling as well as for the retrieval and manipulation of information. An important contrast is that educational databases usually incorporate presentation capability – the capacity to generate graphs – which may not be so critical for commercial or governmental databases.

A number of different types of data-handling programs are commonly used in schools, including:

- branching tree or binary databases;
- flatfile or tabular databases;
- relational databases;
- spreadsheets.

Each of these is structured differently to support different functions.

Branching tree or binary databases

Branching tree or binary databases facilitate the identification of objects, people or plants, for example, by the posing of questions relating to attributes which must be answered 'yes' or 'no' (a binary response). The answer to any question leads to a further question to be answered similarly until only one possible outcome remains (see Figure 11.1).

The structuring of information in binary databases can also provide insights into how binary searches are used in computing to find data or solutions to problems more efficiently. For example, we could play a simple *Guess My Number* game to illustrate this. If I think of a number between 0–50 and invite the children in my class to guess the

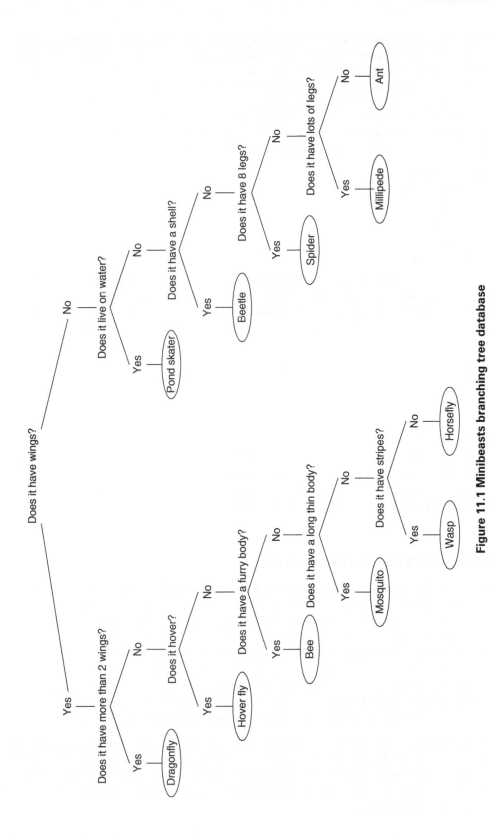

Figure 11.1 Minibeasts branching tree database

number using questions to which I reply 'yes' or 'no' there are various strategies they could use for guessing my number. They could simply search for my number using a linear or sequential strategy, starting at 0 and one-by-one eliminating the numbers until they found my number. This would be fine if I had chosen a low number like 3, but if I had chosen a much higher number such as 35, it would be a very inefficient way of searching for my number. A more efficient strategy would be to choose the middle number of the range each time. For example, if the number 35 is being guessed in the range 0–50, we could find the number in 6 questions, thus:

Is it less than 25? No
Is it less than 37? Yes
Is it less than 31? No
Is it less than 34? No
Is it less than 36? Yes
It must be 35.

This strategy is using a binary search algorithm to locate a piece of data or information as quickly as possible in a set of data, which is something that computers have to do all of the time in relation to the data that is stored in a database. There are many activities away from the computer like this that can be used to illustrate how computers are used to store, organise and search data efficiently. A comprehensive resource (Bell, Witten and Fellows, 2010) for further classroom ideas is available from the Computer Science Unplugged website at the following link: **http://csunplugged.org/**.

PRACTICAL TASK PRACTICAL TASK **PRACTICAL TASK** PRACTICAL TASK

Familiarise yourself with the activity *Battleships* (Bell, Witten and Fellows, 2010, p.43) for exploring different types of searching algorithm. The resources and instructions for this activity can be found at **http://csunplugged.org/**. Try this activity out with a small group of children. Discuss their understanding of the underlying principles of how computers carry out efficient data searches.

Flatfile or tabular databases

Flatfile or tabular databases are perhaps the type of database that most readily come to mind when primary data-handling activity is considered. A datafile comprises a number of records, each containing data arranged in fields. Children will be able to relate to football cards as an analogy. The pack of cards is the datafile and each card is a record. In addition to the player's name, football cards usually include a photograph, the player's age, the name of the club they play for, the position they play, as well as dates of participation in major championships and national representation. Each of these categories is a field. Data are usually entered into a flatfile database through a form, which resembles a questionnaire and includes prompts for data to be added to each field.

Individual records can be viewed on screen (see Figure 11.2). The entire database can usually also be viewed in tabular format, with each column representing a field and each row a record. Sometimes this is called a spreadsheet view. However, the term is misleading as the tabular format does not offer all of the functions of a spreadsheet. 'Table' or 'List' are better alternatives.

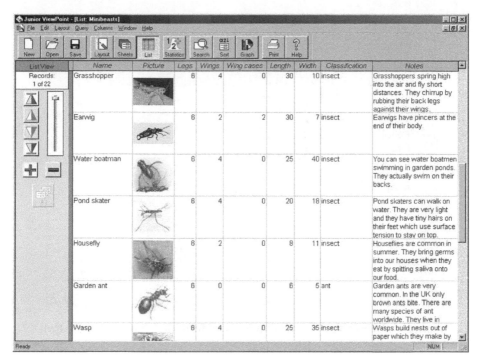

**Figure 11.2 Flatfile database displayed in tabular format
(Junior ViewPoint, Longman Logotron)**

Relational databases

Relational databases have more complex structures than flatfile databases. Rather than data being organised as it is, then entered into records and fields, which then determine the types of interrogation activity the database will support, information is tagged. The tagging interrelates the information in the database. This organisational structure supports greater flexibility in interrogation. Some CD-ROM encyclopaedias and reference works are relevant examples of relational databases used in primary schools. They often feature menus, indexes, keywords and hyperlinks as ways of navigating substantial amounts of related information. It is unlikely that in a primary school the need will arise for teachers to teach and children to learn about the technical aspects of relational databases, but they will need to use them.

Spreadsheets

A spreadsheet appears as a grid made up of cells arranged in rows and columns. Each cell is identified by a co-ordinate conventionally comprising a letter for the column and a number for the row – A3, D4, for example. The column reference is given first. Data, often numeric, are entered into each cell by clicking and typing. The data can be searched, sorted, rearranged and presented in graphical format. More importantly, however, individual cells can be programmed to make and display the results of calculations. In the spreadsheet in Figure 11.3, the cell B12 has been programmed with a formula which instructs it to add 17.5 per cent VAT to the value in cell B10 and display the result.

Teaching with and about databases and spreadsheets involves teachers in the following activities.

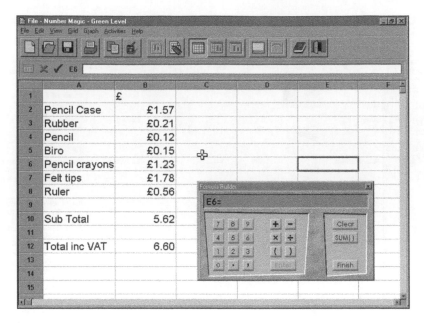

Figure 11.3 Spreadsheet showing entry of formula (Number Magic, RM)

- **Selecting appropriate opportunities** – in which data handling can facilitate, enhance or extend children's learning, such as through a research project that involves interrogating a database, or exploring number patterns and rules with a spreadsheet. In some instances, the focus will be on teaching and learning in computing – how a database can facilitate an investigation. In others, ICT will be used as a resource in the teaching and learning of another curriculum area, for instance using a CD-ROM to research the eating habits of minibeasts.

- **Selecting appropriate resources** – a search tool which enables safe searching of a website or a CD-ROM which supports beginning readers with audio and graphic clues. Both teachers and the children should also make informed choices about when it is worth going through the preparatory work to set up a database, rather than resorting to the quicker option of setting up a spreadsheet.

- **Preparing suitable resources** – although it is instructive for children to construct a database by determining their own fields and records, it may alternatively be appropriate for them to interrogate prepared resources. Many data-files are commercially available, and may be supplied with the database software, but sometimes teachers will wish to prepare their own or customise existing ones to meet their objectives. Similarly, teachers will sometimes design databases in which children can then enter information they have researched or collected.

- **Exploring the full range of data-handling activities** – databases and spreadsheets are not just about the storage and retrieval of information, they facilitate hypothesising, decision-making, organising, analysing and synthesising.

- **Making explicit links between related knowledge, skills and understanding** – knowledge, skills and understanding of databases and spreadsheets have relevance across the primary curriculum. Teachers thus have opportunities to make explicit and reinforce the links between children's previous experiences and new learning across the range of contexts.

- **Modelling appropriate use of ICT** – for instance, how producing a branching tree database in electronic format enables modifications to be made quickly and easily, or how spreadsheet formulae can be replicated using the 'fill down' function.

- **Demonstrating and intervening** – for example, intervening to assist a child to identify the tallest child in a class by sorting height data in descending order, or demonstrating the effect of changing the price of an item in a spreadsheet budget.

The list below attempts to identify the knowledge, skills and understanding of database and spreadsheet software teachers need in order to teach effectively with and about these software packages. The list reflects the features of common software under each of the categories identified. Some software packages may support only a subset of these functions. This is no reflection on their usefulness – in most cases it is a strength, as it may not be helpful for the children to encounter a cluttered interface. However, it does signal that teachers must be aware of the capabilities and limitations of any program as these will be significant in the choice of software for any teaching and learning activity.

Branching tree or binary databases:

- creating, opening, saving, closing, deleting and printing documents;
- adding, modifying and deleting data and questions;
- plotting and replotting branching tree keys;
- inserting titles;
- selecting font and font size;
- exporting branching tree keys into other applications;
- importing information from other applications, e.g. clip art;
- utilising help;
- altering defaults;
- customising the branching tree program, e.g. switching off functions not needed;
- utilising alternative input devices, e.g. overlay keyboards;
- protecting documents.

Flatfile or tabular databases:

- opening, closing, deleting and printing existing datafiles;
- navigating through records using forwards and backwards;
- simple and complex sorting and searching (more than one condition);
- searching to retrieve data;
- plotting and replotting graphs/reports, including:

  - adding text, title, etc.
  - selecting graph type
  - selecting and modifying colours
  - saving
  - exporting graphs to other applications;

- entering data into a prepared datafile, including:

  - selecting a new record/answer sheet
  - entering, modifying and deleting data-saving;

- designing a new datafile, including:

  - opening a form/questionnaire designer
  - selecting font, font size, font colour, background colour
  - inserting and modifying questions, including making appropriate selections for style and format of answer supported:
  - words numbers dates;
  - yes/no multiple choice;

- inserting text, images, borders, arrows;
- saving.

Relational databases (e.g. CD-ROMs):

- loading, including installation prior to first use;
- modifying computer display and volume settings;
- opening and closing;
- navigating using menus, hyperlinks, forwards, backwards, home;
- searching and retrieving information using menus, indexes, keywords and hyperlinks;
- playing audio and video;
- copying and pasting text and graphics into other applications;
- selecting and printing information;
- utilising help;
- critical evaluation.

Spreadsheets:

- creating, opening, saving, closing, deleting and printing documents;
- selecting worksheet and cell size;
- selecting font and font size;
- inserting, modifying and deleting row and column labels;
- inserting, modifying, moving and deleting textual and numerical data;
- inserting, modifying and deleting formulae and functions;
- using fill down and fill right functions to replicate formulae;
- inserting and deleting cells, rows and columns;
- formatting data, e.g. left alignment, centring around decimal point;
- searching and sorting data;
- adding, modifying and deleting borders and shading;
- selecting, modifying and displaying graph types;
- formatting graphs to include axes labels, key and text;
- exporting graphs and spreadsheets to other applications;
- importing information from other applications, e.g. clip art, data;
- utilising help;
- altering defaults;
- customising the spreadsheet program, e.g. switching off functions not needed;
- utilising alternative input devices, e.g. data-loggers;
- protecting cells and documents.

There will be occasions on which other data-handling software, such as graphing programs, will be more suitable. It may also happen that a data-handling project that, on a large scale, would be tackled through a database, could in the context of a classroom activity be more easily implemented through a spreadsheet. Teachers need to be confident in making decisions about the most appropriate application for a particular situation.

What are the key features of databases and spreadsheets?

Branching tree databases:

- support sorting and classification activities at all levels;
- support data-handling activities across a range of subject areas;
- provide opportunities for developing and refining questioning techniques;

- do not replace children using paper- or book-based branching tree keys;
- facilitate the creation, revision and extension of branching tree databases;
- facilitate understanding of how computers search data efficiently;
- often support images as well as text.

Flatfile or tabular databases:

The structure of a flatfile database is determined by the choice of fields and the type of information they contain. These design issues in turn determine the ways in which the database can be used.

Flatfile databases:

- support searching to retrieve information, e.g. the names of the children in the class with blue eyes;
- support understanding of how computers can quickly and efficiently sort and search data;
- support more sophisticated searching, on two variables, e.g. the names of girls whose favourite food is pizza;
- support sorting by field, e.g. to see the distribution of hair colour across the class;
- support sorting and ordering a field, e.g. into descending order to find the name of the child with the smallest feet;
- provide graphical representation of enquiry results where this is appropriate, often called a report;
- support sorting and classification activities at all levels;
- support data-handling activities across a range of subject areas;
- facilitate the development of knowledge and understanding across a range of subject areas;
- provide opportunities for developing and refining searching and sorting techniques;
- often support data held as images as well as text;
- support the rapid retrieval of information.

Relational databases:

- support searching by keyword, index and menu;
- support complex or Boolean searching (see Chapter 16);
- support data-handling activities across a range of subject areas;
- provide opportunities for developing and refining search techniques;
- do not replace children using traditional reference sources;
- facilitate the development of knowledge and understanding across a range of subject areas;
- often support video, audio and animations, as well as images and text;
- support the rapid retrieval of vast amounts of information.

Spreadsheets:

- support data held as text or numbers;
- display and process numerical information;
- enable automated calculations and recalculations;
- support the graphical representation of information;
- support the organisation and reorganisation of data to identify patterns, gaps and correlations;
- support the use of graphs to identify errors in data;
- provide opportunities for developing and refining searching, sorting and modelling techniques;
- support the rapid retrieval of information;
- support rapid calculations;
- sometimes support searching to retrieve information, e.g. chocolate bars available for less than 40p;
- support sorting, e.g. displaying chocolate bars in order of unit cost;
- support data handling activities across a range of subject areas;
- sometimes support images for illustration purposes.

What do databases and spreadsheets contribute to teaching and learning?

In the wider world, the key characteristic of databases is that they facilitate the rapid retrieval of information. This feature is worth discussing with children as the link between the databases they use in the classroom and a commercial database may not be apparent. For example, it is important to discuss how databases are used by banks, the National Health Service (NHS) and the Police. Similarly, discussing the ways in which consumer data are harvested and used commercially is important in developing children's understanding of the role that databases play more broadly in society.

Databases support the development of questioning skills in practical situations. Branching tree databases require very particular types of question, to which the answer can be only 'yes' or 'no', but at the same time they call on children to apply their subject knowledge as well as skills of sorting and classification. Similarly, if children are to interrogate flatfile or relational databases effectively and productively, they need to devise effective questions. Again, these are dependent on experience, knowledge and understanding of the data and structure of the database as well as of the subject itself.

An attribute of spreadsheets is their potential to support 'what if' questions. If the price of every item in the tuck shop is raised by 2p, will profits increase? The answer may appear obvious at first sight, but the children will quickly realise that other variables, such as the effect of the price increase to deter sales, will come into play and the model will need to be modified. Spreadsheets provide opportunities for children to make predictions and hypotheses and test them. For example, is the cheapest way to buy fruit in large pre-packed bags? A spreadsheet can be used to compare the costs of different fruit bought singly, loose and pre-packed from different shops. Decision-making is involved in all sorts of data-handling activity.

Similarly, children may consider what is the best way to interrogate a database to retrieve information. Will keyword searching lead to the required information most quickly? Would using the index lead to information which may not be found by a keyword search?

Databases are organised stores of information. Information collected by one individual or group is of value to others only if it is accessible. The preparation of data for entry into a flatfile database requires children to order and organise and classify material around the database fields. Structuring information has many applications and is a key skill in effective communication. Children can consider the audience for their data and associated tensions, such as quality versus quantity.

Data retrieval is rarely the final outcome of data-handling activity. Often it is the start. Data retrieved from any type of database can be analysed, interpreted, synthesised and presented. The presentation of data graphically is often the first stage in analysis and interpretation. It can also support the identification of relationships and potential errors and inconsistencies.

Progression of knowledge, skills and understanding

Branching tree or binary databases
Identification keys for plants and animals are the most obvious example of branching tree databases. The creation of branching tree databases which are as all-encompassing as this is a very sophisticated activity, requiring high levels of subject knowledge and understanding

together with well-developed questioning skills. It is more appropriate to use a finite set of, perhaps, minibeasts and explore questions which will progressively lead to a positive identification. Does it have six legs? Does it have a hard, shiny shell? Does it fly?

Children need to use examples of prepared branching tree databases, electronic or otherwise, before they can consider designing their own. It is useful to begin by laying out the objects, or cards representing them, on a table or the floor for children to arrange and rearrange as they select and trial questions. Even with only eight minibeasts to contrast with each other, this may take some time. Children may also need to draw on reference material to facilitate their sorting. A considerable amount of work may be involved before the children are ready to use a branching tree program on the computer.

Some of the primary packages, such as FlexiTREE3 (Flexible Software Ltd), come with prepared examples. Children can test these and will soon realise that their datasets are restricted. Increasing the range of minibeasts will require more questions. An extension activity could be to try to reduce the number of questions necessary to differentiate between the minibeasts.

Flatfile or tabular databases

Junior ViewPoint (Logotron) is generic software which can be used across the curriculum. The example in Figure 11.4 provides an appropriate model for work with younger children as the amount of information to be entered of a textual or numeric nature is minimal, with some fields requiring selections to be made from multiple-choice lists by pointing and clicking.

In this example children will enter their own data, perhaps with assistance, into a prepared structure. Then, as a group or class, they can interrogate the data to answer questions (how many people have blue eyes?) or test hypotheses (taller people weigh more).

As with graphing, it is not always necessary or appropriate for children to collect and enter their own data into a flatfile database before they interrogate it, particularly if this information is sensitive, as in the case of weight. They can also work productively with prepared datafiles. A number of software publishers sell prepared datafiles to support a

---

ALL ABOUT ME

1. What is your name? | Daniel |

2. Are you a boy or a girl?   ☒ Boy   ☐ Girl

3. What colour is your hair? ☐ Blonde   ☐ Black   ☒ Brown   ☐ Ginger

4. What colour are your eyes? ☐ Blue   ☐ Grey   ☐ Green   ☒ Hazel   ☐ Brown

5. How tall are you?   142 centimetres

6. How much do you weigh?   28 kilogrammes

7. What did you weigh when   4.0 kilogrammes
    you were born?

**Figure 11.4 An 'ourselves' questionnaire making use of multiple-choice data entry
(Junior ViewPoint, Longman Logotron)**

range of curriculum areas. These have advantages which include effective design, accuracy of information, large numbers of records and saving teacher preparation time.

Children will need plenty of experience with databases before they can begin to design their own. Designing and preparing a database is a time-consuming activity and due thought should be given to long-term outcomes. A class may begin a database of plants and animals living within the school grounds, which could be monitored and expanded by subsequent classes, building into a valuable record of diversity and change over time. Trialling the design and checking the entries for errors are vital stages of the process. Such activity is generally recommended for the latter part of Key Stage 2.

Spreadsheets

Children can be introduced to spreadsheets through the functions they perform. For example, RM's Number Magic spreadsheet software comes complete with a number of prepared examples (see Figure 11.5). These will support a range of activities, mainly mathematics-focused, across Key Stage 2. Children can enter numbers into a spreadsheet set up as a function machine to determine what function the machine supports. The teacher may then draw the children's attention to the formula determining the function and encourage them to experiment with modifying the formula.

Another route into spreadsheet activity is making the link with calculators, placing emphasis on a spreadsheet's potential for supporting and facilitating calculations, especially those of a repeated nature. Children may begin by entering a number and choosing an operation to perform on that number, for instance adding 3. This process can be repeated focusing on emerging patterns, predicting and checking. At this level, spreadsheets have a number of advantages over calculators, the most pertinent being that they are easily checkable, by reviewing the formula for a calculation, or by graphing results to

Figure 11.5 Function machine, a prepared file in RM's Number Magic

identify anomalies. It is important that the copying and pasting of formulae is not offered as a solution too soon, before the purpose and process of formula-writing has been understood. It is also important to make links to computer programming. In creating a spreadsheet with embedded formula to model a particular situation, they are programming the computer and working with inputs, outputs, and algorithms, albeit in a different context.

Children will need opportunities to become familiar with the navigation of spreadsheets, the entry of numeric and textual information, the display of numeric and graphical results, saving and printing.

Spreadsheets can then be used to extend children's knowledge and understanding of number facts and arithmetic laws, supporting mental calculation as children predict and check results as well as deriving generalisations, supporting early algebra work.

As we have seen, spreadsheets are ideal for modelling 'what if?' scenarios. These can be applied to mathematic and scientific situations, particularly in Key Stage 2. Budgets are a popular focus, as are modelling the effect of changing variables in science work. Graphical representation of spreadsheet data can be particularly powerful in this respect.

IN THE CLASSROOM

A Year 6 class was applying their mathematical understanding to the comparison of data from their school weather station with national information for the same period. In order to make comparisons they needed to calculate some weekly and monthly averages from their own data recorded on a daily basis. The teacher reminded the class that, anticipating making eventual use of it, the data had been recorded in a spreadsheet as they were collected. She reminded the children how to enter a formula to calculate the arithmetical mean rainfall over one week in March. The children carefully programmed formulae into other cells to determine median and modal values. The teacher then intervened to demonstrate how formulae could be copied and applied to other cells using the fill handle. A while later the teacher was intrigued to notice that some of the children were busy checking the spreadsheet's calculations with calculators. Questioning determined that this checking regime had been a group decision to ensure that formulae copied from one location to another were actually performing the intended operation.

Relational databases

Most CD-ROM databases make use of multimedia to a greater or lesser extent and whole new concepts in terms of resources have been developed in consequence. *Magic Grandad's Seaside Holidays* (Sherston) supports history teaching at Key Stage 1 by integrating text and images, together with spoken narration and historical video clips, to enable today's children to contrast holidays now with those experienced 50 or 100 years ago. This database requires some quite sophisticated information-handling skills if children are to search in it independently, although the format and navigation are clear and the teacher can control which resources are accessed.

To some extent classroom use of CD-ROMs has inevitably been overtaken by the access that schools enjoy to the internet. However, the authenticity of CD-ROM material, the sharp focus it gives through its content to the children's learning, and the safe environment that is provided all serve to make CD-ROMs preferable for certain purposes. CD-ROM databases are subject to editorial control by their publishers, in the same way as traditional media. No such quality monitors are exercised by the authors of most websites and information retrieved from these should be treated with due caution.

PRACTICAL TASK   PRACTICAL TASK   PRACTICAL TASK   PRACTICAL TASK

Design an A4 help sheet to help children navigate successfully in a specified CD-ROM. What are the key features of effective help sheet design?

What are the capabilities and limitations of databases?

Selecting appropriate databases

The different types of database discussed in this chapter support different types of data-handling activity. Teachers and children will need to make informed decisions about the most appropriate tool for a particular purpose. Again, this is no reflection on the suitability of a particular piece of software as no single program supports all the features and functions discussed.

Keyword searching

Effective keyword searching relies on the choice of appropriate keywords. For most children such selections will require thought, discussion and practice. Some words that have a wide range of applications may not be suitable. Effective keyword selection implies some background knowledge of the search subject. Refining techniques can be used to further narrow the focus of a search.

IN THE CLASSROOM

A group of Year 5 children had been charged with researching and presenting some information on the planet Earth as part of a class science study on the Earth and beyond. Two of the group decided that a CD-ROM encyclopaedia might be a good place to start. They input 'earth' into the search tool and a high number of matches were found. Beginning to explore these in a systematic manner, the children became confused as the first two hits related to soil types and electrical circuits. They had not considered that, even in science, the word 'earth' can have different meanings in at least three contexts: planet Earth, electrical earth and soil.

Spelling is another issue in keyword searching. Incorrectly spelled words are unlikely to prove effective in retrieving the desired information. Some CD-ROMs and websites provide support for children, to help them check their spelling before conducting a search.

One of the strengths of relational databases is that a particular item may be retrieved by searching for any one of a number of keywords. Flatfile or other databases may be more restricted in this respect.

Hypertext literacy

Reading hypertext documents requires a range of skills – many of these have parallels with those associated with traditional texts, while some are different. Many relational databases are navigable by index, as with traditional reference material. The presence of hypertext links, however, means that children's reading of these texts is not linear – they may dart about from one narrative to another to another. Retaining a task focus throughout such a process can be demanding. Similarly, hypertext documents give no sense of geographical location within a text. Children may never know whether they have accessed everything on a particular subject.

CD-ROMs

CD-ROM databases should not be confused with:

- *CD-ROM talking books* – these make use of multimedia but their structure mirrors more closely the linear nature of traditional books. The subject focus of a talking book may be fiction or non-fiction (Oxford Reading Tree, Sherston and Living Books, Broderbund);
- *CD-ROM software* – CD-ROMs are used for the storage and transfer of software. Often when a school buys new software this comes in the form of a CD-ROM. The software is then copied onto the school's computer or network as appropriate and used from there;
- *CD-ROM games and resources* – some games and other resources also come in the form of CD-ROMs. These are not necessarily designed to be copied onto the computer's memory; if space is short, the resources may often be used direct from the disk. Tizzy's Toybox (Sherston) and Mighty Math Number Heroes (Riverdeep) are examples.

CD-ROMs and websites provide access to almost unlimited quantities of information. Sometimes this can be quite daunting as making appropriate selections to satisfy the needs of the task demands that children judge whether particular information is relevant to their enquiry as well as thinking how they might use it.

Copying

Many data-handling activities involve children retrieving information with a view to synthesising or applying it in some way. Teachers have long struggled with children copying information retrieved from reference sources, apparently without engaging with the material. One likely reason for this is that children have difficulty in making sense of the information. Often reference texts are designed with an adult audience in mind and make use of complex sentence structures and sophisticated vocabulary. Information can be useful only if children are able to read it. They also need to deploy associated higher-order reading skills, such as skimming and scanning text.

IN THE CLASSROOM

A Year 5 teacher was encouraging her class to make use of CD-ROM databases to support research across the curriculum. She was discouraged to note that many children merely copied down the text as it appeared on the screen or printed it off. She discussed this issue with the children and suggested a new strategy. Children could print entries or copy and paste them into a word processor, but must then read them through away from the computer, highlighting or underlining words that they did not fully understand, and then looking them up. The children then replaced these elements of the text with their own words to form a narrative that had meaning for them. Some time later she drew one child's attention to the presence of the word 'tectonic' in his work, and was told that it was okay because he now knew what tectonic means.

Data accuracy

Effective interrogation of a database relies on the data held being accurate. It also relies on data being entered in a format in which they can easily be searched or sorted. If a child enters data on the number of their siblings into a flatfile database as text, they could appear as '2brothers' or '2 buthrs'. The data would require considerable checking and modification before it could be used. The phrasing of questions as multiple-choice or yes/no wherever possible minimises the chance of such errors.

Flatfile databases and types of data

Flatfile databases can support data entered in a variety of formats, including:

- text, e.g. the name of a minibeast;
- numeric, e.g. the number of legs the minibeast has;
- dates;
- yes/no, e.g. does the minibeast live the UK?
- multiple-choice, e.g. the life expectancy of a minibeast:

  - a day
  - a week
  - a month
  - 3 months, and so on.

Where text entries are concerned, it is usually possible to limit the length of answers to a specified number of characters. Numeric entries can similarly be limited to a predetermined number of digits, to reduce the chances of inaccurate data being entered in error. In large commercial databases, the limits also serve to minimise the storage space needed – a factor which in the past was significant, but which is not so critical now. The use of multiple-choice and yes/no answers further reduces the risk of inaccurate entries or entries that are difficult to search or sort. Multiple-choice answers rather than open-ended text also make analysis easier.

Spreadsheets and the = sign

Teachers will need to ensure that they make explicit the role of the equals sign in spreadsheet formulae. It does not balance the equation, showing that one side is equal to the other, but provides a function, effectively instructing the software to perform the calculations that follow it. This may also be explained as 'the contents of this cell are equal to'. This is slightly different from the use of the equals sign with calculators, when the calculations are entered first and the = sign instructs the calculator to perform the functions.

Written algorithm:

10 + 4 = 14 (balance, both sides of the equation are equal)

Spreadsheet:

= B3 + B7 (function, add the contents of B3 to B7 and display)

Calculator:

10 + 4 = (function, now add 10 to 4 and display)

Professional use

Spreadsheets have various possibilities for teachers' professional use. Many teachers make a class list at the beginning of the year which they are able to use and reuse many times as mark sheets or for other records.

Data protection

Personal data are governed by the provisions of the Data Protection Act 1998. Although this legislation was not formed with primary school data-handling activities in mind, teachers must ensure that they comply with its requirements where applicable. The key issues are ensuring that data are secure and cannot be accessed by unauthorised individuals and that they are not held any longer than necessary. See Chapter 18 on the professional use of ICT for further information.

Privacy

The collection and interpretation of personal data about children raise issues of privacy and sensitivity – children's height and weight, for instance. Teachers have devised a number of strategies in this respect. Ourselves-type data can be collected for young children's teddies, while with older children it may be appropriate to discuss some of the issues raised, or use datasets that come with the software.

Software selection and advice

Often software and ICT-related resources, such as talking books or non-fiction CD-ROMs, can be obtained from their publishers or software wholesalers on approval or a limited licence for trial purposes. However, with limited budgets and an ever-increasing range of products to choose from, the costs of mistakes can be higher financially and professionally. Software should be evaluated for content and for compatibility. Some software does not sit well with particular operating systems or other software items. It is important to determine whether a software package will cause such problems and, if so, whether the benefits of the software outweigh the problems of overcoming compatibility issues.

Local authority ICT advisers should be a good source of advice and support when purchasing software. In some instances they may have negotiated discounts on recommended titles. TEEM Education maintain a very helpful educational software database, also containing independent reviews and supplier information. This is available online (**www.teemeducation.org.uk**).

Printing issues

It is all too easy with some data-handling programs to print accidentally the entire file rather than the portion intended. Children may decide that it would be useful to print the information they can see on the screen, without considering that that may be a subsection of a very large document. Often it is necessary to detail exactly what is to be printed and to check it with Print Preview if such a facility is available. Sometimes copying and pasting into a word processor or other document may be useful.

The importance of interpreting data

Although using database programs reduces some of the demands on children involved in the manipulation of data, it is important to ensure that value is placed on interpretation and understanding rather than on the presentation of professional-looking graphics. Similarly, use of a database does not ensure successful teaching and learning. This will depend on appropriate task-setting, differentiation and intervention, as in any other teaching and learning situation.

Data-handling and the core subjects

The ideas and activities introduced below are intended to give a feel for the range of ways in which databases can be utilised to support and enhance teaching and learning in mathematics, science and English. They are not intended to be comprehensive, merely to go some way towards illustrating the breadth of possibilities and to provide starting points for the customisation of ideas and the generation of others. Examples introduced under mathematics, for example, may be just as applicable to one or more of the other areas.

There is extensive overlap between science, mathematics, English, ICT and other subject knowledge, skills and understanding in the area of data handling. Teachers need to be clear about their primary teaching objective for any particular task or sequence of activities and maximise the opportunities for making explicit links between learning in the various curriculum contexts.

Data-handling and science

Databases are used extensively in primary science. Data can be collected from children's own observations ('Ourselves' is a good starting point) and experimental results, and then recorded for analysis. Alternatively, a spreadsheet might be used to predict and explore the effect of making changes to variables – for example, recording plant growth measurements against differing quantities of water, light and warmth.

Spreadsheets, and particularly graphs generated from them, can be equally valuable in highlighting errors. The concept of experimental error is often difficult to explore effectively in primary schools owing to the lack of opportunity for repeated experimentation. However, data from a whole class's results entered, compared and analysed might highlight anomalies, leading to discussion and prediction of possible causes and perhaps improvements in experimental technique – the same group member operating the stopwatch each time, for example.

The properties of materials could be a research topic for the compilation of a class datafile resource. Fields might include what the objects are, where they come from and what we use them for, the field structure of the database providing a framework for the children's research. Such resources can be accessed for information later and added to by other classes to build enduring resources over which children have ownership.

CD-ROMs and websites can provide access to high-quality multimedia data. When the USA has a space mission, images are available to children in classrooms around the world as quickly as they are to NASA scientists. Such databases also provide a breadth of resources which would not be available otherwise – slow-motion video of spiders walking or animations of the way the bones or muscles in the leg move as humans walk.

Data-handling and mathematics

Spreadsheets can be used to generate arithmetic and geometric sequences rapidly. Teachers may generate and print these to use away from the computer. A range of problem-solving activities can be supported in this way. For example, using a hundred square, colour in all the cells containing 7s (see Figure 11.6). What do you notice? Now colour all those with numbers ending in 3. What do you notice?

A branching tree database incorporating pictures may be used to support the sorting and classification of shapes with younger children. Does the shape have corners? Does it have four sides?

Mathematical investigations such as the shape of the farmer's field can be modelled using spreadsheets – creating the maximum area with the minimum fencing materials and exploring different shapes of field; working towards generalisations and early algebra.

Data-handling activities which have real relevance for children can be derived from school sporting activities. Recording the results from the netball or football league matches week by week can provide opportunities for statistical analysis: average goals scored per match and comparison of home and away results. Children can be charged with determining the placings of athletics competitors on school sports day: calculating the overall winner based on the average of three long jumps or rounders ball throws.

Figure 11.6 Using the number pattern function (Number Magic, RM)

When you are planning work on databases and spreadsheets, it is helpful to incorporate practical activities into real-life situations around school and in the community. For example, many schools take part in charity and fundraising events, such as sponsored walks or silences, and end-of-term or summer fairs that are open to parents, friends and other members of the community. There are lots of opportunities for older Key Stage 2 children to get involved in organising these. Think of the mathematics in making up a 'float' of change for each stall holder, serving customers and making change, and counting the takings at the end of the fair. A spreadsheet can be used to work out the profit after the floats and any expenditure on purchasing refreshments for sale have been deducted. Children could devise a database of sponsors to record donations or a spreadsheet that keeps a running total as the sponsorship money is collected.

Databases and English

Effective use of a range of databases in the primary school provides opportunities for the teaching and reinforcement of a range of higher-order language skills, such as keyword selection and the skimming and scanning of text.

A class database of book reviews searchable by author, subject matter and reading level may be a valuable ongoing resource. In a whole-school context, children may be involved in the process at varying levels. Older children may be called on to design and trial the structure of the resource. All children could be involved in adding records, with support varying from adult scribes to older children checking the entries for errors and inaccuracies. Similarly, all children might use the database to assist their selection of reading material.

Electronic dictionaries and thesauruses provide alternative reference sources. Some children find these easier to use than paper-based sources because of the combination of audio, images, text and hyperlinks. Most word-processing packages have their own built-in dictionaries and thesauruses.

REFLECTIVE TASK

To provide, in your own mind, a context into which children's work with databases might be lodged, make a list of the databases managed by national and local organisations (commercial, governmental, educational, leisure-related) that hold data about you. Its length may surprise you!

A SUMMARY OF **KEY POINTS**

➤ **Databases enable interaction with data to explore meaning through relationships, patterns and modelling.**

➤ **There is a range of types of data-handling software commonly found in primary schools. These include:**

  • **binary or branching tree databases;**

- flatfile or tabular databases;
- relational databases;
- spreadsheets.

➢ Good database design is essential if the data contained is to be used effectively.

M-LEVEL EXTENSION > > M-LEVEL EXTENSION > > M-LEVEL EXTENSION

Look back over the practical activities suggested in the chapter for helping children to understand the uses of databases and spreadsheets. Divide them into those that could take place in the classroom or other indoor space and those that would be best undertaken outside. How might you use the outdoor classroom and playground areas to best effect in your planning of this aspect? Is it possible to devise a scheme of work with links across a range of subjects that will develop children's capability in the use of databases and spreadsheets?

REFERENCE REFERENCE **REFERENCE** REFERENCE **REFERENCE** REFERENCE

Bell, T., Witten, I.H. and Fellows, M. (2010) *Computer Science Unplugged: An Enrichment and Extension Programme for Primary-aged Children*. Available at **http://csunplugged.org/**.

FURTHER READING FURTHER READING **FURTHER READING** FURTHER READING

Bennett, R. (2006) *Learning ICT with Maths.* London: David Fulton.

Clark-Jeavons, A. (2005) *Exciting ICT in Maths.* Stafford: Network Educational.

DfE (2011) *Teachers' Standards.* Available at **www.education.gov.uk/publications**

Fox, B., Montague-Smith, A. and Wilkes, S. (2000) *Using ICT in Primary Mathematics: Practice and Possibilities.* London: David Fulton.

Leask, M. (ed.) (2000) *Teaching and Learning with ICT in the Primary School.* London: Routledge.

Leask, M. (ed.) (2001) *Issues in Teaching Using ICT.* London: Routledge.

Loveless, A. and Dore, B. (2002) *ICT in the Primary School.* Buckingham: Open University Press.

Meadows, J. (2004) *Science and ICT in Primary Education: A Creative Approach to Big Ideas.* London: David Fulton.

Way, J. and Beardon, T. (2002) *ICT and Primary Mathematics.* Buckingham: Open University Press.

Williams, J. and Easingwood, N. (2004) *ICT and Primary Mathematics.* London: RoutledgeFalmer.

Williams, J. and Easingwood, N. (2003) *ICT and Primary Science.* London: RoutledgeFalmer.

12
Programming and computational thinking

Introduction

As discussed in the Introduction to this book, there has been a shift in emphasis in the latest draft of the National Curriculum for England, with calls for children to be taught more about how computers work. It is argued that as well as learning to use applications children should be given the tools and understanding to create their own applications by learning some of the fundamentals of programming and computational thinking. In this chapter we will provide an introduction to programming in the primary years and consider both what is meant by 'computational thinking' and how children's capacity for computational thinking can be developed within meaningful contexts. We stress the importance of developing appropriate pedagogies and contexts for developing children's understanding of programming and computational thinking. There are many interesting concepts and processes in the subject repertoire that is computer science, but it is vital to consider their appropriateness for the children we are teaching.

We will examine the aspects of the new programme of study for computing in order to clarify some of the key concepts relating to programming and computational thinking. Key software, such as Logo, Scratch, Kodu, Flowol, will also be introduced, with examples of projects and discussion of different pedagogical approaches. While we focus on specific pieces of software, the pedagogical and computing principles can be applied to any of the other programming languages or environments that are being explored to teach programming and aspects of computer science in the primary classroom. The second half of this chapter will also introduce some of the common hardware that can be used in the primary classroom in order to develop children's understanding of the ways in which computers can be utilised to control and automate aspects of our physical environments as well as simulate or create virtual worlds. Throughout the chapter we will refer to specific online resources. However, readers are also advised to make use of the following website: **https://sites. google.com/site/primaryictitt/home**. This website (Berry and Harrison, no date) has been developed by a group of expert teachers and teacher educators, to crowd source a range of resources to support primary teachers in responding to the new curriculum for computing with particular emphasis on the computer science aspects of the programme of study.

What do the programmes of study for Key Stages 1 and 2 include?

Key Stage 1

- Understand what algorithms are, how they are implemented as programs on digital devices, and that programs execute by following precise and unambiguous instructions.
- Create and debug simple programs.
- Use logical reasoning to predict the behaviour of simple programs.

Key Stage 2

- Design, write and debug programs that accomplish specific goals, including controlling or simulating physical systems; solve problems by decomposing them into smaller parts.
- Use sequence, selection, and repetition in programs; work with variables and various forms of input and output.
- Use logical reasoning to explain how some simple algorithms work and to detect and correct errors in algorithms and programs.

One of the most significant changes in the 2014 programme of study for computing in the National Curriculum is its reference to specific specialist language. This specialist language comes from the broader discipline of computer science and signifies the intent within this programme of study to help children understand the distinct nature of computational thinking and how it is utilised within society. Thus in order to develop this understanding in children it is important that as teachers we also have a sound understanding of what is meant by computational thinking and the various processes involved. We will now explore some of the definitions surrounding these processes and various terminology in order to unpick this aspect of the programme of study. The aim of these definitions is to provide teachers with user-friendly working definitions to help them to develop the necessary language when working with children. Consequently, these may differ significantly to the various academic definitions to be found within the discipline of computer science.

Defining terms

Computational thinking – We define computational thinking here broadly as ways of thinking that people engage with as they employ the processes and tools of computing to solve problems. Such problems might exist in the physical world (e.g. an automated vending machine, a pedestrian crossing) or in a simulated/imaginary digital environment of a computer game, or a tablet/smartphone app. That is, computational thinking is, in its broadest sense, a term that encapsulates a number of particular logical thought processes that people employ to utilise a range of computer hardware and software to transform ideas and imagined solutions into reality.

REFLECTIVE TASK

Make a list of all the applications in the world around us that have computational thinking embedded within them. Think about the home as well as the outdoor environment.

Algorithms, inputs, outputs and sequencing – These are fundamental concepts in computing and computer science. A useful way to think about algorithms is that they are the way we teach computers to carry out our ideas or automate aspects of our world. For example, when we press a letter (input) on a keyboard when word processing, the computer reproduces the graphic shape of the letter (output) on the screen. This is because the computer has been pre-programmed (or taught) to carry out this action via a set of instructions (algorithms). The instructions (algorithms) link the turning on of a particular formation of pixels on the screen required for the letter (output), to the physical key or input on the keyboard. So an algorithm is a set of instructions designed to teach computers to execute tasks and ideas. To do this successfully the instructions that the computer processes need to be precise and in the correct order, which is why understanding the importance of sequence when writing algorithms is also highlighted in the programme of study. Imagine for a moment the multiple algorithms operating behind the scenes when you are using a simple word-processing program, not only to reproduce the graphic representations of the letters as you type, but to know what you mean when you select a piece of text to cut, copy, paste, change the font style or size, insert a table, and so on. Understanding the importance of algorithms to computing gives us an appreciation of the complexity of what is involved behind the scenes of any application.

PRACTICAL TASK PRACTICAL TASK **PRACTICAL TASK** PRACTICAL TASK

Watch the Sandwich Bot video by Philip Bagge on YouTube, available at: **www.youtube.com/watch?v= leBEFaVHlIE&feature=youtu.be**

As you watch, see if you can debug or identify the errors in the algorithms or instructions that the children give the Sandwich Bot. What types of errors do they make – sequence, precision, language?

Abstraction, decomposition, repetition, selection and debugging – A useful way to begin to understand these terms is to analyse and engage with examples of computational thinking that are often taken for granted in our physical environment. For example, we can identify these aspects of computational thinking in a system such as a pedestrian crossing (Figure 12.1).

Figure 12.1 Pedestrian crossing

First, let us decompose a pedestrian crossing into the various real-world problems that the crossing is designed to solve. They can be defined thus:

1. Bring the traffic to a stop safely.
2. Enable pedestrians to cross the road safely.
3. Enable partially sighted or blind pedestrians to cross the road safely.

As you can see, we can identify at least three problems in this scenario and by doing so we have begun to use abstraction and decomposition to break the problem down into its key components. Note also that sequence is vital. There is a clear order in which some of the problems need to be addressed. There are various solutions to these problems that we could design which will have varying levels of safety and effectiveness. Let's consider them one by one, i.e. in abstraction.

PRACTICAL TASK PRACTICAL TASK **PRACTICAL TASK** PRACTICAL TASK

To solve the problem of bringing the traffic to a stop safely, consider these two algorithms and decide which is better and why? Possible algorithms to stop the traffic:

Algorithm 1	Algorithm 2
Start	Start
When pedestrian button is pressed (Input 1)	When pedestrian button is pressed (Input 1)
Turn pedestrian wait sign on (Output 1)	Turn pedestrian wait sign on (Output 1)
Turn green light off (Output 2)	Turn green light off (Output 2)
Turn amber light on (Output 3)	Turn amber light on (Output 3)
Wait five seconds	Turn amber light off (Output 3)
Turn amber light off (Output 3)	Turn red light on (Output 4)
Turn red light on (Output 4)	
So Algorithm 1 is safer because the extra instruction to wait for five seconds while the amber light is on will give the motorist more time to slow down and stop safely.	

We can now select Algorithm 1 and develop it further to address the second problem of enabling pedestrians to cross the road safely when the traffic has been stopped safely, for example:

Table 12.1 is one possible solution to the first two problems of stopping the traffic safely and enabling pedestrians to cross. Think of a way that this algorithm could be improved and made safer. Is there a way of warning pedestrians that the green man is about to go off so that they do not set off across the road when there is not enough time to cross? For example, we could incorporate a flashing routine so that after a while the green man begins flashing to indicate that it will shortly turn off.

Computers, like humans are capable of multitasking or carrying out more than one operation at the same time. So we can exploit this to address the third problem of making sure that the pedestrian crossing is also safe for partially sighted or blind people to use. As well as the various visual outputs, such as the red/green man and red/amber/green traffic

Table 12.1 Algorithm to stop traffic and allow pedestrians to cross the road safely

Algorithm 1 developed to stop traffic and enable pedestrians to cross the road safely
Start When pedestrian button is pressed (Input 1) Turn pedestrian wait sign on (Output 1) Turn green light off (Output 2) Turn amber light on (Output 3) Wait five seconds Turn amber light off (Output 3) Turn red light on (Output 4) Turn wait sign (Output 1), amber light (Output 2) and red man off (Output 5) Turn green man on (Output 6) Wait 20 seconds Turn green man off (Output 6) Turn red man (Output 5) and amber light on (Output 3) Wait 5 seconds Turn amber light off (Output 3) Turn green light on (Output 2)

lights, pedestrian crossings have an audio output or signal that acts as a sign that it is safe to cross for those unable to see the visual signs. So it is possible to write a separate algorithm that would run in parallel to the main algorithm to control this audio output. Hence computer scientists sometimes talk of parallel or distributed algorithms. These are simply algorithms within the same system but controlling different outputs or aspects of the system, and exploiting the computer's capacity to multitask.

From this brief exploration of computational thinking and some of the associated concepts, it is possible to see how algorithms are fundamental to computing and why they have been emphasised in the computing programme of study. Clearly, working with algorithms can be challenging when solving complex problems. However, there are child-centred ways of engaging young children at Key Stage 1 with algorithmic thinking and problem solving, as we explore next.

Programmable toys: introducing algorithmic thinking

Despite the recent shifts in the primary National Curriculum to encourage more teaching of aspects of computer science in the curriculum, this is not in fact new. Programming has been introduced into primary classrooms in the past from as early as Key Stage 1. Programmable toys, such as Roamer Classic® (see Valiant Technology, **www.valiant-technology.com/uk/pages/roamer_home.php?cat=1&1**) are common devices that have been used in many primary schools since the 1970s to develop children's problem-solving skills and give children an understanding of the ways in which we can use computers to control or automate the world around us. Children use the arrow keys and numerical values to input simple instructions to move the toys. Figure 12.2 is an example of the latest version called Roamer®. Problem solving using programmable toys can also help to establish and develop some important mathematical concepts in young children, such as an understanding of angle as rotation or turning, and the development of estimation of distance, which is so important in mathematics when developing an understanding of linear measurement. Indeed, the development

Figure 12.2 Roamer® courtesy of Valiant Technology (www.valiant-technology.com/)

of children's mathematical concepts underlies Papert's vision of the Logo programming language on which many programmable toys are based (Papert, 1993).

More recently, other programmable toys, such as Bee-Bot (Figure 12.3) have become available. Programmable toys such as these are an ideal entry point for young and even pre-school children to begin to explore algorithmic thinking; that is, giving simple instructions

Figure 12.3 Bee-Bot programmable toy (left) and Bee-Bot app (right)

to devices and debugging or problem solving when they do not behave in the predicted or expected way. Similarly, apps are available for smartphones and tablets such as the iPad, which allow children to explore giving instructions and writing algorithms to program Bee-Bot in an onscreen game environment (Figure 12.3). The point at which teachers introduce the relevant vocabulary (algorithm, debug, quarter turn, whole turn, etc.) to young children should be left to the teacher's professional judgement, based on their knowledge of the children.

Programmable toys also lend themselves to a range of pedagogical contexts and a search on the internet for teaching ideas will reveal a plethora of imaginative ideas of how to integrate the programming of such toys into the curriculum in meaningful ways. See, for example, Kristine Kopelke's resource *Making Your Classroom Buzz with Bee-Bots*, which is available at the following link: **http://elresources.skola.edu.mt/ wp-content/uploads/2010/06/doc_669_2468_beebotguideA4v2.pdf** (Kopelke, 2012). Programmable toys can be integrated into narrative role-play contexts, by being adapted to take on a character from a popular children's book. Or they can be used within various games scenarios, such as number mats and treasure hunt maps to name but two. While there are many different activity and games mats available to accompany programmable toys such as Bee-Bot, it is also possible to involve the children in designing and creating their own games and scenarios. Involving young children in the designing and exploring of games-based scenarios with programmable toys engages them in the exploration of algorithms to program toys and encounter problems that require debugging. This can provide a sound basis for the further development of computational thinking. Key processes of computational thinking – designing and debugging algorithms, being able to break problems down into their component parts – are relevant whether learners are trying to navigate a Bee-Bot through a maze on the classroom floor or write a program to simulate a satellite orbiting the Earth onscreen, as we will see next. Computational thinking is required to solve the simplest of programming tasks to the most complex.

From Logo to Scratch

Seymour Papert, the mathematician and computer scientist, created the programming language Logo to enable children to explore mathematical concepts and develop problem-solving skills in much the same way that children initially acquire and develop language skills; that is, through immersion in practice. There are various versions of Logo available, but in the Textease Studio CT version, instructions or algorithms can be written straight onto the screen or in the command line to control the turtle's movement around the screen. You can watch a screencast demonstration of programming with this software at the following link: **www.textease.com/demos/turtlect/Turtle/Turtle.html**. Figure 12.4 illustrates a simple simulation of a satellite orbiting the Earth in Textease TurtleCT, which uses Logo as its programming language.

In Figure 12.4 the satellite has been made into a controllable object in the turtle settings. Consequently, the algorithm repeat 180 [fd 1 rt 2] is applied to determine the direction and movement of the satellite. So for every step forward (fd 1) the direction of travel turns 2 degrees to the right (rt 2). As this is repeated 180 times, the satellite travels through 360 degrees back to its starting point. Logo, like Scratch, is what is often termed a 'low threshold, high ceiling' programming environment (Resnick, 2012). That is, it is easy to make things happen on the screen simply by using text-based commands such as forward (fd), backward (bk), right 90 (rt 90), left 90 (lt 90), and so on. For a list of Logo commands, see

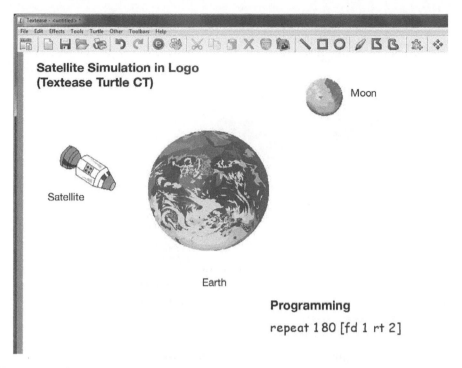

Figure 12.4 Simulation illustrating a simple algorithm in Logo (Textease Turtle CT)

the following link: **www.textease.com/pdfs/guides/turtlecommandguide.pdf**. Of course, Figure 12.4 is a simple simulation that could be developed much further, but there are many possible applications for Logo, including more complex simulations, graphics applications using the turtle to draw as it travels, game creation and animation. See the list of links at the end of this chapter for more examples of how Logo can be developed further.

Let us look now at the same scenario of the satellite orbiting the Earth but this time using Scratch to control the satellite (Figure 12.5).

Figure 12.5 illustrates the Scratch programming language. To program in Scratch, users drag and click together various blocks into a logical sequence to form an algorithm. In the example given, the first block is an 'event' block (when green flag is clicked), the second block is known as a 'control' block because the instruction (repeat 180) is applied to everything within it (it is a repeating loop). The darkest blocks in Figure 12.5 are known as 'motion' blocks because they determine the various motion paths that the object being controlled takes around the screen. The instruction to 'set rotation style to don't rotate' means that the satellite will remain in its current orientation when the program is activated and it orbits the Earth.

Scratch was developed by Mitchell Resnick and researchers at MIT Media Lab. Resnick describes the rationale behind its design as being to make the programming environment 'more tinkerable', as he describes (Resnick, 2012, p.4):

> To create programs in Scratch, you snap together graphical blocks into stacks, just like LEGO bricks, without any of the obscure syntax (square brackets, semi colons etc.) of traditional programming languages.

Figure 12.5 Satellite simulation using Scratch

Thus, the design of the programming blocks, together with the graphical interface, is designed to make it easy for learners to get started and experiment to find out 'what would happen if?' Again, the theory is that it gives learners a low threshold in terms of getting started with exploring and learning how to program, but can also be used to challenge the learner as they create more sophisticated scenarios requiring more complex logical and computational thinking. However, facilitating progression in children's computational thinking can be pedagogically challenging, as we will explore next.

Pedagogies for progression in computational thinking

In this next section we want to consider in more depth how children's computational thinking might be developed through different pedagogical approaches to a programming environment such as Scratch. It is beyond the scope of this text to give readers a course in Scratch programming, and there are already many excellent online resources available to support teachers in the development of their own knowledge of Scratch, including useful video tutorials to get teachers or children started, such as this one by Miles Berry (**www.youtube.com/watch?v=TV0MqrmLpgU**) (Berry, 2011). Another good starting point is the Scratch website for educators at the following link: **http://scratched. media.mit.edu/**. Indeed, the wealth of online video tutorials and support resources available for Scratch could arguably be problematic in terms of the pedagogical issues of developing children's computational thinking with Scratch.

An important part of learning for young children is through practise and mimicking more knowledgeable others within any discipline. But this is problematic if it does not progress

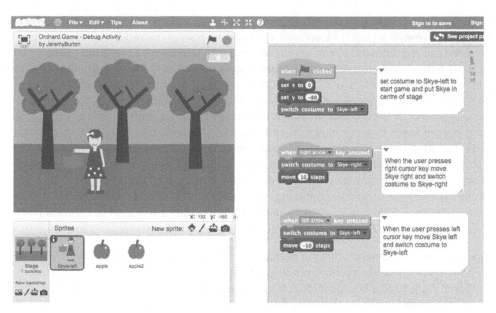

Figure 12.6 Orchard Game – Debug Activity, courtesy of Jeremy Burton, University of Brighton

so that children begin to use their knowledge to express their own ideas or develop their own creativity through programming. Research carried out into the use of Logo programming in education back in the 1980s found that 'children's programs often displayed production without comprehension' together with 'rote use of chunks from other children's programs or those of the teacher' (Pea, 1983, p.5). So how can we ensure progression and development in children's computational thinking when using a tool such as Scratch?

The screenshot in Figure 12.6 illustrates a project called Orchard Game, which was created by Jeremy Burton (Burton, 2013), a senior lecturer in computing education. In the game, apples randomly clone themselves and fall from the trees. The main character, Skye (output) moves left and right across the screen in response to the arrow keys (inputs) to collect the apples in her basket, as they fall. Each time an apple goes into the basket the score (variable) increases by one, but if they hit the ground the score decreases by one. The score is one application of the concept of variables within a computer program. Essentially, variables in a program simply store information monitoring changes in the state of a system; hence the label of variable. Another example is a vending machine which will use variables in its programming so that it registers when a product is sold out and can switch on an output to alert the customer that the product is not available.

PRACTICAL TASK   PRACTICAL TASK   **PRACTICAL TASK**   PRACTICAL TASK

Follow this link to the Scratch profile: http://scratch.mit.edu/users/JeremyBurton/. There are two versions of the Orchard Game. The first version has no bugs in it. Play this to get an idea of how the game works. Now try the Orchard Game – Debugging Activity. In this version of the game, the creator has deliberately made some basic errors in the programming which need debugging. He has also provided some comments that you can open to help you if you get stuck. Try remixing this game to correct the errors in programming.

There are many video tutorials on YouTube of how to create various games in Scratch. There are also many step-by-step walk-throughs of how to recreate various games. For example, see the Whack-a-Witch game, which is available from Code Club at the following link: **http://codeclub-assets.s3.amazonaws.com/public/codeclub-whackawitch. pdf**. Pedagogically, it is clear that when learning how to use any program, children will need to build their repertoire of commands in order to understand how to code or program. However, it is vital that they also understand why a certain piece of code within any program leads to a particular outcome within the system or game being designed. While following instructions on how to achieve certain outcomes within Scratch may be appropriate to familiarise children with the programming environment, this is ultimately limiting, as following others' instruction or video tutorials may actually require little computational thinking or problem solving. The pedagogical model provided by Burton's Orchard Game – Debugging Activity does actually require the learner to engage with solving the problems in the programming and offers a good pedagogical model.

Once children are familiar with the basics of a programming language like Scratch they can be engaged in tasks that will require a deeper level of analysis and that will begin to challenge them to use computational thinking to a greater degree. For example, evaluating other computer games that they enjoy playing can prompt further enquiry and discussion, identifying which bit of code or programming relates to which outputs within the game. In this way, they can see how the various problems within the game have been solved and consider whether they have been solved in the most efficient or effective way. An important aspect of computational thinking is efficiency as the more unnecessarily complex a piece of code or algorithm is, the higher the chance of it conflicting with other algorithms in the program which need debugging.

Ultimately, to develop higher levels of computational thinking children will need exposure to extended projects which require them to design their own games, simulations or scenarios. Much useful work can be done away from the programming environment or computer, getting children to design and devise their own ideas. Indeed, games and software companies spend a great deal of time researching their potential audiences for any new software or games they design and create. The process of designing and creating a new piece of software is multidisciplinary as successful software products require careful research of the target audience, effective design and high-quality graphics as well as effective programming and various testing of the final artefact. This process can offer an effective pedagogical model for children to engage with and can also be embedded within other areas of the curriculum. For example, a task might be to research, design and create a simulation that illustrates the water cycle. Another example might be to create an interactive and animated environment for younger children based on a favourite children's picture book. For more ideas about how programming with Scratch can be embedded in the curriculum, see the *Literacy from Scratch* website (**www.literacyfrom- scratch.org.uk/index.htm**). In order to tackle more open-ended design-based tasks children will need to collaborate to discuss their ideas, sketch or story-board the different scenarios, source or create their own graphics and audio, identify the various algorithms required to control the various inputs and outputs behind their ideas, program their simulation/game, test their game/simulation, evaluate and debug any aspects that can be improved and, re-test the simulation/game.

The important aspect to remember when programming with children is that merely learning a programming language for its own sake can be limiting. Whatever programming language we are using, a key aim is also to build the children's relational understanding of what it means to be a computer scientist. Consequently, children should be engaging in computational thinking both at the computer and away from the computer, utilising the tools creatively to realise their ideas and solutions to practical and imagined problems. Such aims needs to be built into a whole-school approach to computing so that children's knowledge, understanding and skills are built on throughout the primary phase through appropriate challenges and appropriate pedagogies that require them to engage in the various aspects of computational thinking outlined earlier in this chapter.

Alternatives to Scratch

Although Scratch is a common tool for developing children's knowledge and understanding of programming, there are some other programming environments that are worth noting. Kodu (**www.kodugamelab.com**) is a programming environment that enables users to create their own games and narrative environments using a visual programming language. Richard Thomson, a teacher and ICT co-ordinator at St Luke's Primary School in Brighton and Hove uses Kodu in Key Stage 1 and integrates it into classroom practice in a number of ways, as explained in the following example of practice.

IN THE CLASSROOM

We have had a very successful Kodu club this year in which a significant amount of the year group have had some productive programming experience. The following screenshots (Figure 12.7) are from a 'game' in which some of Kodu's comprehensive features have been employed. The programming is entirely the child's own work.

Figure 12.7 Game and example of visual programming in Kodu created by Dylan, Year 2, who explains: *'First, I needed trees to make it harder so I got trees. I got the floor to light up so it was spooky. I wanted to move so I programmed the cycle to move. The world needed some danger so I programmed Kodu to catch me. I needed to get something to make me win so I got a castle.'*

Next year we will be including Kodu in the mainstream Year 2 curriculum in a number of ways:

1. **We will introduce Kodu in the same way as we did in the club using the inbuilt tutorials and allowing them to explore and collaborate to pick up the basics. Cross-curricula links will relate to our WWO programme (working with others) which is part of PSHE. There will be opportunities for the children to develop simple games with the emphasis on building up a repertoire of useful procedures through planning and debugging.**

2. **We then plan to use Kodu as a stimulus for our story writing, in which we will use the features illustrated in the example below (Figure 12.7) to program a simple narrative which the children will then write about. I expect the settings and 'characters' to be especially motivating to our more reluctant boy writers. The speech features will provide a great context to teach using speech in the body of a text.**

3. **Finally, we will promote the use of Kodu at home via links from our VLE and continue to run a weekly club to support the children's wider use of the software.**

In Figure 12.7 the right-hand screen shows the games environment that Dylan has created. The left-hand screen of Figure 12.7 illustrates Dylan's programming as a series of instructions (algorithms) 1 to 5. It is useful to see these as a set of rules that define what happens in the game. So rule 1 can be read as: when the keyboard arrow keys are pressed, move the character. Rule 2 would be: when the 'A' key on the keyboard is pressed shoot. Rules 3–5 assign what happens if the character bumps into any of the identified objects (sputnik, castle, Kodu). If the character bumps into a sputnik or Kodu the game is over. If the character manages to get to the castle (rule 4) then the game is won. From this example it is possible to see how the games environment could be built up from asking the children to imagine and design a simple games environment with various Kodu characters. Next they would have to describe what happens in the games environment. For example, what events lead to the player winning or losing the game? Finally, the children create the environment and characters in Kodu and write the rules using the visual programming language, as illustrated.

Flowol and Mimic Creator

Other educational software that has been used in primary schools for a while to teach aspects of programming and computer science is Flowol and its extension software Mimic Creator. The concept behind these two pieces of software is not unlike Scratch. Like Scratch, this software can be used to program and control preloaded simulations or for children to create their own games and simulations. First, let us examine Flowol in more detail.

In Flowol, a 'mimic' is simply an onscreen visual simulation of a physical scenario, system or game, which is programmed using flow charts. Figure 12.8 is an example of Flowol's preloaded Lighthouse mimic. In the left-hand screenshot all of the inputs and outputs are in the 'off' state, whereas in the labelled right-hand screenshot of the same mimic, all of the inputs and outputs are in the 'on' state. In Flowol, then, the mimic is essentially a graphic representation of a scenario with various 'hotspots' on the simulation that allow the inputs and outputs to be toggled between their 'on' and 'off' states, as we have illustrated in Figure 12.8. So how is the mimic programmed?

Figure 12.8 Flowol Lighthouse Mimic showing inputs and outputs

First, we will examine some of the underlying algorithms that would be needed to automate a lighthouse and then illustrate how these would be represented using Flowol's flow-chart programming environment.

A lighthouse's warning lamp generally flashes on and off throughout the day and the night, with the foghorn warning being added in conditions of poor visibility. Consequently, let us begin with the algorithm for the warning lamp. Because Flowol uses a flow-chart programming environment, once the program is started it will continue to run as a series of flow-chart loops. So the algorithm to make the warning lamp flash could be written simply as follows:

Start
Turn output 1 on (Lighthouse Lamp)
Delay 1 second
Turn output 1 off (Lighthouse Lamp)
Delay 1 second

This algorithm is represented in the first flow-chart – 'Lighthouse Lamp' – in Figure 12.9. Notice that there is an arrow from the last 'Delay 1' box back to the 'Start' of this program, forming a loop, which will continue to run as long as the program is in operation. So what about the Foghorn output and how this is controlled or programmed?

The algorithm for the Foghorn is in many ways similar to the Lighthouse Lamp in that the computer needs to be instructed to turn this output on and off repeatedly during times of poor visibility. Consequently, if you look closely at the third flow-chart in Figure 12.9, labelled 'Foghorn Sub-routine', you will notice that the majority of this flow-chart is very similar to the algorithm and flow-chart for the Lighthouse Lamp. For example:

Start
Turn Foghorn on
Delay 1 second
Turn Foghorn off
Delay 1 second

However, in Flowol, the Foghorn program has been written as a sub-routine because it would only be called on to run if there is poor visibility. Furthermore, this is one example

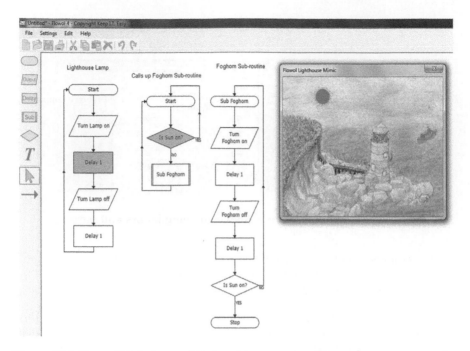

Figure 12.9 Flowol Lighthouse Mimic with example of flow-chart programming

of how the process of selection can work in programming. Consequently, the visibility of the sun (Input 1) in the mimic is what activates the Foghorn. In Figure 12.9, the flow-chart labelled 'Call up Foghorn Sub-routine' has been paused at the point where the program checks whether the sun is visible or not. In programming and algorithmic terms, this is often referred to as an 'if, then statement', or in Flowol, the rhombus shape is referred to as the decision symbol. As the Sun (Input 1) is visible in Figure 12.9, then the program remains in the loop, constantly asking the question and checking if Input 1 is 'on'. If the Sun (Input 1) is clicked on the screen so that the sun is no longer visible (its 'off' state), then the program would 'select' and follow the 'no' path of the flow-chart and activate the 'Foghorn Sub-routine'. What is also evident from analysing the flow-chart programming is that it is helpful to break the various programs down into their component parts or 'decompose' the problem being solved by each of the different parts of the algorithm. In doing so, we can use logical reasoning to solve the various problems faced.

Of course, programmers often remark that computers do exactly as you tell them but often not what you expect, and if you look closely again at the 'Foghorn Sub-routine' you will notice that there is another vital piece of this third flow-chart (Figure 12.9). Once the computer has entered the 'Foghorn Sub-routine', it is essential that it continues to monitor the visibility of the sun in order to turn off the Foghorn when the visibility improves. Consequently, at the end of the 'Foghorn Sub-routine' there is another 'decision symbol' or 'if, then statement' used to check the Sun Input. If the Sun Input is not on, then the program will continue to loop (repetition) around the Foghorn flow-chart, turning the foghorn output on and off. If the Sun Input is 'on', indicating visibility has improved, then the 'Foghorn Sub-routine' will be stopped. Hence the 'Stop' symbol at the end of this flow-chart. So what is Mimic Creator and how does it work with Flowol?

Mimic Creator is an additional piece of software that works with Flowol and allows children to create their own mimics (programmable simulations or scenarios). Children can design their mimic or system and use graphics software to create a background image in which all of their inputs and outputs are represented in the 'off' state, as we illustrated in Figure 12.8 using the Lighthouse mimic. A graphics package is then used to create the graphical representations of the inputs and outputs in their 'on' state, which are then layered over the background image; for example, as we represented in Figure 12.9. Essentially, Mimic Creator is used to assemble the different graphical inputs and outputs of the mimic ready to be programmed in Flowol. There is not space within this chapter to give a detailed introduction to Mimic Creator, but it can offer a useful progression once children are familiar with Flowol and have had experience programming the pre-installed mimics with flow-charts. It offers the opportunity for children to design, develop and simulate their own automated scenarios or games.

In summary, the flow-chart approach to programming is a useful tool educationally in computing because it can help visually illustrate the importance of sequence and logical reasoning when writing programs. While running their programs in Flowol, children can speed up, slow down or pause the program, enabling them to track where the program may have an error that needs debugging. When a program is run in Flowol, the various stages of the program are lit up, making visible the processing of the algorithm (in this case, a flow-chart) by the computer. This can help children to understand the significance and importance of processor speeds in computers and what is actually going on within any computer program as it runs behind the screen.

Physical computing

By physical computing we mean the exploration of physical objects or systems which have computers embedded within them. So, for example, think of the many real-world objects we interact with every day that have computers embedded within them, such as vending machines, lifts, toys, mobile phones, TV remote controls. There are many educational resources available that can be used to develop children's understanding of the ways in which computers can be utilised to automate the physical world. We discussed earlier in this chapter how programmable toys can be used to develop children's understanding of computational thinking as they explore different algorithms through programming toys. However, programmable toys are to a certain extent closed systems in which the inputs and outputs have been predetermined by the makers of the toy.

Lego offer a range of construction kits that can be linked to and controlled by a computer through various interfaces, allowing children to progress to a point where they can devise their own systems or robots that incorporate various light, sound, distance and tilt sensors (inputs) as well as motors, buzzers, LEDs and various outputs. For example, there is a range of Lego WeDo Kits that can be controlled using the Lego visual programming language (Figure 12.10).

In the example of the Hungry Alligator kit (Figure 12.10), the algorithm represented by the short visual program blocks illustrated is:

When the start key is pressed
Wait until motion is sensed
Turn the motor anticlockwise (7 tenths of a second)

Lego WeDo visual programming blocks

Figure 12.10 Lego WeDo Hungry Alligator kit and example of visual program. Images courtesy of LEGO® Education www.LEGOeducation.com ©2014 The LEGO Group

Play sound 17 (a crunching noise)
Turn the motor clockwise (7 tenths of a second)
Repeat

The various programming blocks are combined to create programs that control the outputs and inputs embedded in the alligator. As we saw earlier with Scratch, the blocks snap together in a sequence and the repeat block encapsulates the section of the program that is to be repeated, much like a loop in a flow-chart program we examined earlier. Lego WeDo can also interface and be programmed with Scratch. There are various Lego robotics and control systems available for different levels of competence. For example, the Lego Mindstorms products also offer the opportunity for children to build and control their own robots and controllable systems (**http://mindstorms.lego.com/en-gb/ default.aspx**). In order to design, develop and create their own physical and robotic models with Lego, which can then be programmed and controlled, children will need to develop significant experience over time, sometimes working with kits such as the WeDo examples, and at other times devising their own controllable models or systems. However, there are other ways in which to explore with children the application of computer science and, specifically, programming in physical and electronic devises, as we discuss now in the light of a recent school-based project involving mobile phones.

IN THE CLASSROOM

Lis Bundock and Pippa Totraku, Senior Lecturers in Primary Computing at the University of Brighton, led an app making project at a local partnership school. The aim of the project was to build on the children's experience of programming with Scratch and use the open source software, MIT App Inventor, to explore how computational thinking is embedded within mobile devices and smartphones (see **www.appinventor. org**). App Inventor has a similar visual blocks programming language to Scratch, which is used to design, build and test apps on android smartphones. The project targeted children in Years 5 and 6, as this is a critical age when children, especially girls, make decisions about their aspirations to pursue computer science and ICT-related careers, which was another key aim of the project.

The school-based sessions ran for three hours a week over a 10-week period. The facilitators drew upon a range of teaching methods, including face-to-face, online tutorials, web-based resources and practical workshops to ensure that all children could learn at their own pace. Prior to any programming, the children explored their understanding of computer science, computational thinking and the purpose of apps and their effectiveness. They then developed a range of core programming skills that provided them with the foundations necessary for designing, creating and testing their own mobile phone apps.

Motivation and engagement were high as children developed apps that reflected their own personal interests. Examples of some of the apps were: 'Shake the Beat', which you shook to play random songs that the pupils had recorded; 'I'm Bored', which worked as a Magic 8 ball and offered random ideas on what to do; and a 'Sound Box', which played sound bites of musical instruments. At the end of the project, the children connected their learning by taking the phones home to share and celebrate their apps with family and friends.

Let us have a closer look at how App Inventor works by analysing part of one of the apps that the children in this project created, 'Sound Box'. The screenshots in Figure 12.11 illustrate the Design Interface of App Inventor on the left, which is used by the children to design the various mobile phone screens for their app and then assemble the various digital assets that will be utilised, such as sounds, images, buttons, backgrounds, and so on. From this, it is possible to see that before children proceed to this stage of constructing their app and assembling the digital assets, it is essential for them to have evaluated and discussed a range of different apps, paying attention to the layout and design of the various screens as well as the function of various components and the overall purpose of the app, as discussed in the example of classroom practice. Much of this kind of work can be done away from the computer or software.

The screen on the right of Figure 12.11 shows a screenshot of the Blocks Editor, which is opened from the design interface. The Blocks Editor is where the programming of the various components of the app takes place and is similar to the Scratch interface. The blocks or programming that can be seen in the screenshot control what happens when the various buttons on screen 1 of the app are pressed. Each block of program controls the activation of a particular sound (output) for each button (input), but the algorithm in each program block also ensures that when a new sound is activated any other sounds associated with the other buttons are switched off or stopped.

Raspberry Pi

Other resources for the exploration of physical computing and electronics include the low-cost Raspberry Pi computer (**http://elinux.org/Raspberry_Pi**). Raspberry Pi is a small single board computer that can be linked to a keyboard, monitor and network and runs on the open source Linux operating system. It is referred to as single board because all of the components are contained on one circuit board, as can be seen in Figure 12.12. Raspberry Pi also supports various programming languages, including Scratch and, for more advanced users, a language called Python. The educational advantage of the Raspberry Pi is that it is an open and expandable system. By this we mean that the components are visible and not encased within a metal container like most of the computers we are used to using (see Figure 12.12). This means that children can start

The making of the *Sound Box*
App for mobile phone with
MIT App Inventor

Figure 12.11 App Inventor Design Interface on the left and the Blocks Editor on the right

to become familiar with the components within the computer and begin to develop an understanding of their functions. In addition, Raspberry Pi can be integrated with other physical components. For example, it is possible to connect numerous peripherals, such as expansion boards. Expansion boards, which are also sometimes referred to as 'break-out boards', are electronic circuit boards that allow users to connect LEDs, motors and various sensors to the Raspberry Pi which can then be programmed and controlled either using Scratch or Python programming languages.

Let us consider in more detail what Raspberry Pi offers educationally. It is fair to say that you need to take some time setting up Raspberry Pi. The philosophy behind this computer is that users become familiar with the workings of the computer so it is not designed to simply take out of the box, plug in and go. It is necessary to spend some time downloading the operating system and configuring the SD card (1). Although this may seem daunting at first for those not used to tinkering with computers, it is not as difficult as it sounds and there are numerous start-up demonstrations that can be found on YouTube as well as the helpful and detailed start-up guide available via the official Raspberry Pi website at the following link: **www.raspberrypi.org/quick-start-guide**. This also creates an opportunity to discuss with learners the role of operating systems.

Figure 12.12 Raspberry Pi Computer. Adapted from original Image courtesy of Paul Beech and www.raspberrypi.org

An operating system is 'a collection of software that manages computer hardware resources and provides common services for computer programs' (Wikipedia, 2013). Every digital device requires an operating system for applications software to run on them. Most digital devices, such as smartphones, tablets, laptops and desktop computers, come with the operating systems pre-installed (e.g. Windows 7, Android, Mac OS X, Linux, etc.). Installing the operating system on the Raspberry Pi is an opportunity to explore and discuss the function of operating systems with learners rather than merely taking for granted this aspect of computer architecture. Once the operating system has been downloaded and installed on the SD Card (1), the Raspberry Pi is ready to connect and use. First, it needs a power supply and this can be supplied via a micro USB lead (2) connected to another computer's USB slot. Some mobile phone chargers can also be used to supply power to the Rasberry Pi (see **www.raspberrypi.org/quick-start-guide** for further guidance on this). The Raspberry Pi is connected to a TV or computer monitor via the HDMI output (5) and the USB inputs (4) are used for connecting the mouse and keyboard. Once the initial set-up has been completed, the process does not need to be repeated and the Raspberry Pi can operate as a fully-functioning computer. Various software (e.g. Scratch, Python) come pre-installed within the operating system, as does a simple web browser which can be used for searching the internet when Raspberry Pi is connected to the internet via an Ethernet cable (9). Again, solving the problem of connecting the Raspberry Pi to the internet is an educational opportunity in which learners can be fully involved.

Perhaps where the Raspberry Pi offers the most opportunities for learning about how computers can actually work to control and automate our environment is in the capacity to expand the Raspberry Pi system. If you examine Figure 12.12 again closely you will notice a set of pins, which are labelled General Purpose Input/Output or GPIO pins (8). It is possible to buy connectors which connect these input and output pins to a solder-free breadboard, into which wires can be pushed as well as various other electrical components, such as Light Emitting Diodes (LEDs), push switches and various other sensors which can then be programmed and controlled. While this is not the kind of activity you would undertake with the whole class, it would be worthwhile to establish a computing development area in your classroom where children could explore this application of computing to simple electronics and begin to explore how computing is embedded in various automated systems through the use of various electrical components. There are some helpful blogs that outline how to exploit the Raspberry Pi in these ways. For example, Simon Walter has a series of tutorials on how to use Scratch to control the GPIO Pins on a Raspberry Pi, which is available at the following link: **http://cymplecy.wordpress.com/2013/04/22/ scratch-gpio-version-2-introduction-for-beginners/**.

There are other low-cost devices similar to Raspberry Pi that can be used with children to explore computing and electronics. For example, the Picaxe microcontroller products (**www.picaxe.com/What-Is-PICAXE**) are based on the same principles of an open system and can be used to develop various electronics projects which can then be programmed. Picaxe also make various pre-assembled electronic kits, such as the dice kit below (Figure 12.13). With the dice project, the object is to program the LEDs to light to produce random numbers like traditional dice. The dice is activated by the push button. Picaxe offer a range of cheap kits that introduce children to programming and electronics. For example, the Simple PIC Kit involves three traffic light LEDs and the Safety Light Kit uses high-intensity LEDs that are programmed to flash in various sequences to create a pedestrian or cyclist safety light. The Picaxe microcontrollers embedded in the kits connect to a computer via a USB port and can then be programmed using Logicator, which is a flow-chart programming language not unlike Flowol that we discussed earlier in this chapter. The kits can also be programmed with Flowol.

**Figure 12.13 Picaxe electronic dice kit. Image Courtesy of Revolution Education Ltd
www.picaxe.com**

Another device worth exploring for introducing children to aspects of physical computing in school is Makey Makey (see **www.makeymakey.com**/). Makey Makey is described as an Invention Kit. At its simplest, Makey Makey is an input/output device that enables the user to imagine and create new ways of physically interacting with computer programs. So, for example, it could be linked to Scratch to create a physical interface for an onscreen game that children have created and programmed.

Open systems like the Raspberry Pi computer, Makey Makey, and the various Picaxe products can be used to develop children's understanding of how computing hardware and software is used to monitor and control our physical environment. Building children's hands-on experience of the range of electronic input devices, such as light, sound and motion sensors, and their respective output devices, such as LEDs, motors and buzzers, can offer insights into computer science for children. However, such experiences have to be built over time. There are of course pedagogical and classroom management implications concerning the exploration of physical computing. As we suggested earlier, it is unlikely that teachers will have the resources to explore some of these projects together with a whole class. The advantage of software such as Scratch and Flowol is that it is possible for a whole class to be working on similar projects, such as exploring programming or designing and creating a game at the same time, for example, during a session in the computer suite or on a class set of laptops. However, working with physical objects such as programmable toys like the Lego WeDo kits or exploring programming and electronics with Raspberry Pi lend themselves much more towards focused group work where the teacher can scaffold the children's learning and problem solving, as appropriate.

A SUMMARY OF **KEY POINTS**

➤ Throughout this chapter we have discussed a range of software and hardware, but it is always vital to consider the principles behind why teaching children how to code or program is important. We have stressed that:

➤ Beyond learning how to program in a particular language, children should be encouraged to develop their computational thinking skills, which we have seen involve: being able to solve problems by breaking them down or decomposing them into their constituent parts; writing and debugging algorithms; and using logical and sequential thinking when programming devices or simulations.

➤ Whatever software or programming environment is being explored – from working with programming blocks to flow-charts or text-based programming languages – there are fundamental processes, such as logical reasoning and working with algorithms, which underpin this aspect of computing and are therefore made explicit in the programme of study for primary computing.

➤ Computing is multi-disciplinary in nature, which concurs with Livingstone and Hope's review of this area of the curriculum (Livingstone and Hope, 2011). That is, effective programming and computing is a creative endeavour in which children will also need to draw on their digital literacy skills to create artefacts that others want to engage with and to solve problems drawing on their own and others' resilience and ingenuity. Whether designing and creating a new game in Scratch or designing and developing an app for a smartphone with a program such as App Inventor, children will need to draw on a range of skills, knowledge and understanding. This will at times involve: engaging with the process of design to develop their ideas; applying their digital literacy skills to manipulate various digital media assets, such as images and sound; developing their computational thinking as they work out what algorithms they need to make a game, app or program work; and testing and evaluating what they have created to identify any bugs or ways of improving their work.

> ➤ The role of the teacher and their pedagogical strategies in promoting and helping children to synthesise these dispositions and capabilities should not be underestimated.

M-LEVEL EXTENSION > > M-LEVEL EXTENSION > > M-LEVEL EXTENSION

Find out more about Raspberry Pi (**www.raspberrypi.org**) or Makey Makey (**www.makeymakey.com/**). Familiarise yourself with the different components of the single board computers and their function. Carry out further research online to discover the kinds of projects they have been used to develop. Think about how you could integrate a Raspberry Pi, or Makey Makey developer area into your classroom to enable children to explore the potential of such devices and develop their understanding of physical computing.

REFERENCES REFERENCES **REFERENCES** REFERENCES REFERENCES REFERENCES

Berry, M. (2011) *Scratch Fish Demo*. Available at **www.youtube.com/watch?v=TV0MqrmLpgU**

Berry, M. and Harrison, B. (no date) *Computing Initial Teacher Training and CPD: A Resource Site by Teachers for Teachers*. available at **https://sites.google.com/site/primaryictitt/home**

Burton, J. (2013) *Orchard Game*. Available at **http://scratch.mit.edu/users/JeremyBurton/** (accessed 11 January 2014).

DfE (2011) *Teachers' Standards.* Available at **www.education.gov.uk/publications**

Kopelke, K. (2012) *Making Your Classroom Buzz with Bee-Bots*. Available at **http://elresources. skola.edu.mt/wp-content/uploads/2010/06/doc_669_2468_beebotguideA4v2.pdf**

Livingstone, I. and Hope, A. (2011) *Next Gen. Transforming the UK into the World's Leading Talent Hub for the Video Games and Visual Effects Industries*. London: Nesta. Available at **www.nesta. org.uk/publications/assets/features/next_gen**

Papert, S. (1993) *Mindstorms: Children, Computers and Powerful Ideas* (2nd edn). New York: Perseus.

Pea, R. (1983) Logo programming and problem solving. Paper presented at symposium of the American Educational Research Association, 'Chameleon in the Classroom: Developing Roles for Computers', Montreal, Canada. Available at **http://hal.archives-ouvertes.fr/docs/00/19/05/46/ PDF/A39_Pea_87d_CCT_TR_MS.pdf**

Resnick, M. (2012) *Mother's Day, Warrior Cats, and Digital Fluency: Stories from the Scratch Online Community.* Available at **http://web.media.mit.edu/~mres/papers/mothers-day-warrior-cats.pdf**

USEFUL LINKS

Codeclub, **www.codeclub.org.uk/**

Flowol 4, **www.flowol.com/**

Kodu Game Lab, **www.kodugamelab.com/**

Learning with Scratch, MIT media lab, **http://llk.media.mit.edu/projects/scratch/papers/Learning-with-Scratch.pdf**

Lego WeDo and Scratch, **http://info.scratch.mit.edu/WeDo**

Lego Mindstorms, **www.lego.com/en-gb/mindstorms/?domainredir=mindstorms.lego.com**

Makey Makey, **www.makeymakey.com/**

Mit App Inventor, **www.appinventor.org**

Raspberry Pi, **www.raspberrypi.org**

Raspberry Pi Wiki Hub, **http://elinux.org/Raspberry_Pi**

Picaxe Micro-controllers, **www.picaxe.com/What-Is-PICAXE**

Simon Haughton's website at **www.simonhaughton.co.uk/scratch-programming/**

Terrapin Tools for Thinking, **www.terrapinlogo.com/project-ideas.php#Anchor-project3**

Textease Turtle CT, **www.textease.com/turtle/**

FURTHER READING FURTHER READING **FURTHER READING** FURTHER READING

Brennan, K. and Resnick, M. (2012) New frameworks for studying and assessing the development of computational thinking. Paper presented at annual American

Educational Research Association meeting, Vancouver, BC, Canada. Available at **http://web.media.mit.edu/~kbrennan/files/Brennan_Resnick_AERA2012_CT.pdf** (accessed 4 February 2014).

Richardson, M. and Wallace, S. (2012) *Getting Started with Raspberry Pi*. Sebastopol: Maker Media.

13
Mobile technologies

Introduction

One of the exciting aspects of computing is that the technology itself is evolving quickly and providing opportunities for innovation and experiment. In this chapter we will summarise the different kinds of mobile technology that are currently available, conscious that the picture is constantly changing. We will go on to review some of the ways in which mobile devices might be utilised in primary schools. What we will encounter is considerable variety in the contexts in which mobile technology can be applied, which leads to consideration of the implications for primary teachers and subject leaders in taking strategic decisions about the equipment that is important and relevant for them.

What are mobile technologies?

In the last few years there has been significant development in the range and diversity of ICT equipment that is small enough to be carried around conveniently, and it is to these recent innovations that the term 'mobile technologies' is usually applied. Early developments saw the emergence of what were called personal digital assistants (PDAs), which incorporated various facilities, such as calendars, satellite navigation and internet connectivity. However, many of these applications have now converged into one device, with the development of smartphones, MP3 players such as Apple's iPod, and Apple/Android/ Windows tablets (e.g. iPad, Galaxy, Surface). We will also refer to laptops, or 'notebook' computers, and tablet PCs, although strictly these are 'portable' rather than 'mobile', due in part to their physical size (Anderson and Blackwood, 2004).

What do the programmes of study for Key Stages 1 and 2 include?

The programmes of study for computing do not make any direct reference to mobile technologies. However, mobile technology has become commonplace in our lives. Accordingly, including its use in curriculum activities is only a reflection of what is happening in the world beyond the school gates. How mobile technologies are used to address aspects of the programme of study for computing will depend on how they are integrated into teaching and learning. For example, if a tablet device such as an iPad is used in a history lesson to research the life of a Victorian child using the internet and a note-taking app, then there will be an opportunity to develop children's digital literacy skills as they are taught to:

- Use search technologies effectively, appreciate how results are selected and ranked, and be discerning in evaluating digital content.

However, equally, children might be engaged in programming an onscreen Bee-Bot to navigate a virtual maze on a tablet device and would therefore be focusing on how to:

- Create and debug simple programs;
- Use logical reasoning to predict the behaviour of simple programs.

Essentially, mobile devices can be used to support any aspect of the programme of study for computing, depending on the teacher's pedagogical design of the activities.

What do teachers need to know about using mobile technologies in the classroom?

In considering the use of mobile technologies inside – and outside – the classroom, teachers will need to establish what is practical in terms of funding. This is likely to be a team decision involving all staff. Some schools have made the choice to buy a class set of laptops, or even iPads. Some schools have equipped children with iPads but at present they are a minority, especially in the UK. Other schools have explored schemes – Bring Your Own Device (BYOD) – which actively encourage the children to bring their own mobile devices into schools in order to teach them how to use them appropriately and critically to support their learning. Of course any scheme needs to be carefully considered by the whole school in terms of issues of equal access and safety. It is unlikely that mobile devices will completely replace the school's need for desktop or laptop computers, so if a set of iPads is bought, will staff in the school as a whole have the time and commitment to explore how to appropriate them into their pedagogical practice? If not, then it is questionable whether the devices will be more than an expensive novelty. Apart from cost considerations, the increasing diversity of affordable ICT suggests that teachers in future will need to choose what is most appropriate for their classroom.

The range of mobile technology available is substantial and it may be useful to summarise the features of the main types of mobile equipment that are currently marketed.

A laptop computer in principle has all the functionality of a desktop computer but with the additional benefit of being powered by a rechargeable battery, thus making it transportable. With mobility in mind, the size and weight of laptops are minimised and so they usually have a smaller screen and keyboard. The reduction in size of the components makes laptops more expensive than a desktop computer of comparable specification. Laptops can also be more difficult to use. The keyboard is not raked, which makes typing physically harder, and some users have difficulty using the touch pad to control the pointer. These concerns can be overcome by attaching a standard keyboard and mouse, or by using a docking station and mouse. Laptops have the advantage of being easy to transfer from one location to another. In a school, this potentially enables more effective use of a valuable resource as the laptop is moved from one classroom to another according to need. Some schools have bought class sets of laptops which are stored on a specially designed trolley with recharging facilities, so constituting a portable computer suite. Manufacturers have recently tended to refer to laptops as 'notebooks'.

Tablets are now characterised by having a touch-sensitive screen that also responds to various gestures, for example swiping. These have developed as a variation from what were often referred to as tablet PCs, which often had a pen-shaped stylus as an input device. Tablets such as the iPad can be operated using a stylus and some users find the stylus easier to use than touch and hand gestures. Tablets also incorporate a range of applications (apps) to support many different activities; image capture and manipulation, sound recording and editing and note-taking to name but a few. Another advantage of a tablet device is that it can be passed around a classroom and, using a data projector and wireless connection, children can take their turns to make a contribution which will be shared instantly by the whole class. For more information about the use of tablets in education, see Burden et al.'s *iPad Scotland Evaluation* (Burden, Hopkins, Male, Martin and Trala, 2012).

Smartphones have developed through the convergence of PDAs and mobile phones. PDAs were initially conceived as personal organisers, but their functionality was quickly extended so that they were typically supplied with simple versions of office software, internet connectivity and sound recording facilities. Mobile phone ('smartphone') capability, including photography, was then incorporated into PDAs, leading to what are generally termed smartphones. Smartphones have a pop-up virtual keyboard for input via a touch screen. However, small physical keyboards can also be connected via Bluetooth to both tablets and smartphones, which can be a much easier way of entering text.

The use of **mobile phones** has been considered in relation to teaching and learning. Many schools ban children from bringing their phones into the classrooms, concerned about the possible distraction and also the risk of theft. However, there is an argument that children's enthusiasm for these devices can be harnessed to support the development of their literacy and oracy skills (Attewell, 2005) and, more generally, for communication (Cole, 2003).

MP3 players store and play audio files, usually music. MP3 is a reference to the file format which at one time was dominant for music, but the devices are perhaps better referred to as digital audio players (DAPs), as other formats, such as Windows Media Audio (WMA) and Advanced Audio Coding (AAC), used on Apple's iPod, are now also popular. The hardware itself falls into three main categories. Portable CD players originally could play only purchased (or copied) CDs, but can now usually manage downloaded MP3s or other formats burned onto a CD-R. Some products are now effectively personal media players, capable of capture and playback of video and still images as well as audio files.

What are the key features of mobile technologies?

While the transportability of mobile devices is their obvious shared feature, it is also worth considering how they will be integrated with other equipment. It would probably be a mistake to think of a tablet device such as an iPad as a replacement for a fully functioning desktop (or laptop) computer. Rather, its portability can be exploited, but through synchronisation with the full-size computer; data collected 'on the move' can be processed further in the classroom. For example, if a Calendar entry – a time and date for an appointment – is made on a smartphone during a staff meeting, it can later be synchronised with Calendar on the teacher's home computer (it was this kind of facility, rather than any educational application, that originally drove forward the development of PDAs and smartphones). This procedure effectively backs up the information and also makes it accessible on a large screen.

Data transfer between devices may be set up via cables but, increasingly, wireless connectivity can be established. There is increasing interoperability between devices with many devices offering automatic synchronising via web-based storage and services. These are often referred to as cloud-based services; that is, the principle is that the user's data follows the user rather than being fixed by the location of a particular device. Services such as Dropbox (see **www.dropbox.com/**), Google Drive and SkyDrive are useful in this respect because they enable you to store and save all documents to one location, which is always accessible from any device providing an internet connection is available. This saves working with duplicate files and avoids losing track of the latest version of a document or file. However, it should also be noted that such facilities for cloud-based storage and synchronisation work best when there is personal ownership of the mobile device.

What do mobile technologies contribute to teaching and learning?

Investigations into the opportunities for mobile technologies to support teaching and learning have been ongoing for some time now (see Passey, 1999, for an early influential report). It is arguable, though, that evidence to support the benefits of mobile technologies for teaching and learning remains inconclusive (see Naismith et al., 2004, for an objective overview) and may have depended on resources and time that, though possible in an experimental situation, would not be scaleable. While some educationalists see potential for the use of smartphones for school use, this possibility has not been widely adopted. Technical, financial and practical constraints can all be readily identified. Ironically, it may also be that children and young people see the smartphone and technologies associated with it as representative of their independence from adults. In this case, they may be reluctant to see their phones 'hijacked' for the school's purposes. Crook (2012) identified significant tensions associated with the use of such technologies in schools, and Traxler (2010, p.5) argues that the integration of mobile technologies into education offers opportunities for innovation and inclusion but also warns that it is necessary to resolve several tensions as mobile technologies are 'woven into all the times and places of students' lives'.

Nevertheless, if all these reservations can gradually be overcome, it would seem that mobile technologies offer exciting prospects by extending the classroom both spatially, or geographically, and temporally, so that learning does not have to take place within any fixed parameters of location or time. This shift to what has been dubbed 'anytime, anywhere' learning is consistent with other social trends, such as '24/7' availability of services and flexible working patterns for adults.

Podcasts, which might be either sound or video files that are transferred automatically onto mobile devices (or other computers), could be exploited profitably by education. Files are offered through a feed by the information provider (which would be the school, or individual teacher) to a 'subscriber' (the learner; the idea of a subscription in this instance does not necessarily imply that a payment is made). On the internet, feed readers or 'aggregators', most popularly in RSS (Really Simple Syndication) format, are used to keep subscribers in touch with any changes made to pages. This is particularly helpful for fast-changing news websites. However, the principle could also be applied to release lessons in the form of talks or demonstrations to children which they would download and play back at a time to suit themselves. **Screencasts** use screen-capture apps now available for tablet devices, which can be used for modelling and direct instruction of specific processes, for example in mathematics.

PRACTICAL TASK PRACTICAL TASK PRACTICAL TASK PRACTICAL TASK

Watch the video *Modelling Multiplication* (Turvey, 2013) at the following link: **http://vimeo.com/64421196.** This short video was recorded on an iPad using the app, Explain Everything (**www.explaineverything. com/**), and then edited using videoediting software. It demonstrates how short lessons can be put together to reinforce children's learning of a particular process while also illustrating the process to parents or guardians so they can support the children's learning. Think about other ways you could use a screen-capture app like Explain Everything to model other processes.

THE BIGGER PICTURE THE BIGGER PICTURE THE BIGGER PICTURE THE BIGGER PICTURE

The use of mobile technologies in the primary classroom has many exciting possibilities. The peer- and self-assessment in PE using digital video clips (see Chapter 9) can be extended by utilising a class set of iPod Touches to include the use of videos of good practice in a range of sports and there are apps available, many of which are free to download, that enable children to analyse performance. Relevant material can be projected onto a larger screen, such as the interactive whiteboard (IWB), for wider group or whole-class discussion.

The value of a mobile device for a teacher's professional use should not be underestimated. Apart from providing a portable electronic diary, devices offer a range of possibilities for maintaining records, or creating media-rich digital content. For example, a spreadsheet can be set up so that children's achievement during a lesson can be recorded as it happens rather than retrospectively. A discreet entry into a mobile device, taken as the lesson progresses, is much less obtrusive than making a note into a desktop or laptop computer, and can be made as the teacher moves around the class. Mobile devices' compactness and easy mobility may also be used to carry notes around during a lesson, either of the plan itself or relating to individual children. However, just as mobile technologies tend to pervade all aspects of children and young peoples' lives, the same can be said for teachers' own use of mobile technologies. Thus, careful consideration needs to be given to how the different aspects of teachers' professional and personal lives converge through the use of mobile technologies (Turvey, 2012).

PRACTICAL TASK PRACTICAL TASK PRACTICAL TASK PRACTICAL TASK

The only practical approach to starting to think about the ways in which mobile technologies might be applied in teaching and learning is to explore them thoroughly so that you become familiar with their characteristics and limitations. Once you have done this at a personal level you will be better placed to determine a role for mobile technologies in the classroom, and to persuade others (including those in the school who manage budgets) that what you are proposing is worthwhile. Accordingly, choose one of the mobile technologies that appeals to you, and which, somehow, you can finance, and use it regularly over several weeks to discover its capabilities.

THE BIGGER PICTURE THE BIGGER PICTURE THE BIGGER PICTURE THE BIGGER PICTURE

Many schools are already using mobile technologies to keep in touch with parents, such as when they need to let families know of school closure due to bad weather, reporting safe arrival of a school trip or text messaging when a child is absent from school. There are also services that can text or e-mail school correspondence and newsletters direct to parents. These are further developed by the use of apps. For example, ParentMail's +Pay service (see **www.parentmail.co.uk**) is a mobile phone app that sends parents information about school visits and other events and allows them to send authorisation and pay for the trip electronically, with the school being able to track payments into a central account covering extra-curricular clubs and sports teams' arrangements as well.

REFLECTIVE TASK

Talk with children about mobile technologies. With which technologies are they familiar through personal use? Do you foresee any difficulties in teaching children the technical aspects of mobile technology use? What might be some of the data protection issues with mobile technologies? Also think about e-Safety and the various associated risks that mobile technologies might pose. For example, is there a need for guidelines on the use of mobile devices for taking photographs in school? How and where will the photographs be stored? See Chapter 19 for more guidance on issues relating to e-Safety.

A SUMMARY OF **KEY POINTS**

> There are many mobile technologies that could be used in primary schools, but not all educationalists are convinced of their value and purchasing class sets has obvious financial implications, as does equipping children with devices.

> Some schools have invested in class sets of laptops or notebooks and use them as a mobile computer suite.

> Tablet devices can use simple versions of office software, internet connectivity and rich-media capability. They have touch screens and virtual QWERTY keyboard input but physical peripherals can be added via Bluetooth.

> Mobile phones and smartphones may have uses in the classroom, though some children may prefer to use these independently and their inclusion in schools can be controversial.

> Podcasts/Screencasts of sound or video files could be provided by schools for use out of school hours.

> Research and studies show that the use of mobile technologies has the potential to extend learning beyond the physical boundaries of school.

M-LEVEL EXTENSION > > M-LEVEL EXTENSION > > M-LEVEL EXTENSION

Find out more about the controversy around the use of mobile technologies in the primary classroom. Use the research summaries and studies described in this chapter, together with your own further reading, to examine the debate. What are the advantages and disadvantages of utilising mobile technologies to support children's learning? What are the pros and cons of using them to support your own teaching strategies, including for assessment, recording and reporting to parents? Are there any ethical or safeguarding concerns raised by their use? Overall, what are your conclusions about this issue?

REFERENCES REFERENCES **REFERENCES** REFERENCES REFERENCES REFERENCES

Anderson, P. and Blackwood, A. (2004) *Mobile and PDA Technologies and Their Future Use in Education.* JISC Technology and Standards Watch: **www.jisc.ac.uk/** (accessed 11 May 2011).

Attewell, J. (2005) *Mobile Technologies and Learning.* London: Learning and Skills Development Agency. Available at **www.m-learning.org/docs/The%20m-learning%20project%20%20technology%20update%20and%20project%20summary.pdf** (accessed 11 May 2011).

Burden, K., Hopkins, P., Male, T., Martin, S. and Trala, C. (2012) *iPad Scotland Evaluation.* University of Hull. Available at **www.janhylen.se/wp-content/uploads/2013/01/Skottland.pdf**

Cole, G. (2003) *Ring Tone Revolution.* Available at **http://education.guardian.co.uk/elearning/story/0,,869659,00.html** (accessed 11 May 2011).

Crook, C. (2012) The 'digital native' in context: tensions associated with importing Web 2.0 practices into the school setting. *Oxford Review of Education*, 38 (1), 63–80.

DfE (2011) *Teachers' Standards.* Available at **www.education.gov.uk/publications**

Naismith, L., Lonsdale, P., Vavoula, G. and Sharples, M. (2004) *Literature Review in Mobile Technologies and Learning.* Futurelab series report 11. Available at **www2.futurelab.org.uk/resources/documents/lit_reviews/Mobile_Review.pdf** (accessed 11 January, 2014).

Passey, D. (1999) *Anytime, Anywhere Learning Pilot Programme: Project Report.* Reading: Microsoft UK/Lancaster University.

Traxler, J. (2010) Will student devices deliver innovation, inclusion, and transformation? *Journal of the Research Center for Educational Technology*, 6 (1), 3–15.

Turvey, K. (2012) Questioning the character and significance of convergence between social network and professional practices in teacher education. *British Journal of Educational Technology*, 43 (1), 739–753.

Turvey, K. (2013) *Modelling Multiplication.* Available at **http://vimeo.com/64421196** (accessed 11 January, 2014).

FURTHER READING FURTHER READING **FURTHER READING** FURTHER READING

Futurelab (2006) *Mudlarking in Deptford.* Available at **www.futurelab.org.uk/projects/mudlarking/in-deptford/** (accessed 11 January 2014).

Heppell, S. et al. (2004) *Building Learning Futures... A Research Project at Ultralab within the CABE/RIBA 'Building Futures' Programme* (p9). Available at **http://rubble.heppell.net/places/media/final_report.pdf** (accessed 11 January 2014).

Naismith, L., Lonsdale, P., Vavoula, G. and Sharples, M. (2004) *Literature Review in Mobile Technologies and Learning.* Futurelab series report 11. Available at **www2.futurelab.org.uk/resources/documents/lit_reviews/Mobile_Review.pdf** (accessed 11 January, 2014).

Pachler, N., Bachmair, B. and Cook, J. (2010) *Mobile Learning: Structures, Agency, Practices.* London/New York: Springer.

Perry, D. (2005) *'Learning2Go' Mobile Learning – PDAs in Schools Project.* Wolverhampton LA. Available at **www.wolverhampton-engage.net/sites/anonymous/Learning2Go/Downloads/Evaluation%20-%20Learning2Go%20Phase%202%20Report%20-%20Spring%202006.pdf** (accessed 11 January 2014).

14
Interactive whiteboards

Introduction

Interactive whiteboards (IWBs) have been in use in schools for well over a decade now. As with the introduction of most new technologies into schools, initially a body of anecdotal evidence and small-scale studies emerged suggesting that there are real and significant gains to be made by the use of interactive whiteboards in the classroom. These opportunities were summarised by the National Whiteboard Network, the arm of the Primary National Strategy charged with supporting the introduction of IWBs into schools, as the potential to:

- *Improve the quality of interactions*
- *Improve teacher assessment through the promotion of effective questioning*
- *Enhance modelling*
- *Redress the balance of making resources and planning for teaching*
- *Increase the pace of learning*

National Whiteboard Network (2006)

We will examine some of these claims against some of the more recent evidence and developments in order to help student teachers develop a more critical and reflective approach to the IWB. Also, while the National Whiteboard Network is no longer in existence (and their publications, which were originally available online via their website, are now no longer accessible), there are plenty of online resources where teachers and student teachers can find resources and support for their use of the various types of IWB they may encounter (see further reading at the end of this chapter).

What are interactive whiteboards?

Interactive whiteboards are touch-sensitive boards which allow teachers and children to engage directly with digital content projected onto a screen from a computer via a data projector. They have their conceptual origins in commercial contexts where they were introduced to enliven presentations and dialogue in the boardroom and elsewhere. In large part due to the 1997–2010 Labour government policy, they have now been widely adopted in schools in the United Kingdom. The most common types of IWB found in UK schools are those developed by Smart Technologies, referred to as a SmartBoard (see **http://smarttech.com/gb**), and another type developed by Promethean, referred to as an ActivBoard (**www.prometheanworld.com/gb/english/education/home/**). An exploration of these two companies' websites will also reveal that development in touch-sensitive (haptic) technologies for education is a fast-moving field. One of the latest developments is what is referred to as multi-touch tables, which allow learners to interact synchronously around a horizontal surface. Such technologies are expensive at the moment, and there is not a great deal of research about their educational value. However, it is reasonable to assume that, like IWBs and other educational technologies, once the 'wow' factor has waned it is the pedagogy that is vital if the technology is to be effective.

What do the programmes of study for Key Stages 1 and 2 include?

The interactive whiteboard is akin to the traditional chalkboard or whiteboard in that it is genuinely a cross-curricular tool and it is probably not useful to think of its implementation as grounded in the computing subject content. That said, it is nevertheless arguable that good classroom use of the IWB can contribute to any aspect of the computing programme of study. For example, it could be used to facilitate whole-class or small-group analysis of the programming within a particular Scratch project that a child has created. Equally, another student might use the IWB to explain and model how they have used a variable in their Scratch game to keep the player's score. These examples would address the computer science aspects of the programme of study. However, another example could involve the teacher or a child modelling how to edit a short sequence of digital video or audio to improve part of a short film, thus demonstrating the development of the digital literacy element of the computing programme of study. An interactive whiteboard could be employed to facilitate any aspect of the computing programme of study, again depending on the teacher's pedagogical design of the activity.

What do teachers need to know about using an interactive whiteboard in the classroom?

Technically, interactive whiteboards work by enabling the teacher and children to control the computer by touching the board, either with a special pen or with their finger. The touch is understood by the computer in the same way as it recognises mouse movement and clicks.

There are two main technologies that have been implemented in the design of IWBs used in the classroom, which can broadly be characterised as 'hard' or 'soft' boards. Hard boards have a grid of copper wire behind the solid surface. These boards need special pens which are tracked by the grid using electromagnetism. Soft boards use 'resistive' technology. The board has a polyester surface membrane which is flexible, though strong, and separated from a rigid second layer by a small air gap. As the finger or pen is used to depress the surface, the contact is registered by the board and transmitted to the computer.

The 'feel' of the two different boards is quite distinctive, and teachers usually decide that they have a preference for one type of board rather than the other. Sometimes this partiality may simply be the result of familiarity. It can also be influenced by the software that is provided with the board. The software is not interchangeable, although there has been considerable convergence in functionality as the different manufacturers have recognised the utility of particular tools. Teachers need to consider that, if they build up a bank of resources for one type of board, it will not easily be converted to the other.

Another vital area to consider is the physical set up of the IWB. While you will not have much, if any, control over this as a student teacher, it is worth considering the set up of the IWB you inherit so that you are aware of the issues that can arise and affect your lesson, as we will explore next.

The components of an IWB set-up

In order to use an interactive whiteboard three items of equipment are necessary: the whiteboard itself, a computer and a data projector. The computer is connected to both the projector and to the interactive whiteboard. The physical organisation of this equipment is important. When IWBs were first introduced decisions had to be taken as to whether the equipment should be fixed or mobile, with the IWB held on a trolley and the data projector and computer moved around with it. Schools now tend to arrange for their IWBs to be permanently installed on a wall, as mobile systems proved to be cumbersome and time-consuming. If at all possible, ceiling mounting the data projector is preferable, too, although more recently all-in-one systems have become available, in which the projector is mounted on an arm that reaches out from the whiteboard with a short-throw projector mounted at the end of the arm. The advantage of this is that it is easier to interact with the board, without blocking the projected image. Health and safety concerns would support this option too as there is less risk of the user looking directly into the projector. Trailing leads should always be avoided in the classroom, and trunking used for cables where at all possible. An additional benefit to a fixed installation is that encasing the projector in a ceiling-mounted unit provides security for what is otherwise an attractive, portable target for thieves.

The computer used to control the IWB can be a standard desktop computer. Its positioning will to a certain extent depend on the geography of the classroom; there is no need for it to be close to the whiteboard. Many schools use laptops for this purpose, which have the benefit of enabling teachers to prepare resources away from the classroom. Similarly, it is increasingly becoming possible to link up tablet devices to projection facilities.

The positioning of the board in the classroom needs careful consideration. There must be sufficient space on either side of the board for the teacher or children to stand and avoid being in the path of the projector. The projected light will be affected by other light sources, such as windows and overhead lights. Blinds or curtains may be necessary. The height of the board is also a factor. At the very least the teacher must be able to reach the top of the board, both to calibrate it and to access menu items in program windows, and as far as is practical the children should be able to use as much of the board as possible. However, the board also needs to be visible to the class. In many classrooms, benches or small platforms have been set up so that shorter users can write on the whole board. There is an obvious safety consideration here; balancing on a stool is not an acceptable alternative.

The size of the board is important. Generally speaking, the larger the board, the easier it will be for the class to use. Detail will be difficult to make out on a small board from the back of the room. While this may not be problematical when using resources designed specifically with the whiteboard in mind, the size of text will be a concern when, for example, demonstrating menu items in a program window. Needless to say, there is a cost implication involved in opting for a larger board.

Increasingly, schools are recognising that the full potential of an interactive whiteboard is realised only if good-quality audio equipment has been integrated. Many programs and web pages that might be used on the interactive whiteboard depend to a greater or lesser extent on audio facilities, sometimes to give feedback on choices that the user has made. It is important that the sound can be heard by the whole class, and ideally the source should be close to the board itself, rather than the computer, so that there is close identification of sound and projected image.

The IWB should not be used with conventional whiteboard pens. Although the IWB can be wiped, marks will inevitably be left and will be picked out by the light from the projector. Wherever space has allowed, teachers have tended to retain their old whiteboard, or alternatively use a whiteboard (or paper flipchart) mounted on an easel, in addition to the IWB.

RESEARCH SUMMARY RESEARCH SUMMARY **RESEARCH SUMMARY** RESEARCH SUMMARY

Early research into the use of interactive whiteboards, among the general benefits that are concluded, are motivation, which is widely reported (e.g. Levy, 2002), the efficiency with which teachers are able to present web-based and other resources (Walker, 2003) and the opportunities for interaction and discussion in the classroom. Factors that support effective use include, significantly, the importance of teachers becoming familiar with the technology (Glover and Miller, 2001; Levy, 2002) and also practical considerations such as the position of the boards to avoid sunlight and any obstructions (Smith, 2001). More recently, research has highlighted the importance of distinguishing between levels and types of interactivity, suggesting that interactivity for its own sake may not necessarily lead to increased cognitive engagement with the learning process (Beauchamp, 2011; Kennewell, Tanner, Jones and Beauchamp, 2007).

What are the key ways of using an interactive whiteboard?

There are two main ways in which a teacher may use an interactive whiteboard. It can be used very effectively with the pen or finger simply replacing the mouse. For example, a PowerPoint presentation can be managed at the board, clicking for each new slide, rather than the teacher needing to go to the computer in order to move on. This becomes particularly useful for the children if the presentation has been designed to include choices activated by hyperlinks, so that the children are able to decide or at least to see what option has been taken. Similarly, for the teacher to work at the board to show the children how to use software has more impact, and can help to maintain the momentum of a lesson, compared with the teacher demonstrating remotely, hoping that the children can follow the pointer.

Alternatively, the teacher can use the native software of the whiteboard. At its most straightforward, the software provides a selection of tools that enable annotation and other manipulation, such as gradually revealing parts of the desktop. These tools can be used in 'real time' and, combined with the strong visual impact of what is on screen, perhaps from a web page, can make for lively lessons that engage the children well. However, the software can also be used to prepare resources in advance of the lesson to create files that will be used interactively with the children. In SMART, these files are known as notebooks, while in Promethean they are flipcharts. RM offer an alternative software called Easiteach. Creating notebooks, flipcharts or Easiteach files with interactive features is not difficult, but time spent becoming familiar and adept with the software will be repaid.

PRACTICAL TASK PRACTICAL TASK **PRACTICAL TASK** PRACTICAL TASK

Spend some time exploring the IWB resources at the following websites and consider how you could use them or adapt them for use in your own teaching.

Activ Board Promethean – **www.prometheanplanet.com/en-gb/**

SmartBoard – **http://exchange.smarttech.com/#tab=0**

What do interactive whiteboards contribute to teaching and learning?

It is worth briefly considering the claims noted by the National Whiteboard Network, as quoted in the introduction to this chapter, in relation to the potential of interactive whiteboards highlighted at the start of this chapter. Four of the five refer to gains that may be made over 'traditional' teaching approaches. The judgement that a particular technology offers an improvement over teaching by alternative means is always a good litmus test; if ICT does not bring an enhancement, then why bother with it?

Perhaps the most important of the five gains is the **increased pace of lessons** that IWBs allow, although it should also be remembered that increased pace may not always be desirable or indeed synonymous with increased learning. Sometimes teachers slow the pace of a lesson to try to address misconceptions or deepen the children's understanding of a concept. Nevertheless, the potential for increased pace has been widely reported by teachers. If the lesson is well prepared, the teacher will be able to use resources quickly and smoothly to move from one point to another. File organisation on the computer is important for quick access, and it will usually be helpful to organise desktop shortcuts in advance of the lesson. The teacher also needs to know how to use the resource itself. This is not as straightforward as it may seem. Some resources may have been created with a lot of thought but are not necessarily intuitive to use. Planning, and specifically consultation of the supporting guides, will help to ensure that the lesson itself maintains good pace where desirable.

If the teacher has sufficient digital resources to hand, and knows how they intend to use them, then the pace of the lesson that follows can be varied accordingly to make space for two other of the benefits identified by the National Whiteboard Network, namely: **improving the quality of interactions** and **improving teacher assessment through the promotion of effective questioning**. Indeed, the importance of the quality of pedagogical interactions when using the interactive whiteboard and maintaining a focus on learning goals are important factors, as confirmed by Kennewell et al.'s findings (2007) and also Beauchamp's research (2011).

The final claim of the National Whiteboard Network, that IWBs have the potential to **redress the balance of making resources and planning for teaching**, is perhaps more contentious. Resources are increasingly available for downloading from the internet, and many of these are of high quality or can be adapted easily. There are also some proprietary software titles, designed with IWB use particularly in mind, which may be purchased. However, searching for the right resource takes time and in some circumstances it may be quicker, and provide a tailor-made outcome, to create the resource from scratch. Once the teacher has a file for use on the interactive whiteboard, though, it is recyclable, and the initial effort made to secure exactly the right material will be repaid in subsequent years. Within a school, teachers may also share resources and develop online libraries, using filing systems provided by the IWB software.

Modelling is well suited to work on the interactive whiteboard. For young children, to see and manipulate representational images and icons has a strong impact and will often make the teaching point much more clearly than verbal or textual explanations. The technology self-evidently lends itself to whole-class teaching more than to group work. Even if a teacher decided to work with one group at the IWB while the rest of the class was occupied in other activities, there would be the likelihood of children being distracted, especially if sound and video were involved. As with any whole-class work, the teacher needs to ensure that all of the children are engaged. Planned and targeted questioning will be a key technique to this end. Ironically, the children's physical interactivity with the board may not be as fundamental. In the early days of the introduction of IWBs, it was reckoned that giving the children direct access to the board would be central to the success of the technology. However, it became apparent that bringing young children, especially, frequently to the front of the class incurred a time overhead and distracted from the learning objectives of the lesson – the very benefit that the IWB is supposed to bring. Obviously there is a balance to be struck.

Another surprising consideration is whether the interactive whiteboard is genuinely being used interactively (Beauchamp, 2011; Kennewell et al., 2007). If the data projector is essentially only beaming what is on the computer desktop, or if the interactivity is low level, such as moving on slides sequentially in a PowerPoint presentation, then it is questionable whether the IWB is necessary. At a more sophisticated level, some schools are exploring the potential of wireless devices, such as remote tablet devices or slates, that can be passed around the room but enable the children to interact with the interactive whiteboard. The intention here is for the input equipment to be passed around the class, without the children coming to the board. This provides an interesting alternative approach, but in the primary classroom, at least, there will be a concomitant loss of physical connection directly between the teacher or children and the board, which might represent a pedagogical disadvantage. As we can see, the effective integration of a technology such as the interactive whiteboard is pedagogically complex and requires a critical approach to one's practice.

REFLECTIVE TASK

Break down the elements of a lesson you have observed (or given) in which extensive use was made of the interactive whiteboard. Identify which parts of the lesson were necessarily interactive, and which were more a matter of projecting images or text, or making use passively of other multimedia resources.

Interactive whiteboards and the core subjects

On the face of it, interactive whiteboards are cross-curricular and it is possible to conceive of resources being prepared for any subject. However, it is noticeable that many of the available resources focus on the core subjects.

THE BIGGER PICTURE THE BIGGER PICTURE THE BIGGER PICTURE THE BIGGER PICTURE

When planning and drafting shared writing and going on to develop it further through revising and editing it, the IWB can be integral in engaging and motivating children. It can be used to record their contributions, give vocabulary choices, draft sentences and cut and paste them to re-sequence the piece, until everyone is happy with the result. The children can then move to working further on the same text or developing one of their own in groups on the classroom computer or in your school's ICT suite.

THE BIGGER PICTURE THE BIGGER PICTURE THE BIGGER PICTURE THE BIGGER PICTURE

There are many programs available as secondary sources to illustrate phenomena that are not possible to recreate in the classroom, both for use with the whole class on the IWB and for children to use in groups on the class computer. These can make mathematics and science fun while providing useful models and simulations. Make sure that you know what is available in school and via the local authority's virtual learning environment (VLE), but also consider the internet. When you plan to use secondary sources, remember that there are colleagues in school who can advise you on what is available, and check the school's long/medium-term planning in case it identifies available resources before deciding whether you will need to source any additional materials yourself. Always pre-view video clips and TV programmes, simulations and models and use programs hands-on to ensure that they are appropriate for your requirements and suitable for the children's needs.

Provision of free resources for science is not as well developed. Partly this may be for reasons of cost. Interesting and accurate representations of scientific phenomena and experiments take time to produce. However, there is good proprietary software available from companies such as Sherston, 2Simple, CATS, 4Learning, Kar2ouche, ClicSoft, Boardworks, The Big Bus and Inclusive Technology. Also, when using secondary sources on an IWB it is worth remembering that they are a representation of a real-world artifact or process. So, for example, if you plan to use a science electricity simulation, think about what is lost in comparison to using actual batteries, bulbs and wires. Similarly, a simulated protractor on an IWB is not the actual tool, so think about how modelling the use of a protractor by using a simulated protractor on the IWB might actually confuse some children further rather than help them.

A SUMMARY OF **KEY POINTS**

➢ IWBs are touch-sensitive boards that allow teachers and children to engage directly with material projected on a screen from a computer via a data projector.

➢ There are two main technologies in their design: 'hard' and 'soft' boards.

➢ Most schools invest in one or the other in a whole-school approach.

➢ The positioning of the board, the computer and the data projector requires careful thought to ensure that this is optimal in supporting teaching and learning.

> ➢ There are five main benefits of using IWBs identified by research projects, including the pace of learning, enhancement of modelling, improving the quality of interactions, and of assessment through effective questioning, and redressing the balance between making resources and planning.
>
> ➢ Teachers need to think critically about how they integrate interactive whiteboards into their pedagogical practice.

M-LEVEL EXTENSION > > M-LEVEL EXTENSION > > M-LEVEL EXTENSION

Teachers often liken their 'performance' in the classroom to a stage role in which the success of a lesson is in part gauged by how well they have engaged their audience of children. If teachers include an interactive whiteboard as one of their props, then it is important that it is used effectively and efficiently. This does not mean that the whole lesson is scripted. Indeed, one of the exciting aspects about the use of an interactive whiteboard is that the opportunity is there to respond quickly and easily to the questions or suggestions of the audience, following hyperlinks and creating searches. Make a point of observing a range of colleagues teaching with the IWB in as many subjects as you can make arrangements to see. Read as widely as possible about the IWB as a tool to improve the quality of teaching and learning (see Moss et al., 2007; Somekh et al., 2007).

REFERENCES REFERENCES **REFERENCES** REFERENCES REFERENCES REFERENCES

Beauchamp, G. (2011) Interactivity and ICT in the primary school: categories of learner interactions with and without ICT. *Technology, Pedagogy and Education*, 20 (2), 175–190.

DfE (2011) *Teachers' Standards.* Available at **www.education.gov.uk/publications**

Glover, D. and Miller, D. (2001) Running with technology: the pedagogic impact of the large-scale introduction of interactive whiteboards in one secondary school. *Journal of Information Technology for Teacher Education*, 10 (3), 257–276.

Kennewell, S., Tanner, H., Jones, S. and Beauchamp, G. (2007) Analysing the use of interactive technology to implement interactive teaching. *Journal of Computer Assisted Learning*, 24 (1), 61–73.

Levy, P. (2002) *Interactive Whiteboards in Learning and Teaching in Two Sheffield Schools: A Developmental Study.* Sheffield: Department of Information Studies, University of Sheffield.

Moss, G. et al. (2007) *The Interactive Whiteboards, Pedagogy and Pupil Performance Evaluation: London Challenge.* London: School of Educational Foundations and Policy Studies, IOE. Available at **http://webarchive.nationalarchives.gov.uk/20130401151715/https://www.education.gov.uk/publications/eOrderingDownload/RR816%20Report.pdf** (accessed 12 January 2014).

Smith, H. (2001) *SmartBoard Evaluation: Final Report.* Kent NGfL. Available at **www.kentict.org.uk/kentict/kentict_iwb_smart_final.cfm** (accessed 12 January 2014).

Somekh, B. et al. (2007) *Evaluation of the Primary Schools Whiteboard Expansion Project (SWEEP).* Manchester: Metropolitan University/SWEEP/DfES. Available at **http://webarchive.nationalarchives.gov.uk/20130401151715/https://www.education.gov.uk/publications/eOrderingDownload/SWEEP-Report.pdf** (accessed 12 January 2014).

Walker, D. (2003) Quality at the dockside. *TES Online*, 3 January, pp.66–67.

FURTHER READING FURTHER READING **FURTHER READING** FURTHER READING

Moss, G. et al. (2007) *The Interactive Whiteboards, Pedagogy and Pupil Performance Evaluation: London Challenge.* London: School of Educational Foundations and Policy Studies, IOE. Available at **http://webarchive.nationalarchives.gov.uk/20130401151715/https://www.education.gov.uk/publications/eOrderingDownload/RR816%20Report.pdf** (accessed 12 January 2014).

Smith, A. (2000) *Interactive Whiteboard Evaluation*. Available at **www.mirandanet.ac.uk/publications/ smartboard.htm** (accessed 12 January 2014).

Somekh, B. et al. (2007) *Evaluation of the Primary Schools Whiteboard Expansion Project (SWEEP)*. Manchester: Metropolitan University/SWEEP/DfES. Available at **http://webarchive.nationalarchives. gov.uk/20130401151715/https://www.education.gov.uk/publications/eOrderingDownload/ SWEEP-Report.pdf** (accessed 12 January 2014).

<h1 style="text-align:center">15</h1>

Digital audio and music

Introduction

The intention of this chapter is to introduce a range of ways in which children can utilise digital audio creatively both in computing and in music education. However, throughout the chapter we emphasise the caveat that technology should not replace traditional ways of learning about and making music in the primary school, but offer new opportunities to engage with the subject.

The importance of music and audio or in people's lives is often underestimated. Indeed, creating, performing and listening to music are fundamental activities that can play a significant part in the emotional, social and intellectual development of the individual. The music industry has undergone radical change due to the digitisation of music and the ease with which music can be created, accessed and shared in compressed file formats such as MP3s. Powerful music composition programs connected to an electronic keyboard can enable children to engage immediately with the elements and language of music without necessarily understanding formal music notation. Similarly, the significance of audio seems to be enjoying a resurgence as new forms of expression and communication emerge, such as the podcast. The ease with which quality digital audio recordings can be created through a desktop or laptop computer puts these new forms of communication and expression well within the grasp of primary school children. This chapter will introduce a range of applications, and examine how these can be utilised to support children's learning in music specifically, but also how audio in general can be utilised creatively across the curriculum.

What do the programmes of study for Key Stages 1 and 2 include?

In the aims of the National Curriculum for computing, it is emphasised that the teaching of computing 'ensures that pupils become digitally literate – able to use, and express themselves and develop their ideas through, information and communication technology – at a level suitable for the future workplace and as active participants in a digital world' (DfE, 2013). A key aspect of digital literacy is the ability to make effective and appropriate use of digital audio whether for the sound track of a movie, the audio in a computer game, or creating a musical composition. Much digital audio can also be shared with wider audiences using online services. The specific aspects of the programme of study which relate to this are highlighted as follows.

At Key Stage 1, the new programme of study for computing (DfE, 2013) states that, children should be taught to:

- Use technology purposefully to create, organise, store, manipulate and retrieve digital content;
- Recognise common uses of information technology beyond school.

At Key Stage 2 (DfE, 2013) children should be taught how to:

- Make use of the opportunities offered by internet services for communication and collaboration.
- Use technology safely, respectfully and responsibly; know a range of ways to report concerns and inappropriate behavior.
- Select, use and combine a variety of software (including internet services) on a range of digital devices to accomplish given goals, including collecting, analysing, evaluating and presenting data and information.

Composing and performing music

GarageBand is a piece of software that comes with Apple Mac computers and is particularly suited to music composition activities (see Figure 15.1). The software contains pre-recorded musical loops which can be previewed and then dragged onto the score, building up tracks and layers of music which can then be mixed using the dynamic and balance controls. However, the real creative potential of this software is in the way that live instruments, including the voice, can be recorded. This opens up a number of possibilities, such as creating and recording a rap, a song or creating a soundscape to accompany a poem written by a child or group of children. It is also possible to connect a midi keyboard to the computer so children can create, record and then orchestrate their own melodies.

THE BIGGER PICTURE THE BIGGER PICTURE THE BIGGER PICTURE THE BIGGER PICTURE

When you are planning to use ICT to support children's learning in music, consider using the website **www.singup.org/**. This has a useful 'songbank' with ideas for lesson plans, including using ICT to support the teaching of music and/or music plans.

There are a number of applications that work in a similar way to Garageband, for example with children dragging pre-recorded samples and loops into their own compositions, then adapting these by applying effects and editing them. These include Dance Ejay, Music Maker, RM Music Explorer and 2Simple Music Toolkit. However, it is important that teachers recognise both the limitations and potential of such software and it is useful to ask some key questions.

Figure 15.1 GarageBand Apple Mac – user interface

- How far can any pre-recorded samples be adapted and changed?
- Is there any facility for recording and combining live instruments?
- To what extent can children generate their own melodies, rhythms or soundscapes?
- Does the software support any links between different types of media (sound, still/moving image)?

Another piece of software that is particularly flexible is Audacity (see Figure 15.2). Although there are no sample sounds for children to use, they can record their own sounds into the computer and then edit these by cutting and splicing them as well as applying effects.

Multiple layers of sound can also be built up to create complex textures of sound. This software particularly lends itself to spoken word and music projects, such as creating a soundscape to accompany and add mood to a poem or story. The software is open source and can be downloaded at **http://audacity.sourceforge.net/**.

Figure 15.2 Interface of Audacity

IN THE CLASSROOM

A class of Year 5 children have been working with a trainee teacher, creating the words for a class rap on an anti-bullying theme. Over the course of a week, groups of the children use music composition software to set the words to music. The trainee teacher asks the children to think how they are going to accompany their rap. What kinds of instruments will they use? How will they make sure that as they build up the different layers of music, the all-important words and message they are trying to convey is not lost? What form will their rap take? Will they have a refrain that is repeated at intervals throughout or some other structure? How will the piece end: all instruments fading out together or phasing out the instruments one by one? As the children begin recording their rap, they make mistakes, which become evident as they listen to and evaluate their work as it progresses. At different stages, they decide to rehearse and practise coming in at the correct time before actually recording.

REFLECTIVE TASK

REFLECTIVE TASK

Consider this classroom example in relation to the programmes of study for music and computing.

What aspects of the programmes of study for both subjects could be addressed through the activity described?

Combining audio and visual

Once children become familiar with using musical composition software to compose and record music digitally, this opens up a number of possibilities for exciting projects combining audio with still and moving image. An important aspect of the programme of study for computing at both Key Stage 1 and 2 is using 'technology safely, respectfully and responsibly'. Children should be taught that digital audio, such as sound effects and music, is copyrighted, which can limit how they can or cannot use other people's creative work, including audio/music. There are digital audio libraries that provide downloadable content under different kinds of licences, such as creative commons. One such site is **http:// freeplaymusic.com/**, where music and sound effects can be downloaded for educational use; that is, the original source or composer should be attributed and there should not be any commercial gain from the use of the music. Another useful online media repository that has been built up over a number of years is maintained by Fred Riley and is available at the following link: **www.fredriley.org.uk/callhull/elearning/media**. This repository has links to various sites which make images, video and audio available to users under Creative Commons licences; for example, the Freesound project cited here is particularly useful for sound effects and atmospheric music (see **www.freesound.org/**). In this way it is possible to source audio which can be combined and mixed with the children's images or video to create the required mood and atmosphere.

New software is often not necessary to initiate such projects. PowerPoint supports audio and this facility can be utilised in many ways. One idea might be to create an online gallery of children's artwork for a whole-school assembly by getting them to scan their work or photograph it. They could then create or choose an appropriate short piece of music to accompany their slide and artwork. Windows Movie Maker is also standard on most new PCs these days. Children could create their own pieces of music to accompany a short movie clip they have shot. The key to success with such projects initially is to try this out yourself first and to keep the pieces of music created to a manageable length. The impact of combining music and image is often rewarding and children enjoy experimenting with different types of music to create different moods.

Podcasts and podcasting

Podcasting is a method of publishing files to the internet, allowing users to subscribe to a feed and receive new files automatically by subscription, usually at no cost, whenever they log onto the internet. The latest update is automatically downloaded to the subscribers' preferred device, whether this is an MP3 player, tablet device or mobile phone.

Again, there is a great deal of educational potential with this technology. Teachers might consider creating their own educational podcasts or children themselves could create a podcast to accompany a historical or geographical field trip to their local area. This could be shared more widely with the school community with software such as audioBoo (see **http://audioboo.fm/**). An audioBoo app can be installed on a tablet device or smartphone so that children can record their audio responses while out on a field trip. These are then uploaded to the school or class audioBoo site back in school so that it can be shared more widely. SoundCloud (see **https://soundcloud.com/**) offers a similar facility. Such software enables children to create and broadcast their own podcasts. Devices such as smartphones or tablets usually have a built-in microphone.

IN THE CLASSROOM

Follow this link: **https://audioboo.fm/boos/1332463-e-safety-broadcast**. Listen to the e-Safety broadcast that was made by Year 4 children. They created and composed the short audio advert using the software GarageBand. After a lesson discussing and exploring the issues of e-Safety, their task was to plan and create a short audio advert to make other children in the school aware of e-Safety issues. These were then shared with other children in the school via audioBoo. Think about how this activity addressed some of the aspects of the computing curriculum.

Listening to and appraising music

Many primary school classrooms are equipped with interactive whiteboards (see Chapter 14), which again offer a wealth of opportunities for sharing and discussing ideas about music as they usually have good-quality audio integrated within the system. However, together with rich audio resources to enhance children's experience, there is also the capacity to use a range of media to explore musical ideas. For example, the interactive whiteboard could be used to create a graphic score which the class interpret using percussion instruments.

Alternatively, a class might be asked to appraise a particular Cézanne landscape. How does it make them feel? What is the mood? Is there a clue in the colours used? They could then go on to appraise different pieces of music and decide which is suitable for the painting. Indeed, the opportunity to bring together a rich array of digital media in one place can be a powerful tool in developing children's aesthetic appreciation of music through listening and appraising, as this next classroom example illustrates.

IN THE CLASSROOM

A music advisory teacher is giving a demonstration lesson with a Year 2 class. They are looking at how the elements of music can be used to depict a real event. They begin by performing a poem projected on the interactive whiteboard about a steam train. The teacher draws the children's attention to the sounds created in the poem. Next they watch and listen to a short video clip of a steam train as it blows its whistle and releases steam, finally coupling with its carriages and accelerating gradually out of the station. They talk about the different sounds they have heard in the sequence. In the main part of the lesson they create their

---

own soundscape to accompany the video, using percussion instruments and body sounds, also discussing how to depict the gradual acceleration of the train through tempo. Finally, the teacher introduces the children to a new piece of music – 'The little train of the Caipira' by Villa Lobos, which depicts exactly what they have been creating, using different instruments of the orchestra to represent the different sounds and manipulating tempo to illustrate the train gradually getting up to speed. The children listen carefully, identifying and appreciating the different elements of this piece of music, which they can now understand, having explored this event themselves through text, moving image and audio.

(Peter Walker, Advisory Teacher for Music, Brighton and Hove)

There can be no doubt that the range of ICT tools now available to the primary teacher offers new ways of enabling children to find out about a range of music, as illustrated above. However, to make the most of these new opportunities, a secure subject knowledge of music is essential in order to develop children's understanding further and use the technology effectively.

Some practical issues

There are some important factors concerning file types and saving work when using digital audio. Most software supports MP3 and WAV files. However, MP3 files compress the data more to give smaller file sizes, which is an important factor to consider if children's work needs to be transferred between machines or indeed uploaded to the school website or virtual learning environment. Audacity can be used to convert between file types. There are also numerous online converters available.

There is an array of software and hardware to support children's development of knowledge and understanding in music and the main focus of this chapter has been on those resources, which lend themselves towards more creative uses of technology in music. For teachers to make effective use of ICT in music they must have a critical view of the technology and an understanding of the opportunities it affords both the teacher and the learner in relation to the development of their subject knowledge. It may be, for example, that it is far better for children to beat a real drum to a piece of music or song than create a rhythmic pattern in a computer program if we want to develop their ability to hold a steady beat. Similarly, to develop children's control of pitch they need plenty of opportunities to find their own voice through singing and performing live music together. However, we have also shown through this chapter that working with digital audio is a vitally important aspect in the development of children's digital literacy.

A SUMMARY OF **KEY POINTS**

➤ **ICT should not be used as a substitute for traditional ways of making music.**

➤ **There is a wealth of software and hardware that can be utilised to enrich and develop children's digital literacy when working with audio.**

➤ **It is vital for teachers to develop their own capabilities with audio and music applications before implementing them in the classroom.**

> A sound knowledge and understanding of the music curriculum should underpin any use of technology to support children's learning in music.
> Music and soundscapes can enhance literacy work with poems and stories.
> Podcasts can support teaching and learning in a range of subjects.

M-LEVEL EXTENSION > > M-LEVEL EXTENSION > > M-LEVEL EXTENSION

Understanding sound is an aspect of science that may benefit from setting in a cross-curricular context. An obvious link can be made to music, exploring the sounds made by a range of different instruments, including tuned and untuned percussion, and discussing tone, pitch and timbre. But there are other curriculum areas and subjects that you could consider, for example designing sound-making machines and finding out how microphones, loudspeakers and radios work in technology, and using editing programs to add sound effects to a story or play that the children have written and recorded in their literacy work. How could this be planned for the particular year group you are working with or across each of the primary phases?

REFERENCES REFERENCES **REFERENCES** REFERENCES REFERENCES REFERENCES

Audacity, **http://audacity.sourceforge.net/** (accessed 20 January 2014).

AudioBoo, **http://audioboo.fm/** (accessed 20 January 2014).

DfE (2013) *Digital Technology in Schools.* Available at **www.education.gov.uk/a00201823/digital-technology-in-schools**

Freeplay Music, **http://freeplaymusic.com/** (accessed 20 January 2014).

Freesound, http://freesound.org/ (accessed 15 April 2014).

GarageBand, http://apple.com/uk/mac/garageband/ (accessed 15 April 2014).

Riley, F. (no date) *Media Repositories for E-learning*. Available at **www.fredriley.org.uk/callhull/elearning/media** (accessed 20 January 2014).

Sing Up, http://singup.org/ (accessed 15 April 2014).

Sound Cloud, **https://soundcloud.com/** (accessed 20 January 2014).

FURTHER READING FURTHER READING **FURTHER READING** FURTHER READING

Jones, P. and Robson, C. (2008) *Teaching Music in Primary Schools.* Exeter: Learning Matters

Creating Music, **www.creatingmusic.com/** (accessed 20 January 2014).

Soundhub, Music Education Kent, **http://soundhubkent.com/** (accessed 20 January 2014).

Sound2Picture, **www.ucanplay.tv/** (accessed 20 January 2014).

16
The internet

Introduction

This chapter aims to introduce you to ways in which the internet is used to support and enhance learning, and to give you a basic introduction to how some aspects of the internet and world wide web work. In recent years, larger numbers of teachers and children have been working in spaces which are not open to the wider internet, such as secure password-protected online areas known as virtual learning environments (VLEs) (see Chapter 17). There are also exciting developments which exploit the potential of the internet for collaboration, publication and communication using the tools of 'social software', which we discuss further in Chapter 17. This chapter should be read alongside Chapter 19, *E-safety*. E-safety is such an important issue that it needs more in-depth coverage in a separate chapter.

What are the internet and the world wide web?

In everyday communication, people refer to the internet and/or the world wide web (WWW) interchangeably. Technically, the WWW is in fact only one part of the internet, being made up of hypertext pages containing text, images, sounds and animations interconnected via hyperlinks. These pages provide information, opinion, archive material, music, video and up-to-the moment news and images. Some provide software and games to download, while others act as portals or gateways, existing merely to provide links to a range of other pages. Anyone can publish pages on the WWW. All web pages are written in coding languages such as the original hypertext mark up language (HTML). Your browser (Internet Explorer, Firefox, Google Chrome) interprets the data transferred via the internet and makes it readable and presentable on your device/screen. Thus, an accessible way to conceive of the WWW is that it is the content, whereas the internet is the actual infrastructure of wires, cables, wireless and satellite connections, routers, servers and physical devices that constitute the global network via which data is transferred.

PRACTICAL TASK PRACTICAL TASK PRACTICAL TASK PRACTICAL TASK

Watch the video 'How the Internet Works' at the following link: www.youtube.com/watch?v=VXg_HGgo7Qs&noredirect=1 (Common Craft, 2011). Use the internet to find some more videos that explain how the internet and the WWW work. Familiarise yourself with what 'servers' do and what an IP address is. As you research the question 'how does the internet and world wide web work?' look out for any inaccuracies or discrepancies in the information you find. Think about how you could help children to understanding how the internet and WWW work.

The internet is a communications tool and much of the communication it facilitates takes place via the world wide web. However, a plethora of new forms of communication have emerged with the growth of the internet, for example: e-mail, discussion forums, audio and video conferencing and, more recently, new genres of communication epitomised by social networking tools such as Twitter and Snapchat. With the emergence of different genres of communication, there have also emerged new conventions for how we communicate. For example, conventions associated with electronic mail (e-mail), often referred to as 'netiquette', have grown up, such as a lack of formality, tolerance of spelling errors and a prohibition on spam (unsolicited or junk e-mail). However, it is also true to say that the emergence and establishment of new conventions are not straightforward and tend to be shaped more by the user context. For example, levels of formality may vary greatly between the social use of e-mail and the professional use.

More recently, the potential of the internet to shape the way we engage with our physical world has begun to be explored further. That is, while the internet is essentially a communication tool, it not only enables us to communicate with other people, but can also facilitate increased digital interaction with our physical environment as the objects we engage with can be programmed to respond in different ways, as we explore in the following reflection.

REFLECTIVE TASK

Watch the video 'What is the Internet of Things?' at the following link: **www.youtube.com/watch?v=LVIT4sX6uVs** (FW Thinking, 2013). Think about how we engage with the internet, and how it has changed over the duration of your life. What is your response to some of the future predictions regarding the 'internet of things' highlighted in this video? Think about the ways in which algorithms are currently used to build computational thinking into our physical environment, as discussed in Chapter 12. What could be some of the moral and ethical issues underlying the predictions made in the video 'What is the Internet of Things?'

What do the programmes of study for Key Stages 1 and 2 include?

While we have included the strands referring specifically to e-safety here, these are dealt with in more detail and depth in Chapter 19. What you will notice as you explore the programme of study in relation to the internet is that there is a clear expectation – made more explicit in the Key Stage 2 programme of study – that children are taught about how technologies such as the internet and world wide web actually work as well as developing their digital literacy in order to use these technologies effectively and critically. Think about these two aspects as you explore the relevant parts of the programme of study outlined below.

Key Stage 1

- Use technology purposefully to create, organise, store, manipulate and retrieve digital content.
- Use technology safely and respectfully, keeping personal information private; know where to go for help and support when they have concerns about material on the internet.
- Recognise common uses of information technology beyond school.

Key Stage 2

- Understand computer networks including the internet; how they can provide multiple services, such as the world wide web; and the opportunities they offer for communication and collaboration.

- Use search technologies effectively, appreciate how results are selected and ranked, and be discerning in evaluating digital content.
- Use technology safely, respectfully and responsibly; know a range of ways to report concerns and inappropriate behaviour.
- Select, use and combine a variety of software (including internet services) on a range of digital devices to accomplish given goals, including collecting, analysing, evaluating and presenting data and information.

What does the internet contribute to teaching and learning?

The pervasive nature of the internet make it essential that children develop their knowledge and understanding of both how the internet and the world wide web work to provide a plethora of services and how to make effective and critical use of such facilities. These principles underpin the design of the new programme of study for computing, as highlighted above. It is a given that the internet is now a feature of life within and outside formal settings of education. Its influence is all-pervasive in daily activities, from shopping and banking to downloading music and video. There are increasing numbers of viewers online for the various video-sharing sites, such as YouTube, which are drawing people away from the traditional broadcast media. The latest computers from both Mac and PC vendors place the internet and media-sharing at the heart of their respective operating systems in such a way as to make it seem obvious and inevitable that a user would be part of the online world from the moment the computer is switched on.

While we cannot assume that all learners have access to these all-pervasive facilities and services at home, there are very many ways to be connected to and to use the internet even without personal ownership of a computer. For school children, this is sometimes the computer in the classroom or network room at school, perhaps even after school in community use of the facilities in an extended day or in a local library or internet café. Many mobile devices also provide access. Next we will consider what the internet and world wide web can contribute to teaching and learning before going on to consider the underlying knowledge and understanding that teachers and children need to develop.

Research

The opportunities for finding things out via the internet are almost limitless. Teachers can research subject knowledge, teaching ideas and resources. Accessing such information efficiently and effectively is vital to ensure that they and their classes can benefit from the professional information at their disposal.

Well-organised and well-managed research activities on the world wide web can be visually and intellectually engaging as well as developing children's understanding of electronic texts and the use of a range of media to communicate information effectively. The development and practical application of higher-order reading skills, such as keyword searching, skimming and scanning, are key, as are strategies for effective use of search tools. Caution must, however, be exercised, as already noted, as not all the information accessed may be current, appropriate or even accurate.

E-mail and video-conferencing provide opportunities for asking direct and purposeful questions, as well as making comparisons and collecting data. Similarly, there is a range of 'ask an expert' websites, through which children can seek information directly from historians or authors.

The world wide web also provides children with opportunities to find things out from other children via web pages. This can be valuable in all sorts of ways, such as providing models at levels children can aspire to – children's poems, for instance, as most poems children read are written by adults. Children's science, geography or RE work may be sources of information expressed in language accessible to primary children.

Collaboration and communication

Collaboration is facilitated by communication and the internet provides a variety of channels for this. Children can contribute stories, poems and reviews to a range of websites. They can also respond to others' contributions. Such sites also model authors' story-starts and provide plentiful opportunities for reading online. See Chapter 17 on social media and later in this chapter for further ideas and information on this.

Children may post part-completed or drafted work on school web pages and invite responses to help them develop their work. This might be a D&T design, a poem or a piece of music. Responding to others' work can help children articulate and apply their own knowledge, skills and understanding.

Person-to-person exchanges, such as those by electronic pen friends, are facilitated by the internet. This can add an element of speed to the communication, maintaining interest and relevance for the correspondents.

The global online community works because people are prepared to share information and resources with others, often without charge. There are a number of sites where schools can access environmental data on weather from around the country and the world. Schools can post their own data, either as a *quid pro quo* for utilising information from other schools, or merely for the satisfaction of adding to the wealth of available resources. Similarly, publishing children's project work on the web enables them to share it with people they know, parents and other relatives, as well as people they don't, such as children in an elementary school in the USA. Posting lists of links to useful online resources can save other teachers time and effort.

Understanding computer networks and the internet

We have already discussed in the introductory sections of this chapter some of the core knowledge that teachers and children need to understand regarding the difference between the internet and the world wide web and also how these work, but there are other important features that are useful for teachers and children alike to understand. We will turn to these now.

Synchronous and asynchronous communication

The terms synchronous and asynchronous are used to describe different forms of communication online. Synchronous is 'real-time' communication where two or more people communicate at the same time. Asynchronous communication is when a discussion may occur over a longer period of time, giving participants much more time to think about their responses. Electronic discussion or conferencing takes a variety of forms and formats. There are electronic bulletin boards or newsgroups where information or queries can be posted related to a specific subject or interest. These often lead to detailed exchanges of information and opinion between several contributors. Some individuals find it useful to watch the discussion without necessarily contributing themselves. Access to such asynchronous discussions can be restricted (for instance, to members of a professional association) or they can be open.

A similar function can be provided through e-mail. In this case it is called a 'listserv' and is essentially an e-mail distribution list with all participants automatically being circulated with each contribution. A newsgroup or listserv may be mediated by an individual who checks each contribution for relevance before it is posted.

As highlighted, e-mail and the electronic discussion possibilities described above are known as 'asynchronous'. Users can read others' contributions and respond at a time convenient to them. Communication is not dependent on the contributors being available at the same time.

Access to synchronous discussion, where the participants are online at the same time, is also available through a range of tools, from instant messaging through to video chat (in, for example, Skype or FaceTime). Electronic conferences can be established where specified participants meet online and contribute to a real-time discussion. Conferencing can utilise text, audio or video (video-conferencing). Generally, specific software is used for each of these.

Navigating the world wide web

It is useful to know and understand what is going on behind the scenes when we navigate the world wide web. As you probably already know from your own use of the internet, navigation is via pointing and clicking on hypertext links. These links take the user from one hypertext document to another. The cursor will become a hand symbol when it is moved over a hypertext link. For regular users of the internet this is something that is done without thinking. You may find that there are children who use these interfaces instinctively but there will be others who will need some specific input into simple navigational tasks. So how does navigation work?

Although any website may have any number of pages linked together, each of these pages is essentially a separate document and has its own individual uniform resource locator or URL. This is the web page address and it is this unique URL which enables navigation through the almost limitless range of web pages. URLs may at first appear confusing, although familiarity quickly enables the user to decode and even predict some URLs. Briefly, using as an example the URL **http://www.yorksj.ac.uk/research/**

- http stands for hypertext transport protocol and means the document is being accessed through hypertext. It is a protocol because it is using a recognised set of rules to translate and transform the bits of information transmitted to your computer into the format you see on your screen;
- www.stands for world wide web;
- yorksj is the name of the server being accessed, in this case York St John University, and this is the server on which the web page being accessed is stored;
- ac stands for academic – all academic institutions in the UK have this as part of their URL: **http://www.exeter.ac.uk/** is Exeter University. Find out what .org .com and .sch stand for in URLs;

- .uk means that the site is based in the United Kingdom; similarly .es is Spain; an address without a country designation is usually based in the USA;
- /research is the directory or pathway on the server in which the specific page is located, i.e. where the document is stored.

When you find something, remember that you can do one of two things. First, you can add the site to your list of 'Bookmarks' or 'Favourites' so that you do not have to search for it again. However, if you are on another person's computer this will simply add the link to their personal list of sites. In order to see the link from any computer you will need to set up some online bookmarks with a resource such as del.icio.us (see Chapter 17 on social software).

Searching the world wide web

Locating useful resources on the world wide web may be time-consuming. Search engines such as Google produce hundreds of possible pages as results from plain text searches, only some of which will be relevant and useful. Many teachers search for useful information as part of the planning process and gather together some useful links or pages as a list in advance of a lesson. Unless you are specifically teaching and learning about searching (which is something that is essential to do at some point), it will be a waste of the children's time to use up part of the time for basic resource location.

The reason for their variability is that search engines are huge databases which users can search with keywords or phrases. Search engines automatically trawl the web looking for sites and index them by keyword. This can mean that every word in a website is indexed regardless of context or relative importance, resulting in huge numbers of hits for any word or phrase searched, many of which may not be useful. Results are usually ranked in order of relevance, which can be helpful, although the criteria used to decide relevance may not match with the user's own ideas. Searching with combinations of words or phrases can result in fewer, more appropriate hits. Many search engines support a range of strategies and tools for refining searches. Practice will also improve the user's effectiveness in using a search engine.

Directories are the second common type of search engine and they allow users to progressively narrow down their search area by choosing categories and sub-categories, e.g. Yahoo! (**www.yahoo.com**/). There are some similarities to branching or binary databases that we examined in Chapter 11. Some form of human mediation is usually involved in organising these directories and formulating the searching algorithms by which they operate. Productive searching may as a result be faster. The number of websites included in a directory is likely to be smaller than that covered by a search engine. Most search directories also support keyword or phrase searching.

Children's internet access at school is often filtered by the local authority or regional broadband supplier, meaning that open text searches on the internet are usually (though not always) safer. When using more popular adult search engines in a school setting, where the access is not controlled, there is a greater risk of receiving results in an open text search which may be inappropriate (see also Chapter 19 on e-safety and acceptable use policies). If you are looking for resources with children, and you want them to use a search engine facility themselves, it is a good idea to use the safer junior version of the search engine, such as 'Yahooligans', a cut-down version of 'Yahoo'.

PRACTICAL TASK PRACTICAL TASK PRACTICAL TASK PRACTICAL TASK

Use two different search engines and carry out a keyword search for:

- information related to a specific part of the National Curriculum programmes of study, for example, habitats. Compare how many results (hits) you get from each search engine and how long it takes. Think about how the search engines can return so many results in such a short time. Computer Science Unplugged (see http://csunplugged.org/) is a useful resource for illustrating many principles of computer science, including how computer scientists design fast-searching algorithms to help search vast amounts of data quickly. For example, try the activity, Divide and Conquer at http://csunplugged.org/divideAndConquer.

Advanced searching

Most search tools now support both keyword and categorised searching. For many users, especially when starting out, search tools can be frustratingly unproductive. Perseverance and the use of some advanced or Boolean searching strategies will usually turn up something useful. The term 'Boolean' originates from the nineteenth-century English mathematician George Boole because the search strategies themselves are based on a form of logic that he developed.

Boolean searching involves the use of operators such as AND, OR and NOT. These can be used to refine searches by combining or excluding words or phrases:

AND narrows a search, such that only sites that contain both keywords will be displayed, e.g. information AND technology;

OR widens a search, to include sites containing one or other, or both, of the keywords used, e.g. information OR technology;

NOT narrows a search, by excluding sites containing the keyword which follows it, e.g. information NOT technology.

Often the Boolean operators must be in upper case, although it is important to check in the search tool being used. Some tools use the plus and minus sign to provide similar functions. Other useful strategies supported by a number of search tools include:

- the use of quotation marks around phrases, such as "information technology" – this will ensure that only sites in which the words appear in this order are found;
- wild cards – symbols which can be entered at the beginning or end of keywords or phrases, such as 'tech', and the search engine will then look for matches which contain words beginning with tech, but with a range of endings, such as technology, technologies, techniques and technical. The symbol used varies between search tools.

Search tools vary enormously. They also develop and change. It is worthwhile exploring the guidance given by the tools themselves – there is usually a wealth of information pointing towards more efficient and effective use. You could also use the website **www.searchenginewatch.com**, which is a comprehensive listing of search engines together with tutorials and rankings of the various services. As already mentioned above, the website Computer Science Unplugged (see **http://csunplugged.com/videos**) also has useful resources for teaching children about how search engines use different sorting algorithms to search the vast amount of data available.

There are many sites designed for teachers, providing access to resources, teaching ideas and discussion opportunities. Many of these are free, although there are some commercial services for which a subscription is payable. Searching in sites like these is likely to provide results more quickly than using general search tools. Additionally, the material provided may also be more closely matched to teachers' needs. One example is the BBC site **www.bbc.co.uk/schools/** which provides access to a huge range of curriculum resources.

A search tool with a UK focus can be helpful. This will reduce the range of sites searched, but results may be more closely matched to the user's requirements; using the UK version of Google is one example (**www.google.co.uk**). Similarly, some other search engines and directories will allow the user to search for UK sites only if required.

Information and resources for the core subjects

This is the information age. The world wide web contains unimaginable amounts of information. Some of it is incorrect, some of it is out of date, some of it is not relevant, but some of it is of a high quality and generously shared by its originator with the world-wide online community. Access to such a wealth of information is revolutionising many aspects of day-to-day life.

There is an unprecedented range of resources available via the internet, mostly freely available, including:

- channels for discussion and exchanges with peers with similar interests;
- activities developed by others and shared;
- free software downloads;
- lesson plans and ideas;
- video clips;
- audio clips;
- examples of children's work.

THE BIGGER PICTURE   THE BIGGER PICTURE   THE BIGGER PICTURE   THE BIGGER PICTURE

When you are planning to use the internet to source teaching resources or to discuss issues with colleagues, *TES* is a useful source. The weekly *TES Magazine* often has articles on resources for a range of subjects, especially ICT, and sometimes features 'Web star of the week', focusing on teachers who share resources by posting them on the *TES* website (**www.tes.co.uk**) for you to download. Many of these colleagues are also contributors in the online forums, and have regular blogs and Twitter feeds. But remember that while using resources produced or recommended by other experienced colleagues can save you a lot of valuable time, you must always check them out yourself and ensure that they are suitable for the children you are working with.

The ideas and activities discussed here are intended only to give a brief introductory feel for the range of ways in which the internet can be utilised to support and enhance teaching and learning in mathematics, science and English. They are not intended to be comprehensive, merely to go some way towards illustrating the breadth of possibilities and to provide starting points for the customisation of ideas and the generation of others. Examples introduced under mathematics, for example, may be just as applicable to one or more of the other areas and vice versa.

In English, there are very many websites that support a range of literacy-related activities. For example, Kent National Grid for Learning has developed a range of big books online featuring Sebastian Swan (**www.sebastianswan.org.uk**). These can be read online (see Figure 16.1) and are supported by a range of worked lesson plans and activity ideas and resources. Children are encouraged to e-mail Sebastian with their work, which may be displayed on the pin board. Sebastian also publishes a blog.

Another example is the Children's Story site at **www.childrenstory.com**, which enables the user to select a fairy story and hear it being read. Activities such as these can be followed up in a range of ways away from the computer.

For science, there may well be areas of the subject that are difficult to resource or provide few opportunities for practical activities. These are well catered for with child-centred web resources. The NASAKIDS site at **www.nasa.gov/audience/forkids/home/index.html** is visually engaging, often modelling through video and animation concepts which are counterintuitive and otherwise difficult to communicate.

For mathematics, there is a wide range of activities available online which can reinforce the acquisition of basic skills at the BBC's school portal at **www.bbc.co.uk/schools**. Children and their teachers can access websites to look for mathematics investigations which may then be carried out away from the computer. Such opportunities maximise the use of limited computer resources as well as providing access to well-thought-out activities. There is an increasing range of activities to support young children's mathematical activities, which may also be used to develop hand–eye co-ordination as well as reinforce early mathematics.

Figure 16.1 'Sebastian Swan' home page – direct access at
www.sebastianswan.org.uk

Many of the websites have teachers' areas with worksheets, activity ideas and lesson plans. For an example, see the mathematics area of Teaching Ideas at **www.teachingideas.co.uk**, which contains activity ideas and resources which may help teachers in managing the setting and marking of homework.

THE BIGGER PICTURE THE BIGGER PICTURE THE BIGGER PICTURE THE BIGGER PICTURE

When you are planning homework activities, they must, of course, be purposeful and either extend children's knowledge or understanding or consolidate a skill already learnt in school. You can involve parents in supporting even very young children's learning by sharing in advance the topics or aspects of the areas of learning that you plan to study. Many Nursery and Reception classes and other Early Years settings have regular newsletters for parents and you could ask to put a short article in this. This is helpful as a strategy for involving all parents, especially if you are asking children in Key Stages 1 and 2 to undertake 'finding out' tasks, as parents might plan a trip to their local library or want to supervise children's safe use of the internet.

PRACTICAL TASK PRACTICAL TASK PRACTICAL TASK PRACTICAL TASK

Download a lesson idea, worksheet or other resource from a suitable website. Draw up a lesson plan for a stated age group and subject focus detailing how you would make use of the resource to enhance or extend children's learning. (See Chapter 2 on planning for primary computing as a subject for ideas on how to do this.)

Issues in using the internet

Staying focused

The internet, and especially the world wide web, can be enthralling – the temptation for random exploration can be hard to resist. Teachers will need to manage children's tasks in order to ensure both their safety and the productivity of the activity. Use of bookmarked sites only, tightly focused tasks and time limiting can be appropriate strategies.

Reading level and language issues

The vast majority of web pages are aimed at an adult audience and may thus be difficult for primary children to comprehend. There are a number of strategies teachers can deploy in order to provide access to material which is accessible, including:

- the use of a search tool such as Ask Kids, which is designed to select sites which answer the query posed at an appropriate reading level;
- utilising web pages specifically written for children;
- utilising web pages recommended by other teachers;
- utilising children's work on school web pages.

Teachers may also be concerned about American web pages which display not only differences in vocabulary but also in the spellings of words. Children are exposed to US (and Australian) vocabulary through television, as are adults, and appear to have little difficulty with comprehension. Alternative spellings may provide more of a challenge, although they can also provide a teaching and learning opportunity. Teachers can make explicit the differences and discuss these with children – for instance, searching for information on the theme of 'colour' in a US-based search tool may be unproductive, although a parallel search using the US spelling could also be attempted.

Copyright and the web

Material placed on the world wide web remains the intellectual property of the author and is subject to copyright whether or not this is specifically stated. Copyright extends beyond text to images, animation and sound. However, it is generally accepted that material placed on the web is there for other people to use. Sometimes it will not be possible to copy and paste an image from a web page because the author has arranged the programming to prevent this. Similarly, it may be possible to listen to a sound file, but not to download it. It is good practice to acknowledge the source of any material from the web and to encourage children to do the same. Further information is available from the Copyright Licensing Agency at **www.cla.co.uk** and the Copyright Web Site at **www.benedict.com**/. Children should also be introduced to the concept of sharing content under a Creative Commons license, which allows other people to use and re-use digital content under certain regulations. More information about Creative Commons can be found at the following website: **http://creativecommons.org**/.

Currency and authenticity

There is a lot of concern about the currency and authenticity of materials available on the world wide web. The potential to access up-to-the-moment satellite weather photographs, breaking world news stories, images from space as they are received from missions, or real-time videos of bird eggs hatching is exhilarating. However, there are lots of websites which are not regularly maintained and in which the information displayed may be outdated. This can be frustrating and schools must also do their bit to ensure that their own web pages are current. Many web pages include information giving the date on which they were last updated. This can be a useful guide.

Authenticity is often harder to assess. Anyone can upload information to the world wide web or circulate it via e-mail, newsgroups or listservs. There is no editing process, as there is with any published book, newspaper or magazine, and thus material, particularly from unfamiliar sources, must be viewed critically. It may be partial, misleading or inaccurate. Comparing information from the internet with that from other sources for substantiation and corroboration can be a teaching and learning objective in itself. Some high-quality websites are subject to an editing process, such as the BBC, **www.bbc.co.uk**, and newspapers, e.g. **www.guardian.co.uk**. Children need to be taught about these issues so that they can be critical and discerning in their use of content.

PRACTICAL TASK PRACTICAL TASK **PRACTICAL TASK** PRACTICAL TASK

There are numerous bogus websites such as the one about a so-called tree octopus at this link **http://zapatopi. net/treeoctopus**/. Explore the website and identify the strategies that have been used to make this appear an authentic website. Think about how you could use a site like this to develop children's knowledge and understanding about how to question and validate the information they find on the world wide web.

Vocabulary and jargon

A vast new vocabulary is emerging related to computing and ICT, a lot of it related to the internet and some of it found in this chapter. In common with children's language development in maths or science, it is important that they develop a vocabulary which enables them to articulate their ideas, understanding, intentions and problems. Deciding when and how much vocabulary to introduce is an important professional consideration for teachers.

Printing from websites

Web pages can be printed using the icon on the browser, or selecting Print via a menu. This will print the whole of the current web page, which may be rather more than is expected. There is nothing to limit the length of web pages to the amount visible on screen at any one time, or even to A4. The web page author can make the page any length at all. Printing out long pages can be time-consuming and expensive. It is useful to get into the habit of copying and pasting text and images to be printed into a word processing package and to encourage this strategy with children. This ensures that only the text and images actually required are printed, and the document length can be assessed before a decision on printing is made.

Digital division

There is increasing concern that the internet is leading to a digital division in society in the UK, with information (and skill) haves and have-nots. Concern focuses on the potential for children (and adults) who do not have access to online resources to be seriously disadvantaged as a result. This issue is increasingly relevant for primary schools as home computer ownership continues to expand. Many children live in families for whom computer ownership may not be a reality. Schools are beginning to consider the implications for entitlement and equality of opportunities. Free internet access is available via many public libraries and the availability of such community facilities is increasing. Some schools make computer facilities available before and after school to address this issue.

School websites and publishing on the internet

Many schools have websites which provide a medium of communication and publication for the school community. Over the last few years many of these school websites have been absorbed into virtual learning environments (VLEs) and other social software environments or platforms (see Chapter 17).

Publishing on the internet is available at a number of different levels. If you become interested in publishing for yourself and others, you could consider using one of the social software tools for blogging or you could use a web-publishing package which generates the necessary coding in the web page authoring language HTML. Some schools operate and teachers publish their own blogs using tools such as WordPress, Weebly, Edublogs and Tumblr. There are many possibilities for authoring and publishing on the world wide web which involve creating content from templates, and which are well within the capabilities of primary school children. Some of these tools also allow users to edit both using templates or through writing and editing HTML code (see Chapter 17).

A SUMMARY OF **KEY POINTS**

➤ The internet is a global network of computers supporting communication through the world wide web, e-mail and conferencing, and there are special features which make it useful in supporting teaching and learning.

➤ Schools are increasingly active in the online community, searching, retrieving, analysing and synthesising information as well as developing, trialling and publishing their own.

➤ It is important that teachers and children develop their knowledge and understanding of how the internet and the world wide web work.

➤ Critical evaluation of web-based resources is vital to ensure suitability, accuracy and safety.

➤ Through its many facets the internet has the potential to support teachers in their day-to-day work in the classroom as well as their continuing professional development.

M-LEVEL EXTENSION > > M-LEVEL EXTENSION > > M-LEVEL EXTENSION

Carry out further research on how the internet works. Much of the internet remains a mystery for many adults and children. How is it, for example, that a photograph can be sent from one side of the world to the other in a matter of seconds? Find out about packet switching; for example, why is this important to the transportation of data via the internet? Watch this video by James May about how the internet works: **www.youtube.com/watch?v=C3sr7_0FyPA**. When you have found out more about these aspects of the internet, think about how you could develop children's understanding of how data is transmitted and received across the internet. For example, could you use role play to model this?

REFERENCES REFERENCES **REFERENCES** REFERENCES REFERENCES REFERENCES

BBC schools website at **www.bbc.co.uk/schools/** (accessed 21 January 2014).

Children's Story site at **www.childrenstory.com** (accessed 21 January 2014).

Common Craft (2011) *How the Internet Works*. Available at **www.youtube.com/watch?v=VXg_HGgo7Qs** (accessed 21 January 2014).

Creative Commons, **http://creativecommons.org/** (accessed 21 January 2014).

Computer Science Unplugged, **http://csunplugged.com/videos** (accessed 21 January 2014).

DfE (2011) *Teachers' Standards.* Available at **www.education.gov.uk/publications**

DfE (2013) *National Curriculum in England: Primary Curriculum.* London: DfE. Available at **www.gov.uk/government/publications/national-curriculum-in-england-primary-curriculum**

Delicious social bookmarking site, **www.delicious.com** (accessed 21 January 2014).

FW Thinking (2013) *What is the Internet of Things?* Available at **www.youtube.com/watch?v=LVIT4sX6uVs** (accessed 21 January 2014).

NASA website at **www.nasa.gov/audience/forkids/home/index.html** (accessed 21 January 2014).

Search Engine Watch. Available at **www.searchenginewatch.com** (accessed 21 January 2014).

Sebastian Swan website at **www.sebastianswan.org.uk** (accessed 21 January 2014).

Teaching Ideas. Available at **www.teachingideas.co.uk** (accessed 21 January 2014).

TES (The Times Educational Supplement). Available at **www.tes.co.uk** (accessed 21 January 2014).

Tree Octopus. Available at **http://zapatopi.net/treeoctopus/** (accessed 21 January 2014).

FURTHER READING   FURTHER READING   **FURTHER READING**   FURTHER READING

Bell, T., Witten, I.H. and Fellows, M. (2010) *Computer Science Unplugged: An Enrichment and Extension Programme for Primary-aged Children*. Available at **http://csunplugged.org/sites/default/files/activity_pdfs_full/unpluggedTeachersMar2010-USletter.pdf** (accessed 21 January 2014).

Meadows, J. and Millar, K. (2006) Networking people and computers, in M. Leask and J. Meadows (eds), *Teaching and Learning with ICT in the Primary School*. Oxford: Routledge.

17
Social media:
Tools for communicating, collaborating and publishing

Introduction

Perhaps the greatest opportunities for cross-curricular work as well as deepening understanding of computing and ICT arise from the careful use of 'social media', those online environments which depend on communication, a shared understanding of ways of presenting ideas, resources and, ultimately, of self-publication/broadcast. These include, but are not limited to Twitter, Facebook, WordPress, Edublogs and many, many others. With careful use and regard for pupil safety, these environments can provide authentic and rich experiences for communicating, collaborating and publishing as well as learning about how the internet works. Most importantly, perhaps, social media in the world outside school is likely to be very much a part of the way of life of the children you encounter and teach, just as much as it is a part of yours. To varying degrees, and for better or worse, the children in your immediate care will have access to the wider social media spaces of the internet and they will certainly see their parents experiencing many kinds of all-pervasive communicative media. Even in poorer homes with lower ownership of equipment, the social media world makes inroads in the form of posting and commenting, private instant messaging, and long-distance family relationships are maintained through video call software such as Skype, or similar, and more.

What do the programmes of study for Key Stages 1 and 2 include?

Working with social media across the programmes of study in a range of curriculum contexts to provide an authentic space for enquiry, discussion and collaboration is perhaps the most obvious use. However, there are many key elements of the National Curriculum for computing and ICT which can be explicitly planned for, in order to meet the overarching stated aim of ensuring that pupils 'are responsible, competent, confident and creative users of information and communication technology'.

Key Stage 1

- Use technology purposefully to create, organise, store, manipulate and retrieve digital content.
- Recognise common uses of information technology beyond school.
- Use technology safely and respectfully, keeping personal information private; identify where to go for help and support when they have concerns about content or contact on the internet or other online technologies.

Key Stage 2

- Understand computer networks, including the internet; how they can provide multiple services, such as the world wide web, and the opportunities they offer for communication and collaboration.

- Select, use and combine a variety of software (including internet services) on a range of digital devices to accomplish given goals.
- Use technology safely, respectfully and responsibly; recognise acceptable/unacceptable behaviour; identify a range of ways to report concerns about content and contact.

Starting points for working with social media – what do teachers need to know? What is available to use?

For primary schools, the exploration and use of social media is often thought of as problematic in that many of them are open-ended, open-source and open-use (and therefore open to abuse). However, the tools which have emerged that make these sorts of sites possible have, on occasion, been adopted and adapted into safe environments for education. Such tools as 'blogs' or 'wikis' can and do form parts of virtual learning environments (VLEs), enabling children to produce and edit their own online versions of themselves and their work which, in turn, invites communication from peers in the form of comments, questions, criticisms, etc. What social media offer are increasingly authentic publishing opportunities and rich environments for writing and exhibiting media production.

As noted in the introduction to the chapter, children of primary school age may well encounter some of the tools of 'social media' outside school, even if these are not the same spaces which you use. They are also subject to rapid changes and patterns of use. Examples which younger learners may use more than Facebook include child-friendly spaces such as Club Penguin or Moshi Monsters, which are not unlike social media in some of their functions. These may often have tie-ins to other forms of media products in a world in which media convergence is a given (see Jenkins, 2006). As far as Facebook is concerned, evidence suggests that the generation entering their teens now uses rapid sharing apps such as Snapchat and simple blog publishing like Tumblr instead of the more detailed and formal looking spaces of Facebook. Children whom you teach may well have seen parents, friends or siblings using these social media. Templates in all these spaces enable the creation of sophisticated-looking pages online. It should be stressed at the outset that all of these sites are places where the content is sometimes inappropriate. The onward links from people's pages, however innocent they appear at first, cannot all be vetted and verified. For this reason, there is a tendency for such sites to be blocked for users in schools. However, the principle of one's own desktop and publishing space with the associated freedom to publish, comment and collaborate in a safe way is enshrined in many local and regional VLEs.

Outside the VLE and on the wider internet are a range of blogging services for education which allow for similar experiences of publishing for real audiences. Blogs are online journals or diaries, on any subject, often with rich media content (for more on this see Rettberg, 2008). 'Edublogs' is a blogging space especially created with education users in mind and is built on the same easy-to-use platform as one of the major free blog providers, WordPress (see Figure 17.1).

The Edublogs homepage (**http://edublogs.org/schools/**) has a user-friendly interface and a series of useful global links, although these are dominated by educators and classrooms

Fabulous fractions wp.me/p3gGSV-pTELi
1 week ago

5SC 100 day Ancient Greece.
Olympics animals art assembly
Boccia Book Week Brighton
celebrations changing materials
Childrens Rights
Christmas conscience alley
cooking Creative
writing Dick Whittington
Diwali dress up day DT Easter
eco electricity Fairtrade
fireworks Fractions
geography Great Fire green flag
Harvest history home
learning inclusion independent
learning Juniors learning partners
Lets Dance literacy
London Maths

China and dragons

Today we have been thinking about the country of China. (Beth) We have been learning about differences and the sames. (Bobby)

Our thinking skill was to think of things we know about Chinese dragons. (Izzy) We made a design with our learning partners to make a toy out of recycled stuff. (Beth) learning leaders met to design badges (Mia) We did dragon dancing - we had a dragons head, the body, and the pearl of wisdom to lead the dragon. We played the instruments and even made the videos. Have a look at our lovely day!

Figure 17.1 Teacher, Tracey Bowers' class blog, Hertford Infant and Nursery School, Brighton. Photo by Ruth Simon-House.

in the United States. There are significant numbers of UK educators on there too who wish to administer a live writing and documenting presence for the work they undertake in their classrooms. The claims made for this are that it gives writing an 'authenticity' for the end-user. It is worth stating that it is also possible to be inauthentic in social media, as much as it is anywhere else, and that the technology by itself does not confer any useful agency on the children. Skilled, student-centred pedagogy brings out the best in the children by presenting them with huge opportunities to develop an audience and to reach out and engage with digital culture. The usual repeated caveats about safety are as important here as anywhere.

IN THE CLASSROOM – A RECENT SUCCESSFUL BLOGGING INITIATIVE

One of the most recent and successful examples of blogging is the simple and effective structure devised by David Mitchell, a primary school Deputy Headteacher from Bolton, whose method, known as 'Quadblogging', enables groups of up to four schools at a time to blog between each other over a four-week period, taking it in turns to be the focus and commenters on each other's work. The originating school has passed over a million hits and the main issue with blogs (that they start well but rarely stay maintained) is circumvented by the onward momentum and drive that inheres from having an audience and a purpose. See **www.quadblogging.com** (Mitchell, 2014). Again, this is something which is worthy of investigation while keeping in mind that human agency is what keeps it going; the technology by itself confers no agency nor any guarantee of success in the venture.

Like many social media services, Edublogs are synchronised across devices and enable users to develop a sense of themselves as connected to the outside world and to their developing achievements as writers. For those children who are at the very earliest stages of writing and whom you would nevertheless like to connect with other children and places beyond the school through social media, you could consider using a micro-blogging tool such as the phenomenally popular, Twitter, where, as you probably know, users publish in short, 140-character pieces. This requires an active policy of policing and protecting younger users, but it can be done very effectively, as shown below.

EXAMPLE SOCIAL MEDIA USE WITH YOUNGER LEARNERS: TWITTER

Publishing in the form of a micro-blog of only 140 characters per post, Twitter has received some attention as a social media space which has potential value in the classroom, particularly for younger learners. A teacher called Martin Waller used it with his class of 6 year olds who had a shared Twitter identity which he moderated, effectively making himself the firewall. This is a big responsibility, but he has written of the very positive impact on the children of being able to publish their thoughts and actions to a wide audience, giving their writing a genuine purpose beyond the sometimes limited world of the classroom (see Waller, 2012).

Twitter, Edublogs, Wordpress could also all be used in conjunction with synchronised, note-taking software that is available across desktops and tablets, such as Evernote. A personalised and agentive approach to children's own record-keeping of their work would see a combination of snapped pictures and videos, scrapbooked electronically into spaces such as Evernote for access at home and at school. It has been successfully used in other settings and in other projects, such as Keri Facer and Helen Manchester's Learning Lives project (Facer and Manchester, 2012).

Other kinds of social media sites for sharing content

In addition to the communicative, self-curated and self-broadcasting social media sites, such as Facebook and Twitter, are the websites which host user-generated content, such as, for example, Flickr; this may well be a photo-sharing website that you also make use of from time to time. Indeed, sites such as Flickr are a rich source of digital photographs, uploaded by users and given tags to make them searchable by others, including those uploading and using the same tags. Thus, pictures of, for example, a trip to the Science Museum in London to view a gaming exhibition, 'Game on', could be uploaded to Flickr or similar and given label categories, known as 'tags', of 'London' 'Museum' 'Computer game' 'Science' 'Exhibition'. People viewing Flickr may search for the pictures which you have taken and uploaded by the tag you have used. Furthermore, you and your class may search for pictures taken of the same place – sometimes at the same time – for the purposes of onward communication, shared commentaries on public spaces, and so on.

Flickr and similar sites are a way to share images between home and school with the caveat that you still require a shared internet policy to enable the publication of pictures featuring children who may be recognised. The same sort of sharing and tagging applies to video images in sites such as YouTube, which are popular exhibition spaces for digital video projects. Indeed, the whole vexed issue of blocking YouTube or not is one which confounds many schools. Blocking is a popular way of protecting children from inappropriate content or, more likely, surprisingly offensive and inappropriate comments on highly appropriate content. There is no easy answer to this issue, but one approach is to recognise the unique repository of popular cultural and curriculum-related content on YouTube which is available freely. Inevitably, there is a high cost overhead in terms of your effort to police access to all this in real time (assuming YouTube is not blocked in your school). Many teachers simply conclude that they need to use their own time to download the source video file using one of the many converters available (such as zamzar.com) and show it to their class without any worries from linked content, offensive commenting on the clip or any adverts which are also worthy of blocking. For further reading on social media used in this way, see *DIY Media* (Knobel and Lankshear, 2010) and *New Literacies: Everyday Practices and Social Learning* (Lankshear and Knobel, 2011).

The idea of co-authoring is extended into factual writing by the creation of online reference texts in wikis – collaborative writing tools. Thus, Wikipedia has grown exponentially into an enormous reference resource, edited (and policed) by its creators to allow contributions from a wide range of co-authors, all of whom are writing from personal knowledge and experience. Although generally considered to be one of the safer sites for social software authors to visit, there is by no means universal understanding or approval of the site in formal educational circles. The tools which allow collaborative writing have, however, sometimes been adapted into wikis in shared areas in VLEs.

A further social software tool which you should consider for your own personal use is one of the many sites which allow the tagging and categorisation of particular bookmarked websites. You can create an online collection of websites which you use regularly by tagging them with labels that enable you to locate them more frequently. Examples here would include Delicious and Diigo (which can be found by adding a .com to those names). The advantage over traditional bookmarking is that the list is synchronised across computers, tablets and smartphones. If you move location frequently, or use more than one computer in a day, these sites enable you to keep track of the useful resources you discover. There is also the possibility of enabling sharing, of seeing what other people are finding through their use of a particular tag. As usual, one of the caveats here is a thorough exploration of the safety policy of the school and the site yourself to ensure that children are not at risk and that they will report to you anything that makes them uncomfortable. The other caveat is to remember that sites move and re-purpose themselves; Delicious has been taken over twice, for example. It is always worth checking resource recommendations and functionality for yourself. One suggested purpose of Delicious is to create group lists of resources in an online account administered at the school, perhaps one per class. Again, an important consideration here will be the safety angle and the lack of wishing to duplicate on functions which may have been adapted into your local VLE already.

Conclusion

This brief survey of social media has attempted to provide you with some suggestions and starting points for an exploration of an area of great opportunity for schools to use. Social media allow children to be productive in spaces which really do have an audience, for whom they can learn to write and create. They afford the opportunity of learning beyond the classroom by connecting to other schools and other classes and, safety caveats notwithstanding, allow for your leaners to develop a rich understanding of both the internet as it used every day and of any of the subjects of the curriculum which you choose to make the subject of posts and creative activity.

A SUMMARY OF **KEY POINTS**

➢ Schools and their children are increasingly active in the online community, searching, retrieving, analysing and synthesising information as well as developing, trialling and publishing their own.

➢ There are clear benefits in working in linked spaces across synchronised devices.

➢ It appears that children and young people respond well to real opportunities to publish and to see their work online, and experience the positive impact of others critiquing their work.

➢ Critical evaluation of web-based resources is vital to ensure suitability, accuracy and safety. Try any social media spaces yourself and/or seek the advice of other teachers using them through Twitter or blogs before you use them with children; always do so with permission from parents and school managers.

M-LEVEL EXTENSION > > M-LEVEL EXTENSION > > M-LEVEL EXTENSION

Consider the range of opportunities for the use of the internet in teaching and learning. What is the likely impact of the use of blogging and social software, possibly within a VLE, on your role in the classroom? How might this be a way to join subjects together in cross-curricular projects? What are the issues that must be taken into account when using the internet in this way?

REFERENCES REFERENCES **REFERENCES** REFERENCES REFERENCES REFERENCES

Delicious social bookmarking site, **www.delicious.com** (accessed 21 January 2014).

Diigo social bookmarking site, **www.diigo.com** (accessed 21 January 2014).

Edublogs, **http://edublogs.org/schools** (accessed 4 February 2014).

Facer, K. and Manchester, H. (2012) *Mapping Learner Lives: Final Report*. Manchester: Manchester Metropolitan University Education and Social Research Institute.

Jenkins, H. (2006) *Convergence Culture*. New York: New York University Press.

Knobel, M. and Lankshear, C. (eds) (2010) *DIY Media: Creating, Sharing and Learning with New Technologies*. New York: Peter Lang.

Lankshear, C. and Knobel, M. (2011) *New Literacies: Everyday Practices and Social Learning*. Milton Keynes: Open University Press.

Mitchell, D. (2014) Quadblogging site at **www.quadblogging.com** and **www.quadblogging.net** (older version with background).

Rettberg, J.W. (2008) *Blogging*. Cambridge: Polity Press.

Waller, M. (2012) More than Tweets: developing the 'new' and 'old' through online social networking, in G. Merchant, J. Gillen et al., *Virtual Literacies: Interactive Spaces for Children and Young People*. London: Routledge.

FURTHER READING FURTHER READING **FURTHER READING** FURTHER READING

Buckingham, D. and Willett, R. (eds) (2006) *Digital Generations: Children, Young People and the New Media*. Englewood Cliffs, NJ: Lawrence Erlbaum Associates.

Facer, K. and Manchester, H. (2012) *Mapping Learner Lives: Final Report*. Manchester: Manchester Metropolitan University Education and Social Research Institute.

Gee, J.P. (2004) *Situated Language and Learning*. London: Routledge.

Jenkins, H. (2006) *Convergence Culture*. New York: New York University Press.

Knobel, M. and Lankshear, C. (eds) (2010) *DIY Media: Creating, Sharing and Learning with New Technologies*. New York: Peter Lang.

Lankshear, C. and Knobel, M. (2011) *New Literacies: Everyday Practices and Social Learning*. Milton Keynes: Open University Press.

Merchant, G., Gillen, J. et al. (2012) *Virtual Literacies: Interactive Spaces for Children and Young People*. London: Routledge.

Potter, J. (2012) *Digital Media and Learner Identity: The New Curatorship*. New York: Palgrave Macmillan.

Rettberg, J.W. (2008) *Blogging*. Cambridge: Polity Press.

Section C
ICT and the Professional Teacher

The rapid development of ICT brings a series of challenges to which teachers must respond. In this third section we provide an overview of three aspects of teachers' involvement with ICT which are critical for effective and positive use of ICT in the classroom. These are:

- professional use of ICT;
- e-safety – including health and safety;
- ethical and legal issues.

ICT should be a teacher's helpful ally administratively, for example providing ready means for maintaining records of children's progress as well as offering diverse opportunities for the preparation of resources. In Chapter 18 on the professional use of ICT, we offer some ideas as starting points for both improved personal capability and continuing professional development.

The importance of e-safety has been placed at the core of the new curriculum for computing, featuring prominently in the programme of study both at Key Stage 1 and 2 as illustrated in Chapters 16 and 17. Schools have a responsibility for promoting and teaching children about the safe and responsible use of the internet, which we deal with additionally here in Chapter 19. Teachers also have a clear duty of care for the children in their classroom. Electrically powered equipment in the classroom brings a particular burden of responsibility for safe operation. It would be impractical to provide an exhaustive list of 'dos' and 'don'ts' in respect of health and safety, but Chapter 19 in this section includes guidelines on how to make your classroom as free from risk as possible, as well as referring you to appropriate interpretations of the relevant legislation.

The new ways of communication that ICT offers have raised a range of ethical and legal issues with which we as a society are grappling to come to terms. Many of these are not completely new problems; for example, there have always been opportunities for plagiarism, or for the dissemination of undesirable material. However, the need to take a moral stand and deal with potential threats has been markedly accentuated by the speed and ease with which information can now be transmitted. The earlier chapters on the internet (see Chapters 16 and 17) discussed some of the questions involved. In Chapter 20 on ethical and legal issues, we turn our attention to two other significant areas for ICT in education, copyright and data protection, contributing to the promotion of positive values and attitudes in a pragmatic way and aiming to avoid unnecessary pitfalls.

18
Professional use of ICT

Introduction

The Teachers' Standards require you to:

8. Fulfil wider professional responsibilities

including:

- taking responsibility for improving teaching through appropriate professional development

In order to fulfil your wider professional responsibilities in a timely and effective way, you may consider using ICT to support you. This chapter begins by discussing how ICT can improve efficiency and then considers the use of ICT to support your ongoing professional development.

Personal capability

Selective use of ICT will repay the investment of time made to gain proficiency with the keyboard, other hardware and appropriate software. Facility with the keyboard remains particularly helpful. For those who want to develop typing skills, an electronic tutor such as Mavis Beacon or Accu-Type is invaluable. The course need not necessarily be followed to its conclusion but to a point when you are using most of your fingers and moving around the keyboard with some fluency. Despite the increasing accuracy of speech recognition facilities across devices, the keyboard remains one of the most common forms of input so fluency is vital.

In a similar way, cumulative benefit is derived from learning to use key software. Modern word processors, desktop publishing packages and spreadsheets have wide-ranging functionality. However, it is also reasonable to expect that teachers are able to use a range of media, including video and audio. To a novice, such software may seem daunting, but in time it will prove quicker to use them than relying on 'traditional' pen-and-paper approaches. Effective use of software can be time-saving and also open up educational possibilities. For example:

- using a template in your word processor so that a lesson plan can be called up repeatedly;
- using a spreadsheet to keep children's records that can readily be sorted into order and converted into graphical representations to demonstrate progress;
- using desktop publishing to produce professional-looking worksheets;
- using digital photography (both still and video) to record children's work;
- using the internet for classroom resources and to supplement your subject knowledge;
- modelling a mathematical algorithm with screen-capture software on a tablet device so children can practise at home with parents.

Further ideas are available on a number of websites, including Terry Freedman's useful *ICT in Education* website (see **www.ictineducation.org/**).

Professional development using ICT

In their work in the classroom, teachers will be supporting children in the use of ICT to source information. This is a key skill; the capability to access information is now critical. While reference is often made to a 'knowledge-based' society, there is a strong argument that as well as holding knowledge personally, it is also vital to know how to find unfamiliar information and knowledge when it is needed.

Teachers can help themselves professionally to keep up to date by using ICT in a variety of ways, the most important of which is accessing information via the internet and developing their own PLN, as discussed above. There are a number of key sites with which all teachers should be familiar. A useful starting point is provided by the Department for Education site (**www.education.gov.uk**), not just for its own content – which includes news and discussion of current issues in education – but for links it offers to other key national bodies.

Teachers' TV was a digital television channel for education professionals (heads, teachers, support staff and governors). Programmes covered a range of topics, ranging from the curriculum to more general themes, such as tackling challenging behaviour. The effectiveness of the medium is that it is visual. Watching teaching and learning take place, supported by an informed commentary, provides insights that would be difficult to achieve through the written word alone. Teachers' TV ceased operation in 2011 but most of the resources are available elsewhere. Table 18.1 identifies a number of possible sources.

It is important that teachers should have access to inspection evidence, and foremost among sources for this is the Ofsted site at **www.ofsted.gov.uk**. The site provides access to all of the inspection reports carried out on schools and other educational institutions,

Table 18.1 Teachers' TV sources (from www.education.gov.uk/schools/toolsand initiatives/teacherstv/)

ABA Education Consultancy Ltd	**www.proteachersvideo.com**
Teach Pro Limited	**www.schoolsworld.tv**
Phoenix TTV Limited	**www.teachersmedia.co.uk/**
TSL Education Ltd	**www.tes.co.uk/video**
Laser Learning Ltd	**www.laserlearning.tv**
Axis 12 Limited	**www.teachfind.com/**
RAISEonline.Training	**www.eyfsonline.org**
Creative Education	**www.creativeeducation.co.uk/videos/**
Promethean Planet	**www.prometheanplanet.com/PDTV**

such as local authorities and teacher training providers. This is a huge repository of information. It would be difficult to conceive how it might be made so readily available and kept so up to date other than by the internet. It is also worth remembering that Ofsted produces, and posts on its website, reports on subject and curriculum issues aggregated from its findings in individual schools. This is authoritative research that complements material that teachers might glean from other sources.

There are many other governmental and quasi-governmental sites that hold helpful information for teachers. Most of these are very effective technically; they have been designed carefully and offer an interface that is attractive and intuitive. Not surprisingly, privately produced sites, which tend to offer curriculum resources rather than statutory information and administrative support, can be of less consistently high quality, in terms of both content and presentation. They reflect the somewhat anarchic nature of the internet, and it is worth being circumspect about material when the provenance is uncertain.

Sites referred to in the text were current in February 2014.

A SUMMARY OF **KEY POINTS**

> You can develop your personal ICT capability by improving your own basic skills and by learning to use key office and educational software.

> You can use ICT to support your professional learning by using a range of websites and social networking tools to keep you fully informed of new initiatives and technologies and by also developing your own professional learning network (PLN).

M-LEVEL EXTENSION > > M-LEVEL EXTENSION > > M-LEVEL EXTENSION

Find out more about courses available to you now and in your first few years that include e-learning, distance learning and blended learning. Also find out if there are any local professional development opportunities such as TeachMeets that you could attend. How can you use your findings to best effect in planning your early continuing professional development?

REFERENCES REFERENCES **REFERENCES** REFERENCES REFERENCES REFERENCES

Department for Education website at **www.education.gov.uk**

DfE (2011) *Teachers' Standards.* Available at **www.education.gov.uk/publications**

Freedman, T. (2011) *ICT in Education*, **http://ictineducation.org/** (accessed 12 January 2014).

Ofsted website at **www.ofsted.gov.uk**

FURTHER READING FURTHER READING **FURTHER READING** FURTHER READING

Arthur, J. and Cremin, T. (eds) (2010) *Learning to Teaching in the Primary School* (2nd edn). Abingdon: Routledge.

Duffty, J. (2006) *Primary ICT: Extending Knowledge in Practice.* Exeter: Learning Matters.

19
E-safety

Introduction

In this chapter, we introduce the important and ever shifting issues surrounding the safe use of technologies and the internet. We want to highlight the constantly changing nature of this area, as rapid advances in technological devices and the ways in which people communicate and connect via communications networks mean that new risks go hand in hand with burgeoning opportunities (Livingstone, Haddon, Görzig and Olaffson, 2011). Schools, teachers, parents and children all need to work together to ensure children can safely make the most of the opportunities offered by new technologies. However, schools and teachers in particular have an important role to play in facilitating children's digital literacy and safety skills, which in turn has implications for teachers' professional knowledge and understanding, as we consider in this chapter. We also address more general health and safety considerations that apply to the use of technologies in schools.

The bigger picture

There are many new varieties of electronic text and forms of communication emerging as technology develops. Blogs, vlogs, instant messaging, mobile phone texting, wikis, tweets and social networking sites provide ever-expanding possibilities for sharing information, images and other media. The use of such tools is only just beginning to be explored in educational contexts and there has been concern about privacy and about who can access information outside a person's chosen contacts. One of the risks is that, without hearing or seeing the other person, children cannot identify them or know if their motivation for making contact is innocent. However, it does not have to be a stranger to the child who puts them at risk – peers or indeed family members in some circumstances could be a source of risk.

Social networking can provide a forum for 'cyberbullying'. This is a term used to describe the use of the internet or mobile networks to harass others. It is extremely upsetting for victims because it intrudes into their private space and it can appear that there is no escape. Incidents can take place at all times of day or night, and at any location, even within the safety of the home. There is guidance for schools on managing this issue in the document *Cyberbullying – Safe to Learn: Embedding Anti-bullying Work in Schools* (published by the DCSF in 2007, and available via **www.kidscape.org.uk**). The Child Exploitation and Online Protection (CEOP) Centre is a useful resource for guidance on cyberbullying, and the safe use of the internet and social networking. While the issues of cyberbullying and the grooming of children by online predators are great cause for concern, these risks do not represent the whole picture.

Identifying the risks

A good starting point as a student teacher is to ensure that your own knowledge and understanding of the risks associated with the internet and other communications technologies is up to date. Some of the dangers inherent in the use of the internet or mobile communications networks are widely known and acknowledged. For example, issues such as online grooming of children and young people, or cyberbullying, understandably garner much attention in the media and are a particularly acute concern to children, parents, teachers and the wider community alike. However, equally pervasive is the plethora of wholly inaccurate and pernicious information available online. This includes versions of history which serve extreme political views and are represented as fact (Holocaust deniers, for example). Furthermore, Livingstone et al.'s (2011) comprehensive European survey of children and young people's use of online networks identifies a far more nuanced picture of newer risks emerging via user-generated content, including hate sites, pro-anorexic sites, self-harm sites, drug forums and suicide sites. Childnet International (2007) have developed a range of useful resources for trainee teachers focusing on the issues of e-safety, in which they classify the risks in terms of three broad areas (often referred to as 'the three Cs'):

- **Contact** – this includes online grooming and cyberbullying.
- **Content** – this includes any inappropriate material, such as pornographic, hateful or violent content. It also includes any material that may be dangerous, illegal, age-inappropriate, inaccurate or biased. Under this category, plagiarism and copyright issues are also considered as children, like adults, can put themselves at risk through the illegal use of copyright material.
- **Commercialism** – including issues such as junk e-mail, personal privacy and commercial exploitation of children and young people through aggressive marketing strategies and premium rate services.

PRACTICAL TASK PRACTICAL TASK PRACTICAL TASK PRACTICAL TASK

Download the leaflet *E-safety: An Introduction for Trainee Teachers*, which is available from the Childnet International website at: **www.childnet.com/kia/traineeteachers/trainers.aspx**.

Read through and familiarise yourself specifically with the various areas of risk identified. Discuss your response to this leaflet with other student teachers on your course. ENSURE that you understand your responsibility to report to the designated member of staff in school, any disclosure which indicates that a child may be at risk. You should also make careful notes of any disclosure, which you should sign and date.

Developing a proactive stance towards e-safety

There are various strategies that schools use to ensure, in the first instance, that children are kept safe while using the internet in school. Internet safety policies exist to ensure, as far as possible, safe access and responsible use of the internet for learners within school. All schools making use of the internet should have an appropriate policy, often called an acceptable use policy, which clearly outlines the potential benefits and risks and how these are managed within the school. Policies are usually written and reviewed in consultation with parents and there are model versions available from government websites for education and parents' information sites. Student teachers should familiarise themselves with how these policies operate in their schools and seek further advice from the senior management and/or ICT subject leader.

Since most access to the internet in schools is now supplied under contract by Regional Broadband Consortia (RBCs), the filtering of inappropriate content is often carried out remotely by the local authority or RBC itself. Teachers can often report sites which they feel are harmful, and these are added to the list for blocked access. It may also be appropriate to request the unblocking of sites – as it is quite possible that harmless yet educational sites can be blocked due to the software not discriminating between key words and words contained within words (Sussex, for example). Encouraging a culture where children feel able to report things they see which make them feel uncomfortable fosters a responsible attitude and begins to educate learners about how they would deal with these issues in the wider world beyond the classroom. It is also important to remember that no filtering system is guaranteed to filter out all potentially harmful content.

While the provision for filtering and blocking content together with clear expectations and policies with regard to acceptable internet use in schools can be useful tools in a proactive stance towards e-safety, it is questionable whether, in and of themselves, these can empower children and young people to keep themselves safe online beyond school. Increasingly, children are faced with a plethora of online tools and facilities. These are accessed through mobile technologies such as phones, iPads and other tablet devices, and MP3 players offering connectivity to the internet, social networks and online applications. In addition, domestic and public spaces are increasingly equipped with both secure and open wireless connectivity, which again can be accessed through a range of devices and applications.

RESEARCH SUMMARY RESEARCH SUMMARY **RESEARCH SUMMARY** RESEARCH SUMMARY

There have been two major research studies into e-safety: *The Byron Review* (Byron, 2008), and the EU Kids Online study (Livingstone et al., 2011). A vital message emerging from these two research studies into e-safety is that it is no longer adequate for teachers and schools to only take a banning and blocking approach to inappropriate content or activity on the internet. Livingstone et al. (2011) found that 38 per cent of 9–12 year olds were using social networking sites under age and the authors of the review question the usefulness of blanket age limits altogether. It is clear that policing the internet whether in school or wider society is not in itself sufficient, as Byron points out:

> Children and young people need to be empowered to keep themselves safe – this isn't just about a top-down approach. Children will be children – pushing boundaries and taking risks. At a public swimming pool we have gates, put up signs, have lifeguards and shallow ends, but we also teach children how to swim. (Byron, 2008, p.2)

Livingstone et al. (2011) also focus on the need to empower children and young people to keep themselves safe while making the most of the rich opportunities offered by online collaboration tools. However, they also stress the changing nature of the risks associated with the internet and mobile networks, and the importance of 'listening to children to learn what new risks they are experiencing' (Livingstone et al., 2011, p.29). Against this backdrop, it is clear that schools and teachers have an important role to play in equipping children with the critical knowledge, understanding and skills to keep themselves safe online in school and beyond. As discussed in Chapters 16 and 17, the use of the internet in schools, together with the access to a range of online collaboration tools within a relatively safe environment of a VLE, places schools in a unique position to address issues of e-safety with children.

Professional issues for teachers

If student teachers and teachers are to keep up to date with both the new risks and opportunities that developments in new forms of communication might yield, then their own safe and critical use of such technologies is to be welcomed. Furthermore, social networking sites and tools are used by many student teachers to keep in touch with friends and family while away from home. They are also a useful tool for forming new friendships and networks both professionally and socially. However, it is the tendency of these social and professional networks to converge that can pose risks to student teachers' and teachers' professional reputations alike.

You should take care over what information you share online, including any photographs of your social life. Remember that children and their parents may look you up online. They might also request to become friends with you on social networking sites. To protect your professional reputation, ensure that you understand the privacy settings you use for any online content you upload or any online communities you participate in. Consider carefully what information you include in any online profiles, professional or personal.

It is important to follow all relevant guidelines on communicating with children and their parents/carers, for example on using your own personal mobile or any mobile phone issued by the school, the local authority or nationally. Many schools do now use various text-messaging services to update parents on events at school or even on their child's progress. However, this is very different from using your own mobile phone to contact parents. Many schools have a school mobile phone for use on trips or contacting parents in case of emergency. However, common sense also dictates that in the case of a serious emergency the child's immediate safety should come before the need to follow any school protocol regarding what mobile phone to use.

With the increasing emergence of digital mobile technologies such as smartphones and tablet devices such as iPads, innovative teachers and schools will want to explore the educational potential of these devices. You need to remember that such devices can store a great deal of personal and professional data, which needs to be managed effectively and safely to ensure the protection of those in your care and, ultimately, your own professional reputation.

PRACTICAL TASK   PRACTICAL TASK   **PRACTICAL TASK**   PRACTICAL TASK

Visit the *Know IT All for Trainee Teachers* website at the following link: **www.childnet.com/kia/ traineeteachers/** (Childnet International, 2011).

Work through the three sections (Social Networking, Teachers and Technology, Resources) and use the checklists to carry out an audit of your own knowledge and understanding. Audit your own 'digital identity' by carrying out a search on your name using public search engines. After consulting this material, make some time to discuss your response with other trainees on your course.

Health and safety

So far in this chapter we have examined the safety issues surrounding the use of the internet and new forms of communication tools. However, there are also a number of traditional health and safety considerations that apply to the use of computers and other aspects of ICT equipment in schools. There are legal requirements that student teachers need to be aware of. However, the extent to which legislation deals with specific aspects of the use of ICT in schools is limited and so we will also cover some practical considerations which contribute to the sense of responsibility for health and safety that every good teacher will have in her classroom.

Legal requirements

Under the Health and Safety at Work etc. Act 1974 and the Management of Health and Safety at Work Regulations 1999, employees – which includes classroom teachers – must:

- take reasonable care of their own and others' health and safety;
- co-operate with their employers;
- carry out activities in accordance with training and instructions;
- inform the employer of any serious risks.

While the current health and safety legislation resides primarily in documents issued by the Health and Safety Executive (see Further Reading), and while ultimate responsibility lies with senior leaders, teachers need to think beyond the strictly legal to consider what constitutes good practice.

Room layout

Only a few primary schools were designed from the outset to accommodate computers, and so in many cases the siting of equipment is at best a compromise with the overall physical arrangements of the classroom. The convention in the primary school originally was for computers to be dispersed around the school, usually one, two or possibly three to each classroom. Where they are positioned among the desks, tables, chairs, bookshelves and cupboards will to some extent be dictated by circumstances, but even so there are guidelines worth following. None of these is more than common sense, but they bear summarising.

It is important that the computer is positioned so that the monitor is not subject to reflection, either from artificial light or from sunlight. Not only is glare distracting, but it may also cause headaches and strain if users are subjected to it for long.

The computer should be as close to a power supply as possible, keeping the length of electrical flex to a minimum in order to reduce proportionately the risk of someone tripping over it. If the cable supplied is too long, and an alternative of more appropriate length is unavailable, it is preferable to loop and tape or tie the surplus together (to minimise the build-up of a magnetic field the loop should not be too tight).

For convenience, many schools have bought trolleys so that computers can be moved easily from room to room. These are fine, as long as they are designed well, with the work surface at an appropriate height for the children – which won't be the same throughout a primary school – and with sufficient area for the 'footprint' of your equipment. The dimensions merit checking as trolleys may not have convenient workspace for overflow, especially if the expectation is for more than one child to be using the computer at any time. Again, attention must be paid to ensure that cable is not flapping loosely around the system.

The question of space often becomes even more acute in those schools that have decided to dedicate a room to an ICT suite. The challenge is to accommodate children and computers in a room that was in all likelihood designed with only children in mind. Rows of computers are often arranged around the wall, with little space for writing or source materials – or a coworker.

Additionally, turning to face the teacher is hard for the children. Possibly associated with a lack of space may be problems caused by excessive heat and humidity. Computers give off a significant amount of heat and fumes, especially if grouped together, and consideration of improved ventilation may become important. Schools may need to give consideration to the installation of air-conditioning units.

THE BIGGER PICTURE   THE BIGGER PICTURE   THE BIGGER PICTURE   THE BIGGER PICTURE

When you are planning to reorganise your classroom, keep in mind the requirements of health and safety (of both children and adults, including your own!). Take advice from other teachers and senior staff, and the site manager or caretaker. Also, bear in mind the safeguarding agenda, for example don't cover external or corridor windows and glass panels in doors completely with displays or posters. It is considered safer for children to have sightlines available, and it is also in your best interests as it reduces the possibility of any misunderstanding or false allegations. Always adhere to school policies in these areas.

Setting up the computer

Linking the components that make up a single computer system, one that is either new or has been dismantled for a move, is not difficult and there is no reason to be disconcerted by this task. However, as with all electrical equipment, there is a potential hazard if care is not taken, and the obvious precaution is to ensure that the equipment is disconnected at the mains before making any adjustments to the cables that make up the system.

Computers in operation are not drawing much power from the mains, which means that a single computer, monitor and peripherals can share just one socket without problem. However, a gang, rather than a splitter (which is more likely to become dislodged if leads are accidentally bumped), should provide this access. Also, one gang per socket is the rule, and gangs should not be daisy-chained. In a room in which several stations are planned, professional advice should be sought. Both tidiness and safety will dictate that mains leads, and any data cables for networking, should be concealed in trunking, with as little flex as possible lying on the work surface.

Data from the computer to the monitor are run through an RGB cable, RGB representing red, green and blue – the colours used to make up the picture on the screen. Usually, the cable has 15 pin D-shaped connectors at either end, with the direction of the cable made obvious by the configuration of the pins.

The same is true for the connection of other peripherals. Computer manufacturers over the last few years have gone out of their way to make clear which device goes into which socket, often using colour coding to assist. The keyboard and mouse, which are standard input devices, often have reserved sockets. However, they may alternatively be supplied to connect through USB (universal serial bus) ports. These are a more efficient alternative to the older nine-pin serial port (which you will still find on some computers). Most peripherals – printers, cameras, memory sticks, scanners – are now manufactured with USB connections.

They are usually efficient and require no manual installation of supporting software. All of the above makes the assumption that the equipment is sound and in good working order. Old or frayed leads must be replaced, and you must be vigilant in watching for any accidental damage, such as cuts to plastic insulation or wear to plugs, that may have been sustained. If repairs, rather than connecting and setting up ICT equipment, are involved, then professional help should be sought.

Danger, children at work

Teachers must be clear that, while ultimate legal duty for health and safety in the classroom lies with employers, in practice they are responsible for the safe operation of computers in their classrooms. A cable that has not been correctly attached is a potential hazard and on a daily basis only the teacher is in a position to check this. For the same reason, none of the setting up discussed in the previous section should be delegated to primary age children.

Apart from electrical safety, computer equipment is often heavy and should be moved only by an adult. Yet children are going to be the main computer users in your classroom, and so they too need to know how to work efficiently and safely at the computer. For older Key Stage 2 children, this may extend to switching the computer on themselves, and perhaps even to switching on at the mains too. However, the teacher must be on hand to supervise either of these tasks.

Monitors have improved considerably in quality over recent years but it is still not advisable for children (or adults) to sit in front of a screen for extended periods. There is no substantive evidence that eyesight is adversely affected by spending a long time in front of a VDU (visual display unit), nor is the level of radiation emitted close to breaching safe levels set out in international recommendations. However, reading a screen for long periods without a break can cause a headache.

Teachers need also to be aware of rare, but serious, effects that can arise. A few people suffer from photo-sensitive epilepsy which is triggered by flickering light. However, they can often still work successfully with a monitor, especially given that the quality of this equipment has improved so substantially over the last decade. Similarly, some people experience skin irritations as the result of working with monitors. The cause of this response may be a range of factors, possibly attributable to the computers drying out the atmosphere, in which case air flow and humidity into the room should be improved.

Another reason to discourage extended time in front of the computer is to make it practical for the user to maintain good posture. Slouching, while generally unattractive and unhealthy, will also be detrimental to the relationship of the user's wrists with the keyboard. The lower arms should be held off the desk and be about horizontal. Children in the classroom are unlikely to be using a computer continuously long enough to be susceptible to repetitive strain injury, but if they can be encouraged to sit properly at the computer from early on it will stand them in good stead for the future. For similar reasons, an ergonomic chair with adjustable height and backrest is recommended. This will enable children – who vary tremendously in height – to sit with their feet on the floor (or on a rest) and with their thighs parallel to the ground.

Newer technologies

In recent years there has been an influx of various technologies in the classroom, including interactive whiteboards, visualisers, laptop charging stations or trolleys, handheld devices and, more recently, tablet devices such as iPads. All of the general safety issues raised in this chapter also apply to varying degrees with these newer technologies. Trailing cables, the location and storage of equipment, together with the length of time spent using technological equipment must be managed effectively by the teacher to minimise any risks to children. Equipment with powerful light sources, such as visualisers and data projectors linked to interactive whiteboards, must also be monitored carefully to ensure that children or teachers are not exposed to glare.

It is important when using the interactive whiteboard that both teachers and children are aware of the potential danger of staring directly into the light source. Standing to one side rather than directly between the board and the data projector when facing the class reduces this risk.

Mobile devices, such as handheld devices and iPads, can also pose new safety issues. The fact that these devices are light and carried around easily can lead users to use the devices while on the move. While the technology may be mobile, children should be discouraged from using such equipment on the move.

A SUMMARY OF **KEY POINTS**

> New technologies and applications, whether virtual or real, bring new opportunities and new risks.

> Children need to be empowered to make safe use of new communications technologies within and beyond the school environment.

> Under relevant legislation, you must take reasonable care of your own and others' safety, cooperate with your employer regarding health and safety, carry out acts in accordance with training/instructions provided, and inform the employer of any serious risks.

> You must take care where ICT equipment is placed in your classroom, and how you and your children use it.

M-LEVEL EXTENSION > > M-LEVEL EXTENSION > > M-LEVEL EXTENSION

Consider whether any of the health and safety recommendations provided in this chapter, included in the examples in other chapters of the book, and raised by the reference materials and further reading suggestions provided below, apply more widely than in ICT. What other subjects are likely to need similar levels of attention to the safeguarding of children? How can you increase your awareness of health and safety issues now and when you are awarded QTS?

REFERENCES REFERENCES **REFERENCES** REFERENCES REFERENCES REFERENCES

Byron, T. (2008) *The Byron Review: Safer Children in a Digital World*. London: DCSF. Available at **www.education.gov.uk/publications/standard/publicationdetail/page1/DCSF-00334–2008** (accessed 12 January 2014).

The Child Exploitation and Online Protection Centre (CEOP), **http://ceop.police.uk/** (accessed 12 January 2014).

Childnet International (2007) *E-safety: An Introduction for Trainee Teachers.* Available at **www.childnet. com/kia/traineeteachers/trainers.aspx** (accessed 12 January 2014).

Childnet International (2011) *Know IT All for Trainees and NQTs.* Available at **www.childnet.com/kia/ traineeteachers/** (accessed 12 January 2014).

DCSF (2007) *Cyberbullying – Safe to Learn: Embedding Anti-bullying Work in Schools.* Available at **www.kidscape.org.uk** (accessed 12 January 2014).

DfE (2011) *Teachers' Standards.* Available at **www.education.gov.uk/publications** (accessed 12 January 2014).

Livingstone, S., Haddon, L., Görzig, A. and Olaffson, K. (2011) *EU Kids Online: Full Report.* London: LSE. Available at **www.lse.ac.uk/media@lse/research/EUKidsOnline/Home.aspx** (accessed 12 January 2014).

FURTHER READING FURTHER READING FURTHER READING FURTHER READING

DfE (2011) *Teachers' Standards.* Available at **www.education.gov.uk/publications** (accessed 12 January 2014).

Health and Safety Executive, **www.hse.gov.uk/services/education/index.htm** For information on classroom risk assessment, school trips, work-related stress, slips and trips in school and a range of resources (accessed 12 January 2014).

Health and Safety Executive (2006) *Working with VDUs Revision 3.* Downloadable leaflet from the HSE website at **www.hse.gov.uk** (accessed 12 January 2014).

www.legislation.gov.uk for Acts and Regulations (accessed 12 January 2014).

20
Ethical and legal issues

Introduction

The rapid development of ICT has presented a range of new social and legal challenges. Some of the ethical questions that are raised have already been considered in Chapter 16. However, the innovatory opportunities for learning, working and leisure presented by ICT have further consequences for the legal framework in which they operate, and the rapid pace of change has added an additional layer of complexity to these tangled arrangements.

This chapter aims to provide an awareness of some of the issues involved. However, it is not intended to be a comprehensive guide, and if you have a concern over a particular circumstance in which the legitimacy of an action might be debatable, it is sensible to seek further advice.

Copyright

Even before the advent of computers the question of copyright was a vexed one for schools. The current legislation in the United Kingdom is, though, unequivocal and thorough. It applies to anything published (including text and artistic production, which might itself be literary, musical, graphic or dramatic in nature). It extends, too, to other technological media apart from computers, such as films, audio and televised programmes. In short, the likelihood is that anything you might want to copy is covered by the legislation.

Some of the confusion over copyright for schools may originate in the concept of 'fair dealing' which is embodied in the Copyright, Designs and Patents Act 1988 (this Act still forms the basis of legislation in this country, though its impact has been modified by EU harmonisation). Becta's helpful guidance (Becta, 2000) summarised this idea succinctly:

> 'Fair dealing' is really a permitted form of defence if accused of infringement, limited to particular purposes of which the best known is 'research or private study', but case law has established that producing multiple copies for classes is certainly not 'private study'.

The inference is clear. Educational institutions are not in any way exempt from copyright legislation. However, many schools and colleges have paid a fee to the Copyright Licensing Agency (CLA). This provides limited rights to make copies of some copyright material. Copying is restricted to works published by organisations that have joined the scheme, but this in fact covers most British publishers (a major exception, however, is printed music). More restrictive, though, is the scope of the CLA scheme in applying only to printed material. The exact allowance for copying (usually photocopying) differs between institutions and has been varied in recent years; it would be sensible to check your school's current agreement to ascertain precisely what is permitted.

If we switch our focus more particularly to ICT, the same principles apply. In practice, a computer program should be regarded as a literary work, with its authors and distributors enjoying the same rights and privileges as if they had produced a book. Software publishers are usually very careful to stipulate what the purchaser has bought. In general, 'buying software only gains title to a licence to install and use the software, not to the software itself. The text of the licence will give details about how many copies of the software may be made. The starting point is that only one will be allowed, in order that data may be transferred to a computer's hard disk. However, it is often possible to buy at economic rates licences to cover a whole site, or multiple stations within a purchasing institution.

Teachers have an obligation to ensure that software-licensing conditions are not breached in their school. In some circles the conditions under which software has been purchased are broken with the excuse that additional, illegal copies are not hurting anyone because the transmission is electronic; no physical material is appropriated. However, the disk and packaging are negligible elements of the software bundle. What is at stake is the author's intellectual property, and an unauthorised copy represents its theft. Apart from the ethical argument against software theft, there is also the highly pragmatic consideration that, especially among smaller educational publishers, loss of revenue will jeopardise future development of material.

Several organisations are involved in monitoring the use of software to ensure that breaches of copyright are avoided. Foremost of these in the United Kingdom is the Federation Against Software Theft (FAST), which has its website at **www.fastiis.org**. FAST does not simply act to police software use, however; it is a valuable source of advice and support to computer users.

The internet poses considerable challenges to the enforcement of copyright law, not least in the difficulty of monitoring all the material that is held and is available for download. Nevertheless, copyright laws do apply. Even if copyright ownership is not declared, it should be reckoned as applicable, unless its rightful owner has explicitly placed the material in the public domain.

Creative Commons

As discussed so far, issues surrounding copyright are complex, which can sometimes lead to teachers and children understandably becoming over-cautious in their use of ICT when creating content. In order to address this issue, much digital media and content is also made available under different types of copyright licences courtesy of the organisation Creative Commons, which you can find out more about at the following link: **http://creativecommons.org/about**. Work that is made available under Creative Commons remains the intellectual property of the person who created the original content, but the various different copyright licences allow the owner to be more specific about the permission they grant for others' use of their content. For example, work that is licensed as **CC BY-NC** or **Attribution-NonCommercial** indicates that the owner gives permission for others to 'remix, tweak, and build on' the work 'non-commercially'. In this case, any new work that incorporates, for example, someone else's digital audio must acknowledge the original creator of the audio and be non-commercial. For more detail about different types of licence, visit the following link: **http://creativecommons.org/licenses/**.

PRACTICAL TASK ~~PRACTICAL TASK~~ PRACTICAL TASK ~~PRACTICAL TASK~~

Most search engines allow you to carry out an advanced search in which you can search for digital assets that have been made available under Creative Commons copyright permissions. Using a photo-sharing website such as Flickr (see **www.flickr.com/**), find out how to carry out an advanced search for images that are available with Creative Commons permissions.

THE BIGGER PICTURE ~~THE BIGGER PICTURE~~ THE BIGGER PICTURE ~~THE BIGGER PICTURE~~

There is a useful website that gives information about poetry that is out of copyright or where living contemporary poets have given permission to have their work performed in videos for the site, including poems by Michael Rosen, Roger McGough, Francesca Beard and Benjamin Zephaniah. Set up by Michael Rosen when he was the Children's Laureate (2007–2009), Perform a Poem is an e-safe site for sharing children's poetry performances. The site, a joint project between Booktrust and the London Grid for Learning (LGfL), is also available to be hosted by other UK grids that are part of the National Education Network. For more information, see the website (**http://performapoem.lgfl.org.uk**).

Another useful site providing free access to online resources is Project Gutenberg, which has a choice of over 33,000 free e-books for a variety of platforms, including a 'children's bookshelf' (see **www.gutenberg.org**).

Teachers will need to determine how best to introduce children to the concept of copyright. While this is a more urgent question in secondary schools, the increase in computer use, particularly at home, by primary age children means that breach of copyright as well as plagiarism from the internet or CD-ROM may well arise in your classroom. While it may not be appropriate to introduce a formal system of referencing to young children, spending time to explain why sources should be acknowledged will only be to their long-term benefit. Also teaching children about different licences and Creative Commons is a good way of getting them to engage with the issues when they are creating their own content with digital media. For example, what kinds of permissions do they think they would give others with regards their own content?

Data protection

Teachers and schools need to know of their obligations regarding data confidentiality. These duties are enshrined in data protection legislation. In essence, this dates back to the Data Protection Act 1984, which was introduced in response to growing concern about the impact of advancing computer technology on personal privacy. Considering its vintage, it was far-sighted, providing both rights for individuals and a demand on organisations (or individuals) that hold and use personal information to adopt responsible practices, even for data such as names and addresses, which might not be considered to be particularly sensitive.

Ironically, the original Act was limited to information held on computer, which exempted data records held by 'traditional' methods on hard copy. Another difficulty with the 1984

Act, which perhaps could not be foreseen, was that the growing internationalisation of computer use through the internet would facilitate the unscrupulous transfer of data to locations outside the UK jurisdiction. Partly to improve the regulations in these areas, but also partly in response to an EU directive issued in September 1990 aimed at harmonising legislation across the member states, the 1984 Act was replaced by a revision, formulated in 1998 and taking effect in March 2000.

Like the original Act, the current legislation is based on eight principles. The detail of these has been rearranged from the earlier requirements, primarily to accommodate the new eighth principle. The list was summarised by the Information Commissioner as follows:

> *...anyone who processes personal information must comply with eight principles, which make sure that personal information is:*
>
> - *fairly and lawfully processed;*
> - *processed for limited purposes;*
> - *adequate, relevant and not excessive;*
> - *accurate;*
> - *not kept longer than necessary;*
> - *processed in accordance with the data subject's rights;*
> - *secure;*
> - *not transferred to countries without adequate protection.*

(ICO, 2007)

There remain exemptions to the Act. These include personal data held in connection with domestic or recreational matters and personal data that the law requires the user to make public, such as the electoral register. On the other hand, the principles provide for individuals to be able to access data held about themselves, and to insist on the data being corrected if they are erroneous.

Schools are subject to the Data Protection Act, and it is difficult to envisage a school not being registered. Staff who keep records on children on a home computer, and, indeed, under the 1998 Act, paper records, come under the scope of the legislation, and their schools should be aware of this.

A SUMMARY OF **KEY POINTS**

➢ **Copyright applies to anything published in any medium.**

➢ **Many schools and colleges have paid a fee to the CLA; this provides limited rights to make copies of some copyrighted materials.**

➢ **A computer program should be regarded as a literary work, with the same protection.**

➢ **Children should be taught about copyright and the ethical use of their own and others' content.**

➢ **Schools are subject to the Data Protection Act 1998.**

➢ **You need to comply with the eight principles of the Act.**

M-LEVEL EXTENSION > > M-LEVEL EXTENSION > > M-LEVEL EXTENSION

Find out more about how copyright and data protection apply to schools. How can you teach children about copyright in ways that they can understand so that they are well prepared for the next stages of school and for lifelong learning? How will the requirements of data protection legislation apply to you as a primary teacher in your dealings with children's personal information and records? How can you incorporate within Citizenship the development of children's understanding about their data protection rights, their rights to privacy, and the reasonable measures that they should take to protect themselves from sharing too much information about themselves online?

REFERENCES REFERENCES REFERENCES REFERENCES REFERENCES REFERENCES

Becta (2000) Copyright and ICT Information Sheet (no longer available).

Creative Commons, **http://creativecommons.org/** (accessed 21 January 2014).

Flickr. Available at **www.flickr.com/** (accessed 21 January 2014).

ICO (Information Commissioner's Office) (2007), **www.ico.gov.uk**. Summaries and the full text of the Data Protection Act can be downloaded from this site.

Project Gutenberg. Available at **www.gutenberg.org/** (accessed 21 January 2014).

Rosen, M. with Booktrust (2014) *Perform a Poem*. Available at **http://performapoem.lgfl.org.uk/default.aspx** (accessed 21 January 2014).

FURTHER READING FURTHER READING FURTHER READING FURTHER READING

www.cla.co.uk for information on copyright compliancy (accessed 21 January 2014).

www.fastiis.org/ for information on software rights (accessed 21 January 2014).

www.legislation.gov.uk for relevant Acts and guidelines (accessed 21 January 2014).

Self-assessment questions

Chapter 1 – Organising ICT in your classroom

1. You may hear teachers in schools talking about ICT initiatives using the following acronyms. What do they stand for?

   a) NGfL.
   b) RBCs.
   c) NOF.
   d) VLEs.

2. What is the 'skills gap'?

3. List three models of logon practice that you might encounter in schools.

4. Why is it important for children to save their work before printing?

5. Whole-class demonstrations of new software or introductions to new skills are recommended. What are the main drawbacks of the alternative 'cascade' model?

6. Match the following examples of hardware/peripherals that can be used to support children with additional and special educational needs to their descriptions.

   a) Concept keyboard.
   b) Touch window.
   c) Big keys.
   d) Trackball.

      i) An inverted mouse system based on a large ball.
      ii) A large-format keyboard for children with fine-motor control difficulties.
      iii) A device attaching to the front of a monitor that acts as a touch screen or replacement mouse.
      iv) A device creating touch-sensitive areas to be created on a flat board, allowing users to input text/commands.

Chapter 2 – Planning for primary computing as a subject

1. Why are the following aspects important when thinking about planning in the light of new technologies?

   • High expectations.
   • Designing opportunities for learners to develop and practise their computing skills.

2. List five of the key questions that you should ask yourself to ensure that your planning is effective.

3. Test yourself on the definitions of the following terms: algorithm; input and output; selection; decomposition; debug; variable.

4. Which four aspects of context should be included in a longer-format lesson plan?

5. How can you brief another adult supporting you in the classroom?

6. List three types of possible differentiation that you might make in your planning.

7. How can you ensure that you are well prepared for a lesson?

8. Which three elements should be evaluated at the end of a lesson?

Chapter 3 – Planning for primary ICT in other subjects

1. In what ways could the use of a wiki or Googledoc support the writing process?

2. Where you are using a three-part mathematics lesson, how can the use of ICT support each part?

3. For each of Key Stages 1 and 2, give two examples of the use of ICT to support science.

4. Match the uses of ICT with the appropriate foundation subject.

   a) Art and design.
   b) Geography.
   c) History.
   d) Design and technology.
   e) Music.
   f) RE/PSHE/Citizenship.
   g) PE.
   h) Languages.

      i) Record and assess children's own compositions.
      ii) Use a drill-and-practice vocabulary program.
      iii) Use a digital camera to record in the locality.
      iv) Use the internet to find out about other cultures and faiths.
      v) Use painting software to explore colour, pattern, texture, line and tone.
      vi) Use videos of movements and actions to develop ideas.
      vii) Undertake a virtual museum tour.
      viii) Use a programmable robot to learn about control devices.

Chapter 4 – Planning ICT in the Early Years Foundation Stage

1. Whose theories underpin the organisation of Early Years settings?

2. How did he believe that young children refine their growing understanding?

3. What did he call the environment in which this takes place?

4. How can the use of ICT support talk in the EYFS?

5. In which prime or specific area of learning would each of the following uses of ICT support children's development?

- Experiencing a story via the interactive whiteboard.
- Using graphics software to experiment with shape and colour.
- Using the internet to find out about other countries and cultures.
- Handling a range of ICT equipment requiring various fine-motor skills.
- Sharing and collaborating in the use of ICT equipment.
- Using software that develops counting/number identification.

Chapter 5 – Assessment and recording in primary computing and ICT

1. Why is assessment a vital part of the planning process?

2. Why are samples of children's work insufficient as a record of progress in ICT?

3. What is individual profiling of children in ICT?

4. List six of the important elements of the context of an observation of a child's ICT work.

5. How can a whole-class snapshot support formative assessment?

6. Which assessment strategy described in this chapter would be most appropriate for use in the EYFS and why?

Chapter 6 – Monitoring primary computing and ICT

1. At which three levels are primary computing and ICT monitored?

2. Which body is the main organisation responsible for monitoring computing and ICT nationally?

3. Which organisations have been responsible for the local monitoring of computing and for supporting schools with their development of ICT?

4. Which people in schools might be responsible for monitoring computing and ICT?

Chapter 7 – Word processing and desktop publishing

1. What is the difference between word processing and desktop publishing?

2. What are the two main ways in which teachers apply their knowledge, skills and understanding of word processing?

3. Explain the three key features of word-processing software.
   - editing;
   - formatting;
   - tools.

4. What are the four stages of the writing process that word processing can support?

5. List six ways of text entry into a word processor.

6. What special features are provided in word-processing programs for primary children?

Chapter 8 – Graphics software and digital cameras

1. What are the main purposes of graphics software?

2. What are the two types of graphics software?

3. How are these different?

4. What are the three key features of graphics software that make them useful for primary ICT?

5. List the main possible sources of graphics.

6. In settings with older hardware set-ups, what might be the problems with printing from graphics software?

Chapter 9 – Media production: Video, animation and ICT

1. There are many benefits of using digital video in schools. However, its use raises some issues. What are these?

2. List the ways in which digital video can support assessment.

3. Which two types of work with digital cameras could be starting points for digital video production?

4. When editing films, what features does editing software allow?

Chapter 10 – Graphing programs

1. What are graphing programs?

2. When would it be better to use a database?

3. What are the three types of data that you might collect?

4. What are the potential drawbacks of the following?

   • A pie chart.
   • Line graphs.

5. What are the two categories of graphing programs?

6. Give examples of where a program with set colour order may be inappropriate if not adjusted.

Chapter 11 – Databases and spreadsheets

1. What are databases?

2. What are spreadsheets?

3. What are the four main types of data-handling program commonly used in schools?

4. Match the type of software with its possible use.

   a) Branching tree or binary databases.
   b) Flatfile or tabular databases.
   c) Spreadsheets.
   d) Relational databases.

      i) Contain data arranged in fields, usually input through a form.
      ii) Contain complex data that are tagged to enhance flexibility of interrogation and may have menus, indexes, keywords and hyperlinks.
      iii) Facilitate the identification of objects, people or plants by posing Yes/No questions about their attributes.
      iv) A grid of cells arranged in rows and columns where data and formulae can be entered prior to searching, sorting and presenting graphically.

5. What do the following terms mean?

   - Keyword searching.
   - Hypertext literacy.

6. List the formats of data that can be supported in a flatfile database.

Chapter 12 – Programming and computational thinking

1. Define computational thinking in a way that is accessible to a non-specialist.

2. Identify 3–4 applications of computer science in our physical environment

3. How are the program languages Scratch and Logo different?

4. What strategies could teachers use to ensure there is progression in the development of children's computational thinking through programming?

5. What is Raspberry Pi?

Chapter 13 – Mobile technologies

1. Match the mobile technologies with their key features.

   a) PDA.
   b) Smartphone.
   c) Laptop or notebook.
   d) Tablet PC.
   e) MP3 player/DAP.

      i) Has all of the functionality of a desktop but is portable.
      ii) Has a pen-shaped stylus input device and handwriting-recognition software and comes in 'slate' and rotating screen versions.
      iii) Personal organiser with additional functionality, including versions of office software, internet connectivity, sound recording facility and photographic capability.

iv) Mobile phone with many applications, including internet access, camera, games, and communication via social networking.

v) Originally only for music files, now capable of other media, for example storing still images and video playback.

2. Explain how mobile technologies contribute to 'anytime, anywhere' learning.

Chapter 14 – Interactive whiteboards

1. What are interactive whiteboards (IWBs)?

2. Describe the two main types of technology relating to IWBs?

3. What factors must be taken into account when siting the components of the IWB set-up?

4. What are the five identified benefits of using IWBs?

Chapter 15 – Digital audio and music

1. When considering software to use to support composing and performing music, what important issues should you consider?

2. What is a podcast?

3. Which piece of classroom hardware can be used effectively to support teaching and learning in music?

4. What must you remember to keep in mind when planning to use ICT to support teaching and learning in music?

Chapter 16 – The internet

1. What is the difference between the internet and the world wide web?

2. What is 'netiquette'?

3. What is a web browser?

4. Define the elements of the following URL: http://www.ofsted.gov.uk/reports/

5. What is Boolean searching?

6. What is digital division?

7. Why should you always preview sites found on a search or recommended by colleagues?

Chapter 17 – Social media: Tools for communicating, collaborating and publishing

1. To what should teachers give careful regard when considering using social media in the classroom?

2. What is the name that has been given to a form of blogging which enables groups of up to four schools at a time to blog between each other over a four-week period, taking it in turns to be the focus and commenters on each other's work?

Chapter 18 – Professional use of ICT

1. In which two main ways can you improve your personal ICT capability?

2. How can you use ICT in support of your own professional development?

Chapter 19 – E-safety

1. What are 'the three Cs' of e-safety identified by Childnet International?

2. What are the four main duties placed on you as an employee by the Health and Safety etc. at Work Act 1974 and the Management of Health and Safety at Work Regulations 1999?

3. Which body provides regular updates and guidance on health and safety?

Chapter 20 – Ethical and legal issues

1. Two organisations involved in the monitoring of copyright are CLA and FAST. Give their full titles and say which aspects of copyright they oversee.

2. What are the eight basic principles of data-protection legislation?

Answers to self-assessment questions

Chapter 1 – Organising ICT in your classroom

1. The acronyms stand for:

    a) NGfL   National Grid for Learning
    b) RBCs   Regional Broadband Consortia
    c) NOF   New Opportunities Fund
    d) VLEs   Virtual Learning Environments

2. The 'skills gap' is the perceived difference between the ICT knowledge, skills and understanding of children who are experienced in using ICT at home, including PCs and gaming consoles, and teachers who are lacking in confidence and have a lower level of ICT capability.

3. The three models of logon practice that you might encounter in schools are:

    *   the whole class with the same username and password into a general area for saving work;
    *   group logon names/passwords;
    *   each child has a unique username/password.

4. It is important for children to save their work before printing in case they lose their work or the printer fails.

5. The main drawbacks of the 'cascade' model are:

    *   the teacher and/or child who are shown first may be wrongly perceived as the 'ICT experts';
    *   ICT may be seen as something separate from the rest of children's learning.

6. Match the following examples of hardware/peripherals that can be used to support children with additional and special educational needs to their descriptions.

    a) A concept keyboard – iv) this is a device creating touch-sensitive areas to be created on a flat board, allowing users to input text/commands
    b) A touch window – iii) this is a device attaching to the front of a monitor that acts as a touch screen or replacement mouse
    c) Big keys – ii) this is a large-format keyboard for children with fine-motor control difficulties
    d) Trackball – i) this is an inverted mouse system based on a large ball

Chapter 2 – Planning for primary computing as a subject

1. The following aspects are important when thinking about planning in the light of new technologies.

    *   High expectations – it is important to have high expectations of all children in order to ensure that all are appropriately challenged. Your expectations must be based on knowing what children's knowledge, skills and understanding are already.

- Designing opportunities for learners to develop their computing skills – whether planning for computing as a subject or ICT within another subject, you must always keep in mind that the learning should be purposeful rather than just allowing children to engage with the technology.

2. Look back to the relevant section in the chapter on effective planning – analysing the situation – you should have listed any five of the key questions.

3. Check your definitions against those given in the chapter.

4. The four aspects of context that should be included in a longer-format lesson plan are:

- the school/class context;
- the theoretical context;
- the National Curriculum or Early Years Foundation Stage context;
- the scheme of work context.

5. You can brief another adult supporting you in the classroom by:

- talking to them about the lesson beforehand;
- giving them a copy of your planning;
- making clear their role in the lesson/any assessment that is taking place.

6. Three types of possible differentiation that you might make in your planning are:

- for children of different abilities;
- for those with additional or special educational needs;
- for children with English as another language.

7. You can ensure that you are well prepared for a lesson by:

- planning likely timings;
- checking resources;
- reviewing your own learning needs;
- listing organisational memory joggers.

8. The three elements that should be evaluated at the end of a lesson are:

- operational issues;
- learning objectives/intentions;
- what you would do/change next time.

Chapter 3 – Planning for primary ICT in other subjects

1. A wiki or a Googledoc could support the writing process by enabling children to write collaboratively on a shared document both in school and at a distance.

2. Where you are using a three-part mathematics lesson, the use of ICT can support each part as follows.

- Mental maths starter – resources can be varied by using the IWB.
- Main/group activities – a range of software can be used to explore number patterns, practise and assess skills, handle data, develop subject knowledge in various aspects of maths, transform shapes, develop logical thinking and problem-solving skills.
- Plenary – strands of the lesson can be drawn together by the use of electronic media.

3. Check the answers that you gave for each of Key Stages 1 and 2 in the section on planning ICT in science.

4. The uses of ICT match with the appropriate foundation subject as follows.

   a) Art and design – v) use painting software to explore colour, pattern, texture, line and tone.
   b) Geography – iii) use a digital camera to record in the locality.
   c) History – vii) undertake a virtual museum tour.
   d) Design and technology – viii) use a programmable robot to learn about control devices.
   e) Music – i) record and assess children's own compositions.
   f) RE/PSHE/Citizenship – iv) use the internet to find out about other cultures and faiths.
   g) PE – vi) use videos of movements and actions to develop ideas.
   h) Languages – ii) use a drill-and-practice vocabulary program.

Chapter 4 – Planning ICT in the Early Years Foundation Stage

1. Vygotsky's theories underpin the organisation of Early Years settings.

2. He believed that young children refine their growing understanding through innate 'inner speech' that they verbalise and test/retest in their interactions with others.

3. He called the environment in which this takes place the 'zone of proximal development'.

4. The use of ICT can support talk in the EYFS by providing starting points and stimuli for the inner dialogue and talk in the zone of proximal development, for example in imaginative and role-play scenarios.

5. The areas of learning that each would support are as follows.

   - Experiencing a story via the interactive whiteboard – Communication and language.
   - Using graphics software to experiment with shape and colour – Expressive arts and design.
   - Using the internet to find out about other countries and cultures – Understanding of the world.
   - Handling a range of ICT equipment requiring various fine-motor skills – Physical development.
   - Sharing and collaborating in the use of ICT equipment – Personal, social and emotional development.
   - Using software that develops counting/number identification – Mathematics.

Chapter 5 – Assessment and recording in primary computing and ICT

1. Assessment is a vital part of the planning process because, without proper assessment and recording in a subject, there is no real evidence or knowledge of where children are up to and planning becomes empty and meaningless. This can lead to activities being repeated inappropriately. Assessment allows teachers to track progress and plan for children to achieve.

2. Samples of children's work are insufficient as a record of progress in ICT because ICT is often used to present the best/final copy of the work and printouts of these do not show the drafting process and they may hide any misconceptions. Children often work collaboratively and only by observing individual children working can the teacher really assess their ICT capability accurately.

3. Individual profiling of children in ICT is a means of mapping their progress, linking work samples with detailed observations by the teacher and taking into account the child's own views of their developing capabilities. It includes identification of next steps in learning, thus completing the planning cycle.

4. The important elements of the context of an observation of a child's ICT work include:

   - the hardware being used;
   - the software being used;
   - the relevant unit of work;
   - any other curriculum links;
   - whether they were working independently or with a partner/group;
   - the date/timing of the activity.

5. A whole-class snapshot can support formative assessment because it can help you to gain a picture of the ICT capability of the whole class at a particular time to support your planning. It could help you to group children appropriately and to plan relevant work for each group; therefore, it is a useful part of the planning/assessment cycle.

6. The assessment strategy most appropriate for use in the EYFS is individual profiling because observations of individual children fit in with the style of assessment prevalent in the EYFS and it allows you to assess/record progress towards meeting the Early Learning Goals in all six areas of learning.

Chapter 6 – Monitoring primary computing and ICT

1. The three levels at which primary computing and ICT are monitored are nationally, locally and at school level.

2. Ofsted is the main organisation responsible for monitoring computing and ICT nationally.

3. Local authorities have been responsible for the local monitoring of computing and for supporting schools with their development of ICT.

4. In schools, the following might be responsible for monitoring computing and ICT:

   - senior managers, for example Deputy Heads, Assistant Heads or Assessment Coordinators;
   - subject leaders for computing or ICT, including those who are only responsible for ICT and those with several subject responsibilities.

Chapter 7 – Word processing and desktop publishing

1. **Word processing software** focuses more on the entry, storage, retrieval and manipulation of text, with some formatting features allowing the inclusion of graphics and sound to enhance the layout and presentation of the final document. **Desktop publishing software** focuses more on the design of the documents and usually has less emphasis on the text content; often, designers require a final version of text to be provided before laying out the pages with the graphics and design features.

2. The two main ways in which teachers apply their knowledge, skills and understanding of word processing are:

   - teaching and learning with and about word processing;
   - to support the more general aspects of their role, for example in producing policies and other documentation and for general admin work.

3. The three key features of word-processing software are:

   - editing – this allows entry and manipulation of text, including insertion, deletion, correcting, cutting, copying, pasting, etc.;

- formatting – this allows the use of different fonts, text sizes, styles, page size/ orientation, and use of colour, bullets, tables and boxes, etc.;
- tools – there is a range to support the functions described in editing and formatting, including checking of spelling, grammar and style, speech capability, use of templates, and word count.

4. The four stages of the writing process that word processing can support are:

- planning and drafting;
- editing (both structural and technical);
- proofreading;
- presentation.

5. Ways of text entry into a word processor include:

- via a standard QWERTY keyboard and a mouse;
- via an overlay keyboard;
- using a touch screen;
- using a word bank;
- using voice-input/recognition software;
- with the help of an adult scribe (amanuensis).

6. The special features that are provided in word-processing programs for primary children include:

- a speaking word processor facility;
- spell-checkers and thesauruses;
- grammar and style-checkers.

Chapter 8 – Graphics software and digital cameras

1. The main purposes of graphics software are to enter, store, retrieve and manipulate images and their constituent elements: line, colour and texture.

2. The two types of graphics software are painting programs and drawing programs (or vector graphics programs).

3. **Painting programs** produce bitmap images recording separately every pixel, resulting in very large files. **Drawing programs** store drawings as a series of vectors determining their magnitude and direction. These are more economical, resulting in smaller files.

4. The three key features of graphics software that make them useful for primary ICT are their:

- tools;
- editing functions;
- effects.

5. The main possible sources of graphics are:

- children's own drawings and paintings;
- websites;
- CD-ROMs;
- scanning images/objects;
- downloads from digital cameras;
- clip art.

6. In settings with older hardware set-ups, the problems with printing from graphics software might be the large size of graphics files that can fill up limited printer memory, preventing documents from printing out/backlogging printer queues.

Chapter 9 – Media production: Video, animation and ICT

1. problems of using digital video in schools include that, under the safeguarding agenda, publishing images of children introduces ethical and internet safety issues. Trainees should find out about and adhere to the school's and/or local authority's policies and protocols.

2. Digital video can support assessment in the following ways.

   - Producing evidence for portfolios.
   - For teacher assessment, for example recording science experiments or mathematics investigations.
   - In peer-assessment, for example of movement in PE.
   - In self-assessment, for example of speaking and listening/drama work.

3. Two types of work with digital cameras that could be starting points for digital video production are:

   - using digital still cameras, including their short-movie facility;
   - shooting small amounts of material on solid-state digital video cameras.

4. When editing films, editing software allows:

   - scenes to be trimmed to length;
   - scenes to be joined together along a timeline;
   - titles to be added;
   - music and sound effects to be added.

Chapter 10 – Graphing programs

1. Graphing programs facilitate communication of information through graphical representation, enabling data to be entered, stored, presented and interpreted graphically.

2. It would be better to use a database when the data-handling requires sophisticated sorting, searching or modelling.

3. The three types of data that you might collect are:

   - categorical, for example eye colour;
   - discrete, for example number of siblings;
   - continuous, for example heights of growing seedlings.

4. The potential drawbacks of the following are:

   - a pie chart – they are unable to record a zero value; it can be confusing when there are similar values that are difficult to judge by eye;
   - line graphs – gaps in data collection may be interpreted as a zero value.

5. The two categories of graphing programs are:

   - pictogram programs – these usually represent data as pictograms or block graphs only;
   - more sophisticated graphing programs – these support a wider range of graph types and functions.

6. Examples of where a program with set colour order may be inappropriate if not adjusted include:

   - eye colour;
   - hair colour;
   - favourite colours;
   - colours of cars, bedroom walls, football strips, front doors, etc.

Chapter 11 – Databases and spreadsheets

1. Databases are structured stores of information that allow large amounts of data to be stored, organised, searched and retrieved quickly and easily.

2. Spreadsheets are another kind of data-handling software, sharing some features with databases, but that are more appropriate for the manipulation of numerical data and therefore well suited to mathematical calculations and modelling.

3. The four main types of data-handling program commonly used in schools are:

   - branching tree or binary databases;
   - flatfile or tabular databases;
   - relational databases;
   - spreadsheets.

4. Match the type of software with its possible use:

   a) branching tree or binary databases – iii) Facilitate the identification of objects, people or plants by posing Yes/No questions about their attributes;
   b) flatfile or tabular databases – i) Contain data arranged in fields, usually input through a form;
   c) spreadsheets – iv) A grid of cells arranged in rows and columns where data and formulae can be entered prior to searching, sorting and presenting graphically;
   d) relational databases – ii) Contain complex data that are tagged to enhance flexibility of interrogation and may have menus, indexes, keywords and hyperlinks.

5. The following terms mean:

   - keyword searching – a feature of database software requiring the user to select a keyword to be the focus of a search; keywords must be carefully chosen and correctly spelled;
   - hypertext literacy – the skills required to read and navigate hypertext documents.

6. The formats of data that can be supported in a flatfile database are:

   - text;
   - numeric;
   - dates;
   - yes/no;
   - multiple choice.

Chapter 12 – Programming and computational thinking

1. An accessible way of describing computational thinking is that it is ways of thinking that people engage with as they employ the processes and tools of computing to solve problems.

2. The following are examples of the application of computer science in our physical environment.

   • Traffic lights at a pedestrian crossing.
   • A drinks vending machine.
   • An automated entry and exit point for a car park.

3. Logo is a text-based programming language whereas Scratch is a visual-blocks programming language.

4. Strategies to develop children's computational thinking through programming are:

   • Children should be discouraged from copying chunks of code without understanding what they do as it is vital that they also understand why a certain piece of code within any program leads to a particular outcome within the system or game being designed. Getting children to explain chunks of code and what they do is important.
   • To develop higher levels of computational thinking children will need exposure to extended projects which require them to design their own games, simulations or scenarios.

5. Raspberry Pi is a small single board computer that can be linked to a keyboard, monitor and network and runs on the open source Linux operating system. It is referred to as single board because all of the components are contained on one circuit board.

Chapter 13 – Mobile technologies

1. The mobile technologies match with their key features as follows.

   a) PDA – iii) Personal organiser with additional functionality, including versions of office software, internet connectivity, sound recording facility and photographic capability.
   b) Smartphone – iv) Mobile phone with many applications, including internet access, camera, games, and communication via social networking.
   c) Laptop or notebook – i) Has all of the functionality of a desktop but is portable.
   d) Tablet PC – ii) Has a pen-shaped stylus input device and handwriting-recognition software and comes in 'slate' and rotating screen versions.
   e) MP3 player/DAP – v) Originally only for music files, now capable of other media, for example storing still images and video playback.

2. Mobile technologies can contribute to 'anytime, anywhere' learning by extending the classroom so that learning is not restricted to the school day or site – it can take place at home, in the evenings or at weekends or even in the holidays.

Chapter 14 – Interactive whiteboards

1. Interactive whiteboards(IWBs) are touch-sensitive boards that allow teachers and children to engage directly with material projected onto a screen from a computer via a data projector.

2. The two main types of technology relating to IWBs are:

   - 'hard' boards – these have a grid of copper wire behind a solid surface. Their special pens are tracked by the grid using electromagnetism;
   - 'soft' boards – these use restrictive technology, whereby they have a flexible polyester surface membrane separated from a rigid second layer by a small gap. When your finger/pen depresses the surface, contact is registered.

3. Factors that must be taken into account when siting the components of the IWB set-up include whether it is fixed or mobile.

   If mobile:

   - the need to be recalibrated after being moved;
   - the vulnerability of the components;
   - security from theft;
   - health and safety, for example trailing wires.

   If fixed:

   - the position of the board on the wall, for example its height;
   - the space needed for it to be interactive;
   - the position of other light sources, for example windows;
   - the positioning of the computer or laptop for classroom activities;
   - the secure positioning of the data projector.

4. The five identified benefits of using IWBs are:

   - capacity to vary pace of learning;
   - enhanced modelling;
   - improved quality of interactions;
   - improved quality of assessment due to more effective questioning;
   - redressed balance between making resources and planning.

Chapter 15 – Digital audio and music

1. When considering software to use to support composing and performing music, the important issues that you should consider are as follows.

   - Does it include any pre-recorded samples and how far can these be adapted or changed?
   - Does it have a facility for recording and combining live instruments, including the voice?
   - Does it support any links with different types of media, for example other audio material, still images, video clips, etc.?

2. A podcast is a sound (or video) file that can be transferred onto mobile devices or computers, providing a method of publishing files to the internet that allows users to subscribe to a feed and receive new files and updates automatically. Although the word subscriber is used, this does not mean that there is necessarily a cost.

3. The piece of classroom hardware that can be used effectively to support teaching and learning in music is the IWB.

4. When planning to use ICT to support teaching and learning in music you must remember to keep in mind that ICT should never replace traditional music activities, such as singing a range of genres of song, playing percussion accompaniments to a song or piece of music, etc.

Chapter 16 – The internet

1. **The internet** is a communications tool that includes communication via the world wide web, e-mail, discussion groups, and conferencing. **The world wide web** is part of the internet and is made up of hypertext pages that include text, images, sounds and animations interconnected by hypertext links, providing information, news, opinion, archive material, music and video.

2. 'Netiquette' is the range of e-mail specific conventions such as the level of formality, tolerance of spelling variations, type of greetings, etc. that are acceptable in this form of communication.

4. A web browser is a piece of software that allows the user to locate, view and navigate web pages.

5. The elements of the URL http://www.ofsted.gov.uk/reports/ are:

   - http = hypertext transport protocol;
   - www = world wide web;
   - ofsted = the name of the organisation's server being accessed;
   - gov = shows that this is a government body;
   - uk = shows that this is a site based in the United Kingdom;
   - /reports/ = the directory or path on the server.

6. Boolean searching is an advanced system of searching that involves the use of operators such as AND, OR and NOT:

   - AND narrows the search, requiring sites that contain both specified elements;
   - OR widens the search to include sites that include either term;
   - NOT also narrows the search, but allows you to specify sites that contain a keyword that is not followed by the one specified.

7. Digital division is the term used to describe inequality of access in society to online resources and services.

8. You should always preview sites found on a search or recommended by colleagues to ensure that they are relevant to your children and comply with the safe use policy of the school that you are working in.

Chapter 17 – Social media: Tools for communicating, collaborating and publishing

1. Teachers should show careful use and regard for pupil safety when using social media, but these environments can provide authentic and rich experiences for communicating, collaborating and publishing as well as learning about how the internet works.

2. The term used to describe this form of blogging is 'Quadblogging'.

Chapter 18 – Professional use of ICT

1. The two main ways that can you improve your personal ICT capability are:

   - by developing your keyboard skills;
   - by learning to use key software, including both office/admin programs and educational software.

2. You can use ICT in support of your own professional development by using key websites to keep you up to date and to source resources and find out required information.

Chapter 19 – E-safety

1. The 'three Cs' of e-safety defined by Childnet International are:

    *   **Contact** – this includes online grooming and cyberbullying.
    *   **Content** – this includes any inappropriate material, such as pornographic, hateful or violent content. It also includes any material that may be dangerous, illegal, age-inappropriate, inaccurate or biased. Under this category, plagiarism and copyright issues are also considered as children, like adults, can put themselves at risk through the illegal use of copyright material.
    *   **Commercialism** – including issues such as junk e-mail, personal privacy and commercial exploitation of children and young people through aggressive marketing strategies and premium rate services.

2. The four main duties placed on you as an employee by the Health and Safety etc. at Work Act 1974 and the Management of Health and Safety at Work Regulations 1999 are to:

    *   take reasonable care of your own and others' health and safety;
    *   co-operate with your employer over health and safety issues;
    *   carry out all activities in accordance with training/instructions provided;
    *   inform your employer of any serious risks.

3. The Health and Safety Executive (HSE) provides regular updates and guidance on health and safety.

Chapter 20 – Ethical and legal issues

1. Two organisations involved in the monitoring of copyright are:

    *   Copyright Licensing Agency (CLA) – printed materials, issuing licences to make copies of these;
    *   Federation Against Software Theft (FAST) – monitors software use, gives advice to computer users.

2. The eight basic principles of data-protection legislation are that personal information must be:

    *   fairly and lawfully processed;
    *   processed for limited purposes;
    *   adequate, relevant and not excessive;
    *   accurate;
    *   not kept longer than necessary;
    *   processed in accordance with the data subject's rights;
    *   secure;
    *   not transferred to countries without adequate protection.

algorithm:
  definition 36
  examples *see* programming
animation production 130
  by digital cameras 131
  software-created 130
  stop motion 130
art and design:
  planning primary ICT 59–60
  purposeful use of ICT 59–60
art-tech crossover in ICT 4
assessing ICT setting 21–3
  hardware 21–2
  human resources 22–3
assessment:
  of collaborative work 75
  data 81
  Early Years Foundation Stage 80–1
    individual profiling 80
  focus of 77
  individual profiling 78–9
    pro-forma 79
  level descriptors 75–6
  National Curriculum programme of study for
    computing 76–8
  observation important 75–6
  organisation in schools 75
  peer-assessment 78
  in primary computing and ICT 73–82
  principles 74
  of process and product 74
  purpose 73–4
  reflective task, pro forma 81
  self-assessment 78
  skills matrix 79–80
  tracking through software 75
  tutorial software of limited use 75
  whole-class snapshots 79–80
auditing 3

blog:
  definition 39, 236
  Edublogs for education users 236–7
  Twitter (microblog) 237–8
  writing and literacy 50
bring your own device (BYOD) strategy
  19, 199
British Educational Communications and
  Technology Agency (Becta) 3, 84

calculators, use of 54
Cambridge Primary Review (2010) 3
cascade model of instruction, issues 25–6
CD-ROM databases *see* databases, relational

children's contributions 25
cloud-based services 200–1
Code of Conduct and Practice for Registered
  Teachers 3
collaborative work, assessment of 75
collaborative writing online and literacy 50
competence in ICT, and responsibility for work 25
compression, of images by graphics software
  120–1
computational thinking 174–97
  and curriculum 184
  definition 175
  designing software 184
  evaluating computer games 184
  Key Stages 1 and 2 174–5
  pedagogies for progression 182–5
computer science emphasised in Key Stages 1
  and 2 4
computing:
  ICT renamed to 4
  meaning 1
  physical *see* physical computing
  primary *see* primary computing
  programme of study 8
  role 4
  whole-school approach 185
Computing At School (CAS) 4, 84
confidence in use of ICT:
  children's 12
  teachers' 19
copyright, images 121
Core Professional Standards 3

data-handling:
  and core subjects 170–2
  and English 172
  and mathematics 171–2
  relevance to children 171
  and science 170–1
  see also graphing programs, data handling
databases 153–73
  binary databases 154–6
    creating 162–3
    definition 154
    (figure) 155
    FlexiTREE3 163
  binary search algorithm 154–6
  branching databases *see* databases, binary
    databases
  capabilities 166–70
  copying retrieved information 167–8
  data accuracy 168
  data entering 156, 163, 168
  data preparation 162

databases *cont.*
  data protection 169
  definition 153
  designing 164
  and English 172
  fields 156
  flatfile databases 156
    data entering 163
    data formats 168
    Junior ViewPoint (figure) 157, 163
  hypertext links and task focus 167
  information retrieval 162
  interrogation 153, 157, 158, 162, 163, 168
  key features 160–1
  Key Stages 1 and 2 153–4
  keyword searching 166
    spelling 166
  limitations 166–70
  and mathematics 171–2
  practical activities 172
  practical task
    help sheet for CD-ROM 166
    search algorithms 156
  printing problems 170
  privacy of data 169
  records 156
  reflective task, personal data 172
  relational 157, 165–6
    CD-ROM 165–6, 167
  and science 170–1
  selecting appropriate databases 166
  skills needed by teachers 159–60
  tabular databases *see* databases, flatfile
    databases
  teaching activities 158
  understanding retrieved information 167–8, 170
debug, definition 36
decomposition, definition 37
design and technology, planning primary ICT 61–2
desktop publishing 109–10
  definition 93
differentiation:
  in lesson plan example 41
  master's level extension 44
  sources of advice on 34
digital audio 214–20
  copyright 217
  Key Stages 1 and 2 214–25
  licences to use 217
  podcasts
    audioBoo software 218
    creating 217–18
    SoundCloud software 218
  see also music
digital cameras 111–26
  classroom use 112–13
  definition 111–12
  immediacy of images 113

digital cameras *cont.*
  Key Stages 1 and 2 112
  policies on use 112–13
  professional use by teachers 113
  resolution 113
  storage requirements of images 113
  zoom lens 113
digital literacy 7, 8, 10
digital video:
  assessment, use in 129
  cross-curricular work 132
  curriculum uses 129
  editing 131–2
    software 132
  from digital cameras 130–1
  and literacy 131
  reflective task, examples for analysis 132
  resource, online 133
  sound-recording problems 132
display size, importance of 23
drawing *see* graphics software, drawing
  programs

e-learning:
  defined 11, 32
  using 11
e-safety 248–56
  blocking websites 250
  cyberbullying 248
  empowerment of children 250
  health and safety *see* health and safety
  policies 249–50
  professional aspects 251
    audit own digital identity (practical
      task) 251
    mobile aspects 251
    sharing information online 251
  risks
    classifying 249
    identifying 248–9
The Early Years: Foundations for Life, Health
  and Learning 9, 67, 80–1
Early Years Foundation Stage 9
  changes 1
  cross-area planning 71
  early learning goals (table) 67
  planning primary ICT 66–72
  primary ICT
    arts and design 70
    communication and language
      development 69
    dramatic play 68
    mathematics 70
    personal social and emotional
      development 69
    physical development 69
    understanding of world 70
  reflective task

Early Years Foundation Stage *cont.*
   effect of computer 70–1
   lesson plan sample 52–3
   Vygotsky's early learning theories 68
Early Years Foundation Stage Profile 9
Edublog blogging tool 50
English:
   cross-curricular use 51–2
   and databases 172
   and images 125
   planning primary ICT 46–53
   and word processing 108
English as an additional language, children
   with:
   ICT uses for 29
   in lesson plan example 42
   organising ICT for 28–30
   software for 28
   teacher's responsibilities 28
equality of opportunities, implications of
   access 232

file formats:
   audio 200
   graphics 120–1
   music 219
foundation subjects, planning primary ICT
   59–64
The Framework for the National Curriculum 4
funding, bids for 18

generic software, definition 89
geography, planning primary ICT 60–1
Googledocs collaborative writing 50
government policy 3
graphics software 111–26
   capabilities 119–21
   clip art 122
   colour information 119–20
   compression 120–1
   copyright 121
   definition 111
   drawing programs
      definition 114
      using 119
   editing functions 116–17, (figure) 117
   file formats 120–1
   graphics tablet 119
   images
      copyright 121
      and English 125
      licences 121
      and mathematics 124–5
      and science 124
      sources 121
   key features 115–17
   Key Stages 1 and 2 112
   limitations 119–21

graphics software *cont.*
   manipulation of images 117–18
   optical character recognition 123
   painting programs 114, 115, 116
   poster creation 124
   practical activities using 118–19
   practical task
      painting packages 116
      photograph bank 125
      science activity 123
      size of image files 114
   printers 123
      costs 123–4
      memory 123
      resolution 123
   printing 123–4
   progression of skills 118
   resolution 120–1
      and storage requirements 120
   scanners 122–3
   skills required by teachers 115
   tools 116
   and traditional art media 117–18
   use in classroom 114–15
graphing programs 135–52
   3-D graphs 145–6
   analysis of graphs 147
   bar charts 137
   colours 146
   capabilities 144–7
   colour in bar charts 146
   and core subjects 148–51
   Counter 143
   CounterPlus 142, 143, 145, 147
   Counting Pictures 142, 143, 145, 147
   data, ethical considerations 141
   data collection 136, 147
   data entering 143
   data handling 136–8
      teacher confidence 150
   data presentation 137, 140
   data sorting 140
   data types 136
   data-logging 148–9
      Junior Datalogging Insight 148
   DataCalc 147
   DataPlot 143, 146, 147
   DataSweet 147
   definition 135
   and English 150–1
   frequency tables 141, 143, 145
   grouping data 136–7
   key features 139–40
   Key Stages 1 and 2 135–6
   limitations 144–7
   line graphs 137
   and mathematics 149–50
   Pictogram 3 142, 143, 147

graphing programs *cont.*
  pictogram programs 140, 141–2, 146
  pie charts 137
  practical task
    data-logging 149
    discussion 151
    planning tally charts 145
    scales 150
  printing in colour 146
  progression in 147
  purpose 147
  scales 141
  scatter graphs 137
  and science 148–9
  skills needed by teachers 139
  tally charts 145
  teaching with and about 138–9

hand-held computing devices 18–19
  literacy work using 49
health and safety 251–5
  computer location 252
  interactive whiteboard projectors 255
  legal requirements 252
  mains cables 253
  monitors
    extended usage 254
    photo-sensitive epilepsy 254
  power sockets 253
  seating 254
  temperature in computer suite 252–3
high-resource setting:
  literacy teaching, planning ICT to
    support 51
  mathematics 55
history, planning primary ICT 61

ICT:
  background
    local 19
    national 18–19
  Basic Curriculum component 4
  in classroom, organising 18
  cross-disciplinary nature 4
  informal use outside school 10
  infrastructure 3
  inspection reports 246–7
  interactivity 11
  as learning tool 9–12
    characteristics 11–12
  meaning 1
  multi-modal information 12
  Ofsted website 246–7
  professional use by teachers 245–7
    advantages 245
    master's level extension 247
    and Teachers' Standards 245
    updating knowledge 246

ICT *cont.*
  programme of study 7
  provisionality 11
  renaming to computing 4, 5, 8
  role 3–4
  speed of routine activities 12
  support in school 19
  teachers' approaches to 23
  Teachers' TV sources 246
Information Technology in Teacher Education
    (ITTE) 4, 84
input, definition 37
interactive whiteboards 205–13
  assessment improved by using 209
  benefits reported 208
  cross-curricular tool 206
  interactions, quality of 209
  interactivity 210
  Key Stages 1 and 2 206
  modelling 210
  multi-touch tables 205
  National Whiteboard Network 205, 209
  practical task, website resources 209
  Promethean 205
  reflective task, whiteboard usage 210
  resource availability 209–10
    core subjects 210
    science 211
  secondary sources 211
  set-up guidance 207–8
  shared writing 211
  SmartBoard 205
  software
    Promethean flipcharts 208
    proprietary, sources of 211
    RM Easitech 208
    SMART notebooks 208
  software incompatibility 206
  speed of lessons 209
  technologies 206
  using 208
interactivity of ICT 11
internet 221–34
  collaboration opportunities 224
  conferencing 225
  definition 38, 221
  electronic bulletin boards 225
  instant messaging 225
  Key Stages 1 and 2 222–3
  listserv 225
  newsgroups 225
  pervasiveness 223
  practical task, investigating workings 221
  research opportunities 223–4
    other children as sources 224
  sharing information over 224
  synchronous and asynchronous
    communications 224–5

internet *cont.*
  video chat 225
  vocabulary 232

Key Stage 1:
  changes 1
  QCA Scheme of Work 9
Key Stage 2:
  changes 1
  QCA Scheme of Work 9
Key Stage structure changes 4

languages, planning primary ICT 64
laptops for teachers, subsidised 18
learning environment, strategies for managing 24
legal issues 257–60
  copyright 257–8
    application 257
    children and 259
    Copyright Licensing Agency 257
    Creative Commons 258
    licences 258
    music 257
    poetry 259
    software 258
  data protection 259–60
    exceptions 260
    principles 260
    schools 260
lesson effectiveness research 33
lesson plan using ICT, English and other
    subject 52–3
level descriptors, for assessment 75–6
licences:
  for audio 217
  for images 121
  limited trial 169
  for software 258
literacy:
  cross-curricular use 51–2
  and digital video 131
  group activity
    high-resource setting 49
    low-resource setting 47–8
  planning ICT to support 50–1
    resource settings 51
  and word processing 108
log on and off, procedure 24
low-resource setting:
  literacy teaching, planning ICT to support 51
  mathematics 55

master's level extensions:
  application of health and safety
      recommendations 255
  assessment, analysing records 82
  copyright and data protection 261
  data-handling activities 173

master's level extensions *cont.*
  differentiation 44
  digital video, and schemes of work 133
  Early Years Foundation Stage and Vygotsky's
      theories 72
  graphics software and digital cameras, digital
      literacy 126
  higher-order skills development 65
  impact of social software on teacher's
      role 240
  internet data transport 233
  mathematics and data handling 152
  mobile technologies controversies 203–4
  observation and Oftsted's report 87–8
  observing whiteboard use by colleagues 212
  personal preferred learning style 247
  physical computing, single-board
      computers 196
  planning 44
  sound in science and music 220
  word processing package comparison 110
mathematics:
  ability levels 55
  and data-handling 171–2
  and databases 171–2
  high-resource setting 55
  and ICT skills summary (table) 55
  and images 124–5
  low-resource setting 55
  planning primary ICT 53–6
  programme of study Key Stage 1 and 2 54
  reflective task, activity using ICT 56
  software types 54
  and spreadsheets 165, 171–2
  and word processing 106–7
media production 127–34
  ethical use 128
  introduction 127
  Key Stages 1 and 2 128
  safety 128
memory, printers 123
mobile technologies 198–204
  anytime anywhere learning 201
  cloud-based services 200–1
  cost considerations 199, 201
  definition 198
  Key Stages 1 and 2 198–9
  laptop computer 199
  linking to classroom computer 200
  mobile phones 200
  MP3 players 200
  outside school learning 201
  parental contact 203
  parental payment system 203
  podcasts 201
  practical task
    modelling processes 202
    role for 202

mobile technologies *cont.*
  professional use by teachers 202
  reflective task, children's views 203
  screencasts 201
  smartphones 200
  tablets 199–200
  teaching and learning opportunities 201–2
  videos of good practice 202
monitoring primary computing and ICT 83–8
  Computing At School (CAS) 84
  Information Technology in Teacher Education
    (ITTE) 84
  local authorities 85
  Naace (ICT subject association) 84
  Ofsted 84–5
  practical task, ICT staff and policies 86
  reflective task, reports 85
  research summary 86–7
  school-level 85–7
multi-modal information in ICT 12
music 214–20
  composing 62, 215–7
  file types 219
  and image combination 217
  Key Stages 1 and 2 214–25
  listening to 218–9
  performing 215–7
  planning primary ICT 62–3
  reflective task, composing 217
  software
    2Simple Music Toolkit 215
    Audacity 216
    Dance Ejay 215
    GarageBand 215
    keyboard 215
    loops 215
    Music Maker 215
    recording 215
    RM Music Explorer 215
  songbank website 215
  and video combination 217

Naace (ICT subject association) 4, 84
National Curriculum:
  for computing 76–7
  computing, purpose 35
  for English 46
  for geography 60
  programmes of study comparison (table)
    5–7
  Review (2011) 4
National Grid for Learning (NGfL) 3, 18
National Numeracy Strategy 53
New Opportunities Fund (NOF) 3, 18

observation, and assessment 75–6
Ofsted reports on ICT 84–5
online publishing 50

open source software:
  Audacity music editor 216
  Linux operating system 191
  MIT App Inventor 190–1
organising ICT:
  high resource setting 23–4
  low resource setting 24–6
  rotas 26
output, definition 37

packet switching, definition 38
painting *see* graphics software, painting
  programs
parents' concerns with:
  ICT 23
  photography 112–13
PE, planning primary ICT 63
peer-assessment 78
physical computing 189–95
  on Android smartphones 190–1
  apps 190–1
  definition 189
  Lego Mindstorms 190
  Lego WeDo 189–90
    Hungry Alligator 189–90
    programming 189–90
  Makey Makey 195
  MIT App Inventor 189–90
  operating systems 192–3
  Picaxe microcontroller products 194
  Raspberry Pi 191–5
    as controller 193–4
    peripherals 192
    setting up 193
pixels, definition 119–20
plenary:
  in low resource setting 48
  mathematics 54
podcasts:
  creating 217–18
  mobile technologies 201
presentation:
  of projects 24
  software, plenary example 48
primary computing 31–44
  analysis of situation 33–4
  definitions
    Key Stage 1 36
    Key Stage 2 37–9
  indicative activities
    Key Stage 1 35–6
    Key Stage 2 37–9
  lesson plan for Key Stage 1 39–43
  planning effectively 33–4
  planning principles 32–3
    briefing other adults 33
    high expectations 32
    knowledge of subject 32

primary computing *cont.*
    opportunities for learning 32
    purposeful working environment 32–3
    safe working environment 32
    strategies 32
  programme of study 35
  resources
    Key Stage 1 35–6
    Key Stage 2 37–9
  see also monitoring primary computing
    and ICT
primary ICT:
  art and design 59–60
  design and technology 61–2
  Early Years Foundation Stage *see* Early Years
    Foundation Stage, ICT
  English, 46–53, *see also* English
  English and literacy across curriculum
    51–2
  geography 60–1
  history 61
  languages 64
  literacy 46–53, *see also* literacy
  mathematics 53–6, *see also* mathematics
  music 62–3, *see also* music
  in other subjects 45–6
  PE 63
  RE, PSHE and citizenship 63
  science 56–8, *see also* science
Primary National Strategy:
  for English 46–7
  for Literacy and Mathematics 2
program, definition 37
programmable toys 178–80, 189
  Bee-Bot 179
  Lego WeDo 189–90
  resource for using 180
  Roamer and Roamer Classic 178
programme of study:
  computing 8, 35
  ICT 7
programming 174–97
  algorithm examples
    in Flowol 187–8
    in Lego WeDo 189–90
    in Logo 180
    in Scratch 181
  algorithmic thinking 178–80
  decision 188
  if then statement 188
  Key Stages 1 and 2 174–5
  languages *see* programming languages
  loop 187
  selection 188
  sub-routine 187–8
  terms defined 175–8
    abstraction 177
    algorithms 175–6

programming *cont.*
  debugging 180
  decomposition 177
  inputs 175
  outputs 175
  parallel algorithms 178
  sequencing 176
programming environments:
  blocks 181–2, 189–90
  flow chart 187–9
  Flowol 186–9, 194
    algorithm examples 187–8
  Kodu 185–6
  mimic 186, 189
  Mimic Creator 186, 189
  visual 185–6
programming languages:
  Lego WeDo 189–90
  Logicator 194
  Logo 179, 180–1
  pedagogical model 184
  practical task, debugging 183
  Python 191
  Scratch 181–2, 191
    online resources 182–4
protection of children *see* e-safety
provisionality of ICT 11

QCA Scheme of Work for ICT 2, 8, 36
  Key Stages 1 and 2 9
Qualified Teacher Status (QTS) standard 3

RE, PSHE and citizenship, planning primary
  ICT 63
relational databases *see* databases, relational
repetition, definition 37
resolution:
  digital cameras 113
  graphics software 120–1
  printing 120, 123
resource levels 19–20
  definitions (table) 20–1
responsibility for work, and competence in
  ICT 25
risks *see* e-safety
Rose Review (2009) 3

safety *see* e-safety
scheme of work, computing 36
science:
  and data-handling 170–1
  data-logging 148–9
    Junior Datalogging Insight 148
    sensors 148–9
  and databases 170–1
  and ICT
    Key Stage 1 (table) 57
    Key Stage 2 (table) 58

science *cont.*
    and images 124
    planning primary ICT 56–8
    practical task
        data-logging 149
        planning and assessing 58
    and spreadsheets 170
    and word processing 107
search engine, definition 38
selection, definition 37
self-assessment 78
sequence, definition 37
shared writing, interactive whiteboards 211
sharing ideas online (teachers or children) 50
social media 235–41
    blogs 236–8
    bookmark sharing tools 239
    Club Penguin 236
    Delicious 239
    Diigo 239
    Edublogs 236–7
    Facebook 236, 237, 238
    Flickr 238
    inappropriate content approaches 238–9
    Key Stages 1 and 2 235–6
    Moshi Monsters 236
    photo sharing 238
    Twitter 237–8
    video sharing 238–9
    Wikipedia 239
    WordPress 236, 238
    YouTube 238–9
software:
    2Simple Music Toolkit music editor 215
    Audacity music editor 216
    audioBoo podcast 218
    Counter graphing program 143
    CounterPlus graphing program 142, 143,
        145, 147
    Counting Pictures pictogram program 142,
        143, 145, 147
    Dance Ejay music editor 215
    DataCalc spreadsheet 147
    DataPlot graphing program 143, 146, 147
    DataSweet program collection 147
    Evernote notetaking 238
    FlexiTREE3 database 163
    GarageBand music editor 215
    Junior Datalogging Insight data-logging 148
    Junior ViewPoint database (figure)
        157, 163
    Music Maker music editor 215
    Number Magic spreadsheet 154, 164
    Pictogram 3 142, 143, 147
    RM Music Explorer music editor 215
    selecting 169
    SoundCloud podcast 218
    Wordpress blogging tool 50

special educational needs, children with:
    hardware and software 26–7
    in lesson plan example 42
    organising ICT for 26–8
    overlay keyboards 102
    portable computers 105
    reflective task 27
    writing frames 48
specialist subject, reflective task 64
spreadsheets 153–73
    calculations 164
    data protection 169
    definition 153
    description 157
    equals sign explaining 168
    key features 161
    Key Stages 1 and 2 153–4
    and mathematics 165, 171–2
    Number Magic 154, 164
    practical activities using 172
    prediction testing 162
    printing problems 170
    privacy of data 169
    professional use by teachers 169
    and programming 165
    and science 170
    skills needed by teachers 160
    teaching activities 158
Statutory Framework for the Early Years
        Foundation Stage 66–7
support structure for teachers 19

talk around computers, research on 71
teachers as learners in ICT 26
teachers' standards 3–4
The Teachers' Standards in England
        2–3
tracking through software, use in
        assessment 75
Tumblr blogging tool 50, 236
tutorial software 55, 57, 75

variable, definition 38
videos:
    art and design 59
    dance and gymnastic 63
virtual:
    art galleries 59
    keyboard 200
    learning environments
        221, 236
Virtual Teacher's Centre (VTC) 3
Vygotsky, early learning theories 68

whiteboards, interactive *see* interactive
        whiteboards
whole-class techniques 25
wikis and literacy 50

word processing 93–109
  capabilities 100–4
  classroom use by teachers 95
  and core subjects 106–8
  and databases 107
  definition 93
  and English 108
  grammar-checkers 104
  handwriting as alternative to 101
  Key Stages 1 and 2 94
  keyboard alternatives 100–1
  keyboard skills, developing 101
  laptops 105
  layout 108
  limitations 100–4
  and literacy 108
  and mathematics 106–7
  notebooks 105
  overlay keyboards 102
    children with special educational needs or
        disabilities 102
  portable computers 104–5
    children with special educational needs or
        disabilities 102
  practical task
    templates 109
    word banks 102–3
  professional use by teachers 95
  progression 99–100
  recording information 107
  reflective task, handwriting 102
  saving documents 108
  and science 107
  scribes (adult) 103
  and self-esteem 99
  sequencing text 107
  shared work 108
  skills
    acquiring 105–6
    improving 106
    inefficient practices 106
    required by teachers 95–6
  skills development, identifying 99–100
  software *see* word processors
  speaking word processors 103–4
    limitations 103–4
  spell-checkers 104
  storage requirements of documents 100
  text entry 100–3

word processing *cont.*
  thesauruses 104
  touch screens 103
  touch-typing 101
  voice recognition software 103
  word banks 102
word processors:
  basic knowledge required 100
  with desktop publishing 97
  editing 98
  functions reduced 96
  key features 96
  planning and drafting 97–8
  presenting 98–9
    and content of writing 99
  selecting 94–5
  and writing process 97–9
world wide web:
  authenticity of material 231
  bookmarks 226
  child-accessible material 230
  copyright 231
  Creative Commons content sharing 231
  currency of material 231
  definition 38, 221
  distractions while using 230
  navigation 225
  page address structure 225–6
  parental involvement 230
  practical task
    bogus websites 231
    downloading resource for lesson plan 230
    investigating workings 221
    search comparison 227
  printing from websites 232
  publishing by teachers and children 232
  resources for core subjects 228–30
    English 229
    mathematics 229–30
    science 229
  resources, sourcing 228
  school websites 232
  searching 226
    Boolean 227
    directories 226
    search engines 226
  spelling variations 230–1
  teachers' sites 228
  vocabulary 232